EVIDENCE STANDARDS IN EU COMPETITION ENFORCEMENT

What rules or principles govern the assessment of evidence in EU competition enforcement? This book offers, for the first time, a comprehensive academic study on the topic. Its aim is twofold. Firstly, it produces a typology of evidence standards in competition proceedings at the EU level, thereby systemising the guidance that is currently dispersed in the case-law of the EU Courts. Secondly, it examines the applicable evidence rules and principles with a view to better understanding their role in EU competition enforcement. In so doing, the book illustrates that evidence standards are not mere technicalities and their significance should not be underestimated. Rigorous and engaging, this work provides a much-needed analysis of a key question of EU competition enforcement.

Volume 21 in the series Hart Studies in Competition Law

Hart Studies in Competition Law

Joint Ventures and EU Competition Law
Luis Silva Morais

Sanctions in EU Competition Law: Principles and Practice
Michael Frese

Fairness in Antitrust: Protecting the Strong from the Weak
Adi Ayal

European Merger Remedies: Law and Policy
Dorte Hoeg

Media Ownership and Control: Law, Economics and Policy in an Indian and International Context
Suzanne Rab and Alison Sprague

The Interface between Competition and the Internal Market: Market Separation under Article 102 TFEU
Vasiliki Brisimi

Anti-Cartel Enforcement in a Contemporary Age: Leniency Religion
Edited by Caron Beaton-Wells and Christopher Tran

Public Procurement and the EU Competition Rules
Albert Sánchez Graells

The Concept of Abuse in EU Competition Law: Law and Economic Approaches
Pınar Akman

The Competitive Effects of Minority Shareholdings: Legal and Economic Issues
Panagiotis Fotis and Nikolaos Zevgolis

The More Economic Approach to EU Antitrust Law
Anne C Witt

Private Power, Online Information Flows and EU Law
Angela Daly

The Role of Competitors in the Enforcement of State Aid Law
Fernando Pastor-Merchante

The Legality of Bailouts and Buy Nationals: International Trade Law in a Crisis
Kamala Dawar

A Critical Account of Article 106(2) TFEU: Government Failure in Public Service Provision
Jarleth Burke

Dawn Raids Under Challenge
Helene Andersson

A Framework for European Competition Law: Co-ordinated Diversity
Christopher Townley

Evidence Standards in EU Competition Enforcement

The EU Approach

Andriani Kalintiri

•HART•
OXFORD • LONDON • NEW YORK • NEW DELHI • SYDNEY

HART PUBLISHING

Bloomsbury Publishing Plc

Kemp House, Chawley Park, Cumnor Hill, Oxford, OX2 9PH, UK

HART PUBLISHING, the Hart/Stag logo, BLOOMSBURY and the Diana logo are trademarks of Bloomsbury Publishing Plc

First published in Great Britain 2019

A catalogue record for this book is available from the British Library.

Library of Congress Cataloging-in-Publication data

Names: Kalintiri, Andriani, author.

Title: Evidence standards in EU competition enforcement : the EU approach / Andriani Kalintiri.

Other titles: Evidence standards in European Union competition enforcement

Description: Oxford [UK] ; Portland, Oregon : Hart Publishing, 2019. | Series: Hart studies in competition law

Identifiers: LCCN 2018044753 (print) | LCCN 2018045926 (ebook) | ISBN 9781509919673 (Epub) | ISBN 9781509919666 (hardback)

Subjects: LCSH: Evidence (Law)—European Union countries. | Competition, Unfair—European Union countries. | Antiturst law—European Union countries. | Restraint of trade—European Union countries. | Civil procedure—European Union countries. | BISAC: LAW / Antitrust. | LAW / International.

Classification: LCC KJE3926 (ebook) | LCC KJE3926 .K35 2019 (print) | DDC 343.2407/21—dc23

LC record available at https://lccn.loc.gov/2018044753

ISBN: HB: 978-1-50991-966-6
ePDF: 978-1-50991-968-0
ePub: 978-1-50991-967-3

Typeset by Compuscript Ltd, Shannon

ACKNOWLEDGEMENTS

Matters of evidence assessment in competition enforcement caught my interest for the first time when I was an LLM student in Cambridge. Several years later, it is a topic which I still find fascinating for all the intricacies and challenges that it presents. This book is the product of the doctoral research I conducted from 2011 to 2015 at Queen Mary University of London, whose generous funding is gratefully acknowledged. It also reflects the subsequent evolution of my thinking as a Fellow in the Law Department of the London School of Economics and Political Science, which provided the most stimulating intellectual environment one could hope for. While writing might be a solitary process, this work owes much to the many exceptional scholars I have been fortunate enough to discuss my ideas with. I would like to sincerely thank in particular my supervisors, Professor Takis Tridimas and Professor Norman Fenton, for their invaluable guidance, thoughtful advice and much-appreciated encouragement during my PhD, as well as my examiners, Professor Ioannis Lianos and Dr Albertina Albors Llorens, for their challenging questions and thought-provoking comments during the viva. Special thanks are due to Professor Pablo Ibáñez Colomo for his mentorship and friendship; his genuine passion for competition law and for academic rigour is truly inspirational, and this book would look very different without our many illuminating conversations. I would also like to express my gratitude for the support of several dear friends – especially of Kadir Baş and Eda Şahin for our memorable times at IALS, and of Peppy Kesoglou, Maria Kotsovili and Andria Alexandrou for always being only a phone call away. Last but not least, the biggest 'thank you' goes to my family: my husband, Dimitris, for being the most amazing partner and for standing by my side; my elder brother, Vasileios, for his constant 'legal queries'; my younger brother, Michalis, for bringing so much joy into our life; my father, Konstantinos, for his unconditional love and all his sacrifices; and, finally, my mother, Apostolia, to whom I simply owe everything I am – a sentiment no words can ever express.

CONTENTS

TABLE OF CASES

Judgments of the European Court of Justice of the European Union

Opinions of Advocates General

Judgments of the General Court of the European Union

Judgments of the European Court of Human Rights

Decisions of the European Commission of Human Rights

Judgments of Other Courts

TABLE OF LEGISLATION

Treaties

Regulations

Directives

Commission Guidelines and Notices

Other

1

Introduction

I. Evidence Matters in the Spotlight

The past few decades have witnessed a landscape evolution of European Union (EU) competition law. Covering a wide spectrum of commercial conduct, ranging from anti-competitive agreements to abuses of dominance and concentrations with an EU dimension, the EU competition rules have come a long way and have contributed their share to the proper functioning of the internal market.[1] However, substantive legal rules remain a dead letter in the absence of a fair and workable enforcement system. Therefore, as EU competition law has been becoming mature, the debates over the substantive reach of the competition provisions have been complemented by an increased awareness of the importance of sound procedures.

By and large, the growing attention paid to procedural matters can be traced back to two significant developments in EU competition enforcement: the expansion of the European Commission's powers and the tightening of its fining policy in infringement cases. As is well known, the EU Treaties have vested the responsibility for ensuring compliance with the competition provisions in the Commission.[2] Accordingly, the authority may investigate suspected infringements of Articles 101 and 102 of the Treaty on the Functioning of the European Union (TFEU) or the compatibility of a concentration with an EU dimension with the common market; it may take remedial action as appropriate; and it may impose fines on the perpetrators of antitrust violations.[3] Nevertheless, the detection of certain infringements – mainly cartels – proved to be considerably challenging. In recognition of the difficulties that the authority faces, Regulation 1/2003 on the implementation of the rules on competition laid down in Articles 101 and 102 TFEU not only fully decentralised the enforcement regime, but also expanded the Commission's investigative powers with a view to easing its evidence-gathering efforts and ensuring

[1] See generally Heike Schweitzer and Kiran Klaus Patel (eds), *The Historical Foundations of EU Competition Law* (Oxford University Press, 2013).

[2] Consolidated Version of the Treaty on the Functioning of the European Union [2008] OJ C115/47 (TFEU), art 105. See also Consolidated Version of the Treaty on European Union, Protocols – Protocol (No 27) on the internal market and competition [2008] OJ C115/309.

[3] These powers were first granted through Council Regulation 17/1962 (EEC) implementing Articles 85 and 86 of the Treaty [1962] OJ 13/204.

that it has sufficient tools at its disposal to carry out its enforcement duties.[4] Shortly thereafter, a similar rationale underpinned the adoption of Council Regulation 139/2004 on the control of concentrations between undertakings (hereinafter the EU Merger Regulation (EUMR)). Indeed, the latter also identified a need for the Commission's powers of investigation in the context of merger proceedings to be strengthened so as to ensure that competition will be effectively protected and distortions will be prevented in a timely fashion.[5]

The expansion of the Commission's investigative powers was received with uneasiness by undertakings, which started feeling that the existing procedural safeguards were inadequate to mitigate the far-reaching scope of the tools that the authority now possesses. This feeling became particularly acute when the Commission started imposing higher and higher fines for antitrust violations, sometimes totalling billions of euros.[6] The tightening of the Commission's fining policy triggered claims that antitrust fines amounted to 'criminal charges' within the meaning of Article 6(1) of the European Convention for the Protection of Human Rights and Fundamental Freedoms (ECHR), as interpreted by the European Court of Human Rights (ECtHR).[7] In this context, the question emerged whether EU competition enforcement is sufficiently 'fair' and meets the due process demands of the Charter of Fundamental Rights of the European Union (CFR) and the ECHR. However, the multiple functions of the Commission, which combines the roles of the prosecutor, investigator and adjudicator, and the application of a marginal standard of review by the EU Courts,[8] where a Commission decision entails policy choices or complex economic evaluations, have obscured the answer.[9]

In view of these developments, it is hardly surprising that questions of evidence gradually came into the spotlight. Indeed, evidence standards constitute an intrinsic element of what makes a trial 'fair' and judicial protection 'effective'.[10]

[4] Council Regulation (EC) No 1/2003 of 16 December 2002 on the implementation of the rules on competition laid down in Articles 81 and 82 of the Treaty [2003] OJ L1/1 (Regulation 1/2003), Recital 25. Regulation 1/2003 abolished the compulsory notification system for agreements falling within the scope of the antitrust rules, whereas it provided that national competition authorities and national courts also have the power to apply art 101(3) TFEU.

[5] Council Regulation (EC) No 139/2004 of 20 January 2004 on the control of concentrations between undertakings [2004] OJ L24/1 (EUMR), Recital 38.

[6] See, eg, the Cartel Statistics published on the website of the Directorate General (DG) of Competition, available at http://ec.europa.eu/competition/cartels/statistics/statistics.pdf.

[7] European Convention for the Protection of Human Rights and Fundamental Freedoms (European Convention on Human Rights, as amended) (ECHR).

[8] References to the EU Courts must be understood as references to the Court of Justice of the European Union (CJEU) and the General Court of the European Union (GCEU).

[9] See, eg, Wouter Wils, 'The Combination of the Investigative and Prosecutorial Function and the Adjudicative Function in EC Antitrust Enforcement: A Legal and Economic Analysis' (2004) 27 *World Competition* 201; Ian Forrester, 'Due Process in EC Competition Cases: A Distinguished Institution with Flawed Procedures' (2009) 34 *European Law Review* 81; Ian Forrester, 'A Bush in Need of Pruning: The Luxuriant Growth of Light Judicial Review' in Claus-Dieter Ehlermann and Mel Marquis (eds), *European Competition Law Annual 2009: The Evaluation of Evidence and its Judicial Review in Competition Cases* (Hart Publishing, 2010).

[10] The terms 'evidence standards' and 'standards of evidence assessment' are used throughout this book to collectively refer to the rules and principles that instruct how evidence is, or should be, evaluated.

In this sense, evidence rules and principles form part of the procedural safeguards afforded to undertakings, which find themselves involved in competition proceedings. For this reason, the way in which evidence is assessed and relied on by the Commission must live up to the expectations of the CFR and the ECHR. However, what this means in practice is not entirely clear. For example, the ECHR-criminal nature of antitrust fines, coupled with the EU Courts' settled position that the presumption of innocence applies to proceedings that may culminate in the imposition of high financial penalties for the undertakings concerned, has generated some concern that the standard of proof that the Commission must satisfy in antitrust cases may not be high enough.

In any event, the growing interest in matters of evidence in EU competition enforcement can be also attributed to changes in the way in which evidence is collected, the most important being the adoption of the Commission's Leniency Programme in cartel cases. As one would expect, undertakings which consciously violate the competition rules tend to go to great lengths to eliminate any evidence of their unlawful activities by destroying 'dangerous' records and maintaining an overall secretive profile. Such practices, however, thwart the Commission's efforts to detect unlawful conduct and minimise its chances of retrieving evidence capable of establishing the existence of a violation. Although the broadening of its investigative powers has been helpful in this regard, the problem has remained exceptionally acute in the case of cartels. For this reason, the Commission launched its Leniency Programme with a view to incentivising cartelists to blow the whistle and come forward with evidence of a cartel in exchange for immunity or generous reductions in their fine.[11] This 'carrot approach' – as it is often called – has been very successful in strengthening the Commission's battle against cartels. Yet, at the same time, it has fundamentally reshaped the way in which cartels are proved by often turning leniency statements into the main piece of evidence making the Commission's case. This shift has not gone unnoticed; on the contrary, undertakings and scholars alike have taken issue with both the admissibility and the high probative value usually attributed to evidence proffered by leniency applicants.[12]

Finally, evidence matters in EU competition enforcement have gained considerable prominence in the wake of the so-called 'more economic' approach.[13] Indeed, the early application of the competition rules by the Commission has been criticised as formalistic; the authority tended to equate restrictions in the parties' freedom of action with restrictions of competition, whereas it favoured

[11] Commission Notice on immunity from fines and reduction of fines in cartel cases [2006] OJ C298/17 (Leniency Notice).

[12] See, eg, the early criticisms articulated by Julian Joshua, 'Oral Statements in EC Competition Proceedings: A Due Process Short-Cut?' (2004) 26 *Competition Law Insight* 1.

[13] See generally Jordi Gual et al, 'An Economic Approach to Article 82' (July 2005), available at http://ec.europa.eu/dgs/competition/economist/eagcp_july_21_05.pdf; Anne Witt, *The More Economic Approach to EU Antitrust Law* (Hart Publishing, 2016); Denis Waelbroeck and Jacques Bourgeois (eds), *Ten Years of the Effects-Based Approach in EU Competition Law* (Bruylant, 2012).

an expansive construction of Articles 101 and 102 TFEU.[14] In response to these criticisms, the Commission revisited its approach to the enforcement of the competition rules, progressively moving towards an 'effects-based' analysis, under which the legal treatment of a practice depends on its impact on competition rather than its form.[15] The integration of economics in the application of the competition rules is a positive development. At the same time, however, it has given rise to new challenges from an evidence perspective. On the one hand, it has increased to an extent the complexity of administrative decision-making. On the other hand, it has led to the growing engagement of economic evidence as a means of lending support to the arguments of the authority or of undertaking. Since the assessment of complex economic evidence typically requires specialised knowledge, difficult questions have emerged about its admission into competition proceedings, the criteria of its probative evaluation and its evidential weight vis-a-vis other types of evidence.[16]

II. A Simple Question, an Unclear Answer: What Standards Govern the Evaluation of Evidence?

Naturally, this complicated background – as just outlined – prompts a simple question: how is evidence assessed in EU competition enforcement? Or, to be more specific, what rules or principles inform or should inform its evaluation? The significance of this question cannot be overstated. Indeed, the Commission, when it applies Articles 101 and 102 TFEU, as well as the EUMR and the EU Courts, when they review Commission decisions, rely on evidence. Thus, evidence assessment is hardwired into both the administrative decision-making and the judicial 'decision-checking' process. Nevertheless, despite the significance of the question, the answer remains rather unclear.

To some extent, the uncertainty over the standards which underpin the assessment of evidence in EU competition proceedings can be attributed to the legislative silence on the matter. Indeed, the EU Treaties do not contain evidence rules, whereas – save for Article 2 of Regulation 1/2003, which allocates the burden of proof in disputes concerning the application of Articles 101 and 102 TFEU – there

[14] Valentine Korah, 'EEC Competition Policy – Legal Form or Economic Efficiency' (1986) 39 *Current Legal Problems* 85; Barry Hawk, 'System Failure: Vertical Restraints and EC Competition Law' (1995) 32 *Common Market Law Review* 973.

[15] This shift is manifested in the adoption of several economics-driven Block Exemption Regulations and Guidelines – eg, on vertical restraints, horizontal cooperation agreements and unilateral conduct.

[16] See, eg, Ioannis Lianos '"Judging Economists", Economic Expertise in Competition Litigation: A European View' in Ioannis Lianos and Ioannis Kokkoris (eds), *The Reform of EC Competition Law: New Challenges* (Kluwer Law International, 2010); Nicholas Forwood, 'The Commission's "More Economic Approach" – Implications for the Role of the EU Courts, the Treatment of Economic Evidence and the Scope of Judicial Review' in Claus-Dieter Ehlermann and Mel Marquis (eds), *European Competition Law Annual 2009: The Evaluation of Evidence and its Judicial Review in Competition Cases* (Hart Publishing, 2010).

is no other provision either in Regulation 1/2003 or in the EUMR prescribing rules or principles for the assessment of evidence in competition proceedings.[17] Rather, most guidance on evidence-related matters, such as the operation of the burden of proof, the standard of proof, the use of presumptions and the admissibility or probative value of the evidence, is to be found in the EU Courts' competition jurisprudence. Undeniably, this guidance is highly valuable. Inevitably, however, it has been provided in a fragmentary manner. Therefore, it is at the very least in need of systemisation.

Admittedly, academics have endeavoured to make sense of evidence evaluation in EU competition proceedings over the last few years. Nevertheless, scholarly efforts so far have been rather limited in scope and – sometimes – depth. In terms of scope, the vast majority of the existing studies have explored only a particular aspect of the problem. For instance, some works have examined a specific type of evidence only, such as leniency statements or economic evidence. Others have focused on a particular type of cases, such as cartels or mergers. Last but not least, other commentators have looked only into a specific rule, such as the burden of proof or the standard of proof. As a result, a comprehensive academic study on evidence standards is currently missing from the legal literature on EU competition enforcement.[18] The need for such a study becomes ever more apparent and urgent, given the regularly inaccurate use of the various evidence concepts by both scholars and – occasionally – the EU Courts, which only adds to the general confusion.

III. Purpose, Approach and Scope

A. The Purpose and Approach in this Book

This book examines the standards which inform the evaluation of evidence in EU proceedings concerning the application of Articles 101 and 102 TFEU, as well as the EUMR. In this light, it seeks to answer two questions.

First of all, the book considers what standards govern the assessment of evidence in EU competition enforcement. The primary intention behind this question is to organise the evidence-related case law of the EU Courts and present

[17] The Rules of Procedure of the EU Courts do not address matters of evidence *evaluation*, but rather contain rules on the *production* or *presentation* of evidence (Rules of Procedure of the General Court [2015] OJ L105/1 (RPGC); Rules of Procedure of the Court of Justice [2012] OJ L265/1 (RPCJ)).

[18] The most complete work on evidence assessment in EU competition enforcement so far is the following book: Fernando Castillo de la Torre and Eric Gippini Fournier, *Evidence, Proof and Judicial Review in EU Competition Law* (Edward Elgar, 2017). The present research is different in at least two respects: first, its scope extends to merger control; and, second, it examines evidence standards from a normative perspective too, whereas it also reflects on their implications for EU competition enforcement on a broader level.

it in a systematic, coherent and comprehensive manner. As mentioned, there are almost no rules on evidence in EU legislation. Accordingly, identifying the standards which underpin evidence evaluation in EU competition proceedings becomes possible only through a deductive investigation of the jurisprudence of the EU Courts. For the purposes of conducting this investigation, this book starts from the premise that the process of evidence assessment requires consideration of the following points: (a) what has to be proved; (b) who has to prove it; (c) how much is enough in order for evidence to be treated as 'proof' of an allegation; (d) what evidence the parties may produce to establish their arguments; and (e) how probative value is assigned to specific items of evidence. Except for the first one, which is a matter of substantive EU competition law, the rest of these correspond to the various standards of evidence assessment, namely, the burden of proof, the standard of proof and the principles governing the production of evidence and the appraisal of its probative weight. In practice, the Commission and the EU Courts do not always distinguish among the various evidence standards – at least not explicitly. Nevertheless, being aware of the different stages and elements of the evidence assessment process is essential in order to avoid inaccuracies in the use of the various concepts and properly classify and analyse the guidance provided by the EU Courts.

Second, the book examines the implications of the applicable evidence standards for EU competition enforcement. Academic research on the rules governing evidence assessment in EU competition proceedings has been dominated by debates over their fairness. A possible explanation for this might be that evidence rules are sometimes thought of as mere procedural technicalities that parties must satisfy. However, such a narrow conception of evidence standards is rather shortsighted and fails to do justice to their potential impact on, and contribution in, the enforcement system of which they form part. Therefore, this book takes a broader perspective and seeks to identify the various ways in which the applicable evidence standards may shape, inform or affect the enforcement of the EU competition rules. Specifically, the book considers: (a) their connotations for the allocation of risk in EU competition enforcement; (b) their potential contribution in the fairness of the enforcement system; (c) their implications for the application of the substantive competition rules; (d) their connotations for the Commission and the EU Courts; and (e) their capacity to pave the way for further procedural convergence at the national level.

In considering the above issues, the book takes into account the following parameters, as appropriate. First, the analysis bears in mind the institutional context within which EU competition enforcement is pursued. As will be explained, evidence standards are autonomous, but not independent; while they perform a distinct function within the enforcement system, at the same time they are responsive to its specific features and needs almost by default. Therefore, an examination of evidence standards in EU competition proceedings may not disregard the institutional structure of the system and the administrative model of enforcement which is currently in place. Second, the book takes into account the substantive legal tests that specify when the Commission may intervene in the market. As will be clarified, evidence standards and substantive legal tests are not completely airtight. Whilst the latter are not the main focus of this book, they will be taken into consideration to the extent that this is necessary in order to provide a full picture of the role of evidence standards in EU competition enforcement. Finally, the book is also mindful of the different manifestations of the 'more economic' approach to EU competition enforcement. Indeed, economics may be relevant at multiple levels – including the design of policy priorities, the formulation of legal tests and the assessment of evidence. The present work focuses on the latter issue with a view to better understanding the role that the applicable evidence standards have played or may play in the integration of economics in the application of Articles 101 and 102 TFEU, as well as the EUMR.

The approach of this book is both positive and normative. On a positive level, the analysis identifies the rules and principles that inform the assessment of evidence in EU competition proceedings and considers their impact on, or contribution in, the enforcement of the EU competition rules. On a normative level, it determines what evidence standards should apply in EU competition enforcement and provides certain recommendations.

B. The Scope of the Book

This book focuses on the standards which underpin the process of evidence evaluation, as mostly developed by the EU Courts in the context of their review of Commission decisions concerning the application of Articles 101 and 102 TFEU, as well as the EUMR. However, for the sake of completeness, two related issues are also explored.

First of all, part of the book is dedicated to the presumptions which are most commonly invoked and relied on in EU competition proceedings. One might argue that, strictly speaking, presumptions are not evidence *standards*, that is, *rules* or *principles* governing the evaluation of evidence. Yet, they are one of the main mechanisms through which a party may satisfy its standard of proof and thus discharge its burden of proof too. Cartel enforcement specifically is heavily reliant on presumptions, which have been developed by the EU Courts and are frequently employed by the Commission in its decision-making. Therefore, an analysis of evidence standards in EU competition enforcement would be incomplete without at least a brief consideration of presumptions as a tool for meeting the standard of proof. Second, part of the analysis is dedicated to the interaction between evidence standards and standards of judicial review. Matters of judicial review in EU competition enforcement merit their own separate investigation and, as such, they fall outside the scope of this book. Nonetheless, evidence standards are typically engaged as part of the scrutiny to which the EU Courts subject the Commission's decisions. For this reason, issues of proof and issues of judicial review cannot be entirely disentangled. In this sense, in order to fully appreciate the function of evidence standards in the enforcement of the EU competition rules, some thought must be paid to the subtleties of their symbiosis with the applicable standards of judicial review.

By contrast, a number of issues are not considered in this book. First of all, matters of evidence production and evidence presentation are excluded from the analysis, save where they may have an impact on the formulation of standards for the evaluation of evidence. In this regard, the words 'assessment' or 'evaluation' or 'appraisal' are used interchangeably throughout the book as umbrella terms describing all the different aspects of the process through which evidence is examined and relied upon, first, in order to justify a Commission decision finding a *violation* of Articles 101 and 102 TFEU or declaring the compatibility or incompatibility of a concentration with an EU dimension with the common market, and, second, in order to enable the EU Courts to verify the legality of such a Commission decision.

Second, this book does not consider the Commission's decisional practice. As mentioned earlier, with the exception of Article 2 of Regulation 1/2003, which allocates the burden of proof in antitrust cases, there are no evidence rules in EU legislation. For this reason, the development of specific standards of evidence assessment in EU competition proceedings has been predominantly left in the hands of EU judges. However, the judgments of the EU Courts are binding upon the Commission. Indeed, the lawfulness of the Commission's decision-making is – among other things – dependent on the authority's compliance with the applicable evidence standards as understood by the EU Courts. Therefore, to the extent – and on the assumption – that it deviates from the evidence standards developed by the latter, the Commission's practice in relation to matters of evidence assessment will not be examined.

Third, and rather obviously, the focus is exclusively on evidence standards in EU *competition* proceedings. As such, questions or problems of evidence evaluation in other fields of EU law are not examined in this book. That said, some of the issues addressed herein may be present or of relevance in other areas of EU law too. However, the field of EU competition law was chosen owing to its unique cumulative combination of the following distinct features. First, Commission decisions finding a violation of Articles 101 and 102 TFEU or declaring the incompatibility of a concentration with an EU dimension with the common market have a direct adverse effect on individuals.[19] Second, where an infringement of Article 101 and/or 102 TFEU has been established, the fines that the Commission may impose are of at least a quasi-criminal nature. Third, EU competition enforcement typically requires the performance of complex economic evaluations. Last but not

[19] In contrast, in other areas of EU law, the adverse effects on individuals are typically indirect, such as in the field of risk regulation, or the Commission decisions are principally addressed to a Member State rather than an individual, such as is the case with state aid. Because of these differences, other fields of EU law do not give rise to fairness concerns similar to those arising in competition proceedings.

least, individuals who have been adversely affected by a Commission decision may bring an action for annulment before the GCEU, which has jurisdiction to review the legality of the said decision.

Fourth, this book does not examine questions of institutional reform. The consistent trend of record fines being imposed by the Commission for violations of the antitrust rules has prompted several commentators to question whether the current administrative model is appropriate to secure the effective judicial protection of the sanctioned undertakings and their right to a fair trial. In the wake of these concerns, various proposals for institutional reform have been put on the table. Nonetheless, the focus of the present research is on the applicable evidence standards. Therefore, issues of institutional reform associated with fairness concerns will be addressed only where necessary and merely in an ancillary way, the reference point of the analysis being the current administrative model of EU competition enforcement.

Finally, the book does not examine evidence standards in the enforcement of the EU competition rules at the *national* level, ie, by national competition authorities (NCAs), national courts and private parties. As briefly mentioned earlier, the applicable evidence standards are informed by – and sensitive to – the wider context within which they operate. However, the procedural and institutional framework within which private or decentralised public EU competition enforcement occurs may differ significantly from that of the EU. Accordingly, evidence standards in national proceedings concerning the application of the EU competition provisions will not be considered in this book, except where necessary.

IV. Structure

Chapter 2 sets the scene for the analysis in the rest of the book. To this end, it asks two questions. The first of these is what evidence rules are for? The second is what features of EU competition enforcement may affect the design and content of the standards which inform the evaluation of evidence in that context? The chapter first offers a primer on evidence law and theory in order to highlight a somewhat underestimated point: that evidence rules have an autonomous function in legal proceedings. Specifically, they serve as fact-finding and decision-making devices with a view to enabling adjudicators to deal with uncertainty and evade deadlocks. However, the fact that evidence standards are autonomous does not mean they are completely independent; rather, the second point that the chapter emphasises is that their content is inevitably informed by the features of the enforcement system within which they operate. In EU competition enforcement in particular, regard must be had to the following aspects thereof: the prevailing administrative model, the consequences that Commission decisions may have for the undertakings involved, and the interplay between competition law and economics.

With these preliminary remarks in mind, Chapters 3, 4 and 5 turn their attention to the specific rules and principles which underpin the various stages of the evidence assessment process. Chapter 3 starts with the burden of proof and analyses how this is – or should be – allocated in EU competition enforcement. After providing a brief account of its forms and significance, the chapter examines how the burden of proof is divided between the Commission and the investigated undertakings in infringement and merger proceedings alike, and cautions against the implications of the current bifurcated allocation for the scope of the EU competition rules, as well as its incompatibility – in Article 101 and 102 TFEU proceedings – with the presumption of innocence. Chapter 4 then shifts its focus to the standard of proof in EU competition enforcement. Although the question whether the produced evidence has been 'sufficient' stands at the very core of evidence evaluation, the applicable standard of proof has been rather elusive. Mindful of this elusiveness, the chapter draws on the case law of the EU Courts in order to infer how the standard of proof is, or should be, regulated in infringement and merger proceedings, while it also sheds some light on the factors which may ease or complicate its discharge. Chapter 5 then examines how evidence is admitted and weighed in EU competition proceedings.[20] Indeed, not all items of information may qualify as 'evidence' and not all evidence will bear the same probative value. The chapter inspects the case law of the EU Courts in order to set out the principles and criteria that determine the admissibility and probative value of the evidence in EU competition proceedings, while it also considers potential shortcomings in the applicable admissibility and evaluative standards.

For the sake of completeness, Chapters 6 and 7 are then dedicated to two peripheral, yet highly pertinent issues: the use of presumptions in EU competition enforcement and the interaction between evidence standards and standards of judicial review. Although – technically speaking – presumptions are not a core evidence *rule* or *principle*, they still play a crucial role in the evidence assessment process by providing the party who bears the burden of proof with an expedient mechanism for satisfying the standard of proof and by re-allocating the evidential onus between the claimant and the defendant. For this reason, Chapter 6 takes a closer look at the presumptions that the EU Courts have developed over the years in their competition jurisprudence and examines their function in the evidence evaluation process, as well as their implications. In any event, because evidence standards are engaged as part of the control that the EU Courts exercise over the Commission's decisions, issues of proof and issues of judicial review cannot be entirely detached. For this reason, Chapter 7 examines the interaction between

[20] The choice to discuss the admissibility and probative value of the evidence after the burden and standard of proof is justified by the fact that the burden and the standard of proof are decision-making *rules* applying to the *totality* of the evidence and, as such, their regulation is informed by similar considerations (mainly fairness and risk allocation). By contrast, the admissibility inquiry, as well as the probative weight analysis, are governed by *principles* (rather than rules, strictly speaking) and apply to *individual* items of information rather than the body of the evidence as a whole. Accordingly, it makes sense to identify first the general threshold that needs to be satisfied in order for evidence to amount to proof and then the factors that guide the assessment of specific pieces of evidence.

evidence standards and standards of judicial review and expounds the subtleties, but also importance, of their symbiosis.

Finally, Chapter 8 draws upon the previous analysis in order to illuminate the implications of the applicable evidence standards for EU competition enforcement from various angles. Indeed, this book shows that the rules and principles which inform the evaluation of evidence in EU competition proceedings are not dry technicalities; rather, they are essential components of an underlying framework which complements the substantive legal tests and shapes enforcement in its own right. As Chapter 8 explains, the applicable evidence standards have multifaceted connotations and implications. First of all, they may provide insights into the enforcement system's proclivity towards risk. Second, coupled with the standards of review, they have the capacity to compensate for the 'fairness deficit' in the administrative model of enforcement and may contribute to its overall compatibility with the principle of effective judicial protection. Third, from a substantive point of view, they may accommodate the 'more economic' approach, whilst serving as a 'quality filter' for the integration of economics in the analysis, and at the same time, they may affect the scope of the EU competition rules. Fourth, from a practical standpoint, they can be translated into specific obligations for – or expectations from – the Commission and the EU Courts. And last but not least, they are prone to paving the way for further procedural convergence in the application of the EU competition rules at the national level.[21]

[21] This book has examined the case law of the EU Courts as at 25 June 2018.

2

Evidence Standards in EU Competition Enforcement

Autonomous, But Not Independent

I. Introduction

Academic works on evidence standards in EU competition enforcement sometimes fall into a 'paradox'. On the one hand, because evidence rules are an intrinsic feature of legal decision-making, their presence is sometimes taken for granted and little thought is paid to the function of – or need for – such rules in the first place. On the other hand, the recurring anguish to ensure their fairness or retain their effectiveness might result in evidence standards being examined in disregard of the broader enforcement system of which they form part. Wary of this 'paradox', this chapter sets the scene for the analysis to follow by highlighting that evidence standards in EU competition enforcement are autonomous, but not independent. As section II expounds, evidence rules fulfil specific needs in legal proceedings: they serve as fact-finding and decision-making devices, thereby enabling adjudicators to manage uncertainty and evade deadlocks. In this sense, they perform an autonomous function. At the same time, however, evidence standards are not completely independent: their content becomes inevitably informed by the specific features of the context within which they operate. Section III outlines the reasons for this contextual dependency and submits that in relation to EU competition enforcement, special attention must be paid to: the prevailing administrative model; the consequences that Commission decisions may have for the undertakings involved; and the interplay between competition law and economics.

II. A Primer on Evidence Law and Theory

Much of the uncertainty which surrounds evidence standards in EU competition enforcement derives from misconceptions about the actual function of evidence rules in adjudication. The various evidential concepts are often used indistinctly or interchangeably – as if they were one and the same – and their precise role is shrouded in a cloud of confusion. For this reason, this section offers a brief account of the objectives that evidence law is committed to.[1] The intention is twofold: first, to clarify the raison d'être of evidence rules; and, second, to highlight that most of the evidence problems that have troubled competition scholars are not unique to EU competition enforcement – rather, similar difficulties exist in almost every area of law.

To begin with, evidence is not assessed in legal proceedings for the sake of it. Adjudication consists in applying the pertinent rules to the facts as established.[2] Accordingly, evidence evaluation in this context has a specific purpose: to figure out what happened in order to conclude whether the conduct in question satisfies the conditions for the application of the relevant legal provision. Arguably, the distinction between questions of fact and issues of law may be ambiguous at times.[3] Nevertheless, getting the facts right is still crucial. These remarks already reveal what evidence law aims for in the first place: accuracy in fact-finding. Judges – or decision-makers generally – are looking for the 'truth' and rely on the available evidence in order to discover it. Unsurprisingly, the notions of 'knowledge' and 'belief' and the human ability to reach the 'truth' have been long debated.[4] However, irrespective of the philosophical reflections on these matters, accuracy in fact-finding remains a core objective of evidence law. In this sense, 'truth' is its holy grail. Nevertheless, the quest for the 'holy grail' is fraught with significant challenges. In the overwhelming majority of cases, factual certainty is simply unattainable. Accordingly, complete accuracy in the fact-finding becomes a utopian goal. In these circumstances, the central problem that evidence law is called to deal with is *uncertainty*. Since the rendering of justice cannot be halted, judges may not refuse to adjudicate and are obliged to decide one way or another.[5] Therefore, the question of how to handle uncertainty becomes translated into the question of how to decide under conditions of incomplete information. This is not a problem to be taken lightly. Because it is so closely attached to legal reasoning, the assessment of the evidence ultimately indicates whether the decision-maker is justified in believing a proposition.[6] From this perspective, the problem of

[1] There is a wealth of scholarship on evidence. See especially William Twining, 'Evidence and Legal Theory' (1984) 47 *Modern Law Review* 261; William Twining, *Theories of Evidence: Bentham and Wigmore* (Weidenfeld & Nicolson, 1985); Richard Lempert, 'The New Evidence Scholarship: Analysing the Process of Proof' (1986) 66 *Boston University Law Review* 439; William Twining, *Rethinking Evidence: Exploratory Essays*, 2nd edn (Cambridge University Press, 2006); Michael Pardo, 'The Nature and Purpose of Evidence Theory' (2013) 66 *Vanderbilt Law Review* 547.

[2] Hock Lai Ho, *A Philosophy of Evidence Law: Justice in the Search for Truth* (Oxford University Press, 2008) 33.

[3] Ronald Allen and Michael Pardo, 'The Myth of the Law-Fact Distinction' (2003) 97 *Northwestern University Law Review* 1769.

[4] Willard Van Orman Quine and Joseph Silbert Ullian, *The Web of Belief*, 2nd edn (McGraw-Hill Humanities/Social Sciences/Languages, 1978); Richard Bernstein, *Beyond Objectivism and Relativism: Science, Hermeneutics, and Praxis* (University of Pennsylvania Press, 1983).

[5] Alex Stein, *Foundations of Evidence Law* (Oxford University Press, 2005) 34, 56.

[6] Ho (n 2) 71.

uncertainty boils down to two fundamental questions: first, how to find out what can be found; and, second, how to decide when no conclusion can be reached on the facts of the case.

The first question – that is, how to find out what can be found – has been the subject of systematic study in philosophy, psychology and mathematics. All three fields have contributed their share to the development of various models of deductive or inductive inferential reasoning in an effort to make sense of the proof process.[7] In this regard, significant attention has been given to probabilistic approaches, which require the fact-finder to consider the probability of the facts being 'true' on the basis of the available evidence. Various strands have emerged with a view to capturing these evaluative processes mathematically – such as Bayes' theorem – and have been both strongly supported and fiercely criticised in the literature.[8] However, probabilistic reasoning is not the only option. In reaction to its weaknesses, other theories have evolved – such as the relative plausibility theory, which maintains that the parties' arguments should be examined as a whole and then their relative plausibility should be considered vis-a-vis the alternative counterfactual.[9] Yet, despite one's best efforts, the danger remains: sometimes, adjudicators may still find themselves unable to decide on the 'truth' of the contested facts. Since 'adjudication can never be halted in indecision',[10] the second fundamental question that evidence law addresses is how to decide when the fact-finding exercise has failed to yield fruitful results. In practice, a fact-finding failure entails that one of the litigants must bear the risk of an erroneous ruling. Evidence rules allocate that risk between the parties and offer a way out of the deadlock.[11] The most effective risk-allocation mechanisms are the burden of proof and the standard of proof, both of which provide *who* and *under what conditions of uncertainty* will be forced by law to take the risk of a mistaken ruling in the case of a fact-finding failure.[12]

[7] See, eg, Jonathan Cohen, *An Introduction to the Philosophy of Induction and Probability* (Clarendon Press, 1989); Jonathan Cohen, *An Essay on Belief and Acceptance* (Clarendon Press, 1992); Ronald Allen and Brian Leiter, 'Naturalised Epistemology and the Law of Evidence' (2001) 87 *Virginia Law Review* 1491.

[8] See John Kaplan, 'Decision Theory and the Fact-Finding Process' (1968) 20 *Stanford Law Review* 1065; Richard Lempert, 'Modeling Relevance' (1976–77) 75 *Michigan Law Review* 1021; Jonathan Cohen, *The Probable and the Provable* (Clarendon Press, 1977); Peter Tillers and Eric Green (eds), *Probability and Inference in the Law of Evidence* (Kluwer Academic Publishers, 1988); David Schum, *The Evidential Foundations of Probabilistic Reasoning* (Northwestern University Press, 2001). *cf* Laurence Tribe, 'Trial by Mathematics: Precision and Ritual in the Legal Process' (1971) 84 *Harvard Law Review* 1329.

[9] Ronald Allen, 'The Nature of Juridical Proof' (1991) 13 *Cardozo Law Review* 373; Ronald Allen, 'Factual Ambiguity and a Theory of Evidence' (1994) 88 *Northwestern Law Review* 604.

[10] Stein (n 5) 34.

[11] ibid 107.

[12] For a brief account of the traditional burden of proof theory, see Ronald Allen, 'Burdens of Proof' (2014) 13 *Law, Probability & Risk* 195, 196–206.

In this sense, evidence rules perform an autonomous function in litigation: they provide adjudicators with specific fact-finding and decision-making tools. That said, however, their operation is subject to two important qualifications: *efficiency* and *fairness* considerations. Indeed, efficiency as a theme features prominently in evidence scholarship.[13] Although accuracy in fact-finding remains the ultimate goal, neither resources nor time are infinite. As Friedman put it, 'evidence does not simply show up in the courtroom. It must be produced, sometimes at a significant cost'.[14] In addition, more evidence does not always guarantee more accuracy; sometimes, the extra piece of information may simply not be worth the effort.[15] Therefore, every fact-trier is forced to stop at some point and make a decision based on the available evidence. These 'external constraints' of the fact-finding inquiry have best been illustrated in economic analyses of evidence law.[16] Usually, the latter adopt a cost-benefit perspective and seek to determine the extent to which the various evidence rules minimise cost or maximise wealth.[17] By perceiving evidence rules as economising devices, economic analyses of evidence law may protect the legal system from a futile waste of resources or never-ending trials.[18] However, despite their merits, they have been strongly criticised for failing to account for other non-economic values, which are equally – if not more – important.[19] Indeed, truth and efficiency are not desirable at *any* price; rather, they are subject to the overriding demands of justice. In practice, this means that evidence rules must be fair.[20] This is why evidence obtained through illegal means will normally not be taken into consideration in the fact-finding process, even if it could illuminate what happened, or why rules which may be inefficient in economic terms may nevertheless be preserved.[21]

All in all, this brief account shows that, by serving as fact-finding and decision-making devices, evidence rules perform an autonomous function in legal proceedings. Unsurprisingly, their content is principally driven by the need to ensure accuracy in fact-finding. However, efficiency and fairness considerations weigh in equally heavily. It is in view of these broad observations that the rest of this book identifies and evaluates the standards which govern the assessment of evidence in EU competition enforcement.

[13] See Stein (n 5) ch 5.

[14] Richard Friedman, 'Economic Analysis of Evidentiary Law: An Underused Tool, an Underplowed Field' (1998) 19 *Cardozo Law Review* 1531, 1532.

[15] Louis Kaplow, 'The Value of Accuracy in Adjudication: An Economic Analysis' (1994) 23 *Journal of Legal Studies* 307, 357.

[16] See Richard Posner, 'An Economic Approach to the Law of Evidence' (1999) 51 *Stanford Law Review* 1477.

[17] ibid 1480–87.

[18] Friedman (n 14) 1537–38.

[19] Richard Lempert, 'The Economic Analysis of Evidence Law: Common Sense on Stilts' (2001) 87 *Virginia Law Review* 1619.

[20] Stein (n 5) 26.

[21] Lempert (n 19) 1631–32.

III. Evidence Standards and EU Competition Enforcement

A. The Contextual Dependency of Evidence Standards

While evidence standards may well be autonomous, this does not mean they are completely independent; rather, their content is informed by the features of the enforcement system of which they form part.

The reasons for this contextual dependency are threefold. First of all, the fact-finding and decision-making process does not follow the same route in every enforcement model; rather, it differs according to its specific characteristics. For instance, in inquisitorial proceedings, the fact-finder assumes full responsibility for the fact-finding and actively engages in evidence production. By contrast, in adversarial settings, the fact-finder bases their decision only upon the evidence produced by the parties.[22] Likewise, the structure and function of civil litigation are very different from that of criminal enforcement: in the former case, both parties are private and priority is given to efficient dispute resolution, whereas in the latter case, one party is the prosecutor (that is, the state) and the emphasis is placed on protecting the public and securing justice, punishment and deterrence. In practice, this divergence means that in fulfilling their function, evidence standards cannot but be responsive to the specific features of the fact-finding and decision-making process in the enforcement model within which they operate.

Second, the contextual dependency of evidence standards derives from the fact that the fairness of the applicable evidence standards is impossible to determine in the abstract. Indeed, there is a consensus that evidence standards must be 'fair'. In the EU context specifically, this imperative emanates from the principle of effective judicial protection, as encapsulated in the CFR. Article 47 CFR dictates that 'everyone is entitled to a fair and public hearing within a reasonable time by an independent and impartial tribunal previously established by law', whereas Article 48 CFR expressly recognises the application of the presumption of innocence and the rights of defence 'for everyone who has been charged'.[23]

[22] The superiority of the inquisitorial over the adversarial system and vice versa has been extensively debated (see Allan Lind, John Thibaut and Laurens Walker, 'Discovery and Presentation of Evidence in Adversary and Nonadversary Proceedings' (1972) 71 *Michigan Law Review* 1129, 1140–43; John Anthony Jolowicz, 'Adversarial and Inquisitorial Models of Civil Procedure' (2003) 52 *International & Comparative Law Quarterly* 281). In reality, however, 'pure' versions of the models are rare and most systems combine elements of both, but are classified according to their predominant nature (Francesco Parisi, 'Rent-Seeking through Litigation: Adversarial and Inquisitorial Systems Compared' (2002) 22 *International Review of Law and Economics* 193).

[23] Articles 47 and 48 CFR constitute the EU equivalent of the right to a fair trial as enshrined in art 6 ECHR. Since the attribution to the CFR of the same legal value as the Treaties by virtue of art 6 of the Treaty on European Union (TEU), the EU Courts have stressed that 'Article 47 of the Charter secures in EU law the protection afforded by Art 6(1) of the ECHR' and 'it is necessary, therefore, to refer only to Article 47' (Case C-386/10 P *Chalkor v Commission*, ECLI:EU:C:2011:815, para 51; Case C-439/11 P *Ziegler v Commission*, ECLI:EU:C:2013:513, para 126).

Arguably, no provision – or the equivalent Article 6 ECHR – contains specific evidence prescriptions. However, evidence assessment constitutes a core aspect of legal decision-making. In this sense, evidence standards are essentially an integral part of the 'trial' itself.[24] Nevertheless, the fact that evidence standards are part of what makes judicial protection 'effective' does not reveal what evidence rules and principles are fair in the first place. Rather, the level of protection that Articles 47 and 48 CFR – as well as Article 6 ECHR – afford to individuals depends on the implications of enforcement action for their rights and interests, and the balance of power among the parties involved. Therefore, in order to evaluate the fairness of the applicable evidence standards, one must take into account the seriousness of the consequences of law enforcement for the individuals concerned and the power dynamics among the various stakeholders.

Finally, evidence standards are inevitably susceptible to the policy choices and practical challenges that underpin the enforcement of the field of law in question. An illustrative example of this may be found in employment discrimination cases. In view of the often insurmountable difficulties for employees to prove that they have been discriminated against by their employer, various jurisdictions around the world – including the EU – have reversed the burden of proof in order to ensure the effective enforcement of the principle of equal treatment by introducing a presumption of discrimination where the employee succeeds in establishing a prima facie case.[25] A different but equally representative example may be found in areas of law enforcement which involve specialised knowledge, such as healthcare or environmental protection. In these circumstances, the proper interpretation and application of the legal rules are often contingent on the latest scientific or technical knowledge. In order for their function to be effective, evidence standards must accommodate these external dependencies, whilst preserving the robustness and quality of legal decision-making.

B. The Specific Features of EU Competition Enforcement

In view of these remarks, attention must be paid to three important features of EU competition enforcement before identifying and analysing the standards which inform the evaluation of evidence in EU competition proceedings. These are: the prevailing administrative model; the consequences that Commission decisions

[24] Theodosios Karvounakis, 'Fair Criminal Evidence in Europe: From the European Convention on Human Rights to EU Criminal Law' (Queen Mary University of London, 2012) has correctly pointed out that the right to a fair trial is 'evidence-related' and 'can be read with respect to evidence law' (at 270–71). In *Otis*, the CJEU explained that the principle of effective judicial protection 'comprises various elements', including the rights of defence, the equality of arms principle and the presumption of innocence. (Case C-199/11 *Otis and Others*, ECLI:EU:C:2012:684, para 48). As will be shown, all three play a key role in the formulation of appropriate evidence rules and principles.

[25] Directive 2006/54/EC of the European Parliament and of the Council of 5 July 2006 on the implementation of the principle of equal opportunities and equal treatment of men and women in matters of employment and occupation (recast) [2006] OJ L204/23, Recital 30 and art 19.

may have for the undertakings involved; and the interplay between competition law and economics.

i. The Administrative Model of Enforcement

Different enforcement models may call for different evidence standards. At the EU level, the enforcement of the competition rules has been based on traditional systems of administrative justice. As such, it comprises two distinct phases. At first instance, decisions on the compatibility of a firm's conduct with Articles 101 and 102 TFEU or the EUMR are made by the Commission. Then, the Commission's decisions may be challenged before the EU Courts. Therefore, a few remarks are necessary about both the administrative and the judicial leg of EU competition enforcement and the role of the Commission and the EU Courts respectively.

a. The Administrative Phase

The Commission is the institution in charge of ensuring the application of the EU competition rules. To this end, it has been equipped with extensive powers not only to investigate suspected infringements of Articles 101 and 102 TFEU or notified concentrations, but also to decide whether it should intervene in the market and how. Accordingly, in the administrative phase of EU competition enforcement, the Commission combines – as has been rightly observed – the roles of the prosecutor, the investigator and the adjudicator.[26] Unsurprisingly, this combination of roles is not without its implications. Its broad powers to gather evidence and decide on whether the EU competition rules have been violated have turned the Commission into the leading fact-finder in both infringement and merger proceedings. Because of this, the latter are often characterised are inquisitorial in nature.[27] However, it should be noted that such classification is not entirely accurate. Putting the debates over the superiority of the inquisitorial or adversarial model of evidence production to one side,[28] the inquisitorial features of the administrative phase of EU competition enforcement have been mitigated by the adversarial principle.[29] As has been long recognised by the EU Courts, this principle applies to competition proceedings and requires that 'the undertakings concerned must have been afforded the opportunity, during the administrative procedure, to make known its

[26] Wouter Wils, 'The Combination of the Investigative and Prosecutorial Function and the Adjudicative Function in EC Antitrust Enforcement: A Legal and Economic Analysis' (2004) 27 *World Competition* 201.

[27] Damien Neven, 'Competition Economics and Antitrust in Europe' (2005) 21 *Economic Policy* 741, 763.

[28] See n 22.

[29] In principle, the EU Courts do not search for the truth of their own motion; rather, they decide on the facts based on the pleas made and the evidence proffered by the parties. For more on this, see ch 7, section III.A.

views on the truth and relevance of the facts and circumstances alleged and on the documents used by the Commission to support its claim that there has been an infringement of the EC Treaty'.[30]

The adversarial principle has somewhat tempered the inquisitorial nature of administrative competition proceedings. Nevertheless, in order for the right to challenge the evidence to be truly effective, both parties must be on an equal footing in accordance with the principle of equality of arms.[31] As the EU Courts have explained, the latter 'is no more than a corollary of the very concept of a fair hearing'[32] and implies that 'each party must be afforded a reasonable opportunity to present his evidence, under conditions that do not place him at a substantial disadvantage vis-a-vis his opponent'.[33] Such 'substantial disadvantage' must not be understood formalistically and may arise where one party's resources and powers outweigh the other's means.[34] Seen through this prism, however, competition proceedings appear to suffer from what Roberts and Zuckerman have aptly called the 'adversarial deficit'.[35] By default, the Commission is in a much better position than undertakings to produce evidence due to its wide investigative powers, whereas several features of the administrative proceedings – such as the tight deadlines for replying to the Statement of Objections or the fact that not all collected evidence is communicated to the investigated undertakings – place the latter at a substantial disadvantage vis-a-vis the authority.[36]

The disparity of arms between the Commission and the investigated undertakings should not be taken lightly. By contrast, the principle of effective judicial protection and the right to a fair trial require that restorative measures be adopted to reverse the 'substantial disadvantage' at which undertakings may find themselves.

[30] Case C-413/06 P *Bertelsmann and Sony Corporation of America v Impala*, ECLI:EU:C:2008:392, para 61. For the ECtHR's position, see *Ruiz-Mateos v Spain*, ECLI:CE:ECHR:1993:0623JUD001295287, para 63.

[31] *Barberà, Messegué and Jabardo v Spain*, ECLI:CE:ECHR:1988:1206JUD001059083, para 78; *Brandstetter v Austria*, ECLI:CE:ECHR:1991:0828JUD001117084, paras 66–67; *Rowe and Davis v United Kingdom*, ECLI:CE:ECHR:2000:0216JUD002890195, para 60.

[32] Joined Cases C-514/07 P, C-528/07 P and C-532/07 P *Sweden and Others v API and Commission*, ECLI:EU:C:2010:541, para 88.

[33] *Otis* (n 24) para 71; Case C-580/12 P *Guardian Industries and Guardian Europe v Commission*, ECLI:EU:C:2014:2363, para 31. For the ECtHR position, see *Salov v Ukraine*, ECLI:CE:ECHR:2005:0906JUD006551801, para 78.

[34] John Jackson, 'The Effect of Human Rights on Criminal Evidentiary Processes: Towards Convergence, Divergence or Realignment?' (2005) 68 *Modern Law Review* 737, 751–52; Mark Janis, Richard Kay and Anthony Bradley, *European Human Rights Law*, 3rd edn (Oxford University Press, 2008) 792, 797–98.

[35] Paul Roberts and Adrian Zuckerman, *Criminal Evidence*, 2nd edn (Oxford University Press, 2010) 15.

[36] James Venit, 'Human All Too Human: The Gathering and Assessment of Evidence and the Appropriate Standard of Proof and Judicial Review in Commission Enforcement Proceedings Applying Articles 81 and 82' in Claus-Dieter Ehlermann and Mel Marquis (eds), *European Competition Law Annual 2009: The Evaluation of Evidence and its Judicial Review in Competition Cases* (Hart Publishing, 2010) 229–30.

Such restorative measures typically take the form of different defence rights and properly adjusted evidence rules.[37] Indeed, the EU Courts have consistently confirmed that the rights of defence should be respected 'in all proceedings initiated against a person which are liable to culminate in a measure adversely affecting that person'.[38] However, evidence standards in EU competition enforcement must also account for the inequality of arms that emanates from the Commission's role as the leading fact-finder in administrative competition proceedings.[39] This is all the more crucial considering that the Commission's investigative powers are complemented with far-reaching decision-making powers as well. This symbiosis of a fact-finding and a decision-making function within the same body has been frequently criticised as depriving the Commission of its independence and impartiality, and increasing the risk of prosecutorial and other biases.[40] This risk becomes amplified by the fact that the Commission is not only an administrative agency, but also a political institution; eventually, the ultimate decision on the finding of an infringement of Articles 101 and 102 TFEU or on the compatibility of a concentration with the common market is for the College of Commissioners to make, ie, a political body with minimal (if any) involvement in the actual administrative process.[41]

Therefore, the applicable standards of evidence assessment must be tailored to the distinct features of the administrative phase of EU competition enforcement – as just described – and must compensate for the implications arising from the Commission's multiple roles.

b. The Judicial Phase

Administrative proceedings constitute only the first part of EU competition enforcement. Once a Commission decision has been adopted in relation to either Articles 101 and 102 TFEU or the EUMR, it may then be appealed before the EU Courts.[42] Broadly speaking, judicial review reflects the 'control exercised by the [EU] Courts to ensure the proper and lawful enforcement of the competition rules' by the authority.[43] However, such control is subject to two important limitations.

[37] Roberts and Zuckerman (n 35) 14–15, 59.

[38] Case C-32/95 P *Commission v Lisrestal and Others*, ECLI:EU:C:1996:402, para 21. See also Regulation 1/2003, Recitals 16, 32 and arts 12(3) and 27(2); EUMR, Recitals 36–37.

[39] This conclusion is not weakened by the fact that during the judicial phase, EU judges enjoy significant case management powers and may order a variety of measures of organisation and inquiry. The EU Courts are under no obligation to actively engage in fact-finding.

[40] Ian Forrester, 'Due Process in EC Competition Cases: A Distinguished Institution with Flawed Procedures' (2009) 34 *European Law Review* 817, 821, 831.

[41] ibid 831–32. *cf* Yannis Karagiannis, 'The Causes and Consequences of the Collegial Implementation of European Competition Law' (2013) 19 *European Law Journal* 682.

[42] Art 263 TFEU; Regulation 1/2003, Recital 33; and EUMR, art 21(2).

[43] David Bailey, 'Scope of Judicial Review under Article 81 EC' (2004) 41 *Common Market Law Review* 1327, 1330.

By default, Commission decisions are 'presumed to be valid'[44] and can only be challenged on specific grounds concerning their lawfulness.[45] Furthermore, EU judges cannot go as far as substituting their opinion for that of the authority: if a Commission decision is found to be defective, all they can do is merely to annul it.[46]

In view of these restrictions, the rigorousness with which the EU Courts review the legality of the Commission decisions becomes of the utmost importance. In principle, the intensity of judicial control fluctuates depending on its subject matter. According to settled case law, questions of fact and issues of law are subject to comprehensive review and the EU Courts are expected to thoroughly scrutinise Commission decisions for errors in the authority's factual findings or its interpretation of the legal rules.[47] By contrast, policy choices and complex assessments are in principle subject to marginal review.[48] This is thought to be a less strict standard of judicial control which allows the Commission some latitude and entails checking 'whether the relevant procedural rules have been complied with, whether the statement of the reasons for the decision is adequate, whether the facts have been accurately stated and whether there has been a manifest error of appraisal or misuse of powers'.[49] That said, however, the EU Courts have explained that despite the Commission's appreciation in relation to economic matters, they will not 'refrain from reviewing the Commission's interpretation of information of an economic nature'. By contrast, they will carefully examine 'whether the evidence relied on is factually accurate, reliable and consistent, but also whether that evidence contains all the information which must be taken into account in order to assess a complex situation and whether it is capable of substantiating the conclusions drawn from it'.[50]

The EU Courts' deferential attitude towards the Commission's policy choices and complex economic assessments has been criticised, especially in proceedings

[44] Case T-12/89 *Solvay v Commission*, ECLI:EU:T:1992:34, para 347; Case T-310/00 *MCI v Commission*, ECLI:EU:T:2004:275, para 55; Case T-282/06 *Sun Chemical Group and Others v Commission*, ECLI:EU:T:2007:203, para 59.

[45] Art 263(2) TFEU. However, it should be noted that with respect to penalties and financial sanctions, the EU Courts retain unlimited jurisdiction and may cancel, reduce or increase the fine or periodic penalty imposed (art 261 TFEU; Regulation 1/2003, art 31; EUMR, art 16).

[46] Case T-210/01 *General Electric v Commission*, ECLI:EU:T:2005:456, para 312.

[47] Case C-386/10 P *Chalkor v Commission*, ECLI:EU:C:2011:815, para 62.

[48] See, for example, Case T-201/04 *Microsoft v Commission*, ECLI:EU:T:2007:289, paras 87–88; Case T-21/05 *Chalkor v Commission*, ECLI:EU:T:2010:205, para 63. See also Case C-12/03 P *Commission v Tetra Laval* (*Tetra Laval II*), ECLI:EU:C:2004:318, Opinion of AG Tizzano, para 85.

[49] Case 42/84 *Remia v Commission*, ECLI:EU:C:1985:327, para 34; Joined Cases 142/84 and 156/84 *British American Tobacco and Reynolds Industries v Commission*, ECLI:EU:C:1987:490, para 62; Case T-271/03 *Deutsche Telekom v Commission*, ECLI:EU:T:2008:101, para 185; Case T-336/07 *Telefónica and Telefónica de España v Commission*, ECLI:EU:T:2012:172, para 70; Case T-360/09 *E.ON Ruhrgas and E.ON v Commission*, ECLI:EU:T:2012:332, para 69.

[50] *Chalkor* (n 47) para 54.

concerning the application of Articles 101 and 102 TFEU.[51] The thrust of the expressed objections can be synopsised in the claim that the EU Courts' control over Commission decisions falls short of the prescriptions of the principle of effective judicial protection and the right to a fair trial, insofar as it fails to compensate for the 'fairness deficit' in the administrative competition proceedings.[52] Since evidence assessment constitutes an intrinsic part of the control that the EU Courts carry out, these debates cannot be ignored. For this reason, Chapter 7 is devoted to analysing the interplay between standards of judicial review and standards of evidence assessment.

ii. The Consequences of Commission Decisions for Undertakings

In addition to the prevalent model of enforcement, one must also be mindful of the consequences that Commission infringement or merger decisions may have for the undertakings involved. The reason is simple: the greater the potential adverse effects of a Commission decision, the higher the level of procedural protection that the undertakings concerned are entitled to in competition proceedings. Two remarks are necessary in this regard: first of all, EU competition law inevitably interferes with the economic freedom of undertakings, to the extent that it proscribes certain forms of commercial conduct; and, second, the fines that the Commission may impose for violations of Articles 101 and 102 TFEU are of at least a quasi-criminal nature.

a. Competition Law as a Limit to Economic Freedom

The need for rules on competition was recognised early on in the history of the EU. Adopted as a complement to the 'four freedoms', the competition rules were intended to contribute to the creation of the internal market by preventing individuals from reinstating barriers to trade.[53] However, while market integration remains a core aspect of EU competition enforcement, competition law has now evolved into an autonomous branch of EU law. Articles 101 and 102 TFEU prohibit anti-competitive agreements and abuses of dominance, whereas the EUMR sets up a system of merger control aimed at monitoring the compatibility of concentrations

[51] Similar issues have been raised in the context of merger control, although they have not gained as much prominence. See George Cumming, *Merger Decisions and the Rules of Procedure of the European Community Courts* (Kluwer Law International, 2011) 228–29; Anca Daniela Chirita, 'Procedural Rights in EU Administrative Competition Proceedings: Ex Ante – Mergers' in Caroline Cauffman and Quian Hao (eds), *Procedural Rights in Competition Law* (Springer, 2015).

[52] See ch 7, section II.B.

[53] Giuliano Marenco, 'The Birth of Modern Competition Law in Europe' in Armin von Bogdandy, Petros Mavroidis and Yves Mény (eds), *European Integration and International Coordination: Studies in Transnational Economic Law in Honour of Claus-Dieter Ehlermann* (Kluwer Law International, 2002) 297–98; Joanna Goyder and Albertina Albors-Llorens, *Goyder's EC Competition Law*, 5th edn (Oxford University Press, 2009) 24–39.

with an EU dimension with the common market. The precise goals of EU competition law have been vigorously debated.[54] Yet, beyond this discussion, the point that this section intends to emphasise is that the competition rules regulate the behaviour of firms in the market by imposing restrictions on certain types of commercial conduct that an undertaking would be otherwise allowed to engage in.[55] This holds true both in antitrust and in merger cases. However, economic freedom is central to the conception of the EU as a free market. Although the ECHR does not contain an explicit legal basis for its protection, it has been correctly observed that this may be easily deduced from the combined interpretation of the right to respect for private life, the freedom of association, the right to receive and impart information and the right to property.[56] Similar protection is afforded by the CFR: Article 17 enshrines the traditional right to property, whereas Article 16 expressly provides for the freedom to conduct a business.

Admittedly, economic freedom is not absolute; its exercise may be subject to limitations.[57] Nevertheless, any restrictions must be 'necessary and [must] genuinely meet objectives of general interest recognised by the Union or the need to protect the rights and freedoms of others'.[58] Examining the applicant's property-based plea in his Opinion in *Masterfoods*, AG Cosmas explained that:

> [T]here is no doubt that Articles [101 and 102 TFEU] occupy an important position in the system of the [EU] legal order and serve the general interest which consists in ensuring undistorted competition. Consequently, it is perfectly comprehensible for restrictions to be placed on the right to property ownership pursuant to Articles [101 and 102 TFEU], to the degree to which they might be necessary to protect competition.[59]

However, the fact that the protection of competition and the effectiveness of competition enforcement constitute an objective of general interest capable of placing lawful limitations on the economic freedom of undertakings[60] does not eliminate the need to ensure the legitimacy of such limitations. According to the

[54] There is an abundance of scholarship on this issue. See generally Daniel Zimmer (ed), *The Goals of Competition Law* (Edward Elgar, 2012); Oles Andriychuk, *The Normative Foundations of European Competition Law* (Edward Elgar, 2017).

[55] *cf* Renato Nazzini, *The Foundations of European Union Competition Law: The Objective and Principles of Article 102* (Oxford University Press, 2011) 20.

[56] Articles 8, 11 and 10 ECHR and art 1 of Protocol I to the ECHR. These rights can be claimed by both physical and legal persons. See art 1 ECHR; and Marius Emberland, *The Human Rights of Companies: Exploring the Structure of ECHR Protection* (Oxford University Press, 2006) 33–35. See also *Markt Intern Verlag GmbH and Klaus Beermann v Germany*, ECLI:CE:ECHR:1989:1120JUD001057283, para 26; *Niemietz v Germany*, ECLI:CE:ECHR:1992:1216JUD001371088, para 29; and Arianna Andreangeli, *EU Competition Enforcement and Human Rights* (Edward Elgar, 2008) 16.

[57] Articles 8(2) and 10(2) ECHR, art 1 of Protocol I to the ECHR and art 17(1) CFR. See also Case 5/88 *Wachauf*, ECLI:EU:C:1989:321, para 18; Case C-292/97 *Karlsson and Others*, ECLI:EU:C:2000:202, para 45.

[58] Art 52(1) CFR.

[59] Case C-344/98 *Masterfoods and HB*, ECLI:EU:C:2000:249, Opinion of AG Cosmas, para 105.

[60] Wouter Wils, 'EU Antitrust Enforcement Powers and Procedural Rights and Guarantees: The Interplay between EU Law, National Law, the Charter of Fundamental Rights of the EU and the European Convention On Human Rights' (2011) 34 *World Competition* 189, 202.

ECtHR, the latter will depend on whether 'a "fair balance" has been struck between the demands of the general interest of the community and the requirements of the protection of the individual's fundamental rights'.[61] Yet, striking a 'fair balance' requires considering, inter alia, 'the degree of protection from arbitrariness that is afforded' in the proceedings through which the measures in question have been adopted, as well as the possibility for the individual to appeal the decision in question.[62] Therefore, in the EU competition context, the applicable standards of procedural fairness – evidence standards included – should account for the regulatory effect of the Commission's decision-making.[63]

This remark is particularly important in the context of merger control. As will be explained shortly, the ECHR-criminal nature of Commission decisions imposing a fine for violations of Articles 101 and 102 TFEU has accentuated the need for adequate procedural safeguards in antitrust infringement proceedings. By contrast, the applicability of the principle of effective judicial protection to merger proceedings[64] and the potential implications of a Commission merger decision for the undertakings involved are not always fully appreciated.[65] Nevertheless, one must bear in mind that Commission decisions declaring a concentration with an EU dimension as incompatible with the common market also interfere with the merging entities' economic freedom.[66] The absence of financial penalties does not eliminate the fact that the merging entities may suffer significant financial consequences if their transaction does not survive the Commission's investigation.[67] Consequently, as Steenbergen rightly pointed out, 'public authorities should be required to make very good arguments if they intend to prohibit such transactions'.[68]

b. The at Least Quasi-criminal Nature of Antitrust Fines

Proceedings concerning the application of Articles 101 and 102 TFEU and the EUMR share many common features. Nevertheless, merger control is built upon

[61] *Chassagnou and Others v France*, ECLI:CE:ECHR:1999:0429JUD002508894, para 75.

[62] *Hentrich v France*, ECLI:CE:ECHR:1994:0922JUD001361688, paras 45, 49.

[63] See also Arianna Andreangeli, 'Between Economic Freedom and Effective Competition Enforcement: The Impact of the Antitrust Remedies Provided by the Modernisation Regulation on Investigated Parties' Freedom to Contract and to Enjoy Property' (2010) 6 *Competition Law Review* 225, 229–34.

[64] Andreangeli ((n 56) 29–30) justifies the engagement of the civil head of art 6(1) ECHR by paralleling merger proceedings with state procedures of authorisation of land transactions (see the therein referred cases: *Ringeisen v Austria*, ECLI:CE:ECHR:1971:0716JUD000261465; and *Sramek v Austria*, ECLI:CE:ECHR:1984:1022JUD000879079). At any rate, art 47 CFR does not distinguish between 'civil rights and obligations' and 'criminal charges' (Wils (n 60) 202). On this point more generally, see Piero Leanza and Ondrej Pridal, *The Right to a Fair Trial: Article 6 of the European Convention on Human Rights* (Kluwer Law International, 2014).

[65] See exceptionally Mihalis Kekelekis, *EC Merger Control Regulation: Rights of Defence* (Kluwer Law International, 2006); and Chirita (n 51).

[66] Justin Coombs and Jorge Padilla, 'The Use of Economic Evidence before the Courts of the European Union' in Ehlermann and Marquis (n 36) 482.

[67] David Bailey, 'Standard of Proof in EC Merger Proceedings: A Common Law Perspective' (2003) 40 *Common Market Law Review* 845, 867.

[68] Ehlermann and Marquis (n 36) 50.

a system of *ex ante* intervention driven by precautionary deliberations, whereas intervention on the basis of Articles 101 and 102 TFEU takes place entirely *ex post*. This divergence has crucial implications for the possible content of Commission decisions. Decisions based on the EUMR may either allow or prohibit the notified concentration to proceed. Accordingly, fines and other periodic penalty payments may be imposed only to ensure compliance with the EUMR.[69] By contrast, Commission decisions finding a violation of Articles 101 and 102 TFEU are typically accompanied by heavy financial penalties which aim at ensuring compliance with the competition rules and have both a deterrent and a punitive function.[70] The strict fining policy pursued by the Commission over the past few years is reflected in the steady increase in the level of monetary sanctions for engagement in anti-competitive conduct and has given rise to complaints that antitrust fines go far beyond typical administrative sanctions and amount to 'criminal charges'.[71] This discussion is not merely theoretical; on the contrary, it has profound implications for the identification of appropriate standards of procedural fairness to be guaranteed in infringement proceedings. Where criminal charges are involved, Article 48 CFR complements the protection provided by Article 47 CFR, whereas when Article 6(1) ECHR is engaged under its criminal head, Article 6(2) and (3) ECHR applies as well. In this light, it is necessary to consider the arguments that antitrust fines are criminal in nature and thus call for criminal standards of procedural protection.

1. Antitrust Fines as 'Criminal Charge' under Article 6 ECHR

Naturally, this debate brings to the forefront the question what constitutes a 'criminal charge'. Having consistently emphasised the autonomous meaning to be attributed to this notion,[72] in the *Engel* case, the ECtHR identified three conditions for classifying a sanction as a 'criminal charge'.[73] According to the *Engel* criteria, in order to determine whether a penalty is of a criminal nature, account must be taken of the following: the classification of the charge in national law; the nature of the offence; and the degree of severity of the penalty that the person concerned risks incurring.[74]

However, these conditions are not cumulative. The ECtHR was careful to emphasise that the classification of the sanction under national law is merely the starting point. When the rest of the criteria are satisfied, the exclusion of the penalty from the national list of criminal charges is irrelevant. Similarly, the administrative

[69] EUMR, Recital 43 and art 15.

[70] Regulation 1/2003, art 23(2).

[71] *cf* Wouter Wils, 'The Increased Level of EU Antitrust Fines, Judicial Review, and the European Convention on Human Rights' (2010) 33 *World Competition* 5, 10–12. On the criminalisation of competition law, see Wouter Wils, 'Is Criminalization of EU Competition Law the Answer?' (2005) 28 *World Competition* 117.

[72] *Adolf v Austria*, ECLI:CE:ECHR:1982:0326JUD000826978, para 30.

[73] *Engel and Others v The Netherlands*, ECLI:CE:ECHR:1976:0608JUD000510071, para 82.

[74] ibid.

nature of the national proceedings in question has not prevented the ECtHR from applying the *Engel* criteria and from finding a number of penalties – ranging from road traffic violations to tax surcharges and disciplinary sanctions – as falling within the notion of a 'criminal charge'.[75] Similar conclusions have been reached regarding competition fines. For instance, in its report in *Société Stenuit*, the now defunct European Commission of Human Rights took the view that in light of its severity, the competition fine in question was a criminal charge.[76] More recently, in its *Menarini* ruling, the ECtHR examined the financial penalty imposed by the Italian competition authority in the light of the *Engel* conditions and verified that the Italian competition rules were intended to protect an interest of a general nature, that is, the maintenance of undistorted competition on the market, and that the imposed fine was of both a punitive and a deterrent character.[77] On these grounds, the ECtHR found that Article 6(1) ECHR was engaged under its criminal head.[78]

2. The Position of the EU Courts

Contrary to the ECtHR's rather expansive understanding of criminality,[79] the EU Courts' approach to arguments that antitrust fines are criminal in nature has been more reserved. Referring to Article 23(5) of Regulation 1/2003 in *Volkswagen*, the CJEU confirmed that decisions imposing a fine for participation in an infringement of the competition rules 'are not of a criminal law nature' and rejected the applicant's argument on the ground that – were it to be upheld – 'this would impinge seriously on the effectiveness of Community competition law'.[80] Likewise, in *Compagnie Maritime Belge*, the GCEU repeated that 'the effectiveness of Community competition law would be seriously affected if the argument that competition law formed part of criminal law were accepted'.[81] By the same token, the EU Courts have consistently underlined that, insofar as the purpose of the procedure before the Commission is to apply the competition rules, 'even where it

[75] See, eg, *Öztürk v Germany*, ECLI:CE:ECHR:1984:0221JUD000854479; *Bendenoun v France*, ECLI:CE:ECHR:1994:0224JUD001254786; *Janosevic v Sweden*, ECLI:CE:ECHR:2002:0723JUD003461997; *Jussila v Finland*, ECLI:CE:ECHR:2006:1123JUD007305301; *Dubus v France*, ECLI:CE:ECHR:2009:0611JUD000524204.

[76] *Société Stenuit v France*, Report of the European Commission of Human Rights of 11 July 1989, para 64 (note that the fine in question corresponded to five per cent of the undertaking's annual turnover). See also *M & Co v Germany*, European Commission of Human Rights' Decision of 9 February 1990.

[77] *Menarini Diagnostics SRL v Italy*, ECLI:CE:ECHR:2011:0927JUD004350908, paras 40–42. *cf OOO Neste St Petersburg v Russia*, European Commission of Human Rights' Decision of 3 June 2004.

[78] See also *Société Bouygues Telecom v France*, ECLI:CE:ECHR:2012:0512JUD000002324, where the applicability of art 6(2) ECHR was not even questioned.

[79] Renato Nazzini, 'Administrative Enforcement, Judicial Review and Fundamental Rights in EU Competition Law: A Comparative Contextual-Functionalist Perspective' (2012) 49 *Common Market Law Review* 971, 979 ff.

[80] Case C-338/00 P *Volkswagen v Commission*, ECLI:EU:C:2003:473, paras 96–97. See also Case T-83/91 *Tetra Pak v Commission* (*Tetra Pak I*), ECLI:EU:T:1994:246, para 235.

[81] Case T-276/04 *Compagnie Maritime Belge v Commission*, ECLI:EU:T:2008:237, para 66.

may lead to the imposition of fines, it is an administrative procedure'.[82] Advocates General, on the other hand, have been more open to acknowledging the ECHR-criminal nature of antitrust fines. In his Opinion in *Rhône-Poulenc*, AG Vesterdorf took into account the ECtHR's interpretation of Article 6(1) ECHR and noted that antitrust fines 'have a criminal law character'.[83] Similarly, in his Opinion in *Baustalhgewebe*, AG Léger asserted that the case law of the ECtHR leaves no doubt that antitrust fines amount to a 'criminal charge'.[84] Last but not least, in her Opinion in *KME v Commission*, AG Sharpston accepted that 'the procedure whereby a fine is imposed for breach of the prohibition on price-fixing and market-sharing agreements in Article [101(1) TFEU] falls under the "criminal head" of Article 6 ECHR' as defined by the ECtHR.[85]

However, despite their reluctance to expressly recognise the ECHR-criminal nature of antitrust fines, the EU Courts have stressed on numerous occasions that 'the observance of the rights of the defence constitutes a fundamental principle of Community law which must be respected in all circumstances, in particular in any procedure which may give rise to penalties, even if it is an administrative procedure'.[86] In addition to the rights of defence, the EU Courts have also introduced traditional criminal law guarantees into infringement proceedings. Not only have they confirmed the relevance of 'the principle of non-retroactivity, in any administrative procedure capable of leading to fines under the Treaty rules on competition',[87] but EU judges have also recognised that 'given the nature of the infringements in question and the nature and degree of severity of the ensuing penalties, the principle of the presumption of innocence applies to the procedures relating to infringements of the competition rules applicable to undertakings that may result in the imposition of fines or periodic penalty payments'.[88] Finally, although it did not explicitly endorse the *Engel* criteria as set out by the ECtHR, in *Schindler Holding* the CJEU referred to *Menarini* and took note of the fact that in its ruling, the ECtHR found that the competition fine imposed in this case fell within the criminal sphere.[89]

[82] See Case 45/69 *Boehringer Mannheim v Commission*, ECLI:EU:C:1970:73, para 23. More recently, see Case T-99/04 *AC-Treuhand v Commission*, ECLI:EU:T:2008:256, para 113.

[83] Joined Cases T-1/89 to T-4/89 and T-6/89 to T-15/89 *Rhône-Poulenc v Commission*, ECLI:EU:T:1991:38, Opinion of AG Vesterdorf, 885.

[84] Case C-185/95 P *Baustahlgewebe v Commission*, ECLI:EU:C:1998:37, Opinion of AG Léger, para 31.

[85] Case C-272/09 P *KME v Commission*, ECLI:EU:C:2011:63, Opinion of AG Sharpston, para 64; however, note para 67.

[86] Case T-314/01 *Avebe v Commission*, ECLI:EU:T:2006:266, para 49; Case T-58/01 *Solvay v Commission*, ECLI:EU:T:2009:520, para 223.

[87] Case T-220/00 *Cheil Jedang v Commission*, ECLI:EU:T:2003:193, para 44; Joined Cases T-117/07 and T-121/07 *Areva and Others v Commission*, ECLI:EU:T:2011:69, para 133.

[88] Case C-199/92 P *Hüls v Commission*, ECLI:EU:C:1999:358, paras 149–50; see also Case C-235/92 P *Montecatini v Commission*, ECLI:EU:C:1999:362, paras 175–76.

[89] Case C-501/11 P *Schindler Holding and Others v Commission*, ECLI:EU:C:2013:522, para 33.

This complicated picture begs the question as to how much procedural protection undertakings must be afforded in infringement proceedings. The jurisprudence of both the ECtHR and the EU Courts suggests that high standards of protection are called for. However, what is not entirely clear is how high exactly such standards should be. The answer to this question becomes further complicated if one considers the ECtHR's ruling in *Jussila*. Having found that a tax surcharge amounted to a criminal charge for the purposes of Article 6(1) ECHR, the ECtHR went on to state that 'it is self-evident that there are criminal cases which do not carry any significant degree of stigma' and that 'there are clearly "criminal charges" of differing weight'. Observing then that the autonomous interpretation of the notion of a 'criminal charge' in accordance with the *Engel* criteria has broadened the criminal head of Article 6(1) ECHR 'to cases not strictly belonging to the traditional categories of the criminal law', such as competition law, the ECtHR remarked that such cases 'differ from the hard core of criminal law' and therefore 'the criminal-head guarantees will not necessarily apply with their full stringency'.[90]

Unsurprisingly, *Jussila* gave rise to difficult questions as to what constitutes 'hard-core' and peripheral criminal law, and what criminal-head guarantees will be necessary in each case. It is probably for this reason that the ECtHR carefully omitted any reference to it in *Menarini*. Nevertheless, the question remains: should the full length of criminal procedural safeguards be activated in infringement proceedings? In *Schindler Holding*, the EU Courts acknowledged for the first time the ECHR-criminal dimension of competition fines. While this is a welcome development, it does not automatically mean that all criminal procedural standards apply to antitrust proceedings; rather, the EU Courts have consistently balanced fairness arguments with the need to secure the effectiveness of the enforcement system. It is against this background that the following chapters examine the fairness of the applicable evidence standards.

iii. The Interplay between Competition Law and Economics

Last but not least, when analysing the standards which underpin the assessment of evidence in EU competition enforcement, one must be mindful of the close interplay between competition law and economics. In this regard, it should be clarified that 'economics' may refer to two different types of analysis in competition enforcement: on the one hand, the assessment of the effects of firm conduct on competition – also known as *industrial organisation*;[91] and, on the other hand, the evaluation of the costs and benefits of law in light of its potential impact on business behaviour and competition – also known as *economic analysis of law*.[92]

[90] *Jussila* (n 75) para 43.
[91] See Dennis Carlton and Jeffrey Perloff, *Modern Industrial Organisation*, 4th edn (Pearson, 2015).
[92] See, eg, Richard Posner, *Economic Analysis of Law* (Aspen Publishers, 2011).

Both types of economics may influence enforcement in multiple ways.[93] For instance, they may inform the design of enforcement priorities. Since administrative agencies' resources are limited, it makes sense to focus only on those practices which harm competition and, in particular, on the most injurious among them, so as to deter such conduct. Economics may also instruct the interpretation of the competition rules and the formulation of legal tests. Articles 101 and 102 TFEU, as well as the EUMR, prohibit 'restrictions of competition', 'abuses of a dominant position' and 'concentrations which would significantly impede effective competition' in the common market if allowed to proceed. However, these proscriptions are too vague to be operational as such and are thus in need of further elaboration. In this context, economics may provide valuable insights into whether a rule of prima facie illegality should be preferred over a case-by-case evaluation of the lawfulness of a practice, given the nature of the conduct and the potential impact of the law on firm behaviour.[94] The prohibition of cartels as 'by object' violations of antitrust law, for example, rests on the premise that conduct of this kind lacks any efficiency justification and thus a rule of prima facie illegality is not likely to chill procompetitive behaviour; on the contrary, it may deter harmful practices. Likewise, the 'by effect' analysis of exclusive dealing under Article 101(1) TFEU is explained by the potential efficiencies that such practices may entail and the risk of discouraging conduct which may be beneficial. Last but not least, economics may be employed at the level of adjudication too – for instance, for the production of complex economic evidence to empirically support the parties' arguments, alongside 'traditional' types of evidence, such as documents or statements.[95]

These remarks are crucial from an evidence perspective. The early application of the EU competition rules by the Commission was rather formalistic. The authority favoured an expansive interpretation of the scope of the provisions and tended to equate restrictions on the parties' freedom to act with restrictions of competition.[96] As a result, its enforcement was attacked as being error-prone and as lacking economic sophistication.[97] In response to these criticisms, the

[93] See Maarten Pieter Schinkel, 'Forensic Economics in Competition Law Enforcement' (2008) 4 *Journal of Competition Law & Economics* 1; Christopher Decker, *Economics and the Enforcement of European Competition Law* (Edward Elgar, 2009).

[94] See generally Louis Kaplow, 'Rules versus Standards: An Economic Analysis' (1992) 42 *Duke Law Journal* 557; Frederick Beckner and Steven Salop, 'Decision Theory and Antitrust Rules' (1999) 67 *Antitrust Law Journal* 41; Daniel Crane, 'Rules versus Standards in Antitrust Adjudication' (2007) 64 *Washington and Lee Law Review* 49.

[95] Peter Freeman, 'The Significance of Economic Evidence in Competition Cases' (IEA Beesley Lecture Series, 2009), available at: www.rpieurope.org/Beesley/2009/Peter%20Freeman.pdf.

[96] See generally Heike Schweitzer and Kiran Klaus Patel (eds), *The Historical Foundations of EU Competition Law* (Oxford University Press, 2013); David Gerber, *Law and Competition in Twentieth-Century Europe: Protecting Prometheus* (Oxford University Press, 2001).

[97] Valentine Korah, 'EEC Competition Policy – Legal Form or Economic Efficiency' (1986) 39 *Current Legal Problems* 85; Barry Hawk, 'System Failure: Vertical Restraints and EC Competition Law' (1995) 32 *Common Market Law Review* 973.

Commission gradually revisited its policy in various areas, including vertical restraints, horizontal cooperation agreements and unilateral conduct, by adopting new Block Exemption Regulations and by publishing several sets of guidelines. In these documents, the authority committed itself to a 'more economic' approach to the application of the competition rules by proclaiming consumer welfare as the driving goal of its enforcement and by identifying market power as the trigger for intervention. The precise implications of this shift are still the subject of debate.[98] In any event, it is clear that the multifaceted integration of economics in competition enforcement raises interesting – and significant – questions from the perspective of evidence standards, which are explored throughout this book.

For instance, must the economics underlying the choice between a rule of prima facie illegality or case-by-case analysis meet a standard of proof? Should the selection of one theory of harm over another be justified on the basis of adequate evidence?[99] How is the probative weight of econometric evidence to be ascertained? Is such evidence prioritised over more conventional forms, such as documents? The answer to these questions, which raise complex issues, becomes further complicated by the fact that engaging with economics is subject to an important caveat: it assumes a greater or lesser degree of sophistication in the discipline. While competition agencies have invested in strengthening their capacity in economics over the years, judges hearing antitrust or merger cases often have a generalist background.[100] Naturally, this begs the question whether and, if so, how courts in general and the EU Courts in particular may meaningfully integrate economics in legal analysis and determine the probative merits of economic evidence – especially where conflicting expert testimonies are involved.[101] These concerns are amplified by the fact that ever since the turn to a 'more economic' approach to competition enforcement and the modernisation of the enforcement regime with the adoption of Regulation 1/2003, Commission decisions have become more intricate, at least if their increased length is any indication thereof.[102]

[98] See, eg, Anne Witt, 'The Enforcement of Article 101 TFEU: What Has Happened to the Effects Analysis?' (2018) 55 *Common Market Law Review* 417.

[99] See generally Hans Zenger and Mike Walker, 'Theories of Harm in European Competition Law: A Progress Report' in Jacques Bourgeois and Denis Waelbroeck (eds), *Ten Years of the Effects-Based Approach in EU Competition Law* (Bruylant, 2012) 185–209.

[100] See the criticisms in Frank Easterbrook, 'The Limits of Antitrust' (1984) 63 *Texas Law Review* 1. See also Frank Easterbrook, 'Allocating Antitrust Decisionmaking Tasks' (1987–88) 76 *Georgetown Law Journal* 305.

[101] See, eg, Ioannis Lianos, '"Judging Economists", Economic Expertise in Competition Litigation: A European View' in Ioannis Liannos and Ioannis Kokkoris (eds), *The Reform of EC Competition Law: New Challenges* (Kluwer Law International, 2010); Juan David Gutiérrez-Rodríguez, 'Expert Economic Testimony in Antitrust Cases: A Comparative Law and Economics Study' (2009) 14 *International Law, Revista Colombiana de Derecho Internacional* 221.

[102] Anne Witt, 'From *Airtours* to *Ryanair*: Is the More Economic Approach to EU Merger Law Really about More Economics?' (2012) 49 *Common Market Law Review* 217, 231.

IV. Conclusion

Evidence standards do not exist just for the sake of it, nor do they operate in a vacuum. Therefore, in order to properly investigate the rules and principles which instruct the assessment of evidence in EU competition enforcement, it is important to have a clear understanding both of the mission that the evidence rules seek to fulfil in adjudication and of the pertinence of the specific context within which they operate.

With this in mind, the aim of this chapter has been to set the scene for the analysis to follow by drawing attention to the fact that evidence standards have an autonomous function, but are not completely independent of the enforcement system of which they form part. Indeed, evidence rules fulfil a particular role in legal proceedings: they serve as fact-finding and decision-making devices with a view to enabling adjudicators to deal with uncertainty and evade deadlocks. In line with this, their design is principally driven by the need to ensure accuracy in the outcome of the factual inquiry, although efficiency and fairness considerations weigh in equally heavily. However, the fact that evidence standards are autonomous does not mean that they are completely independent; rather, their content is informed by the features of the enforcement system within which they are embedded. Looking at EU competition enforcement in particular, the rules and principles that inform the assessment of evidence are inevitably responsive to and must accommodate, first, the specific characteristics of the administrative model in place and the dynamics among the undertakings, the Commission and the EU Courts; second, the adverse consequences that infringement and merger decisions may have for the undertakings involved – especially where financial penalties are involved; and, third, the challenges arising from the close interplay between competition law and economics.

Bearing these remarks in mind, the next chapter will now examine the burden of proof and its allocation in EU competition enforcement.

3

The Burden of Proof in EU Competition Enforcement

I. Introduction

In theory, the notion of the *burden of proof* is fairly simple: in order to conclude whether an argument has been established, the judge must examine *who* has to prove it. The real difficulty, however, lies in properly allocating the burden of proof, ie, in determining who *should* bear it. This decision is prone to have direct repercussions on the outcome of litigation and typically reflects policy choices, efficiency considerations and fairness concerns. Against this backdrop, this chapter analyses how the burden of proof is, or should be, allocated in EU competition enforcement. Despite the significance of the matter and with the exception of Article 2 of Regulation 1/2003, the issue has been largely left to the interpretation of the EU Courts. By means of preliminary remarks, section II briefly explores the concept of the burden of proof, the forms it may take and its importance in the decision-making process. Bearing this account in mind, section III considers in detail how the burden of proof is divided between the Commission and the investigated undertakings in infringement proceedings, and explores the intricacies of its interaction with the substantive legal tests of Articles 101 and 102 TFEU, as well as its compatibility with the presumption of innocence.[1] Section IV then turns its attention to the allocation of the burden of proof in merger proceedings and contemplates its implications for the scope of the 'significant impediment to effective competition' legal test and the operation of doubt in merger control.

II. The Concept of the Burden of Proof and its Significance

Before examining the allocation of the burden of proof in EU competition enforcement, it is necessary to briefly describe how the burden of proof operates

[1] Some of the ideas explored in this chapter have been discussed in Andriani Kalintiri, 'The Allocation of the Legal Burden of Proof in Article 101 TFEU Cases: A "Clear" Rule with Not-So-Clear Implications' (2015) 34 *Yearbook of European Law* 232.

and what considerations may influence its regulation. As explained in Chapter 2, the burden of proof – along with the standard of proof – is a mechanism through which the risk of an erroneous decision is dispersed between the parties.

Despite some differences in the way in which common law and civil law jurisdictions conceive it, generally the burden of proof has a twofold essence: the *burden of persuasion* (or *legal burden*) and the *burden of adducing evidence* (or *evidential burden*).[2] Normally, the legislature does not explicitly distinguish between these two dimensions of the burden of proof. However, its twofold nature is of crucial practical importance for the following reasons: first, contrary to the burden of persuasion, which remains stable and rests upon a specific party throughout the proceedings, the evidential burden may shift to and fro the litigants several times;[3] and, second, what truly matters at the end of litigation is who bears the *legal* burden of proof, as this party will essentially bear the risk of *non*-persuasion.[4]

That said, the question of the *allocation* of the burden of proof should not be confused with the distinct question of its *discharge*. Indeed, the allocation of the burden of proof answers the question 'who should bear it?'.[5] In a nutshell, the traditional rule for its allocation is that *ei incumbit probatio qui dicit, non qui negat*.[6] In other words, the starting point is that 'he or she who asserts something must prove it' – irrespective of their procedural capacity as claimant or defendant. Nevertheless, efficiency and fairness considerations may qualify this maxim and refine the way in which the burden of proof is assigned. From an efficiency perspective, for instance, it is sensible to place the burden of proof on the party with the better information so as to address asymmetries and minimise costs. On the other hand, fairness concerns may also influence its distribution. Where the presumption of innocence applies, for example, it is for the prosecutor to prove

[2] James Thayer, 'The Burden of Proof' (1890) 4 *Harvard Law Review* 45, 48 was the first to distinguish the two meanings of the burden of proof. This distinction was then further analysed by John McNaughton, 'Burden of Production of Evidence: A Function of a Burden of Persuasion' (1955) 68 *Harvard Law Review* 1382.

[3] This shifting of the evidential burden is sometimes referred to as the 'tactical burden of proof' (see, eg, Henri Prakken and Giovanni Sartor, 'Presumptions and Burdens of Proof' in Tom van Engers (ed), *Legal Knowledge and Information Systems* (JURIX, 2006) 24–26).

[4] Marc Brealey, 'The Burden of Proof before the European Court' (1985) 10 *European Law Review* 250, 257; Mojtaba Kazazi, *Burden of Proof and Related Issues: A Study on Evidence before International Tribunals* (Kluwer Law International, 1995) 29.

[5] This question has troubled scholars, who have taken different positions. See, eg, James Flemming, 'Burdens of Proof' (1961) 47 *Virginia Law Review* 51; Hay Bruce, 'Allocating the Burden of Proof' (1997) 72 *Indiana Law Journal* 651; Louis Kaplow, 'Burden of Proof' (2012) 121 *Yale Law Journal* 738; Ronald Allen and Alex Stein, 'Evidence, Probability, and the Burden of Proof' (2013) 55 *Arizona Law Review* 557.

[6] In short, this maxim is further translated into the following sub-principles: first, that *actori incumbit probatio*, the underlying assumption being that the person who asks for a change in the status quo should be responsible for proving why such a change should take place; and, second, that *reus in excipiendo fit actor*, which implies that with respect to defences, the burden is on the party claiming their benefit. See Anne-Lise Sibony and Eric Barbier de la Serre, 'Charge de la Preuve et Theorie du Controle en Droit Communautaire de la Concurrence: Pour un Changement de Perspective' (2007) 43 Revue *Trimestrielle de Droit Europeen* 205, 217–18.

the defendant's guilt rather than for the defendant to establish its innocence. By contrast, the question of the *discharge* of the burden of proof follows the question of its allocation and examines how the person bearing it may satisfy it. The short answer is by providing evidence to the applicable standard of proof. In practice, however, discharging the burden of proof will be easier or more difficult depending on how high the standard of proof is, what has to be proved, what evidence is available or used to this end, and any mechanisms in place for that purpose, such as presumptions.[7]

This chapter considers the question of the allocation of the burden of proof in EU competition enforcement. Matters relating to its discharge are examined in Chapters 4, 5 and 6.

III. The Burden of Proof in Antitrust Cases

A. The Burden of Proof in Article 101 TFEU Cases

i. Article 2 of Regulation 1/2003

Considering the general lack of evidence rules in EU competition law, the existence of a rule on the burden of proof in Regulation 1/2003 might seem surprising at first glance. Being an exception to the principle of national procedural autonomy, Article 2 applies to national and EU proceedings alike. Clause one states that:

> In any national or [EU] proceedings for the application of Articles [101 and 102] of the Treaty, the burden of proving an infringement of Article [101(1)] or of Article [102] of the Treaty shall rest on the party or the authority alleging the infringement.

Then, clause two establishes a shift of the burden of proof in cases concerning the application of Article 101(3) TFEU and provides that the undertakings that claim its benefit 'shall bear the burden of proving that the conditions of that paragraph are fulfilled'.

To understand why Regulation 1/2003 adopted a rule on the burden of proof, it is necessary to briefly recall the features of the enforcement regime prior to its coming into force. Its predecessor – Regulation 17/62 – had envisioned a predominantly centralised system, under which undertakings were required to notify their agreements which fell within the scope of Articles 101 and 102 TFEU to the Commission. Upon the parties' request, the authority could then adopt a negative clearance decision finding that there are no grounds for action on its part, or a

[7] Presumptions have the effect of redistributing the burden of proof, as initially allocated. In this sense, they are a mechanism for both discharging and (re)assigning the burden of proof. Nevertheless, their operation will be examined separately in ch 6, because presumptions pertain to specific issues (rather than a finding of an infringement as a whole), whereas their procedural consequences are ambiguous.

decision 'pursuant to Article [101(3)]', commonly called an 'exemption decision'.[8] The latter was the prerogative of the Commission, which had the sole power to examine whether a notified agreement satisfied the conditions of Article 101(3) TFEU and could thus benefit therefrom. This enforcement regime allowed the authority to tightly control how the antitrust rules were interpreted and enforced during the crucial stage of the formation of the EU and the establishment of the single market. At the same time, however, it was particularly burdensome and costly, insofar as the Commission soon became flooded with notifications of agreements, which were often innocuous. In order to deal with these challenges, the authority adopted several Block Exemption Regulations granting the benefit of Article 101(3) TFEU to categories of agreements which fulfilled certain criteria, whereas it also started issuing 'comfort letters', namely informal decisions that the notified agreement either did not infringe Article 101(1) TFEU or satisfied the conditions of Article 101(3) TFEU.

Against this background, it is apparent that, were it required to investigate in depth agreements whose notification did not contain all the necessary information for their assessment, the Commission would become completely paralysed. Accordingly, in *JCB Service*, the GCEU stressed that it was 'incumbent on the applicant undertaking to submit all the evidence necessary to substantiate the economic justification for an exemption and to prove that it satisfies each of the four conditions laid down in Article [101(3) TFEU]'.[9] Nevertheless, whilst helpful, placing the burden of proof with respect to Article 101(3) TFEU on the undertakings concerned could not resolve the problem of managing the large volumes of applications that the authority was receiving. Eventually, the Commission proposed a number of reforms that would decentralise competition enforcement by abolishing the compulsory notification system in place, by removing negative clearance and exemption decisions, and by extending the power to enforce Article 101(3) TFEU to national authorities and national courts. These changes, as now implemented through Regulation 1/2003, have afforded the authority greater freedom in designing its priorities and in deciding how best to use its limited resources. However, in order to secure this freedom, it was necessary to ensure that the Commission's legal burden in the enforcement of Article 101 TFEU would not become too heavy following the elimination of the notification system and of exemption decisions. In this light, and as Recital 5 explains, it was deemed necessary to explicitly regulate the burden of proof 'in order to ensure an effective enforcement of the [EU] competition rules and at the same time the respect of fundamental rights of defence'.

Having said that, Article 2 of Regulation 1/2003 seems at first sight to accord with the general rule that *ei incumbit probatio qui dicit, non qui negat*, whilst it also aligns the burden of proof in Article 101 TFEU cases with the two-level structure

[8] Regulation 17/62, arts 4(1), 5–9. See also art 8(3)(d).
[9] Case T-67/01 *JCB Service v Commission*, ECLI:EU:T:2004:3, para 162.

of the legal test established therein. Indeed, at the first level, Article 2 bestows the responsibility for proving an infringement of competition law on the party initiating an action to this effect. Then, at the second level, where the justification of Article 101(3) TFEU is invoked, the burden of proof rests on the undertaking claiming its applicability.

ii. The EU Courts' Jurisprudence

The question whether the rules relating to the burden of proof have been observed 'constitutes a question of law which is amenable to judicial review on appeal'.[10] Accordingly, the EU Courts have frequently considered allegations that the rules on the burden of proof have been violated and have elaborated on their operation. In so doing, they have endorsed the bifurcation of the legal burden, as envisioned in Article 2 of Regulation 1/2003. In *Aalborg Portland*, for instance, the CJEU reiterated Recital 5, confirming that:

> [I]t should be for the party or the authority alleging an infringement of the competition rules to prove the existence thereof and it should be for the undertaking or association of undertakings invoking the benefit of a defence against a finding of an infringement to demonstrate that the conditions for applying such defence are satisfied, so that the authority will then have to resort to other evidence.[11]

Therefore, the burden of persuasion under Article 101(1) TFEU rests on the Commission, while the burden of persuasion under Article 101(3) TFEU rests on defendant undertakings.

Nevertheless, the operation of the burden of proof is more sophisticated in practice. The starting point is that the party that bears the burden of persuasion also bears the burden of adducing evidence. In *Baustalgewebe*, for instance, the CJEU explained that 'it is incumbent on the Commission to prove the infringements found by it *and* to adduce evidence capable of demonstrating to the requisite legal standard the existence of the circumstances constituting an infringement' (emphasis added).[12] However, once the evidential burden of proof has been sufficiently discharged, it shifts onto the other litigant.[13] As AG Kokott observed in her Opinion in *FEG*, such shift constitutes 'the normal operation of the respective burdens of adducing evidence'.[14] On similar grounds, the EU Courts have rejected the argument that shifting the evidential burden violates the presumption

[10] Joined Cases C-239/11 P, C-489/11 P and C-498/11 P *Siemens AG, Mitsubishi Electric Corporation and Toshiba Corporation v Commission*, ECLI:EU:C:2013:866, para 130.

[11] Joined Cases C-204/00 P, C-205/00 P, C-211/00 P, C-213/00 P, C-217/00 P and C-219/00 P *Aalborg Portland and Others v Commission*, ECLI:EU:C:2004:6, para 78.

[12] Case C-185/95 P *Baustahlgewebe v Commission*, ECLI:EU:C:1998:608, para 58.

[13] Sibony and Barbier de la Serre ((n 2) 218) illustratively liken this to a tennis game.

[14] Case C-105/04 P *Nederlandse Federatieve Vereniging voor de Groothandel op Elektrotechnisch Gebied (FEG) v Commission*, ECLI:EU:C:2005:751, Opinion of AG Kokott, para 74. See also para 73.

of innocence.[15] As explained in *Aalborg Portland*, irrespective of how the *legal* burden of proof is allocated, 'the factual evidence on which a party relies may be of such a kind as to require the other party to provide an explanation or justification, failing which it is permissible to conclude that the burden of proof has been discharged'.[16]

Once the burden of production has been transferred onto the other litigant, the latter is confronted with two options. It can either accept the argument of the opponent, in which case this is considered as established, or it can refute it. However, as AG Kokott clarified in *FEG*, if the conclusions of the Commission are based on 'objectively verifiable evidence from stated sources, the undertakings concerned cannot refute the Commission's findings simply by unsubstantiatedly disputing them'; in this case, 'it falls to them to show in detail why the information used by the Commission is inaccurate, why it has no probative value, if that is the case, or why the conclusions drawn by the Commission are unsound'.[17] The same point was made more recently in *Telefónica*. As explained by the GCEU:

> [A]n undertaking cannot transfer the burden of proof to the Commission by relying on circumstances which it is not in a position to establish. In other words, when the Commission relies on evidence which is in principle sufficient to demonstrate the existence of the infringement, it is not sufficient for the undertaking concerned to raise the possibility that a circumstance arose which might affect the probative value of that evidence in order for the Commission to bear the burden of proving that that circumstance was not capable of affecting the probative value of the evidence. On the contrary, except in cases where such proof could not be provided by the undertaking concerned on account of the conduct of the Commission itself, it is for the undertaking concerned to prove to the requisite legal standard, on the one hand, the existence of the circumstance relied on by it and, on the other, that that circumstance calls in question the probative value of the evidence relied on by the Commission.[18]

Therefore, an undertaking cannot escape its evidential burden simply by denying the Commission's allegations, but is expected to produce counter-evidence to this effect.

Nevertheless, discharge of the burden of production by the party other than the one bearing the burden of persuasion does not require establishing a positive case. As AG Sir Gordon Slynn suggested in his Opinion in *Musique Diffusion Française*, the undertakings accused of an infringement do not 'have to go so far as to show that the Commission's decision was wrong. It may suffice if [they] can show that it was unsafe or insufficiently proven'.[19] Therefore, to shift the evidential burden back

[15] Case C-235/92 P *Montecatini v Commission*, ECLI:EU:C:1999:362, para 181.

[16] *Aalborg Portland* (n 11) para 79; and Case T-168/01 *GlaxoSmithKline Services v Commission*, ECLI:EU:T:2006:265, para 236.

[17] See *FEG*, Opinion of AG Kokott (n 14) para 74.

[18] Case T-216/13 *Telefónica v Commission*, ECLI:EU:T:2016:369, para 130.

[19] Joined Cases 100 to 103/80 *Musique Diffusion française v Commission*, ECLI:EU:C:1983:29, Opinion of AG Sir Gordon Slynn, at 1931.

to the Commission, the defendant is expected only to produce evidence capable of 'calling into question' the Commission's argument rather than positively disproving it. Evidence showing that the Commission's decision relies on insufficient data or that the conclusions inferred from the evidence produced are not sound would suffice to satisfy the undertaking's evidential burden.[20]

The jurisprudence of the EU Courts suggests that this division of evidential labour between the Commission and defendant undertakings is driven by the presumption of innocence and its corollary *in dubio pro reo* principle. As explained in Chapter 2, the presumption of innocence applies to competition infringement proceedings, particularly where high penalties are involved.[21] A main consequence flowing from the presumption of innocence and affecting the burden of proof is that the investigated undertakings cannot be forced to establish their non-participation in an infringement of Article 101(1) TFEU. On the contrary, at the end of the day, it is for the Commission to demonstrate all the elements of the prohibition, even if the evidential burden shifts to and fro between the litigants. In this light, the GCEU stressed in *JFE Engineering* that:

> Where there is doubt, the benefit of that doubt must be given to the undertakings accused of the infringement. The Court cannot therefore conclude that the Commission has established the existence of the infringement at issue to the requisite legal standard if it still entertains doubts on that point, in particular in proceedings for the annulment of a decision imposing a fine.[22]

Therefore, the application of the *in dubio pro reo* principle in Article 101 TFEU proceedings is understood by the EU Courts as preventing a finding of an infringement where there remain doubts as to whether the Commission has successfully discharged its burden of proof by producing evidence demonstrating the conditions of the substantive test to the applicable standard of proof.[23]

Nonetheless, once the Commission has established the applicability of Article 101(1) TFEU, the burden of persuasion shifts on undertakings. In the context of the old enforcement regime, the CJEU confirmed as early as in *VBVB* that 'in the event of an exemption's being applied for under Article [101(3)] it is

[20] Maurice Guerrin and Georgios Kyriazis, 'Cartels: Proof and Procedural Issues' in Barry Hawk (ed), *Fordham Corporate Law Institute: International Antitrust Law and Policy* (Juris, 1993) 796.

[21] Case C-199/92 P *Hüls v Commission*, ECLI:EU:C:1999:358, paras 149–50; *Montecatini* (n 15) paras 175–176.

[22] Joined Cases T-67/00, T-68/00, T-71/00 and T-78/00 *JFE Engineering v Commission*, ECLI:EU:T:2004:221, para 177. For a recent reiteration, see Case T-154/09 *MRI v Commission*, ECLI:EU:T:2013:260, para 106.

[23] However, it should be noted that this operation of doubt is difficult to disassociate from the typical operation of the burden of proof. The latter serves as a risk allocation mechanism in situations where there is uncertainty as to whether the issue in question has been sufficiently proved and dictates that the risk of uncertainty should be borne by the person responsible for proving it. See also Fernando Castillo de la Torre, 'Evidence, Proof and Judicial Review in Cartel Cases' in Claus-Dieter Ehlermann and Mel Marquis (eds), *European Competition Law Annual 2009: The Evaluation of Evidence and its Judicial Review in Competition Cases* (Hart Publishing, 2010) who observes (at 328) that the presumption of innocence in essence reflects the main rationale for allocating the burden of proof.

in the first place for the undertaking concerned to present to the Commission the evidence intended to establish the economic justification for an exemption, and if the Commission has objections to raise, to submit alternatives to it'.[24] This rule has been consistently reaffirmed in subsequent jurisprudence. In *Van den Bergh Foods*, *GlaxoSmithKline*, *MasterCard* and *Lundbeck*, the EU Courts have repeated that the only option for a defendant against whom a finding of an infringement of Article 101(1) TFEU has been reached is to rely on the defence provided for in Article 101(3) TFEU and to 'demonstrate that those conditions are satisfied, by means of convincing arguments and evidence'.[25] Thus, where Article 101(3) TFEU is invoked, both the burden of persuasion and the burden of production fall upon the defendant undertaking who seeks to benefit from its application.

B. The Burden of Proof in Article 102 TFEU Cases

In contrast to Article 101 TFEU, the apportionment of the burden of proof in cases concerning the application of Article 102 TFEU appears to be less straightforward, in the absence of an equivalent Article '102(3)' Treaty provision. As explained earlier, Article 2 of Regulation 1/2003 provides that 'the burden of proving an infringement … of Article [102] of the Treaty shall rest on the party or the authority alleging the infringement'. Therefore, it is clearly incumbent upon the Commission to establish the conditions of the existence of an abuse of dominance. Yet, Article 2 does not clarify the allocation of the burden of proof regarding efficiencies or other justifications. In the absence of an explicit provision, the arising question is who bears the respective onus of proof.

i. The Enforcement Priorities Guidance

The Commission's position on the issue can be found in its Guidance on the enforcement priorities in applying Article 102 TFEU to abusive exclusionary conduct by dominant undertakings.[26] Although in its Guidance the Commission abandoned the use of the procedurally heavy word 'defence' which it had employed in its Discussion Paper – possibly mindful of its insinuations for the burden of proof[27] – its approach in the section entitled 'Objective Necessity and Efficiencies'

[24] Joined Cases 43/82 and 63/82 *VBVB and VBBB v Commission*, ECLI:EU:C:1984:9, para 52.

[25] Case C-552/03 P *Unilever Bestfoods v Commission*, ECLI:EU:C:2006:607, paras 102–03; *GlaxoSmithKline* (n 16) para 235 (confirmed on appeal: Joined Cases C-501/06 P, C-513/06 P, C-515/06 P and C-519/06 P *GlaxoSmithKline Services and Others v Commission and Others*, ECLI:EU:C:2009:610, para 82); Case T-111/08 *MasterCard and Others v Commission*, ECLI:EU:T:2012:260, para 196; Case T-472/13 *Lundbeck v Commission*, ECLI:EU:T:2016:449, paras 710–11.

[26] Guidance on the Commission's enforcement priorities in applying Article 82 of the EC Treaty to abusive exclusionary conduct by dominant undertakings [2009] OJ C45/02 (Enforcement Priorities Guidance).

[27] DG Competition Discussion Paper on the application of Article 82 of the Treaty to exclusionary abuses (2005), available at: http://ec.europa.eu/competition/antitrust/art82/discpaper2005.pdf.

leaves little doubt about its intentions. In an attempt to align the analysis under the two Treaty provisions on competition, namely Articles 101 and 102 TFEU, the Commission made it clear that it expects from the dominant undertaking to put forward claims that its conduct is justified by demonstrating either that it 'is objectively necessary' or that it 'produces substantial efficiencies which outweigh any anti-competitive effects on consumers'.[28] Likewise, it clarified that 'it is incumbent upon the dominant undertaking to provide all the evidence necessary to demonstrate that the conduct concerned is objectively justified'.[29]

Moreover, although Article 102 TFEU does not imitate the bifurcated structure of Article 101 TFEU, the impression of an unwritten Article '102(3)' provision is reinforced by the striking similarity of the constituent conditions of the efficiencies justification – as set out by the Commission – with the elements of Article 101(3) TFEU.[30] Indeed, an undertaking wishing to benefit from the efficiencies justification in order to escape a finding that it has abused its dominance must demonstrate that: (i) the efficiencies have been, or are likely to be, realised as a result of the conduct; (ii) the conduct is indispensable to the realisation of those efficiencies; (iii) the likely efficiencies brought about by the conduct outweigh any likely negative effects on competition and consumer welfare in the affected markets; and (iv) the conduct does not eliminate effective competition by removing all or most existing sources of actual or potential competition.[31] Therefore, by placing the burden of putting forward and substantiating objective justifications and efficiencies on the dominant undertaking, and by setting out conditions similar to those contained in Article 101(3) TFEU, the Commission seems to understand the division of the burden of proof in Article 102 TFEU cases as echoing its apportionment under Article 101 TFEU.

Admittedly, in its Guidance the Commission adds that, once the dominant undertaking has discharged these two burdens (of pleading and of evidence production), it then falls to it 'to make the ultimate assessment of whether the conduct concerned is not objectively necessary and, based on a weighing-up of any apparent anti-competitive effects against any advanced and substantiated efficiencies, is likely to result in consumer harm'.[32] However, confining its duty to a 'more-likely-than-not' weighing-up exercise, the Commission instead places the legal burden of establishing the pro-competitive impact or the justified nature of its conduct on the dominant undertaking and retains for itself only the legal burden of demonstrating the restrictive impact of the behaviour at hand.[33]

[28] Enforcement Priorities Guidance (n 26) para 28.
[29] ibid para 31. See also paras 29, 30, 43, 62, 74, 89, 90.
[30] See also Discussion Paper on the application of Article 82 EC, para 8.
[31] Enforcement Priorities Guidance (n 26) para 30.
[32] ibid para 31.
[33] See also Robert O'Donoghue and Jorge Padilla, *The Law and Economics of Article 102 TFEU*, 2nd edn (Hart Publishing, 2013) 289–90.

ii. The EU Courts' Jurisprudence

As far as the legal burden of establishing the existence of an abuse of dominance is concerned, at first sight the EU Courts' jurisprudence appears to be aligned with Article 2 of Regulation 1/2003. As confirmed in *Telefónica*, 'it is incumbent on the Commission to prove the infringements found by it and to adduce evidence capable of demonstrating to the requisite legal standard the existence of the circumstances constituting an infringement'.[34] By contrast, the EU Courts' approach to the burden of proof regarding efficiencies or other justifications has been less obvious.

Admittedly, the absence of an Article '102(3)' provision has not prevented the EU Courts from assessing whether a conduct which the Commission found to be abusive may escape the application of Article 102 TFEU on the ground that it is justified.[35] For instance, in *United Brands*, the CJEU considered it necessary to ascertain whether the discontinuance of supplies by United Brands was justified, although it ultimately dismissed the merits of the latter's claim that its conduct was merely intended to protect its own commercial interests which had been attacked.[36] In addition to this 'meeting competition' argument, other justifications, such as public interest considerations, have also been examined by EU judges. For example, in *Hilti*, the GCEU assessed whether safety concerns could excuse exclusionary conduct, although eventually it agreed with the Commission that Hilti's behaviour was not genuinely driven by its wish to protect users of its products.[37] Similarly, in *Tetra Pak*, the GCEU evaluated whether abusive conduct in the form of tied sales of filling machines and cartons was objectively justified 'by the concern to protect public health', although the merits of such a claim were again dismissed.[38] Furthermore, in *Microsoft*, the GCEU considered whether Microsoft's refusal to provide its competitors with access to interoperability information could be justified based on its intellectual property rights and the impact that an obligation to supply would have on the firm's incentive to innovate.[39] Later, in *AstraZeneca*, the Court examined – but dismissed as lacking any factual basis – the dominant firm's argument that its decision to deregister the marketing authorisation for its drug was not abusive because it was driven, among other things, by the fact that maintaining such marketing authorisation would impose onerous pharmacovigilance obligations on it.[40] Finally, in addition to these considerations, the EU Courts have

[34] Case T-336/07 *Telefónica and Telefónica de España v Commission*, ECLI:EU:T:2012:172, para 67.

[35] For an early reference, see Case 40/70 *Sirena v Eda*, ECLI:EU:C:1971:18, para 17.

[36] Case 27/76 *United Brands Company v Commission*, ECLI:EU:C:1978:22, paras 184–91. A similar argument was examined in Joined Cases C-468/06 to C-478/06 *Sot Lélos kai Sia*, ECLI:EU:C:2008:504, paras 50, 76, where the CJEU considered whether GlaxoSmithKline's refusal to supply medicinal products could be justified on grounds of limiting parallel trade in view of the economic and regulatory context of the pharmaceuticals sector.

[37] Case T-30/89 *Hilti v Commission*, ECLI:EU:T:1991:70, paras 102–19, 135.

[38] Case T-83/91 *Tetra Pak v Commission* (*Tetra Pak I*), ECLI:EU:T:1994:246, paras 83–84, 138.

[39] Case T-201/04 *Microsoft v Commission*, ECLI:EU:T:2007:289, paras 627, 689 ff.

[40] Case C-457/10 P *AstraZeneca v Commission*, ECLI:EU:C:2012:770, paras 129–41.

been open to arguments that the conduct should be allowed on the ground that it gives rise to efficiencies. For instance, in *British Airways*, the Court was willing to examine whether there was 'an objective economic justification for the discounts and bonuses granted', accepting that 'an undertaking is at liberty to demonstrate that its bonus system producing an exclusionary effect is economically justified'.[41] The possibility to raise such arguments has been further confirmed in, among others, *France Télécom*, *TeliaSonera*, *Post Danmark I*, *Post Danmark II* and *Intel*.[42]

This brief summary of the case law indicates that the EU Courts are not opposed to claims of 'objective justification', although the latter are hardly ever successfully pleaded and the taxonomy of possible arguments is far from clear.[43] Nevertheless, this does not answer the question of the allocation of the burden of proof. Do such claims amount to defences, in which case the legal burden of their proof is borne by the dominant undertakings? Or are they part of the substantive test of 'abuse of dominance', in which case the burden of persuasion remains with the Commission? The judicial wording in *Microsoft* seems to suggest that the legal burden of proving an abuse of dominance falls on the Commission as a whole. Although the GCEU explained that 'it is for the dominant undertaking concerned and not for the Commission … to raise any plea of objective justification and to support it with arguments and evidence', it went on to clarify that 'it then falls to the Commission, where it proposes to make a finding of an abuse of dominant position, to show that the arguments and evidence relied on by the undertaking cannot prevail, and accordingly, that the justification put forward cannot be accepted'.[44] Nonetheless, *Post Danmark I* appears not to be fully aligned with *Microsoft*. Having observed that 'it is open to a dominant undertaking to provide justification for behaviour that is liable to be caught by the prohibition under Article [102 TFEU]' by demonstrating 'either that its conduct is objectively necessary or that the exclusionary effect produced may be counterbalanced, outweighed even, by advantages in terms of efficiency that also benefit consumers', the CJEU took the view that 'it is for the dominant undertaking to show that the efficiency gains likely to result from the conduct under consideration counteract any likely negative effects on competition

[41] Case C-95/04 P *British Airways v Commission*, ECLI:EU:C:2007:166, para 69.

[42] Case C-202/07 P *France Télécom v Commission*, ECLI:EU:C:2009:214, para 111; Case C-52/09 *TeliaSonera Sverige*, ECLI:EU:C:2011:83, para 75; Case C-209/10 *Post Danmark* (*Post Danmark I*), ECLI:EU:C:2012:172, para 42; Case C-23/14 *Post Danmark* (*Post Danmark II*), ECLI:EU:C:2015:651, paras 48–49; Case C-413/14 P *Intel v Commission*, ECLI:EU:C:2017:632, para 140.

[43] For instance, Giorgio Monti, *EC Competition Law* (Cambridge University Press, 2007) 204 ff identifies four types of 'defences': (i) economic justification; (ii) meeting competition; (iii) economic efficiency; and (iv) public policy. Ekaterina Rousseva, 'Abuse of Dominant Position Defences: Objective Justification and Article 82 EC in the Era of Modernisation' in Giuliano Amato and Claus-Dieter Ehlermann (eds), *EC Competition Law: A Critical Assessment* (Hart Publishing, 2009) 417 ff, on the other hand, distinguishes between: (i) objective justifications comprising both reasons of objective necessity and public policy considerations; and ii) the efficiency defence. Tjarda van der Vijver, 'Objective Justification and Article 102 TFEU' (2012) *World Competition* 55 identifies three types of arguments: (i) legitimate business behaviour; (ii) public interest considerations; and (iii) efficiency arguments.

[44] *Microsoft* (n 39) para 688.

and consumer welfare'.[45] Therefore, *Post Danmark I* suggests that at least as far as efficiencies are concerned, the legal burden falls on the dominant undertaking. This position seems to be echoed in *Intel* and *Post Danmark II* too.[46]

C. Taking a Closer Look at the Allocation of the Legal Burden in Antitrust Cases

The allocation of the legal burden of proof contained in Article 2 of Regulation 1/2003 is well embedded in the jurisprudence of the EU Courts, which have progressively produced a wealth of case law clarifying the specifics of its operation. In proceedings concerning an infringement of Article 101 TFEU, the EU Courts have fully approved of the bifurcated division of the burden of persuasion in Article 2, whereas in abuse of dominance cases, they have gone a step further by effectively recognising the existence of an equivalent Article '102(3)' defence in relation to efficiencies.

On the whole, this twofold allocation of the legal burden in antitrust cases has not been seriously challenged. To a great extent, this can be attributed to the strong intuitive appeal of a shared apportionment of the burden of persuasion. The pair 'prohibition-defence' is a familiar structure in adjudication, and assenting to a matching twofold burden of proof comes naturally. In this respect, alleging that the Commission should bear the burden of proving the elements of the infringement, whereas the undertakings should bear the legal burden of proving efficiencies sounds sensible. Nevertheless, a bifurcated allocation of the burden of persuasion in EU competition enforcement should not be accepted at face value. On the contrary, it is necessary to carefully examine its implications for the operation of the legal tests contained in Articles 101 and 102 TFEU, as well as its compatibility with the presumption of innocence, which, according to the EU Courts, applies to proceedings that may culminate in financial penalties for the undertakings involved.

i. The Interplay between the Burden of Persuasion and the Legal Tests of Articles 101 and 102 TFEU

Being an evidence rule, the burden of proof stands independent of the substantive tests contained in Articles 101 and 102 TFEU, which delineate antitrust liability. Nevertheless, there is a deeply complementary relationship between the two.

[45] *Post Danmark I* (n 42) paras 40–42. Note that the CJEU did not cite the GCEU's earlier judgment in *Microsoft*. See also Case T-155/06 *Tomra Systems and Others v Commission*, ECLI:EU:T:2010:370, para 224.

[46] Case T-286/09 *Intel v Commission*, ECLI:EU:T:2014:547, para 94; *Post Danmark II* (n 42) paras 48–49.

On the one hand, how Articles 101 and 102 TFEU are read instructs how the burden of persuasion should be shared between the parties.[47] Conversely, however, how the legal burden has been allocated in the first place may modify how Articles 101 and 102 TFEU are to be enforced.[48] To a great extent, the interplay between substantive legal tests and the burden of persuasion in competition enforcement touches on the broader challenge of how to integrate into the analysis the restrictive effects and any benefits stemming from the conduct under examination.[49] Because of their broad wording, the letter of Articles 101 and 102 TFEU may in principle accommodate multiple interpretations and diverse analytical approaches. Therefore, it is important to consider how the allocation of the burden of persuasion may affect the scope of the antitrust rules.

a. The Implications for the Application of Article 101 TFEU

Article 101(1) TFEU prohibits agreements and concerted practices, as well as decisions of associations of undertakings, which 'have as their object or effect the prevention, restriction or distortion of competition'. However, this terse prohibition is in need of further elaboration. What is a 'restriction of competition'? What does 'by object' mean? How is it different from the term 'by effect'? What criteria must one apply in order to decide whether a practice falls within one limb or the other limb of Article 101(1) TFEU? Unsurprisingly, these questions have been much debated over the years.[50] Yet, looking at this issue from the perspective of the onus of proof, the equal division of the burden of persuasion between the Commission and the undertakings may in principle support two different approaches to legal analysis under Article 101 TFEU.

Under the first possible option, the bifurcated legal burden contained in Article 2 of Regulation 1/2003 might be understood as replicating the intuitive splitting of the possible effects of a conduct into anti-competitive and pro-competitive. In this scenario, the Commission bears the responsibility for proving that the agreement or concerted practice in question constitutes a 'restriction of competition' by

[47] In relation to art 101 TFEU, see Craig Callery, 'Should the European Union Embrace or Exorcise Leegin's "Rule of Reason"?' (2011) 32 *European Competition Law Review* 42, 47, who rightly remarked that 'how Article 101(1) is read, can completely change which party carries the burden of proof'.

[48] *cf* Eddy de Smijter and Ailsa Sinclair, 'The Enforcement System under Regulation 1/2003' in Jonathan Faull and Ali Nikpay (eds), *The EU Law of Competition*, 3rd edn (Oxford University Press, 2014) 98.

[49] The terms 'benefits', 'advantages' and 'efficiencies' are used loosely to describe the various economic and non-economic arguments that undertakings may advance to contest liability.

[50] See especially Pablo Ibáñez Colomo, 'Market Failures, Transaction Costs and Article 101(1) TFEU Case Law' (2012) 37 *European Law Review* 541; David Bailey, 'Restrictions of Competition by Object under Article 101 TFEU' (2012) 49 *Common Market Law Review* 559; Luc Peeperkorn, 'Defining "by Object" Restrictions' (2015) 3 *Concurrences* 40; Pablo Ibáñez Colomo and Alfonso Lamadrid de Pablo, 'On the Notion of Restriction of Competition: What We Know and What We Don't Know We Know' in Damien Gerard, Massimo Merola and Bernd Meyring (eds), *The Notion of Restriction of Competition: Revisiting the Foundations of Antitrust Enforcement in Europe* (Bruylant, 2017).

object or by effect and may discharge its burden by considering only its 'negative' aspects. Once a 'restriction of competition' has then been established, the legal burden shifts onto the defendant undertaking, which must demonstrate the existence of efficiencies or other benefits capable of outweighing the restrictive aspects identified by the authority. This understanding of the practical operation of the symmetrical legal burden contained in Article 2 of Regulation 1/2003 may find support in *BIDS*, where the CJEU held that legitimate objectives or similar considerations are relevant only in connection with Article 101(3) TFEU.[51]

At first glance, completely detaching efficiencies or other benefits from the Commission's legal burden might seem appealing, if anything because such a bifurcated distribution of the burden of persuasion appears to match the twofold structure of Article 101 TFEU. However, a closer look immediately casts serious doubts on the merits of such an approach.

First of all, if understood as reducing the Commission's legal burden to an obligation to examine only the negative aspects of a practice before finding an infringement of Article 101(1) TFEU, the current bifurcated allocation of the burden of persuasion is prone to lead to an overly expansive construction of what qualifies as a 'restriction of competition'. The reason for this is rather obvious: if the Commission is entitled to confine its analysis under Article 101(1) TFEU to an investigation of only the restrictive aspects of the conduct, because the burden of persuasion with respect to efficiencies or other benefits rests exclusively with the undertakings at the level of Article 101(3) TFEU, then more agreements or concerted practices will be classified as 'restrictions of competition', irrespective of whether an examination of all their aspects would have led the authority to a different conclusion. Accordingly, a bifurcated allocation of the burden of persuasion as envisaged in this scenario would be prone to increase the number of false convictions, resulting in over-enforcement. While this risk will obviously be minimal in relation to practices such as cartels, which only rarely – if ever – generate efficiencies, it will be much more tangible with respect to conduct with mixed effects, such as distribution agreements.[52]

This approach to competition analysis under Article 101 TFEU might perhaps be seen in the early decisional practice of the Commission. At that time, the authority did not specify whether the conduct in question restricted competition 'by object' or 'by effect'; rather, it used to examine its negative effects under Article 101(1) TFEU in order to decide whether it amounted to a 'restriction of

[51] Case C-209/07 *Beef Industry Development Society and Barry Brothers* (BIDS), ECLI:EU:C:2008:643, para 21. See also Case T-112/99 *M6 and Others v Commission*, ECLI:EU:T:2001:215, paras 74–77; Andreas Scordamaglia-Tousis, *EU Cartel Enforcement: Reconciling Effective Public Enforcement with Fundamental Rights* (Kluwer Law International, 2013) 286–87.

[52] As the Commission itself recognises in its Guidelines on vertical restraints, 'if a vertical restraint falls within Article 101(1), it is necessary to examine whether it fulfils the conditions for exemption under Article 101(3)'. But if consideration of art 101(3) TFEU is necessary in this case in the authority's view, one may well wonder whether placing the legal burden of proof on defendant undertakings is appropriate, to say the least.

competition'. Then it considered any efficiencies exclusively under Article 101(3) TFEU upon the parties' request. Because of the different features of the old regime, as described earlier, the latter provision was enforced regularly – both formally and informally, which tempered to some extent the risk of over-enforcement. Nowadays, however, the Commission has no obligation to adopt an 'exemption decision'.[53] At most, it may make a finding of inapplicability in accordance with Article 10 of Regulation 1/2003, although this power has never been exercised so far. Given that there is no longer a legal framework for the compulsory application of Article 101(3) TFEU, the risk of false convictions would be even higher nowadays under a bifurcated legal burden understood as matching the splitting of the effects of a conduct into anti-competitive and pro-competitive.

In any event, such an approach is unconvincing for a second reason: it does not sit well with the jurisprudence of the EU Courts. Indeed, the latter abounds with examples of cases, where pro-competitive arguments have already been taken into account in the context of Article 101(1) TFEU. From the early judgments in *Société Technique Minière*,[54] *Metro I* and *Metro II*,[55] *Nungesser*,[56] *Pronuptia*,[57] *Delimitis*[58] or *Gøttrup-Klim*[59] to more recent rulings in *Football Association Premier League*,[60] *Pierre Fabre*,[61] *Coty*[62] and *Cartes Bancaires*,[63] it is clear that Article 101(1) TFEU analysis may entail consideration of pro-competitive arguments, which may lead to the conclusion either that the conduct in question falls outside the scope of the prohibition altogether or that it does not amount to a restriction of competition 'by object', and thus an assessment of its concrete effects is necessary.[64] However, if the

[53] For an early discussion of the implications of this, see Phaedon Nicolaides, 'The Balancing Myth: The Economics of Article 81(1) & (3)' (2005) 32 *Legal Issues of Economic Integration* 123.

[54] Case 56/65 *Société Technique Minière v Maschinenbau Ulm*, ECLI:EU:C:1966:38, p 450 (where the CJEU explained that an exclusive distribution agreement may not interfere with competition if it 'seems really necessary for the penetration of a new area by an undertaking').

[55] Case 26/76 *Metro v Commission (Metro I)*, ECLI:EU:C:1977:167; and Case 75/84 *Metro v Commission (Metro II)*, ECLI:EU:C:1986:399 (where the CJEU examined restrictions in the context of selective distribution systems).

[56] Case 258/78 *Nungesser v Commission*, ECLI:EU:C:1982:211, paras 56–58.

[57] Case 161/84 *Pronuptia*, ECLI:EU:C:1986:41 (where the CJEU held that provisions which are necessary to protect the franchisor's know-how and to maintain the identity and reputation of its network in the context of a franchising agreement do not restrict competition within the meaning of art 101(1) TFEU).

[58] Case C-234/89 *Delimitis*, ECLI:EU:C:1991:91, paras 10–13.

[59] Case C-250/92 *Gøttrup-Klim*, ECLI:EU:C:1994:413 (where the CJEU held that a clause prohibiting the members of a joint purchasing association from participating in competing associations falls outside the scope of art 101(1) TFEU so long as it is restricted to what is necessary to ensure that the cooperative functions properly and maintains its contractual power in relation to producers).

[60] Joined Cases C-403/08 and C-429/08 *Football Association Premier League and Others*, ECLI:EU:C:2011:631, para 140.

[61] Case C-439/09 *Pierre Fabre Dermo-Cosmétique*, ECLI:EU:C:2011:649, para 40.

[62] Case C-230/16 *Coty Germany*, ECLI:EU:C:2017:941, paras 23–24.

[63] Case C-67/13 P *CB v Commission*, ECLI:EU:C:2014:2204, para 75.

[64] Ibáñez Colomo (n 50) 549, who explains that in drawing the line between 'object' and 'effect' restrictions of competition, the EU Courts take account of whether the agreement or practice in question is a 'plausible source of efficiency gains'. See further David Bailey, 'Restrictions of Competition by Object under Article 101 TFEU' (2012) 49 *Common Market Law Review* 559, 579–81. *cf* Case C-551/03P *General Motors v Commission*, ECLI:EU:C:2006:229, para 64.

application of the legal test of Article 101(1) TFEU already requires at least some consideration of the beneficial aspects of the conduct at hand, then the airtight demarcation of the legal burden between the Commission and the undertakings in Article 2 of Regulation 1/2003 is rather confusing.

That said, it is important to appreciate that the bifurcation of the burden of persuasion in Article 2 of Regulation 1/2003 is not compelled by the two-level structure of Article 101 TFEU. Indeed, Article 101(3) TFEU simply reads that 'paragraph (1) may be declared inapplicable', where the agreement or concerted practice in question: (i) contributes to improving the production or distribution of goods or to promoting technical or economic progress; (ii) allows consumers a fair share of the resulting benefit; (iii) does not impose on the undertakings concerned restrictions which are not indispensable; and (iv) does not afford the undertakings the possibility of eliminating competition in respect of a substantial part of the products in question. Nothing in the letter of this provision forces the conclusion that it should be for defendant undertakings to prove any advantages flowing from their agreement or concerted practice.[65]

Nevertheless, the current allocation of the legal burden in Article 2 of Regulation 1/2003 may support a second approach to Article 101 TFEU analysis. Indeed, it has been suggested that Article 101(1) TFEU and Article 101(3) TFEU are concerned with different aspects of competition and thus different efficiencies.[66] AG Trstenjak opined, for instance, in *BIDS* that 'different aspects of consumer welfare are taken into account under [Article 101(1) TFEU] and under [Article 101(3) TFEU]' and that:

> [F]actors which are not capable of casting doubt on the existence of a restriction of competition, in particular efficiencies in production as a result of economies of scale, may not be taken into account in the context of [Article 101(1) TFEU], but only in the context of [Article 101(3) TFEU].[67]

This idea was more recently reiterated in *MasterCard*, where the CJEU explained that a measure which is 'liable to have an appreciable adverse impact on the parameters of competition, such as the price, the quantity and quality of the goods or services' is covered by the prohibition of Article 101(1) TFEU. Economic advantages in the form of an improvement of production or distribution, or of promotion of technical or economic progress – such as those allegedly

[65] *cf* Ekaterina Rousseva, 'Reflections on the Relevance and Proof of Efficiency Defences in Modern EU Antitrust Law' in Jacques Bourgeois and Denis Waelbroeck (eds), *Ten Years of Effects-Based Approach in EU Competition Law: State of Play and Perspectives* (Bruylant, 2012) 283–85.

[66] Okeoghene Odudu, *The Boundaries of EC Competition Law: The Scope of Article 81* (Oxford University Press, 2006) 102–127, who argues that art 101(1) TFEU is concerned with allocative inefficiency. See also Renato Nazzini, 'Article 81 EC between Time Present and Time Past: A Normative Critique of "Restriction of Competition" in EU Law' (2006) 43 *Common Market Law Review* 497; Ginevra Bruzzone and Marco Boccaccio, 'Impact-Based Assessment and Use of Legal Presumptions in EC Competition Law: The Search for the Proper Mix' (2009) 32 *World Competition* 465, 473–77.

[67] Case C-209/07 *Beef Industry Development and Barry Brothers*, ECLI:EU:C:2008:467, Opinion of AG Trstenjak, paras 50–58.

stemming from the MasterCard Interchange Fee in view of the two-sided nature of the payment system in question – 'can be considered only in the context of Article [101(3) TFEU]'.[68] Therefore, it may be argued that the Commission bears the burden of proving that the practice in question constitutes a restriction of competition by object or by effect, but such a finding requires consideration not only of its restrictive potential or effects, but also of – at least some of – its beneficial aspects. Then, once an infringement of Article 101(1) TFEU has been established, the burden of persuasion is placed on the defendant undertaking to demonstrate that there are *other* objective advantages which justify the exemption of the conduct.

This interpretation of the bifurcated burden of persuasion vis-a-vis the analysis under Article 101 TFEU is more sensible than the first scenario and also better aligned with the EU Courts' jurisprudence. As noted earlier, there is an abundance of case law showing that efficiency arguments are examined under Article 101(1) TFEU and may lead to the conclusion either that the practice falls outside the scope of Article 101(1) TFEU altogether or that it may not be prohibited as a restriction of competition by object, and thus its actual or likely anti-competitive effects need to be established. This is unsurprising; according to settled jurisprudence, 'in order to assess the anticompetitive nature of an agreement … regard must be had inter alia to the content of its provisions, its objectives and the economic and legal context of which it forms a part'.[69] In this regard, there is nothing to suggest that the examination of the 'economic context' is confined only to the restrictive aspects of the conduct. This further confirms that the Commission's burden of persuasion under Article 101(1) TFEU entails consideration of at least certain efficiencies.

Nevertheless, this second approach is not without its challenges either; understood in this way, the bifurcated apportionment of the legal burden in Article 2 of Regulation 1/2003 carries two non-negligible risks.[70] The first one is essentially a risk of over-enforcement, insofar as correlating the notion of 'restriction of competition' with only some aspects of firm rivalry – such as prices and product quality – connotes that the Commission's legal burden does not compel the authority to account for all the possible ways in which the agreement or concerted practice may benefit competition. This risk may be amplified by the fact that any consideration

[68] Case C-382/12 P *MasterCard and Others v Commission* (*Mastercard II*), ECLI:EU:C:2014:2201, paras 93, 180. See also Case C-67/13 P *Groupement de Cartes Bancaires (CB) v Commission*, ECLI:EU:C:2014:2204, para 51.

[69] Case C-32/11 *Allianz Hungária Biztosító and Others*, ECLI:EU:C:2013:160, para 36.

[70] *cf* Massimo Merola and Denis Waelbroeck (eds), *Towards an Optimal Enforcement of Competition Rules in Europe: Time for a Review of Regulation 1/2003?* (Bruylant, 2010) 35–46, where the bifurcation of art 101 TFEU is considered to be merely an evidence law issue. Although the authors accept that 'Article 81 EC should be interpreted following a global approach taking into account both anticompetitive and procompetitive effects before finding the existence of a competition law infringement', they submit that what distinguishes the two paragraphs of the provision is 'the methods of assessment of consumer harm'; under art 101(1) TFEU, only an abstract intuitive analysis is necessary, whereas under art 101(3) TFEU, a more detailed cost-benefit inquiry is necessary, the risk of which is 'on the defendant that argues this possibility of justification' (at 43).

of pro-competitive arguments at the level of Article 101(1) TFEU is largely abstract; the authority's legal burden does not extend to an obligation to engage in some sort of weighing exercise.[71] By contrast, the undertakings' burden of persuasion under Article 101(3) TFEU appears much heavier, insofar as defendants are expected to quantify the claimed benefits and demonstrate that these outweigh the restrictive nature or effects of the agreement. In any event, there is a second risk: Article 2 of Regulation 1/2003 might have the unintended consequence of downgrading productive or dynamic efficiencies to pro-competitive effects of a 'lesser quality'. This stems from the fact that the bifurcated allocation of the burden of persuasion between the Commission and the undertakings essentially turns Article 101(3) TFEU into a 'defence': the parties may invoke its application in order to be absolved of their liability under Article 101(1) TFEU. However, labelling Article 101(3) TFEU as a defence hints at a narrow perception of 'competition' under Article 101(1) TFEU, insofar as it implies that productive and dynamic efficiencies have no role to play when assessing whether this has been 'restricted'. In this sense, the bifurcated allocation of the burden of persuasion in Article 2 of Regulation 1/2003 appears to discriminate against productive and dynamic efficiencies by minimising their significance in the competitive process.

GlaxoSmithKline exemplifies to some extent these issues, although the circumstances surrounding the case are admittedly rather special. GlaxoSmithKline notified its distribution arrangements with Spanish wholesalers to the Commission seeking a negative clearance or an exemption under the old regime. However, the authority rejected the request, finding that the dual pricing mechanism that the agreements envisaged with a view to preventing the parallel trade of GlaxoSmithKline's medicines to other Member States restricted competition by object and by effect in violation of Article 101(1) TFEU, and that the conditions of Article 101(3) TFEU had not been satisfied. Challenging the Commission's decision before the EU Courts, GlaxoSmithKline argued that, in view of the features of the pharmaceutical sector, parallel trade resulted in a loss in efficiency, insofar as it affected its capacity to innovate, whereas the dual pricing mechanism was apt to enable a gain in efficiency by improving innovation. Accordingly, in the undertaking's view, the Commission's classification of the practice as a 'by object' restriction of competition was mistaken, as was its conclusion that the conditions of Article 101(3) TFEU had not been demonstrated.

Hearing these pleas, the GCEU largely agreed with GlaxoSmithKline. Noting that parallel trade merits protection on the assumption that consumers benefit from 'the advantages of effective competition in terms of supply or prices', the Court took the view that, considering the specific features of the pharmaceutical industry, the dual pricing mechanism could not be held to restrict competition by object merely because it affected parallel trade. The Commission's finding that

[71] See, eg, Case T-111/08 *MasterCard and Others v Commission*, ECLI:EU:T:2012:260, para 80. See also Ibáñez Colomo (n 50) 559.

the practice violated Article 101(1) TFEU was eventually sustained, insofar as the authority had demonstrated that the practice had the effect of restricting competition. Nevertheless, its decision to reject the request for an exemption under Article 101(3) TFEU was annulled on the ground that it failed to seriously examine GlaxoSmithKline's arguments concerning the impact of parallel trade on its capacity to innovate and the increase in dynamic efficiency to be achieved through the dual pricing mechanism. Considering these claims on appeal, the CJEU noted that the GCEU made an error of law in requiring direct consumer harm for an agreement to have an anti-competitive object, although this error was ineffective. Examining the authority's complaint that the GCEU reversed the burden of proof with respect to Article 101(3) TFEU by requiring it to show that parallel trade would not lead to a loss in efficiency by altering GlaxoSmithKline's ability to innovate, and that the dual pricing mechanism was not apt to enable a gain in efficiency by improving innovation, the CJEU digressed, stressing that the GCEU had merely found that the Commission failed to adequately deal with the arguments and evidence provided by the undertaking. Although the case presents particularities, insofar as it concerned proceedings under the old enforcement regime and touched on European integration, the pleas raised in *GlaxoSmithKline* illustrate how the allocation of the burden of persuasion with respect to efficiencies may shrink or expand the scope of Article 101(1) TFEU, whereas it may also determine their relative significance.[72]

In any event, it is important to note that Article 101(3) TFEU is articulated in terms of the *inapplicability* of Article 101(1) TFEU, as opposed to *exemption* of the conduct in question. This wording may well suffice to question the nature of Article 101(3) TFEU as a 'defence', despite the prescription to the contrary which is inherent in the current distribution of the legal burden in Article 2 of Regulation 1/2003. In essence, this choice of words suggests that where the conditions of Article 101(3) TFEU are satisfied, the motive for prohibiting an agreement or concerted practice under Article 101(1) TFEU becomes extinct. In this respect, the Commission's perception of the operation of Article 101 TFEU is particularly illustrative as well. As the authority has itself explained, Article 101(1) and Article 101(3) TFEU constitute the two sides of the *same* analytical framework on the basis of which the Commission must conclude whether the agreement or concerted practice in question should be prohibited. Indeed, at the end of the day, the question that is to be answered is whether a given agreement or concerted practice must be prohibited because it harms competition or not. In cases where the analysis does not evolve beyond Article 101(1) TFEU, a finding of a 'restriction of competition' marks the end of the Commission's inquiry. Where, however, Article 101(3) TFEU becomes engaged, an additional step is necessary. In particular, it is necessary to examine whether consumers receive a 'fair share' of

[72] See also *Lundbeck* (n 25) paras 710–720, dismissing, among other things, Lundbeck's arguments that the settlement agreements in question encouraged its incentive to innovate.

the resulting benefits. To this end, 'the positive effects of an agreement must be balanced against and compensate for its negative effects on consumers', in which case 'consumers are not harmed' and the agreement is 'on balance pro-competitive and compatible with the objectives of the Community competition rules'.[73]

Since under the current allocation of the legal burden in Article 2 of Regulation 1/2003 it is for the undertakings to establish the conditions of Article 101(3) TFEU, their burden of persuasion effectively amounts to an obligation to demonstrate that their conduct is eventually beneficial. However, this obligation is in direct conflict with the Commission's legal burden to establish that the conduct in question violates the competition rules. The root of this conflict lies in the fact that the allocation of the burden of proof endorsed in Article 2 of Regulation 1/2003 fails to appreciate that segregating the effects – whether established or inferred – of a conduct into anti-competitive and pro-competitive is, in a sense, artificial. Despite its practical value for the purposes of structuring competition analysis under Article 101 TFEU, to the extent that such segregation extends to a matching splitting of the burden of persuasion, it results in an unjustified shift of the legal burden from the Commission onto the undertakings. This is particularly so, considering that it is ultimately the authority that must weigh up 'the advantages expected from the implementation of the agreement and the disadvantages which the agreement entails for the final consumer, owing to its impact on competition' and that in conducting this balancing exercise, the authority enjoys a margin of discretion.[74]

For these reasons, allocating the burden of persuasion with respect to Article 101(3) TFEU upon undertakings is at best confusing and at worst prone to distort the application of Article 101 TFEU. It is therefore submitted that the *legal* burden should remain with the Commission throughout all the stages of an investigation of whether an agreement or concerted practice should be prohibited.

b. The Implications for the Application of Article 102 TFEU

Having contemplated the implications of the bifurcation of the burden of persuasion for the application of Article 101 TFEU, the same exercise will now be carried out in relation to Article 102 TFEU. According to the legal test contained therein,

[73] Commission Guidelines on the application of Article 81(3) of the Treaty [now Article 101(3)] [2004] OJ C101/97, paras 85 and 33.

[74] *GlaxoSmithKline* (n 16) para 244 (see also para 248); Case 42/84 *Remia v Commission*, ECLI:EU:C:1985:190, Opinion of AG Lenz, 2563–64: 'Here the Commission has imported into the proceedings elements of the burden of proof where they do not belong. A proceeding for an exemption under Article [101(3)], unlike a proceeding for the grant of negative clearance, is governed by the principle of official determination of the facts. The Commission must examine whether the information set out in the notification is true and complete and, where necessary, undertake further investigations. It is true that the undertakings concerned are under a duty to provide information but *the Commission is not entitled to place upon them the burden of proving that the conditions for an exemption are met*' (emphasis added).

conduct by one or more undertakings which amounts to an abuse of a dominant position is prohibited. As far as the burden of proof is concerned, Article 2 of Regulation 1/2003 simply provides that 'the burden of proving an infringement of … Article [102] of the Treaty shall rest on the party or the authority alleging the infringement'. In the absence of a bifurcated burden of persuasion similar to that currently governing Article 101 TFEU, in principle the legal burden in abuse of dominance cases should remain with the Commission at all times. Nonetheless, the EU Courts' jurisprudence, as described earlier, reveals some deviation from Article 2 of Regulation 1/2003, to the extent that it seems to match the Commission's burden of proving the existence of an abuse of dominance with a respective burden on the dominant firm to demonstrate the existence of efficiencies.

The bifurcation of the burden of persuasion in abuse of dominance cases has found some support in the literature. Indeed, it has been argued that Article 2 of Regulation 1/2003 must be read in the light of Recital 5, which provides that 'it should be for the undertaking or association of undertakings invoking the benefit of a defence against a finding of an infringement to demonstrate to the required legal standard that the conditions for applying such defence are satisfied'. On this basis, it has been submitted that a bifurcated legal burden in abuse of dominance cases does not constitute an unlawful reversal of the burden of proof as regulated in Article 2 of Regulation 1/2003.[75] Several other arguments have been articulated in support of a shared legal burden in Article 102 TFEU proceedings. For example, Paulis has justified the twofold division of the burden of proof in abuse of dominance cases on the ground that the implicit 'rule of reason' analysis under Article 102 TFEU calls for a 'coherent approach for the allocation of the burden of proof' in both Article 101 and 102 TFEU cases.[76] Moreover, in his opinion, an 'Article 101-like' division of the burden of persuasion in abuse of dominance cases is necessary to ensure that the dominant firm will indeed provide all the relevant information at an early stage of the administrative procedure, thereby enabling the Commission to perform an overall assessment of the conduct in question.[77] Paulis further observed that a burden of proof which would oblige the Commission to establish not only the existence of anti-competitive effects but also the lack of any objective justifications and efficiencies would amount to a 'devil's proof', thereby undermining the effectiveness of public enforcement.[78] Along the same lines, Rousseva has similarly favoured a bifurcated apportionment of the legal burden in

[75] Rousseva (n 43) 425. *cf* Denis Waelbroeck, 'The Assessment of Efficiencies under Article 102 TFEU and the Commission's Guidance Paper' in Federico Etro and Ioannis Kokkoris (eds), *Competition Law and the Enforcement of Article 102* (Oxford University Press, 2010) 121.

[76] Emil Paulis, 'The Burden of Proof in Article 82 Cases' in Barry Hawk (ed), *Fordham Competition Law Institute: International Antitrust Law and Policy* (Juris, 2007) 471–72. *cf* Paul-John Loewanthal, 'The Defence of "Objective Justification" in the Application of Article 82 EC' (2005) 28 *World Competition* 455, 462–63.

[77] Paulis (n 76) 473. *cf* Waelbroeck (n 75) 126.

[78] Paulis (n 76) 474.

Article 102 TFEU cases.[79] Relying on the traditional rule *ei incumbit probatio qui dicit, non qui negat*, she adds that the use of 'negative expressions' with respect to objective justifications 'has the effect of shifting the burden of proof of the presence of such a justification on to the dominant undertakings'.[80]

There is certainly some merit to these arguments. Nevertheless, whether or not dominant undertakings should bear the burden of persuasion with respect to objective justifications and efficiencies depends on whether the latter qualify as 'defences' within the meaning of Recital 5.[81] Only in this scenario would a bifurcated allocation of the legal burden be warranted. However, in order to answer this question, it is necessary to consider how such arguments interact with the legal test of Article 102 TFEU. It should already be noted that the meaning of the latter provision has proved highly contentious. In any event, based on the jurisprudence of the EU Courts, three types of claims may be identified: first, that the conduct is not abusive because the dominant firm's motives are legitimate and thus not anti-competitive; second, that the conduct is not abusive because it gives rise to efficiencies which outweigh any restrictive effects; and, third, that the conduct is not abusive because it is aimed at protecting public interests beyond those with which Article 102 TFEU is concerned.

The first category of arguments encompasses a variety of claims, ranging from allegations that the conduct was necessary to protect the dominant firm's commercial interests, such as in *United Brands* and *Sot Lélos*, to other objective grounds, such as product shortages, intellectual property rights, regulatory burdens and so forth.[82] However, despite their differences, all these arguments share a common feature: they are intended to explain the motives driving the conduct of the dominant firm so as to demonstrate that it does not deviate from competition on the merits and thus is not abusive. However, in view of the definition of the notion of abuse in *Hoffmann-La Roche*, it is for the Commission to demonstrate that the dominant undertaking's behaviour falls outside the range of permissible behaviour and the standards of 'normal competition'.[83] Accordingly, it is difficult to see how such considerations can be detached from the very test of 'abuse of dominance'.[84] As AG Jacobs insightfully explained in his Opinion in *Syfait*, 'the two-stage analysis

[79] Rousseva (n 43) 427–28.

[80] ibid 426 (for example, 'unless objectively justified' or 'in the absence of objective justification').

[81] The EU Courts have refrained from explicitly determining the concept of 'objective justification', which is generally used as an umbrella term to refer to all arguments other than the existence of efficiencies. *cf* Renato Nazzini, 'The Wood Began to Move: An Essay on Consumer Welfare, Evidence and Burden of Proof in Article 82 EC Cases' (2006) 31 *European Law Review* 518, 530, who remarks that 'the concept of "objective justification" can be as wide as to include any efficiencies brought about by the behaviour under review and any form of competition on the merits'.

[82] eg, Case 77/77 *BP v Commission*, ECLI:EU:C:1978:141, para 33; *United Brands* (n 36) paras 184–91; *Sot Lélos* (n 36) paras 50–51; and the arguments raised in *Microsoft* (n 39) paras 111, 670 and *AstraZeneca* (n 40) paras 635–36.

[83] Case 85/76 *Hoffmann-La Roche v Commission*, ECLI:EU:C:1979:36, para 91.

[84] Michael Collins, 'The Burden and Standard of Proof in Competition Litigation and Problems of Judicial Evaluation' (2004) 1 *ERA Forum* 66, 68.

suggested by the distinction between an abuse and its objective justification is … somewhat artificial', since 'the very fact that conduct is characterised as an "abuse" suggests that a negative conclusion has already been reached'.[85] Consequently, placing the legal burden with respect to such arguments on the dominant firm would effectively shrink the scope of conduct that qualifies as 'normal competition' on the part of dominant undertakings and would amount to a reversal of the Commission's burden to establish the existence of an infringement of Article 102 TFEU. On this ground, the position in *Microsoft* is sound and must be upheld, insofar as the GCEU placed on dominant firms only an evidential burden with respect to objective justifications rather than a burden of persuasion.[86]

Examining the second category, this encompasses arguments that the conduct is not abusive because it gives rise to efficiencies which outweigh its restrictive effects. Indeed, the EU Courts have acknowledged that 'a dominant undertaking may demonstrate that the exclusionary effect arising from its conduct may be counterbalanced, or outweighed, by advantages in terms of efficiency which also benefit the consumer'.[87] In this case:

> [I]t is for the dominant undertaking to show that the efficiency gains likely to result from the conduct under consideration counteract any likely negative effects on competition and consumer welfare in the affected markets, that those gains have been, or are likely to be, brought about as a result of that conduct, that such conduct is necessary for the achievement of those gains in efficiency and that it does not eliminate effective competition, by removing all or most existing sources of actual or potential competition.[88]

This case law confirms the operation of an 'efficiency defence' in the echo of Article 101(3) TFEU. However, an equivalent Article '102(3)' provision raises all the problems identified earlier with respect to allocating the burden of persuasion under Article 101(3) TFEU on defendant undertakings.[89] Indeed, such an approach would imply either that the Commission is entitled to discharge its legal burden and conclude that a dominant firm's conduct amounts to an abuse of dominance only by reference to its restrictive aspects, or would hint at an unjustifiably narrow and compartmentalised perception of 'competition' under which only some efficiencies are accounted for, the rest being for the dominant undertaking to establish.[90]

[85] Case C-53/03 *Syfait and Others*, ECLI:EU:C:2004:673, Opinion of AG Jacobs, para 72. As the AG suggested, 'it is more accurate to say that certain types of conduct on the part of a dominant undertaking do not fall within the category of abuse at all'.

[86] In refusal to deal and tying cases, this is further confirmed by the fact that the lack of an objective justification for the conduct is one of the conditions of the substantive legal test.

[87] See nn 45 and 46.

[88] *Post Danmark II* (n 42) para 49.

[89] *cf* David Wood, 'Proving it: The Standard and Burden of Proof in Article 82 EC Cases' (2008) 7 *Competition Law Insight* 4, 6, who advocates for a twofold division of the legal burden also on the ground that imposing the burden of persuasion exclusively on the Commission 'will lead to a greater risk of false negatives and smaller risk of false positives' than the current system.

[90] See also Albertina Albors-Llorens, 'The Role of Objective Justification and Efficencies in the Application of Article 82 EC' (2007) 44 *Common Market Law Review* 1727, 1760; Waelbroeck (n 75) 119, 127;

Finally, the third type of claims entails public interest considerations of the kind made in *Hilti* or *Tetra Pak II*. Since such arguments are not frequently raised before the EU Courts, there is insufficient jurisprudence at the moment to draw safe conclusions about their operation. One could take the view that they are similar to claims falling within the first category, insofar as they are intended to show that the dominant firm's motives were not anti-competitive. However, because they pertain to non-economic benefits stemming from the conduct at hand, it might make sense to treat them as a separate category. The extent to which public interests – beyond competition – may be taken into account in the application of Articles 101 and 102 TFEU has been debated.[91] Yet, irrespective of one's position on this issue, the balancing of such arguments is eventually a political choice, responsibility for which may be hardly placed on a private entity. Rather, it should be for the Commission – a political institution – to explain why competition should be given priority over other public interests or – vice versa – why consumer protection, public health or similar aims should trump competition.

All in all, it is submitted that the allocation of the burden of persuasion should always remain with the Commission in abuse of dominance cases too.

ii. The Incompatibility of the Bifurcated Legal Burden with the Presumption of Innocence

In any event, the bifurcation of the burden of persuasion as envisaged in Article 2 of Regulation 1/2003 must comply with the presumption of innocence, which applies according to settled jurisprudence to antitrust proceedings. Therefore, it is necessary to examine whether a shared division of the legal burden to the effect that the Commission must demonstrate the existence of an infringement under Articles 101(1) and 102 TFEU, whereas undertakings must prove the elements of Article 101(3) TFEU or an equivalent Article '102(3) TFEU', adheres to the principle that 'every person should be considered to be innocent, unless proven guilty'.

The protective scope of the presumption of innocence has been extensively discussed in the academic scholarship.[92] However, from an evidence perspective, three fundamental prescriptions are traditionally understood as stemming from it: first, no one may be forced to prove their innocence; second, any doubt as to the guilt of the defendant must operate in their favour; and, third, the defendant

Hans Friederiszick and Linda Gratz, *Hidden Efficiencies: On the Relevance of Business Justifications in Abuse of Dominance Cases* (European School of Management and Technology Working Paper No 10/2013) 22–23.

[91] See especially Giorgio Monti, 'Article 81 EC and Public Policy' (2002) 39 *Common Market Law Review* 1057; Christopher Townley, *Article 81 EC and Public Policy* (Hart Publishing, 2009); Okeoghene Odudu, 'The Wider Concerns of Competition Law' (2010) 30 *Oxford Journal of Legal Studies* 599.

[92] See Andrew Stumer, *The Presumption of Innocence: Evidential and Human Rights Perspectives* (Hart Publishing, 2010) ch 3; Hock Lai Ho, 'The Presumption of Innocence as a Human Right' in Paul Roberts and Jill Hunter (eds), *Criminal Evidence and Human Rights: Reimagining Common Law Procedural Traditions* (Hart Publishing, 2012) 259–81.

may be exceptionally burdened with proving the elements of a defence only if the standard of proof[93] that they must satisfy is the lowest one, that is, the balance of probabilities – or the equivalent threshold of subjective confidence.[94] These prescriptions have important implications both for the burden and the standard of proof. Issues pertaining to the latter are discussed in detail in Chapter 4, but the following remarks may be made already. First of all, insofar as the legal burden of proving an infringement falls on the Commission, the first clause of Article 2 of Regulation 1/2003 is fully aligned with the presumption of innocence.[95] Second, the EU Courts have taken the view that if there is doubt as to whether the Commission has sufficiently established the elements of an antitrust violation, 'the benefit of that doubt must be given to the undertakings accused'.[96] Therefore, insofar as the discharge of the burden of proof in infringement proceedings is indeed governed by the *in dubio pro reo* principle, the second prescription of the presumption of innocence appears to be satisfied as well. By contrast, the compatibility of the current bifurcated distribution of the burden of persuasion with the third prescription is not as straightforward. In principle, the latter implies that undertakings may be lawfully burdened with proving the elements of Article 101(3) TFEU or an equivalent Article '102(3)' only if their burden is confined to an obligation to demonstrate that on the facts, their conduct is 'more likely than not' pro-competitive.

Inevitably, this begs the question as to what standard of proof defendant undertakings are subject. The next chapter examines this issue in detail.[97] However, for the purposes of the current analysis, it should be emphasised that the standard of proof which defendant undertakings must satisfy under Article 101(3) TFEU or

[93] On the conceptualisation of the standard of proof, see ch 4, section III.B.

[94] Barbara Underwood, 'The Thumb on the Scales of Justice: Burdens of Persuasion in Criminal Cases' (1977) 86 *Yale Law Journal* 1299, 1331–38; Alex Stein, 'Criminal Defences and the Burden of Proof' (1991) 28 *Coexistence* 133, 140. See also Alex Stein, *Foundations of Evidence Law* (Oxford University Press, 2005) 181–82. Even the proposition that a defendant may be legally burdened with establishing the elements of a defence on a mere preponderance of the evidence has been criticised as incompatible with the presumption of innocence, this issue being still debated (eg, Andrew Ashworth, 'Four Threats to the Presumption of Innocence' (2006) 123 *South African Law Journal* 63; Paul Roberts and Adrian Zuckerman, *Criminal Evidence*, 2nd edn (Oxford University Press, 2010) 265–90; Jonathan Levy, 'A Principled Approach to the Standard of Proof for Affirmative Defenses in Criminal Trials' (2013) 40 *American Journal of Criminal Law* 281). Nevertheless, the analysis will proceed on the assumption that placing a legal burden on a defendant to demonstrate the elements of a defence to a civil standard of proof is not incompatible with the presumption of innocence.

[95] Koen Lenaerts, 'Some Thoughts on Evidence and Procedure in European Community Competition Law' (2006) 30 *Fordham International Law Journal* 1463, 1471–72. *cf* Jürgen Schwartze, Rainer Bechtold and Wolfgang Bosch, *Deficiencies in European Community Competition Law: Critical Analysis of the Current Practice and Proposals for Change* (2008), available at: http://ec.europa.eu/competition/consultations/2008_regulation_1_2003/gleiss_lutz_en.pdf, 31, who argue that the Leniency Notice contravenes the presumption of innocence because it results 'in the burden of proof being reversed to the effect that it is not the authorities which must provide evidence of an infringement, but rather the accused undertaking itself which must exonerate itself from the accusation'.

[96] See n 22.

[97] See ch 4, section IV.A.ii.

Article '102(3)' is much higher than the balance of probabilities – or its equivalent level of persuasion. In fact, it corresponds to the 'firm conviction' threshold to which the Commission must demonstrate the existence of a restriction of competition under Article 101(1) TFEU. The reason for this – as will be explained shortly – lies in the conditions of the defence: both in Article 101 and Article 102 TFEU cases, defendant undertakings must establish not only that their conduct gives rise to objective advantages, but also that these outweigh the identified restriction of competition, so that the net impact of the practice remains at least neutral.[98] However, if the authority has produced evidence supporting the firm conviction that the conduct restricts competition, then defendant undertakings have no real prospect of having their claims upheld, unless they produce evidence supporting an *at least equally* strong conviction that any benefits stemming from their behaviour offset the restriction of competition.[99] This will be even more difficult in the case of object violations, where the Commission is not required to prove actual or likely restrictive effects, but may intervene as soon as the conduct has occurred. Accordingly, to the extent that the successful discharge of their legal burden requires that undertakings satisfy a standard of proof higher than the balance of probabilities, a bifurcated apportionment of the burden of persuasion in infringement proceedings is incompatible with the presumption of innocence.[100]

iii. The Way Forward: Refining the Allocation of the Burden of Proof in Antitrust Cases

Despite its intuitive appeal, the shared allocation of the legal burden in infringement proceedings may have important repercussions for the analysis under Articles 101 and 102 TFEU, as well as for the effective judicial protection of the undertakings concerned. In order for these repercussions to be sufficiently addressed, it is submitted that the burden of persuasion should remain with the Commission throughout all the stages of the decision-making process.[101] However, this conclusion forces the double question of what should become of the second clause of Article 2 of Regulation 1/2003, as well as of the EU Courts' jurisprudence on the burden of proving efficiencies or other benefits in antitrust cases. To this end, it is proposed that Article 2 of Regulation 1/2003 and the relevant case law be

[98] This requirement is implicit in the condition of art 101(3) TFEU that consumers must receive 'a fair share of the resulting benefit' and explicit in the art 102 TFEU case law (nn 41 and 42).

[99] For similar reasons, in the context of art 102 TFEU, a number of authors have admitted that in practice, the efficiencies defence is never successful (see O'Donoghue and Padilla (n 33) 287; Monti (n 43) 203; Rousseva (n 43) 415), whereas Waelbroeck ((n 75) 126–27) further takes the view that demanding the dominant undertaking to establish a defence which is hardly ever successful comes as close as admitting the existence of a *probatio diabolica*.

[100] *cf* Hanns Peter Nehl, 'Article 48: Presumption of Innocence and Rights of Defence' in Steve Peers et al (eds), *The EU Charter of Fundamental Rights: A Commentary* (Hart Publishing, 2014) 1284–85.

[101] See also Nazzini (n 81) 530–36; Ioannis Lianos, 'Categorical Thinking in Competition Law and the "Effects-Based" Approach in Article 82 EC' in Ariel Ezrachi (ed), *Article 82 EC: Reflections on its Recent Evolution* (Hart Publishing, 2009) 27.

'read down' to impose only an evidential burden on the undertakings concerned, that is, an obligation to claim and bring forward any evidence of justifications and efficiencies in their sphere of knowledge and possession. Under this suggested approach, the legal burden will rest with the authority at all times.

The proposed refinement of the burden of proof is not of mere academic interest; rather, it differs from the current shared division of the burden of persuasion in at least two fundamental respects. First of all, it has the effect of streamlining the distribution of the legal burden with the Commission's obligation to take into account 'all the relevant information' when applying Articles 101 and 102 TFEU – irrespective of the source of that information.[102] In practice, this means that although the main responsibility for producing evidence of efficiencies under Article 101(3) TFEU or an equivalent Article '102(3)' will still be on the undertakings concerned, the authority will have its own active duty to assess whether the conduct gives rise to benefits which may outweigh its restrictive nature or effects. As a consequence, the Commission will no longer be able to further decline to investigate reliable indications of objective advantages on the ground that the burden of proving the conditions of such a 'defence' falls on undertakings. Second, the proposed revision of the distribution of the legal burden ensures that any uncertainty about the beneficial nature of the conduct in question will actually operate in the undertakings' favour in accordance with the presumption of innocence. Indeed, because the legal burden of proving the conditions of Article 101(3) TFEU or an equivalent Article '102(3)' is currently placed on defendants, any doubt as to the overall positive nature of the conduct effectively turns against them and operates in their disfavour.[103] The herein advocated re-reading guarantees that undertakings will be granted the benefit of the doubt at all levels of the legal analysis under the antitrust rules.

In any event, while the suggested distribution of the burden of proof presents clear advantages, it is worth addressing possible objections as well. The most obvious criticism one could raise against the proposed refinement of the allocation of the burden of proof consists in the claim that information about the beneficial aspects of an agreement or unilateral conduct typically lies with undertakings. Accordingly, it could be argued that the burden of persuasion with respect to Article 101(3) TFEU or an equivalent Article '102(3)' should be placed on the latter as a means of mitigating the information asymmetries that exist between themselves and the authority. At first glance, this argument seems convincing. Indeed, it has been suggested that a reversal of the legal burden might be tolerated in circumstances where the protection that the presumption of innocence affords defendant undertakings is not compromised – for instance, where it is extremely

[102] This obligation is part of the standard of judicial review to which the EU Courts subject complex economic assessments (eg, Case C-272/09 P *KME Germany and Others v Commission*, ECLI:EU:C:2011:810, para 94).

[103] See also Case C-382/12 P *MasterCard and Others v Commission (MasterCard II)*, ECLI:EU:C:2014:42, Opinion of AG Mengozzi, paras 146–47; and ch 4, section IV.A.ii.

easy for an innocent defendant to produce the evidence required in order to benefit from the defence.[104] However, in the context of Article 101(3) TFEU or an equivalent Article '102(3)' provision, it is doubtful whether ease of proof considerations might justify a reversal of the burden of persuasion. Although defendant undertakings may well be in possession of evidence of the *existence* of objective advantages, they will rarely – if ever – possess evidence that the net impact of the conduct on consumers is neutral or positive.

In any event, if the concern is really the existence of information asymmetries with respect to pro-competitive arguments between undertakings and the Commission, the proposed refinement of the burden of proof eliminates this problem, insofar as it places upon the defendant the obligation to plead *and* furnish evidence of justifications, efficiencies or other benefits. Such an evidential burden fully resonates with the principle of 'proof proximity' – to use Volpin's wording – which dictates that the party in whose possession the evidence is should bear the burden of producing it.[105] Indeed, the latter is well entrenched in the EU Courts' jurisprudence. In *AstraZeneca*, for instance, the CJEU stressed that placing the evidential burden on the dominant firm is necessary 'where the undertaking concerned is alone aware of that objective justification or is naturally better placed than the Commission to disclose its existence and demonstrate its relevance'.[106] Therefore, the first criticism against the proposed refinement of the burden of proof in antitrust proceedings is rather weak.

The second – and more serious – objection to the advocated re-allocation of the legal and evidential burden consists in the claim that placing the whole burden of persuasion on the authority will compromise its ability to apply the antitrust rules by forcing it to 'disprove' the existence of objective advantages in relation to every conduct that it investigates, even though a preliminary case of illegality will already have been made. This concern is not invalid, but it is submitted that it is unduly exaggerated. First of all, it disregards that – as noted earlier – a finding of illegality under Article 101(1) or Article 102 TFEU already entails an assessment of efficiencies, insofar as such arguments are embedded in the applicable legal test. Indeed, prohibiting a practice by object conveys that it lacks an economic justification and is presumed to be inherently capable of harming competition.[107] On the other hand, barring a practice by effect connotes that while its impact may be generally both positive and negative, in the circumstances of the case, it has actually harmed competition or such harm is likely to arise. Accordingly, both 'by object' and 'by effect' findings of illegality encompass a preliminary conclusion on the beneficial aspects – or, better, lack thereof – of the conduct. While undertakings may bring forward relevant arguments and evidence, the burden of

[104] Stumer (n 92) 167–76.
[105] Cristina Volpin, 'The Ball is in Your Court: Evidential Burden of Proof and the Proof-Proximity Principle in EU Competition Law' (2014) 51 *Common Market Law Review* 1159.
[106] *AstraZeneca* (n 40) para 686.
[107] On this, see also ch 6.

persuasion already rests with the authority. In this regard, the proposed approach will not affect the Commission's ability to enforce the antitrust rules.

This concern might have some merit in relation to Article 101(3) TFEU or an equivalent Article '102(3)'; placing the burden of persuasion on the authority in this case may indeed force the latter to engage in a more detailed examination of the overall impact of the conduct, beyond the preliminary finding of illegality. Nevertheless, the ensuing increase in the cost of enforcement is unlikely to fundamentally impair the Commission's ability to apply the antitrust rules. For one thing, the Commission's burden of persuasion will become activated only when undertakings have made a reliable case of objective advantages and have produced evidence thereof such as to cast doubt on the restrictive nature or effects of the conduct. In properly classified as 'by object' cases, arguments of this kind will rarely be substantiated and can be refuted with relatively little effort. Insofar as cartels – the typical example of 'by object' violations – constitute the vast majority of cases pursued by the authority, the concern that the proposed refinement of the legal and evidential burden will undermine the effectiveness of enforcement seems exaggerated. In all other cases, the need for a detailed Article 101(3) TFEU or Article '102(3)' analysis will largely depend on the robustness of the Commission's finding of illegality. The stronger the preliminary conclusion of the authority, the less likely it is that undertakings will be able to make a reliable case of objective advantages such as to call for a concrete and detailed examination of the net impact of the practice. Where, however, undertakings have pleaded benefits stemming from the conduct substantiating them with adequate evidence, it is difficult to see how cost considerations may justify placing the burden of persuasion on them. One must not forget that producing evidence about the net impact of a conduct is expensive not only for the authority, but also for the undertakings involved. In any event, the legal burden will determine the outcome of adjudication only in those truly borderline cases where no conclusion can be reached. Yet, if the evidence is such as to cast doubt on the overall impact of the practice, it should be for the authority to explain why there is a violation of the antitrust rules.[108]

IV. The Burden of Proof in Merger Cases

Beyond antitrust infringement proceedings, merger cases also showcase the difficulties in answering the phenomenally simple question 'who should prove what'. Since Regulation 1/2003 is not applicable to merger proceedings, Article 2 cannot be of help.[109] Moreover, there is no provision in the EUMR allocating the legal

[108] This argument is even stronger in the case of non-economic benefits, to the extent that they may be taken into account under art 101(3) TFEU or art '102(3)'.

[109] EUMR, art 21(1).

burden between the Commission and the merging entities. Therefore, the answer to the question of how the burden of persuasion is divided has to be retrieved from the structure of the EUMR, the Commission's Guidelines on the assessment of horizontal and non-horizontal mergers, and the EU Courts' jurisprudence.

A. The EUMR and the Horizontal and Non-Horizontal Merger Guidelines

The EUMR complements Articles 101 and 102 TFEU and provides the framework for the Commission's evaluation of concentrations with an EU dimension. More specifically, Article 2(2) and (3) establishes a symmetrical substantive legal test, pursuant to which 'a concentration which would not significantly impede effective competition in the common market … shall be declared compatible with the common market', whereas conversely 'a concentration which would significantly impede effective competition in the common market … shall be declared incompatible'. This double test has crucial implications for the allocation of the burden of persuasion. Indeed, it denotes that, at the end of its inquiry, the Commission must adopt a positive decision to the effect of either prohibiting or authorising the notified transaction.[110] Therefore, the Commission bears the legal burden for both prohibition and clearance decisions.

Nevertheless, the scope of the Commission's double burden of persuasion is not immediately apparent. Does it involve an obligation to examine efficiencies or is the legal burden with respect to the latter on the merging entities? Neither the EUMR nor the Commission Guidelines on the assessment of horizontal and non-horizontal concentrations – which introduced for the first time a structured framework for integrating efficiencies in merger analysis – are entirely clear on this point.[111] According to Recital 29 of the EUMR, 'in order to determine the impact of a concentration on competition in the common market, it is appropriate to take account of any substantiated and likely efficiencies put forward by the undertakings concerned'. Article 2(1)(b) EUMR then dictates that in appraising the compatibility of a concentration with the common market, the Commission is bound to take a number of factors into account, including whether the concentration favours 'the development of technical and economic progress, provided that it is to customers' advantage and does not form an obstacle to competition'. Furthermore, several passages in both the Horizontal and the Non-Horizontal Merger

[110] ibid arts 6 and 8.

[111] On the 'efficiency defence', see generally DG Economic and Financial Affairs, *The Efficiencies Defence and the European System of Merger Control* (European Economy, Reports and Studies No 5, 2001); Liam Colley, 'From "Defence" to "Attack"? Quantifying Efficiency Arguments in Mergers' (2004) 25 *European Competition Law Review* 342; Fabienne Ilzkovitz and Roderick Meiklejohn (eds), *EC Merger Control: Do We Need an Efficiency Defence?* (Edward Elgar, 2006).

Guidelines underline that the Commission is expected to carry out an 'overall assessment of the foreseeable impact of the merger'.[112]

Moreover, although the Guidelines contain several clauses to the effect that if the parties desire to claim the existence of any efficiencies which should form part of the Commission's analysis, the burden rests with them to invoke the relevant allegations and produce evidence thereof, at first sight these clauses seem to impose only an evidential burden on the merging entities.[113] As the Guidelines explain, the reason for this is that 'most of the information, allowing the Commission to assess whether the merger will bring about the sort of efficiencies that would enable it to clear a merger, is solely in the possession of the merging parties'.[114] On this ground, section 9 of the Form that must be filled in when a transaction is notified to the Commission expressly invites the merging parties to claim any anticipated efficiencies and provide relevant evidence from the very beginning of the administrative proceedings.[115] However, as the Commission is careful to stress, a failure on the part of the notifying parties to provide evidence on efficiencies 'will not be taken to imply that the proposed concentration does not create efficiencies'.[116]

In view of the above, one might be tempted to conclude that although the Guidelines impose a burden on the merging entities to provide evidence of any efficiencies in their possession, the overall legal burden remains with the Commission.[117] However, such a conclusion would be at odds with the Guidelines' prescription that it is incumbent upon the notifying parties 'to provide in due time all the relevant information necessary to demonstrate that the claimed efficiencies are merger-specific and likely to be realised' and 'to show to what extent the efficiencies are likely to counteract any adverse effects on competition that might otherwise result from the merger, and therefore benefit consumers'.[118] Indeed, if it is for the merging firms not only to produce evidence of the existence of efficiencies, but also to demonstrate that the existing efficiencies offset all restrictive effects and

[112] See, eg, Commission Guidelines on the assessment of horizontal mergers under the Council Regulation on the control of concentrations between undertakings [2004] OJ C31/5 (Horizontal Mergers Guidelines), paras 13, 76. See also Commission Guidelines on the assessment of non-horizontal mergers under the Council Regulation on the control of concentrations between undertakings [2008] OJ C265/6 (hereinafter Non-Horizontal Mergers Guidelines), para 21.

[113] Horizontal Merger Guidelines (n 112) paras 12, 77, 85, 86; Non-Horizontal Merger Guidelines (n 112) paras 52, 53, 77 and 115.

[114] Horizontal Merger Guidelines (n 112) para 87.

[115] Commission Regulation (EU) No 1269/2013 of 5 December 2013 amending Regulation (EC) No 802/2004 implementing Council Regulation (EC) No 139/2004 on the control of concentrations between undertakings, Annex I: Form CO relating to the notification of a concentration pursuant to Regulation (EC) No 139/2004, section 9.

[116] ibid fn 1.

[117] A shift of the evidential burden is not problematic in itself. Presumably, merging entities would be happy to provide authorities with any relevant data at their disposal in order to have their transaction cleared. However, even if the undertakings concerned are unwilling to assist in the Commission's investigation, the latter disposes of a wide toolkit of powers to tackle such 'difficulties' (see arts 11 and 14 EUMR; Christoph Luescher, 'Efficiency Considerations in European Merger Control: Just Another Battle Ground for the European Commission, Economists and Competition Lawyers?' (2004) 25 *European Competition Law Review* 72, 80) *cf* Peter Ormosi, 'Diminishing Incentives to Reveal Efficiency-Related Evidence: An Empirical Analysis of EC Merger Cases' (2011) 34 *World Competition* 615.

[118] See n 114.

cannot be achieved through other, less anti-competitive means, their evidential burden seems to become transformed into a much heavier, legal one.

B. The EU Courts' Jurisprudence

Any gap resulting from the lack of legislation on the allocation of the burden of proof in merger proceedings has been filled in by the EU Courts. On several occasions, the EU Courts have confirmed that the legal burden of demonstrating that a concentration would significantly impede effective competition, if allowed to proceed, rests with the Commission. For example, in *Airtours*, the GCEU stressed that 'the Commission is obliged to assess, using a prospective analysis of the reference market, whether the concentration which has been referred to it leads to a situation in which effective competition in the relevant market is significantly impeded'.[119] Moreover, in *Impala*, the CJEU seized the opportunity to clarify that, in view of the legal test in Article 2(2) and 2(3) EUMR, the Commission's burden of proof is twofold. Where the authority has been notified of a proposed concentration, it is 'in principle, required to adopt a position, either in the sense of approving or of prohibiting the concentration, in accordance with its assessment of the economic outcome attributable to the concentration which is most likely to ensue'.[120] As further explained by the Court, in prohibiting or clearing a merger, the Commission is subject to the same standard of proof and no 'presumption' of either merger compatibility or incompatibility with the common market applies.[121] Consequently, the burden of persuasion rests with the Commission under both Article 2(2) and Article 2(3) EUMR.

Nevertheless, this conclusion still leaves open the question as to whether the authority's legal burden entails an examination of efficiencies. Jurisprudence on this matter has been scarce, in part due to the fact that most concentrations are cleared in Phase I or Phase II. In this regard, the GCEU judgment in *Ryanair* is a notable exception. In the context of Ryanair's action for annulment against the Commission's decision to prohibit it from launching a public bid for the entire share capital of Aer Lingus, the Court was called to examine, among other things, whether the authority had failed correctly to assess Ryanair's efficiency claims.[122] In rejecting the applicant's plea, the GCEU agreed with the authority that 'most of the information allowing the Commission to assess efficiencies is solely in the possession of the parties to the concentration and that it is, therefore, incumbent upon the notifying parties to provide in due time the relevant information'.[123] Furthermore, it fully upheld the Guidelines' four conditions for an efficiency claim

[119] Case T-342/99 *Airtours v Commission*, ECLI:EU:T:2002:146, para 59.

[120] Case C-413/06 P *Bertelsmann and Sony Corporation of America v Impala (Impala II)*, ECLI:EU:C:2008:392, para 52.

[121] ibid paras 46, 48.

[122] Case T-342/07 *Ryanair v Commission*, ECLI:EU:T:2010:280, paras 386–444.

[123] ibid para 407.

to be accepted, including the requirement for merger-specificity and consumer benefit.

The same approach was followed in *Deutsche Börse*.[124] Dismissing the applicant's plea that the Commission had committed errors of law and assessment in its evaluation of the efficiencies that the notified merger between NYSE Euronext and Deutsche Börse would allegedly generate, the GCEU once again endorsed the Guidelines and confirmed that it is for the merging parties to demonstrate that the claimed efficiencies are merger-specific and 'likely to counteract any adverse effects on competition that might otherwise result from the merger'.[125] Equally interesting in this regard is the GCEU's dismissal of Deutsche Börse's argument that, by requiring the merging parties to demonstrate that they cannot 'claw back' efficiencies, the Commission shifted the burden of proving anti-competitive effects onto the merging parties. As the GCEU clarified, 'the fact that the evaluation of the efficiencies is one of the factors to take into account in the context of the overall examination of the merger' does not preclude a two-stage analysis of its harmful effects and efficiency gains. Indeed, 'the issue of the demonstration of anti-competitive effects, which is a matter for the Commission, differs from the issue of the demonstration of the fact that the efficiencies benefit consumers, are merger-specific and verifiable, which is a matter for [the merging] parties'.[126]

Accordingly, the EU Courts' jurisprudence seems to point towards a bifurcated legal burden similar to that operating in antitrust infringement proceedings.

C. Taking a Closer Look at the Allocation of the Legal Burden in Merger Cases

The symmetrical nature, on the one hand, and the bifurcation, on the other hand, of the legal burden in merger control merit closer examination. In this context, two issues deserve special mention: first, the interaction of the legal burden with the substantive legal test of the EUMR; and, second, its implications for the operation of doubt in merger enforcement.

i. The Implications of the Bifurcated Burden of Persuasion for the Legal Test of the EUMR

As noted above, the way in which the legal burden is distributed may influence how the competition rules are enforced. The EUMR is no exception in this regard. According to the EUMR, the substantive legal test for prohibiting or authorising a notified transaction is whether the concentration would significantly

[124] Case T-175/12 *Deutsche Börse v Commission*, ECLI:EU:T:2015:148.
[125] ibid para 262.
[126] ibid para 275.

impede effective competition in the common market or not. In this sense, *Impala* embraces an allocation of the burden of persuasion, which brings it into line with the substantive tests of the EUMR, insofar as it recognises the existence of a double legal burden on the Commission to demonstrate either that the concentration should be prohibited or that it should be cleared.

Nevertheless, *Impala* must be considered in conjunction with the GCEU's judgments in *Ryanair* and *Deutsche Börse*, insofar as the latter endorse the Guidelines' framework for analysing efficiency claims and recognise an obligation on the merging entities not only to produce evidence of the existence of efficiencies but also to demonstrate that these are merger-specific and offset all restrictive effects. Conceptually, placing a legal burden with respect to efficiencies on the merging entities is not necessarily in conflict with the Commission's obligation to either prohibit or authorise a notified concentration. Yet, it has critical implications for how the 'significant impediment to effective competition' test of the EUMR is to be understood. Indeed, detaching efficiencies from the Commission's burden of persuasion implies that the authority is allowed to reach a finding of a 'significant impediment to effective competition' – or lack thereof – solely by examining the restrictive aspects – if any – of the transaction.[127] Accordingly, a bifurcated allocation of the legal burden might – as a corollary – broaden the range of conduct which comes within the prohibitive scope of the EUMR.

However, such an outcome would be objectionable. On the one hand, it fails to appreciate the significance of efficiencies as a vital component of merger analysis and the fact that, as the Commission recognises, mergers – and particularly non-horizontal ones – are generally pro-competitive and constitute a legitimate business activity.[128] On the other hand, it contravenes the Commission's stated commitment to performing an 'overall assessment' of the impact of the notified concentration before prohibiting or authorising it.[129] In any event, even if one disregards the implications of placing the legal burden with respect to efficiencies on the merging entities for the operation of the substantive legal test of the EUMR, such an approach would raise concerns from a proportionality point of view.[130]

[127] For a criticism of the Commission's approach towards efficiency claims, see François-Charles Laprévote, 'Abandon All Hope, Ye Who Enter Here? Efficiencies in European Merger Control: A Few Lessons from Recent Decisional Practice' (2014) *e-Competitions* N° 65580, 60, 62–69.

[128] See the Merger Statistics published on the website of the DG Competition, available at: http://ec.europa.eu/competition/mergers/statistics.pdf. See also Non-Horizontal Mergers Guidelines (n 112) para 11. In relation to conglomerate mergers specifically, the Commission's position is that 'in the majority of circumstances [they] will not lead to any competition problem' (Non-Horizontal Merger Guidelines (n 112) para 92). This led Alexandr Svetlicinii ('Assessment of Non-Horizontal Mergers: Is There a Chance for the Efficiency Defence in EC Merger Control?' (2007) 28 *European Competition Law Review* 529, 537) to take the view that by not distinguishing between horizontal and non-horizontal mergers, the Commission unjustifiably imposes an equal burden of proof on the parties.

[129] Christian Fackelmann, 'Dynamic Efficiency Considerations in EC Merger Control: An Intractable Subject or Promising Chance for Innovation' (University of Oxford, Centre for Competition Law and Policy, 2006) 49, available at: http://papers.ssrn.com/sol3/papers.cfm?abstract_id=910465.

[130] Most commentators accept or take for granted that the legal burden of proving efficiencies should fall on the merging parties and instead express strong concerns about the conditions of the 'efficiency

While the conditions of the 'efficiency defence' may be appropriate for integrating pro-competitive arguments in merger analysis where the primary responsibility for the final evaluation thereof falls on the Commission, when the burden of persuasion is placed on the merging firms, it becomes extremely difficult, if not impossible to satisfy.[131]

Therefore, it is submitted that the whole legal burden should remain with the authority at all times, although the merging parties should still bear a burden of producing evidence of any efficiencies in their sphere of knowledge. In practice, this will mean that if the Commission comes across indications of efficiencies, it may not decline to examine them on the ground that they have not been claimed by the parties.[132]

ii. The Implications of the Commission's Symmetrical Legal Burden for the Operation of Doubt in Merger Enforcement

In any event, even the otherwise proper allocation of the legal burden in *Impala* is not entirely devoid of peculiarity. As explained above, the Commission bears a double burden of persuasion: it must either prohibit a notified concentration on the ground that it would significantly impede effective competition in the common market or it must authorise it on the ground that it would not. This means that the authority is forced to make a decision either way. The GCEU emphasised this point in *General Electric* by explaining that:

> [I]t is not the case that the Commission must find in favour of a concentration falling within its jurisdiction in a case in which it might entertain doubts but rather that it must always make an actual decision one way or the other.[133]

defence'. See, eg, Pierre-Emmanuel Noel, 'Efficiency Considerations in the Assessment of Horizontal Mergers under European and U.S. Antitrust Law' (1997) 18 *European Competition Law Review* 498, 507; Peter Camesasca, 'The Explicit Efficiency Defence in Merger Control: Does it Make the Difference?' (1999) 20 *European Competition Law Review* 14, 25; Damien Gerard, 'Merger Control Policy: How to Give Meaningful Consideration to Efficiency Claims?' (2003) 40 *Common Market Law Review* 1367, 1392–93; Jrissy Motis, Damien Neven and Paul Seabright, 'Efficiencies in Merger Control' in Fabienne Ilzkovitz and Roderick Meiklejohn (eds), *European Merger Control: Do We Need an Efficiency Defence?* (Edward Elgar, 2006) 313; Lars-Hendrik Röller, Johan Stennek and Frank Verboven, 'Efficiency Gains from Mergers' in Fabienne Ilzkovitz and Roderick Meiklejohn (eds), *European Merger Control: Do We Need an Efficiency Defence?* (Edward Elgar, 2006) 144 and 177.

[131] OECD, *Competition Policy and Efficiency Claims in Horizontal Agreements* (Competition Policy Roundtables, 1995) 53, available at: http://www.oecd.org/competition/mergers/2379526.pdf. Concerning the merger specificity condition in particular, Mitja Kocmut ('Efficiency Considerations and Merger Control: *Quo Vadis*, Commission?' (2006) 27 *European Competition Law Review* 19, 26) observed that 'the absence of available alternatives is in principle even harder to prove than the existence of the efficiencies themselves', whereas Joseph Brodley ('Proof of Efficiencies in Mergers and Joint Ventures' (1996) 64 *Antitrust Law Journal* 575, 593) similarly stressed that 'it would be oppressive to require the participants to prove that the transaction is preferable to any conceivable alternative'.

[132] As Lars-Hendrik Röller ('Efficiencies in EU Merger Control: Do They Matter?' in Philip Lowe and Mel Marquis (eds), *European Competition Law Annual 2010: Merger Control in European and Global Perspective* (Hart Publishing, 2013) 66) observes, there have been cases where the Commission was prepared to consider efficiencies, but did not do so because they had not been claimed by the parties.

[133] Case T-210/01 *General Electric v Commission*, ECLI:EU:T:2005:456, para 61.

By the same token, in *EDP* the GCEU clarified that if the Commission is uncertain about the pro-competitive nature of the notified transaction, 'it could not conclude that where there is doubt it must prohibit the concentration', as Article 2(2) EUMR demands that a case of incompatibility must be positively made.[134]

Undeniably, the EU Courts' jurisprudence is fully aligned with the identical wording of Article 2(2) and (3) EUMR. Nevertheless, the symmetrical nature of the Commission's double legal burden has serious implications for the operation of doubt in merger enforcement. Contrary to infringement proceedings, where the Commission's burden is confined to establishing that the conduct in question *is* a restriction of competition or an abuse of dominance, in merger control the authority's burden of persuasion also extends to establishing that the notified concentration will *not* significantly impede effective competition in the common market, if authorised. Accordingly, where the Commission fails to discharge its burden of proof under Article 2(2) EUMR, it automatically acquires a mirroring burden of proof under Article 2(3) EUMR, and vice versa. In practice, this means that the Commission must be always convinced about the anti-competitive or pro-competitive nature of the merger and is not allowed to entertain any doubts whatsoever.

However, this double legal burden can theoretically turn merger decision-making into a vicious circle, where no conclusion about the competitive impact of the notified transaction can be positively reached. Instead of enabling the Commission to decide in situations of genuine factual uncertainty, in merger enforcement the symmetrical legal burden instead deals with doubt by calling for more time and resources to be invested in the evaluation of the concentration, until an affirmative conclusion can be reached.[135] As will be demonstrated in Chapter 4, combined with a high standard of proof for prohibition and clearance decisions alike, the imposition of a double burden of proof on the Commission reveals a precautionary approach to merger control and a judicial dislike for both false convictions and false acquittals.[136] It is submitted that it is in view of this prophylactic attitude that the EU Courts' persistent rejection of a 'presumption' of merger compatibility or incompatibility should be understood. Indeed, the principle of merger neutrality which underpins merger evaluation accords with both the symmetrical structure of Article 2(2) and (3) EUMR and the double legal burden of the Commission.

To the extent that this approach minimises decision-making errors and equally safeguards the merging entities' rights and the public interest, it must be commended. Nevertheless, the fact remains that such a symmetrical burden

[134] Case T-87/05 *Energias de Portugal SA v Commission* (*EDP*), ECLI:EU:T:2005:333, para 64.

[135] For instance, uncertainty in Phase I requires initiating Phase II. It should also be noted that in the context of merger control, the annulment of a merger compatibility decision does not allow the automatic conclusion that the concentration is anti-competitive, nor does the annulment of a merger incompatibility decision permit the inference that the notified transaction is pro-competitive. In both cases, all it means is that the Commission must re-examine the case and come back with better arguments and evidence (see art 10(5) EUMR).

[136] See Recitals 4 and 5 of the EUMR. See also ch 4, section IV.B.ii.

of persuasion is not entirely realistic; in exceptional circumstances, it may be genuinely impossible for the Commission to reach a decision to either effect. As AG Tizzano observed in his Opinion in *Tetra Laval*:

> As a matter of fact, I consider that the symmetry of those requirements cannot be absolute, seeing that there is, between the cases in which the notified transactions would very probably create or strengthen a dominant position within the meaning of Article 2 and the cases in which those transactions very probably would not create or strengthen such a dominant position, a 'grey area': an area, that is to say, in which cases are to be found where it is especially difficult to foresee the effects of the notified transaction and where it is therefore impossible to arrive at a clear distinct conviction that the likelihood that a dominant position will be created or strengthened is significantly greater or less than the likelihood that such a position will not be created or strengthened. The system laid down by Regulation 4064/89 must therefore necessarily provide a yardstick for the solution of those cases which are of doubtful or difficult classification.[137]

Therefore, these 'grey' situations beg the question how the case must be resolved. Inevitably, the answer to this seems to turn into a policy choice. When the difficult question is posed at the end of Phase II proceedings and once all time limits and investigative measures have been exhausted, only two options are available: either the Commission will choose to err on the safe side and will prohibit the concentration, mindful of the risk of a false conviction, or it will authorise the transaction, accepting the possibility that a false acquittal might occur.

AG Tizzano positioned himself in favour of authorisation – and rightly so. To this end, he invoked three arguments: first, he drew inspiration from Article 10(6) EUMR, which establishes a presumption of compatibility with the common market in situations where the Commission fails to adopt a decision within the prescribed time limits;[138] second, he relied on the 'parties' freedom of economic activity'; and, third, he remarked that, even in the case of a wrong clearance, Articles 101 and 102 TFEU provide us with the necessary tools for *ex post* corrective intervention.[139] The last two arguments are crucial. Generally, the Commission's symmetrical burden of proof favours the elimination of both false convictions and false acquittals in merger enforcement. However, in truly exceptional circumstances, where a conclusion is impossible, one should take account of the consequences of a prohibition decision for the parties involved, as well as the *ex ante* nature of merger control. With this in mind, a finding of merger illegality in cases of genuine uncertainty would contravene the explicit prescription that the EUMR 'does not go beyond what is necessary in order to achieve the objective of ensuring that competition in the common market is not distorted, in

[137] Case C-12/03 P *Commission v Tetra Laval* (*Tetra Laval II*), ECLI:EU:C:2004:318, Opinion of AG Tizzano, para 76.

[138] *cf Impala II* (n 120) para 49; Bo Vesterdorf, 'Standard of Proof in Merger Cases: Reflections in the Light of the Recent Case Law of the Community Courts' (2005) 1 *European Competition Journal* 3, 29–30.

[139] *Tetra Laval II* (n 137) Opinion of AG Tizzano, paras 78–81.

accordance with the principle of an open market economy with free competition'.[140] Therefore, it is submitted that in deadlock situations where all efforts to reach a definite conclusion have proved unfruitful, a finding of merger compatibility should be accepted.[141]

V. Conclusion

The simplicity of the question as to *who* should bear the responsibility for proving an allegation stands in stark contrast to the difficulty in answering it. Far from being a mere technicality, the allocation of the burden of proof reflects specific policy choices, fairness concerns and efficiency considerations, and might prove determinative of the outcome of litigation. The aim of this chapter has been to examine how the burden of proof is – or should be – regulated in EU competition enforcement. Given its central role in the process of evidence assessment, understanding this issue is crucial. That said, the allocation of the burden of persuasion seems to follow the same twofold pattern across the spectrum of EU competition enforcement. Indeed, the Commission is responsible for demonstrating that the conduct in question amounts to a 'restriction of competition' under Article 101(1) TFEU or an 'abuse of dominance' within the meaning of Article 102 TFEU or to a 'significant impediment to effective competition' under the EUMR. By contrast, the undertakings concerned bear the legal burden of establishing the existence of justifications or other benefits, which outweigh the restrictive nature or effects of their conduct. The bifurcation of the burden of persuasion is explicitly endorsed in the second clause of Article 2 of Regulation 1/2003, as far as Article 101 TFEU is concerned, and is implied in *Post Danmark I* and *Ryanair* as regards Article 102 TFEU and the EUMR respectively.

At first sight, the division of the legal burden between the Commission and undertakings appears sensible and has a strong intuitive appeal. Nevertheless, a more careful look suggests otherwise. Indeed, the bifurcation of the burden of persuasion fails to appreciate the fact that while the segregation of the various aspects of a conduct into anti-competitive and pro-competitive may be useful for the purposes of structuring competition analysis, it remains an artificial exercise. Detaching all or some efficiencies and justifications from the Commission's legal

[140] EUMR, Recital 6. See also Case C-202/06 P *Cementbouw Handel & Industrie v Commission*, ECLI:EU:C:2007:814, para 52.

[141] For commentators in favour of a presumption of merger compatibility, see Tony Reeves and Ninette Dodoo, 'Standards of Proof and Standards of Judicial Review in European Commission Merger Law' (2005) 29 *Fordham International Law Journal* 1034, 1047; Luca Prete, 'Standard of Proof and Scope of Judicial Review in EC Merger Cases: Everything Clear after *Tetra Laval*?' (2005) 26 *European Competition Law Review* 692, 698; Vesterdorf (n 138) 31. *cf* David Bailey, 'Standard of Proof in EC Merger Proceedings: A Common Law Perspective' (2003) 40 *Common Market Law Review* 845, 875–78.

burden might expand the range of conduct which may qualify as a 'restriction of competition', an 'abuse of dominance' or a 'significant impediment to effective competition', insofar as it enables the authority to intervene in the market without considering all the aspects of the conduct at hand. However, such an approach finds no support in the letter of Articles 101 and 102 TFEU, or the EUMR, while it could arguably result in over-enforcement of the competition rules. Moreover, as far as infringement proceedings are concerned, a bifurcated division of the burden of persuasion is objectionable for a further reason: it takes issue with the presumption of innocence, which according to settled case law applies hereto. Indeed, the latter prevents the imposition of a legal burden on defendants, where the standard of proof they must satisfy is higher than the balance of probabilities or an equivalent level of conviction. However, as will be expounded shortly, the standard of proof that undertakings must satisfy mirrors that of the Commission and is higher than the civil threshold. Consequently, a bifurcated burden of persuasion in antitrust proceedings is also not sustainable because it is at odds with the evidential prescriptions of the presumption of innocence.

For these reasons, it was submitted that the overall legal burden should be borne by the Commission across the spectrum of EU competition enforcement and throughout the various stages of the decision-making process. To this end, it was suggested that Article 2 of Regulation 1/2003, *Post Danmark I* and *Ryanair* must be 'read down' as imposing only an evidential burden on the undertakings concerned, that is, a mere obligation to plead efficiencies and other justifications or benefits and produce evidence of their existence. This refined approach to the distribution of the legal and evidential burden in EU competition enforcement has multiple advantages. First of all, it is fully aligned with the principle that the party in whose possession the evidence is should bring it forward, thereby accounting for problems of information asymmetry between the Commission and undertakings. Second, it decreases the risk of over-enforcement by ensuring that, before ultimately prohibiting a conduct as restrictive of competition, as abusive or as significantly impeding effective competition, the authority will take into account *all* its aspects and not merely its restrictive impact or only some of its advantages. Finally, in antitrust infringement proceedings, the proposed refinement in the distribution of the legal burden has the additional advantage that it ensures that doubt will operate in the undertakings' favour in all circumstances, contrary to the current bifurcated allocation which confines the benefit of doubt to the first step of the two-level analysis.

That said, the analysis yielded an interesting conclusion about the operation of doubt in merger control. As explained above, in merger enforcement the Commission bears a symmetrical, double burden of persuasion under which it is required to either prohibit a notified concentration on the ground that it would significantly impede effective competition or authorise it on the ground that it would not. This double burden is certainly aligned with the legal tests of Article 2(2) and (3) EUMR. However, it presents a noteworthy peculiarity: instead of allocating the risk of non-persuasion as per the usual function of the burden of proof, it effectively calls for more time and resources to be invested in the evaluation of notified transactions with unclear competitive impact. On the upside, this symmetrical double burden of proof is prone to eliminate both false convictions and false acquittals, while it reveals an overall risk-averse and precautionary attitude towards merger enforcement for the benefit of both merging entities and the public. However, on the downside, it is not entirely realistic, as there may be exceptional cases in which no decision can be reached. In such deadlock situations, it was submitted that a finding of merger compatibility should be accepted.

In any event, once allocated, the question that emerges is how the burden of proof can be discharged. The short answer is by providing evidence to the standard of proof. Therefore, it is necessary to consider what standard of proof the Commission and undertakings must satisfy to establish their arguments. This is the issue to which Chapter 4 now turns.

4

The Standard of Proof in EU Competition Enforcement

I. Introduction

At the very core of evidence evaluation stands the question whether the produced evidence has been 'sufficient'. Technically, this issue is translated into the standard of proof that one must satisfy in order to discharge one's legal burden and have the case decided in one's favour. The significance of the matter cannot be overstated. As with the burden of proof, the way in which the standard of proof has been set may determine the outcome of litigation, whereas it exposes how fairness and effectiveness considerations are traded off within the enforcement system in question. Nevertheless, detecting the appropriate standard of proof in EU competition enforcement has proved rather challenging. Despite the share of attention that the issue has attracted in recent years, definite conclusions are yet to be drawn, save for a universal acknowledgement that setting proper thresholds of evidence sufficiency is a complicated enterprise. Against this backdrop, the aim of this chapter is to analyse what is – or should be – the standard of proof in EU competition enforcement. To that end, section II offers a brief account of the meaning of the concept and explains its function in the decision-making process. Section III then illuminates some of the reasons for the persisting ambivalence over the applicable threshold of evidence sufficiency. Section IV examines how the standard of proof is regulated in antitrust infringement and merger cases, drawing on the jurisprudence of the EU Courts. Finally, section V discusses the separate question how the standard of proof may be satisfied and contemplates what factors may amplify or alleviate the difficulty of the task.

II. The Concept of the Standard of Proof and its Significance

In a nutshell, the standard of proof prescribes the minimum threshold that litigants need to surpass in terms of both quality and quantity of their evidence in order for their arguments to be established.[1] As explained in Chapter 2, decision-making takes place in circumstances of incomplete information. Because of this, absolute certainty in fact-finding is typically not feasible, whereas even if it is exceptionally attainable, it cannot be a general prerequisite. In this light, the added value of the standard of proof is that by indicating 'how much is enough' for a claim to be established, it determines the minimum degree of factual certainty that the decision-maker may lawfully settle for. However, compromising with anything less than certainty implies accepting the possibility of an error occurring. In this sense, the standard of proof constitutes – along with the burden of proof – a decision-making device through which the risk of a mistaken ruling is allocated in adjudication.[2]

In view of its core mission, the regulation of the standard of proof unsurprisingly depends on how one balances the costs of a false conviction or a false acquittal.[3] Indeed, at the case-specific level, a false conviction interferes with the freedom and rights of the person involved, whereas a false acquittal exposes a society to the harmful impact of the behaviour in question. The balancing of these two costs – namely, of undue interference with individual freedom and of ad hoc societal harm in the case of a failure to convict – through the mechanism of the standard of proof hinges on efficiency and fairness thoughts. In criminal enforcement, for instance, the operation of the presumption of innocence and the ensuing idea that 'it is better that ten guilty persons escape, than that one innocent suffer' have traditionally entailed a preference for false acquittals over false convictions, despite the increased risk of wrongful conduct going unpunished and the associated cost for society. On the contrary, in civil proceedings, it has been suggested that because both parties are on the same level playing field and no criminal charges are involved, the risk of an error should be allocated equally between them and that there is no reason to prioritise the cost of a false conviction over that of a false acquittal, and vice versa.[4]

Arguably, administrative models of enforcement – such as that of EU competition enforcement – are peculiar. On the one hand, they are not purely

[1] See also Case C-8/08 *T-Mobile Netherlands*, ECLI:EU:C:2009:110, Opinion of AG Kokott, fn 60: 'the standard of proof determines the requirements which must be satisfied for facts to be regarded as proven'.

[2] Alex Stein, *Foundations of Evidence Law* (Oxford University Press, 2005) 122, 143.

[3] Jeffrey Parker and Bruce Kobayashi, 'Evidence' in Boudewijn Bouckaert and Gerrit de Geest (eds), *Encyclopedia of Law and Economics* (Edward Elgar, 2000) 298.

[4] See generally James Brook, 'Inevitable Errors: The Preponderance of the Evidence Standard in Civil Litigation' (1982) 18 *Tulsa Law Review* 79, 85; Ronald Allen, 'Burdens of Proof, Uncertainty and Ambiguity in Modern Legal Discourse' (1994) 17 *Harvard Journal of Law & Public Policy* 627, 634; David Hamer, The Civil Standard of Proof Uncertainty: Probability, Belief and Justice (1994) 16 *Sydney Law Review* 506, 509; Mike Redmayne, 'Standards of Proof in Civil Litigation' (1999) 62 *Modern Law Review* 167, 171.

civil, since administrative authorities typically possess extensive investigative, decision-making and sanctioning powers, which they may exercise against natural and legal persons. On the other hand, they are not purely criminal either, since the powers of administrative agencies usually fall short of those of public prosecutors, whereas sanctions may at most take the form of financial penalties rather than imprisonment. These differences suggest that in administrative settings, where the 'dispute' is between a person and an authority which enjoys significant powers and where fines are involved, the balancing of the costs of false acquittals and false convictions must compensate for the inequality of arms between the parties.[5] At the same time, however, the trade-off between the different error costs is subject to the need to preserve the overall effectiveness of the enforcement system of which it forms part. In this regard, the allowed margin for false convictions may not be so narrow as to jeopardise the very ability of an enforcement authority to protect the public interest in accordance with their vested role.

In this light, the standard of proof should balance the minimum threshold of evidence sufficiency that can be tolerated from a fairness perspective against the maximum threshold respectively, beyond which the sustainability of the enforcement system becomes threatened. That said, the question of the regulation of the standard of proof should not be confused with the ensuing question of its discharge. As was mentioned in passing in Chapter 3 and as will be explained in further detail shortly, how easy or difficult it will be for a person to satisfy the standard of proof depends on what has to be proved, what evidence is available or used to this end and what mechanisms there are in place for that purpose – for example, presumptions.

III. The Main Reasons for the Ambivalence Over the Applicable Standard of Proof

While the standard of proof governing EU competition enforcement has been extensively debated in recent years, its content remains rather ambivalent. The complexity of the matter is certainly to 'blame' for this. Nevertheless, much of the vagueness in which the standard of proof is shrouded could be dispelled through a careful exposition of the main causes of the current lack of clarity. This section identifies the following three: the legislative silence on the matter, coupled with the vagueness of the judge-developed concept of 'requisite legal standard'; the 'probabilities versus inner conviction' dilemma surrounding the conceptualisation of the standard of proof; and the tendency to confuse the latter with substantive legal tests.

[5] See also Stein (n 2) 152–53 on the operation of an intermediate 'clear and convincing evidence' standard of proof in cases involving fraud and deprivations of civil liberties.

A. The Legislative Silence and the Vagueness of the 'Requisite Legal Standard'

Much of the uncertainty over the applicable standard of proof in EU competition enforcement would be removed if there were a specific rule governing its regulation. Contrary, however, to the burden of proof, which is exceptionally allocated with respect to antitrust proceedings in Article 2 of Regulation 1/2003, there is no equivalent provision for the standard of proof either in the Treaties or in Regulation 1/2003 or in the EUMR. The only relevant reference one might find is paragraph 5 of the Preamble to Regulation 1/2003, which reads as follows:

> [I]t should be for the party or the authority alleging an infringement of Article [101(1)] and Article [102] of the Treaty to prove the existence thereof to the *required legal standard* ... This Regulation affects *neither national rules on the standard of proof* nor obligations of competition authorities and courts of the Member States to ascertain the relevant facts of a case, provided that such rules and obligations are compatible with general principles of Community law. (Emphasis added)[6]

However, this excerpt is of little help. While it clarifies that in national competition proceedings the standard of proof is subject to the principle of national procedural autonomy,[7] it sheds no light on the standard of proof that governs competition enforcement at the EU level. Therefore, how the 'required legal standard' should be understood remains unclear.

In any event, the legislative silence would not be an issue if the competition jurisprudence of the EU Courts allowed a clear conclusion on the applicable threshold of evidence sufficiency. However, the language employed by EU judges has been criticised as vague and ambiguous.[8] It is remarkable that, contrary to its frequent use in the literature, the term 'standard of proof' appears only in about 50 competition law judgments – either in connection with the parties' arguments or interchangeably with the equally unclear notion 'legal standard'.[9] Instead, the EU Courts have routinely been referring to the 'requisite legal standard' to which arguments must be established to be upheld.[10] Due to its resemblance to the 'required legal standard' wording in paragraph 5 of the Preamble to

[6] Preamble of Regulation 1/2003, para 5.

[7] On this, see ch 8, section V.

[8] This led Ortiz Blanco to characterise the EU Courts' articulations as the 'usual clichés' and 'empty phrases' (Luis Ortiz Blanco, 'Standards of Proof and Personal Conviction in EU Antitrust and Merger Control Procedures' in Claus-Dieter Ehlermann and Mel Marquis (eds), *European Competition Law Annual 2009: The Evaluation of Evidence and its Judicial Review in Competition Cases* (Hart Publishing, 2010) 18, 177). Similarly, Ó Caoimh criticised the EU Courts for using 'language of doubtful value' (Claus-Dieter Ehlermann and Mel Marquis (eds), *European Competition Law Annual 2009: The Evaluation of Evidence and its Judicial Review in Competition Cases* (Hart Publishing, 2010) 58).

[9] As at 24 June 2018. See, eg, Case C-609/13 P *Duravit and Others v Commission*, ECLI:EU:C:2017:46, para 17; Case T-321/05 *AstraZeneca v Commission*, ECLI:EU:T:2010:266, para 343; Case C-413/06 P *Bertelsmann and Sony Corporation of America v Impala (Impala II)*, ECLI:EU:C:2008:392, paras 45, 51.

[10] This expression appears in more than 320 competition law judgments of the EU Courts (as at 24 June 2018).

Regulation 1/2003, this reference has been understood to correspond to the applicable standard of proof. Yet this expression does not reveal anything about the applicable threshold of evidence sufficiency.

That said, it is worth noting that in both infringement and merger cases, the EU Courts often speak of the need for 'convincing evidence', 'consistent evidence', 'sufficiently precise and consistent evidence', 'cogent/objective/reliable and consistent proof', 'solid evidence', 'specific and credible evidence' and 'firm conviction'.[11] These phrases do not rule out one another; usually, they appear cumulatively in the body of the same judgment. Such language, however, obscures the fact that, as Parr and Burrows rightly observed, 'the concept of the standard of proof and the cogency of the evidence required for the standard of proof to be met are two separate matters'.[12] Indeed, what *is* the standard of proof is a distinct question to be answered only by reference to its function as a decision-making and risk-allocation device.

B. The 'Probabilities v Inner Conviction' Dilemma

Beyond the lack of an explicit rule on the standard of proof and the intrinsic vagueness of the 'requisite legal standard' wording, the ambivalence over the applicable threshold of evidence sufficiency may be attributed – at least in part – to the diverse conceptualisation of the notion in different legal systems. On the one hand, common law jurisdictions perceive the standard of proof as indicating the degree of likelihood that the evidence must accord to the issue to be proved in order for the latter to be considered as established. Accordingly, they tend to articulate it in probabilistic terms and distinguish between the balance of probabilities – as the applicable threshold in civil enforcement – and the 'beyond any reasonable doubt' standard – for criminal enforcement. By contrast, civil law systems deem that the evidence is sufficient when the judge has been convinced. As such, they are generally unfamiliar with the notion of the standard of proof and simply refer to the 'intimate conviction' of the judge.[13]

Scholars have tried to explain the divergence in the conceptualisation of the standard of proof in common law and civil law jurisdictions by reference to the values which are arguably prioritised in each system. In this regard, it has been suggested that civilian countries may be more concerned with legitimacy, while

[11] See, for example, Case T-336/07 *Telefónica and Telefónica de España v Commission*, ECLI:EU:T:2012:172, para 67; Case T-214/06 *Imperial Chemical Industries v Commission*, ECLI:EU:T:2012:275, para 53; Case T-79/12 *Cisco Systems and Messagenet v Commission*, ECLI:EU:T:2013:635, para 62.

[12] Nigel Parr and Euan Burrows, 'Burdens and Standards of Proof in European Community Competition Law' in *Issues in Competition Law and Policy: ABA Antitrust Section*, vol 1 (ABA Book Publishing, 2008) 171.

[13] Kevin Clermont and Emily Sherwin, 'A Comparative View of Standards of Proof' (2002) 50 *American Journal of Comparative Law* 243, 245–55.

common law countries place more emphasis on implementing an error-minimising policy.[14] However, EU proceedings are unique in the sense that they favour the mingling of common law and civil law traditions due to the participation of national judges and lawyers, who reasonably tend to approach the matter through the lens of their own legal training.[15] Because of this, classifying them as similar to either common law or civil law jurisdictions would be inaccurate. As Lasok eloquently observed, EU proceedings allow for 'a pot-pourri of national standards which might differ in terms of formulation, if not also in degree' to evolve.[16]

In any event, the 'probabilities versus inner conviction' dilemma goes beyond the classification of the jurisdiction at hand as common law or civil law-based. Rather, it boils down to a fundamental question: should the standard of proof be articulated in the form of several probabilistic thresholds? Or should it be conceived as a single benchmark based on the 'inner conviction' of the judge? Unsurprisingly, there are arguments both in favour and against each option. The case for probabilistic standards of proof often rests on the premise that the use of specific percentages promotes legal certainty, insofar as it creates a sense of objectivity. Nevertheless, the prosecutor's fallacy illustrates that people may sometimes have too much confidence in numbers,[17] whereas the question still remains how to set the probabilistic threshold in the first place. Even with regard to the well-established 'criminal standard', the underlying feeling is that this is neither quantified nor easily quantifiable.[18] On the other hand, the 'intimate conviction of the judge' approach can be equally problematic. Its key advantages – namely uniformity and flexibility – can be seriously compromised by the vagueness of the term, which leaves little room for concrete *ex ante* guidance, whereas at a theoretical level, it is debatable how far from absolute certainty the 'inner conviction' standard really stands.[19]

This brief juxtaposition shows that there is no trouble-free conception of the standard of proof. In a sense, the dilemma between a probabilistic and

[14] ibid 269–74. *cf* Michelle Taruffo, 'Rethinking the Standards of Proof' (2003) 51 *American Journal of Comparative Law* 659.

[15] Eric Gippini Fournier, 'The Elusive Standard of Proof in EU Competition Cases' in Ehlermann and Marquis (n 8) 295–97.

[16] Paul Lasok, *The European Court of Justice: Practice and Procedure*, 2nd edn (Butterworths, 1994) 431.

[17] William Thompson and Edward Schumann, 'Interpretation of Statistical Evidence in Criminal Trials: The Prosecutor's Fallacy and the Defence Attorney's Fallacy' (1987) 11 *Law and Human Behaviour* 167.

[18] See generally Jonathan Cohen, 'The Role of Evidential Weight in Criminal Proof' in Peter Tillers and Eric Green (eds), *Probability and Inference in the Law of Evidence: The Uses and Limits of Bayesianism* (Kluwer Academic Publishers, 1988); David Kaye, 'Do We Need a Calculus of Weight to Understand Proof Beyond a Reasonable Doubt?' in Peter Tillers and Eric Green (eds), *Probability and Inference in the Law of Evidence: The Uses and Limits of Bayesianism* (Kluwer Academic Publishers, 1988); Michael Zander, 'The Criminal Standard of Proof: How Sure is Sure?' (2000) 150 *New Law Journal* 1517; *cf* Harry Saunders, 'Quantifying Reasonable Doubt: A Proposed Solution to an Equal Protection Problem' (bepress Legal Series, 2005), available at http://law.bepress.com/expresso/eps/881.

[19] The criticism is that if the judge is eventually convinced about the truth of an allegation, effectively they must be sure about it. However, a counter-argument is that certainty is not what the standard demands. What is necessary is that the judge, having heard all of the evidence, must be able to

a conviction-based articulation might become philosophical. In essence, both options serve flexibility and legal certainty in equal measure, albeit in different ways.[20] In this light, it has been rightly noted that 'the distinction may be more one of words than of substance'.[21] From an external standpoint, the emphasis is placed on the likelihood thresholds which can 'objectively' justify the making of a factual finding. From an internal point of view, on the other hand, the focus is on the subjective level of confidence that the fact-finder is expected to achieve before deciding.[22] Accordingly, the standard of proof may be best understood as a scale – irrespective of whether it is eventually articulated in probabilistic terms or as varying levels of confidence.[23] It is on this premise that the analysis in this book proceeds.

This remark is important for the discussion on the applicable standard of proof in EU competition enforcement. Indeed, it has been suggested that such a discussion is of little value, if any; at the end of the day, what matters is that the EU Courts are convinced. However, such an approach disregards the fact that one of the grounds on which Commission decisions may be annulled is that the authority failed to satisfy the standard of proof. Yet, if an administrative decision may fail judicial scrutiny on the ground that the standard of proof was not met, the latter should be at the very least made explicit – whether as a probabilistic threshold or as an *ex ante* defined level of confidence that the first instance decision-maker must attain in order to lawfully conclude that – on the facts of the case – the legal rule at hand does apply.[24]

C. The Tendency to Conflate the Standard of Proof with Substantive Legal Tests

Finally, the ambivalence over the applicable standard of proof in EU competition enforcement may be explained to some extent by the tendency to confuse this with

conclude with *confidence* as to the truth or not of the invoked allegations. See Paul Roberts and Adrian Zuckerman, *Criminal Evidence*, 2nd edn (Oxford University Press, 2010) 226, 247.

[20] See Dorothy Kagehiro and Clark Stanton, 'Legal vs Quantified Definitions of Standards of Proof' (1985) 9 *Law and Human Behavior* 159, 175, who explain that 'quantification of standard of proof merely makes explicit what is implicit in the original legal definition'.

[21] Julian Joshua, 'Proof in Contested EEC Competition Cases: A Comparison with the Rules of Evidence in Common Law' (1987) 12 *European Law Review* 315, 318. See also the results of the study conducted by Mark Schweitzer, 'The Civil Standard of Proof – What is it, Actually?' (2016) 20 *International Journal of Evidence & Proof* 217.

[22] See the 'external' and 'internal' analysis of the standard of proof in Hock Lai Ho, *A Philosophy of Evidence Law: Justice in the Search for Truth* (Oxford University Press, 2008) 173*ff*. Note also Christoph Engel, 'Preponderance of Evidence versus Intime Conviction: A Behavioural Perspective on a Conflict between American and Continental European Law' (2009) 33 *Vermont Law Review* 435, 458. *cf* Kevin Clermont, 'Standards of Proof Revisited' (2009) 33 *Vermont Law Review* 469, 477–82.

[23] The concepts 'civil standard', 'balance of probabilities', 'preponderance of the evidence' are merely used for convenience rather than in order to advocate for a probabilistic conceptualisation of the standard of proof.

[24] Paul Craig, *EU Administrative Law*, 2nd edn (Oxford University Press, 2012) 465.

the substantive legal tests that the Commission must satisfy in order to intervene in the market. Indeed, before it adopts an antitrust infringement or merger decision, the authority must demonstrate to the standard of proof that the conditions of the applicable substantive legal test are fulfilled. However, the distinctiveness of the two thresholds has been poorly grasped in competition scholarship and occasionally in the jurisprudence of the EU Courts.

Admittedly, there are several explanations for this. First of all, the lack of an explicit rule on the standard of proof governing EU competition enforcement and the vagueness of the judicial references to the 'requisite legal standard', as discussed earlier, do not help, insofar as they create fertile ground for misconceptions about the function of each threshold. A second explanation may be found in the fact that law-making in EU competition enforcement largely occurs in the context of adjudication. Indeed, the conversion of the broad proscriptions of Articles 101 and 102 TFEU, as well as of the EUMR, into concrete legal tests is not the outcome of an abstract legislative procedure; rather, it takes place in a random and incremental fashion whenever the EU Courts are called to review the legality of a Commission decision following an action for annulment or an appeal. However, the fact that the proper construction of the competition rules is contested in a predominantly adversarial setting and considered within the circumstances of particular cases sometimes further obscures the already-blurred divide between law and fact. This, in turn, may contribute to the misimpression that substantive legal tests and standards of proof overlap.

Yet, the main reason for the observed confusion probably lies in the fact that both standards of proof and substantive legal tests are often articulated in probabilistic language – or may be thought of in such terms. As explained above, in common law jurisdictions, the standard of proof is understood as indicating the required degree of likelihood for a claim to be accepted as true, whereas research has demonstrated that qualitative expressions of evidence sufficiency may also be correlated to probabilistic values.[25] At the same time, probabilistic vocabulary is intrinsic to the articulation of substantive legal tests in antitrust and merger enforcement as well. Indeed, a conduct may be prohibited as anti-competitive even in the absence of 'actual effects' on competition and consumers; some degree of risk of harm may well suffice for the Commission to intervene in the market. For instance, the EU Courts have clarified that 'Article [101(1)] of the Treaty prohibits both actual anticompetitive effects and purely *potential* effects'.[26] Similarly, in the context of Article 102 TFEU, it is settled case law that 'for the purposes of establishing an infringement of Article [102] TFEU, it is sufficient to show that the abusive conduct of the undertaking in a dominant position *tends to* restrict competition or in other words that the conduct is *capable* of having, or *likely* to have, that effect'.[27] Last but not least, in merger control, the use of probabilistic language is inevitable in view of the prospective nature of the analysis that the

[25] See n 20.
[26] Case T-35/92 *Deere v Commission*, ECLI:EU:T:1994:259, paras 61 and 92.
[27] Case 322/81 *Michelin v Commission*, ECLI:EU:C:1983:313, para 239.

Commission must perform. Accordingly, the authority may prohibit or clear a notified concentration only if – having envisaged the most plausible chains of cause and effect[28] – it reached the conclusion that the merger *would or would not* significantly impede effective competition in the market.

Clearly, the expressions used by the EU Courts do not have exactly the same meaning. Indeed, there is a greater or lesser difference in degree between 'capability', 'potential', 'plausibility', 'probability' or 'likelihood'. This difference has not been always acknowledged by EU judges, who have employed these concepts in a rather intuitive manner and sometimes even interchangeably, thereby causing some ambiguity about the reach of the competition rules. In any event, it is important to appreciate that these expressions refer to the substantive legal test rather than the standard of proof. They do not specify the degree of factual certainty that the decision-maker must attain, but rather indicate the level of harm – whether presumed (as in the case of by object violations) or established ad hoc (as in the case of by effect infringements and mergers) – which is required for the Commission to lawfully intervene in the market. Bearing this distinction in mind is crucial. First of all, confusing the two thresholds may result in the misleading impression that EU competition enforcement is governed by several 'standards of proof'. Most importantly, however, the function of substantive legal tests and standards of proof is different, as are the considerations which inform their design.

Indeed, in principle, both devices are driven by a common goal, ie, to manage errors when deciding under conditions of uncertainty – either in the form of false acquittals or in the form of false convictions. However, beyond this commonality, they present marked differences. First of all, they target distinct causes of erroneous decision-making: substantive legal tests are focused on managing legal errors, whereas standards of proof are concerned – as mentioned in Chapter 2 – with factual errors. Second, they balance different error costs. With regard to substantive legal tests, the relevant question is how to discourage anti-competitive behaviour without chilling pro-competitive conduct, insofar as false convictions are prone to deter behaviour which is beneficial for competition, whereas false acquittals may encourage harmful activity by generating the impression that the conduct is tolerated under the competition rules. By contrast, standards of proof aim to balance – as already noted – the cost of undue interference with an individual's freedom as a result of a false conviction against the cost of ad hoc societal harm in the case of a false acquittal. Third, the weighing of the different error costs within each mechanism is informed by distinct considerations. As explained, the regulation of the standard of proof in administrative settings eventually hinges on fairness considerations and the need to preserve the effectiveness of enforcement. In the context of substantive legal tests, on the other hand, the balancing of the costs of false acquittals and false convictions is driven by policy goals, economic insights into the nature of the practice at hand, and the need to

[28] On this, see section IV.B below.

promote the efficiency of enforcement and to ensure the administrability of the law.[29] Therefore, it is important to bear in mind the difference between substantive legal tests and standards of proof.

IV. The Regulation of the Standard of Proof in Antitrust and Merger Cases

Arguably, the almost mechanical appearance of a plethora of evidence-related wording in the case law has not helped dispel the ambivalence over the applicable standard of proof. Nevertheless, the EU Courts' jurisprudence still offers useful guidance on how the matter is regulated in EU competition enforcement.

A. The Standard of Proof in Articles 101 and 102 TFEU Cases

i. The Standard of Proof for the Commission

The discussion about the standard of proof to which the Commission should be subject in infringement proceedings concerning the application of Articles 101 and 102 TFEU has been dominated by fairness concerns due to the quasi-criminal features of antitrust enforcement. As explained in Chapter 2, antitrust fines qualify as 'criminal charges' within the meaning of the ECtHR's case law. In this context, the argument arose that the ECHR-criminal nature of infringement proceedings calls for the application of a 'beyond any reasonable doubt' standard of proof. For example, when challenging the Commission's decision in the gas insulated switchgear cartel, Hitachi claimed that 'the evidence relied on by the Commission in the contested decision is not sufficient to prove the existence of an infringement of Article [101 TFEU] beyond reasonable doubt'.[30] Similar arguments have been advanced in other cases as well.[31]

Admittedly, certain indications in the jurisprudence of the EU Courts appear to point towards the operation of a criminal standard of proof for the Commission. First of all, it has long been recognised that the presumption of innocence, which is typically manifested in a 'beyond any reasonable doubt' threshold of evidence sufficiency, applies 'to the procedures relating to infringements of the competition

[29] See generally Marina Lao, 'Ideology Matters in the Antitrust Debate' (2014) 79 *Antitrust Law Journal* 649; the literature cited in ch 2, n 94; and Pablo Ibáñez Colomo, *The Shaping of EU Competition Law* (Cambridge University Press, 2018) 29–32.

[30] Case T-112/07 *Hitachi and Others v Commission*, ECLI:EU:T:2011:342, para 278.

[31] See, eg, Joined Cases C-204/00P, C-205/00P, C-211/00P, C-213/00P, C-217/00P and C-219/00P *Aalborg Portland and Others v Commission*, ECLI:EU:C:2004:6, para 216; Case C-70/12 P *Quinn Barlo and Others v Commission*, ECLI:EU:C:2013:351, para 33.

rules applicable to undertakings that may result in the imposition of fines'.[32] Accordingly, in *Dresdner Bank and Others*, the GCEU rejected the Commission's claim that 'any manifest error is precluded if the assessment of the facts made by the Commission is more likely than that proposed by the applicants' and highlighted that 'any doubt in the mind of the Court must operate to the advantage of the undertaking to which the decision finding an infringement was addressed'.[33] Further elaborating on this, the Court explained that it 'cannot therefore conclude that the Commission has established the infringement at issue to the requisite legal standard if it still entertains any doubts on that point, in particular in proceedings for annulment of a decision imposing a fine'.[34] In the circumstances of the case, the Commission was eventually found to have failed to demonstrate to the requisite legal standard the existence of facts constituting a concurrence of wills showing an agreement on the ways of charging exchange commissions during the meeting of 15 October 1997.[35] The position taken in *Dresdner Bank and Others* was reiterated in *Toshiba*, where the Court underlined that 'the evidence submitted by the Commission must … permit the conclusion beyond all reasonable doubt that there was an infringement'.[36]

In this light, one might infer that the Commission's decision-making in infringement proceedings is subject to a criminal standard of proof.[37] Nevertheless, in other cases, EU judges seem to have dismissed such an approach. In *JFE Engineering*, for instance, while the Court confirmed the operation of the presumption of innocence, it declined to endorse the criminal 'beyond any reasonable doubt' threshold, explaining instead that 'the Commission must produce sufficiently precise and consistent evidence to support the *firm conviction* that the alleged infringement took place' (emphasis added).[38] A few years later in *BPB*, the GCEU reiterated its position and explicitly rejected the assertion that 'the Commission must adduce proof "beyond any reasonable doubt" of the existence of the infringement in cases where it imposes heavy fines'.[39]

[32] Case C-199/92 P *Hüls v Commission*, ECLI:EU:C:1999:358, paras 149–150; Case C-235/92 P *Montecatini v Commission*, ECLI:EU:C:1999:362, paras 175–76.

[33] Joined Cases T-44/02 OP, T-54/02 OP, T-56/02 OP, T-60/02 OP and T-61/02 OP *Dresdner Bank and Others v Commission*, ECLI:EU:T:2006:271, paras 59–60.

[34] ibid. See also *AstraZeneca* (n 9) para 475; Case T-379/06 *Kaimer and Others v Commission*, ECLI:EU:T:2011:110, para 47.

[35] *Dresdner Bank* (n 33) para 166. Similarly, in Case T-36/05 *Coats Holdings and Coats v Commission*, ECLI:EU:T:2007:268, para 91, the Court annulled the Commission's decision on the ground that the allegedly anti-competitive nature of the meeting on 11 February 1993 had not been established 'beyond doubt'.

[36] Case T-519/09 *Toshiba v Commission*, ECLI:EU:T:2014:263, para 36.

[37] See, for instance, Denis Waelbroeck and Donald Slater, 'The Scope of Object vs Effect under Article 101 TFEU' in Jacques Bourgeois and Denis Waelbroeck (eds), *Ten Years of Effects-Based Approach in EU Competition Law: State of Play and Perspectives* (Bruylant, 2012) 155–56.

[38] Joined Cases T-67/00 T-68/00, T-71/00 and T-78/00 *JFE Engineering v Commission*, ECLI:EU:T:2004:221, paras 177–79 In the context of art 102 TFEU, see *AstraZeneca* (n 9) para 477; and Case T-286/09 *Intel v Commission*, ECLI:EU:T:2014:547, para 64.

[39] Case T-53/03 *BPB v Commission*, ECLI:EU:T:2008:254, para 64.

The EU Courts' jurisprudence on the standard of proof governing infringement cases has had a mixed reception. Schweitzer, for instance, has criticised the rejection of the criminal threshold of evidence sufficiency as reflecting the EU Courts' failure to 'systematically integrate the fundamental rights dimension' in proceedings concerning the application of Articles 101 and 102 TFEU.[40] At the same time, several scholars have espoused more nuanced positions. Castillo de la Torre, for instance, has pointed out that there is no essential difference between earlier formulae used by the EU Courts and the criminal standard of proof, albeit taking note of the judicial unwillingness to explicitly articulate a 'beyond any reasonable doubt' threshold.[41] Similarly, Venit has argued that in Articles 101 and 102 TFEU cases, 'the application of the "strong and convincing evidence" civil standard and the "beyond reasonable doubt" criminal standard should yield the same result'.[42] Last but not least, Bellamy considered that 'in practice, we are applying something very close to the criminal standard but perhaps subconsciously making some allowance in cartel cases for the inherent difficulty of proving collusion'.[43]

This brief account illustrates that there exists some divergence of views regarding the applicable – and appropriate – articulation of the standard of proof. In this regard, it should be stressed, first of all, that framing the search as a choice between the balance of probabilities and the 'beyond any reasonable doubt' benchmark turns the inquiry into a false dilemma. As explained earlier, the standard of proof may be best conceptualised as a scale rather than a binary. The EU standard of proof may thus fall somewhere between these two options. Indeed, it is submitted that the EU Courts' jurisprudence indicates the emergence of an intermediate threshold of evidence sufficiency, which is best encapsulated in the concept of 'firm conviction'.[44] As early as in *Riviera Auto Service*, the GCEU explained that the Commission must produce evidence supporting the 'firm conviction' that the alleged infringement took place.[45] Since then, this wording has been reiterated in several judgments and in a variety of contexts.[46]

That said, the question remains whether a 'firm conviction' standard of proof suffices to ensure the effective judicial protection of the undertakings concerned in

[40] Heike Schweitzer, 'The European Competition Law Enforcement System and the Evolution of Judicial Review' in Ehlermann and Marquis (n 8) 107.

[41] Fernando Castillo de la Torre, 'Evidence, Proof and Judicial Review in Cartel Cases' in Ehlermann and Marquis (n 8) 345–46.

[42] James Venit, 'Human All Too Human: The Gathering and Assessment of Evidence and the Appropriate Standard of Proof and Judicial Review in Commission Enforcement Proceedings Applying Articles 81 and 82' in Ehlermann and Marquis (n 8) 252–53.

[43] Christopher Bellamy, 'Standards of Proof in Competition Cases' in *Judicial Enforcement of Competition Law* (OECD Competition Policy Roundtable, 1996) 107.

[44] John Ratliff, 'Before the European Courts: Avoiding Double Renvoi Judicial Review in EC Competition Cases' in Ehlermann and Marquis (n 8) 458; Ortiz Blanco (n 8) 177.

[45] Joined Cases T-185/96, T-189/96 and T-190/96 *Riviera Auto Service v Commission*, ECLI:EU:T:1999:8, para 47.

[46] It should be noted that the CJEU has only implicitly endorsed the 'firm conviction' standard of proof in Joined Cases C-239/11 P, C-489/11 P and C-498/11 P *Siemens v Commission*, ECLI:EU:C:2013:866, para 217.

view of the quasi-criminal nature of antitrust fines. Scordamaglia-Tousis answers this question affirmatively by examining the 'beyond any reasonable doubt' standard of proof that the ECtHR applies to its own proceedings.[47] According to the ECtHR:

> The level of persuasion necessary for reaching a particular conclusion and, in this connection, the distribution of the burden of proof are intrinsically linked to the specificity of the facts, the nature of the allegation made and the Convention right at stake. The Court is also attentive to the seriousness that attaches to a ruling that a Contracting State has violated fundamental rights.[48]

In agreement with other scholars, Scordamaglia-Tousis reads this passage as illustrating that the ECtHR's 'beyond reasonable doubt' threshold is not 'synonymous to the common law criminal standard, but should be interpreted as having an autonomous meaning'.[49] On this basis, he takes the view that 'the recurrent argument that the current probatory threshold should be enhanced to meet the criminal law requirements in order to comply with the ECHR is in principle erroneous'.[50] However, this justification for excluding the application of the criminal standard of proof to EU competition infringement cases does not seem persuasive, insofar as it disregards the fact that the ECtHR proceedings are not criminal and that the presumption of innocence does not apply to them.[51] Therefore, the fact that the standard of proof that the ECtHR applies to *its own* proceedings concerning the responsibility of the Contracting States under the ECHR is not the criminal threshold of evidence sufficiency, as traditionally understood, does not explain why anything less than a criminal standard of proof in infringement proceedings is in compliance with the ECHR – and, by association, with the CFR.

The answer rather lies elsewhere. As noted earlier, the standard of proof should balance the minimum threshold of evidence sufficiency that may be tolerated from a fairness perspective against the maximum threshold respectively, beyond which the effectiveness of enforcement might become jeopardised. Therefore, the 'firm conviction' threshold must be evaluated in light of these considerations.[52] Reflecting on the fairness of the 'firm conviction' standard of proof, the following

[47] Andreas Scordamaglia-Tousis, *EU Cartel Enforcement: Reconciling Effective Public Enforcement with Fundamental Rights* (Kluwer Law International 2013) 300–02.

[48] *Nachova and Others v Bulgaria*, ECLI:CE:ECHR:2005:0706JUD004357798, para 147.

[49] Scordamaglia-Tousis (n 47) 302; also Loukis Loucaides, 'Standards of Proof in Proceedings under the European Convention of Human Rights' in *Essays on the Developing Law of Human Rights* (Martinus Nijhoff Publishers, 1995) 157–69.

[50] Scordamaglia-Tousis (n 47) 305.

[51] Juliane Kokott, *The Burden of Proof in Comparative and International Human Rights Law: Civil and Common Law Approaches with Special Reference to the American and German Legal Systems* (Kluwer Law International, 1998) 199–200; Loukis Loucaides and Françoise Tulkens, *Judge Loukis Loucaides: An Alternative View on the Jurisprudence of the European Court of Human Rights: A Collection of Separate Opinions (1998–2007)* (Martinus Nijhoff Publishers, 2008) 287–89.

[52] See also Philip Lowe, 'Taking Sound Decisions on the Basis of Available Evidence' in Ehlermann and Marquis (n 8) 157–58.

remarks are helpful. First, while antitrust fines may well qualify as 'criminal charges' within the meaning of the ECHR, the notion of 'criminality' is understood by the ECtHR in a rather expansive manner, as Nazzini has observed.[53] Accordingly, the ECHR-criminal nature of antitrust penalties does not necessarily require the full extent of criminal procedural safeguards to be automatically activated.[54] In this regard, it should be stressed that the judicial imperative for 'firm conviction' based on accurate, reliable, consistent and sufficient evidence indicates anything but a low standard of proof. On the contrary, the 'firm conviction' threshold is flexible enough to be stretched almost to a 'beyond any reasonable doubt' standard.[55] Indeed, the readiness of EU judges to wholly or partially annul Commission decisions where the evidence does not eliminate doubts about the alleged facts confirms that a particularly heightened level of persuasion must be achieved before a finding of infringement is lawfully reached.[56] It is thus submitted that the 'firm conviction' standard is compatible with the principle of effective judicial protection – especially if combined with a refined approach to the burden of proof as advocated for in Chapter 3, under which the burden of persuasion shall remain with the Commission at all times.[57] In this light, a judicial endorsement of the criminal standard of proof might carry a risk of jeopardising the effectiveness of EU competition enforcement. As the EU Courts have acknowledged, discovering evidence of anti-competitive behaviour in fact-intensive cases – especially cartels – is particularly difficult, due to the covert nature of those infringements and the participants' conscious efforts to eliminate incriminating information.[58] Although the Commission does dispose of a vast array of fact-finding tools, it does not possess criminal investigative powers.[59]

With this in mind, the 'firm conviction' threshold offers the optimal solution: it safeguards the effective judicial protection of the undertakings concerned by being flexible enough to be stretched to an almost criminal standard, whilst preserving the small distance from the latter which might be vital to the effectiveness of the EU competition enforcement system.[60]

[53] Renato Nazzini, 'Administrative Enforcement, Judicial Review and Fundamental Rights in EU Competition Law: A Comparative Contextual-Functionalist Perspective' (2012) 49 *Common Market Law Review* 971, 979 ff.

[54] *Jussila v Finland*, ECLI:CE:ECHR:2006:1123JUD007305301, para 43. *cf Menarini Diagnostics SRL v Italy*, ECLI:CE:ECHR:2011:0927JUD004350908, Dissenting Opinion of Judge Pinto de Albuquerque, para 9.

[55] See below section IV.B.ii and n 104.

[56] See Fernando Castillo de la Torre and Eric Gippini Fournier, *Evidence, Proof and Judicial Review in EU Competition Law* (Edward Elgar, 2017) 34–41, in particular 39–40.

[57] *cf* Maria João Melicias, '"Did They Do it?" The Interplay between the Standard of Proof and the Presumption of Innocence in EU Cartel Investigations' (2012) 35 *World Competition* 471, 495–98.

[58] See, for instance, Case T-68/09 *Soliver v Commission*, ECLI:EU:T:2014:867, para 59.

[59] Ortiz Blanco (n 8) 176.

[60] *cf* Schweitzer (n 40) 5, who criticises what she considers being the prioritisation of the Commission's enforcement duties over individual rights.

ii. The Standard of Proof for Undertakings

As explained in Chapter 3, Article 2 of Regulation 1/2003 places the burden of persuasion with respect to Article 101(3) TFEU on undertakings. A similarly bifurcated legal burden operates in the context of Article 102 TFEU as well – assuming that one accepts the existence of an equivalent Article '102(3)' defence. Therefore, it is necessary to examine the threshold of evidence sufficiency that undertakings must satisfy in order to discharge their legal burden. If this is higher than the balance of probabilities or its equivalent level of subjective confidence, then the shared division of the burden of persuasion between the Commission and undertakings would contravene the presumption of innocence. The analysis will focus on Article 101(3) TFEU, but the same conclusions apply mutatis mutandis with respect to a similar Article '102(3)' provision as well.

That said, and somewhat surprisingly, the question as to what standard of proof defendant undertakings are subject when invoking the benefit of Article 101(3) TFEU has troubled the EU Courts only exceptionally. Cursorily touching upon this question in *Compagnie Générale Maritime*, the GCEU upheld the Commission's conclusion that the members of the Far Eastern Freight Conference (FEFC) had furnished no evidence showing that price fixing for inland transport services contributed to technical or economic progress and agreed that 'it appears more likely that the restriction of competition resulting from the price-fixing agreement, instead of stimulating the introduction of new technology, will discourage new investment'.[61] Similarly, in *Van den Bergh Foods*, the GCEU confirmed that 'it is for the undertakings concerned in the first place to present to the Commission the evidence intended to establish that the agreement fulfils the conditions' laid down by Article 101(3) TFEU and found that no 'concrete evidence' had been furnished to show that the Commission made a manifest error of assessment in asserting that it is 'unlikely that HB would definitely cease to supply freezer cabinets to retailers … if its power to impose an obligation of exclusivity in respect of those freezers were to be restricted'.[62] The GCEU's judgment in *GlaxoSmithKline* delivered a few years later is perhaps the closest that the EU Courts have come to articulating an explicit standard of proof for Article 101(3) TFEU. As clarified by the GCEU, 'a person who relies on Article [101(3) TFEU] must demonstrate that those conditions are satisfied by means of convincing arguments and evidence'.[63] However, considered in conjunction with the CJEU's clarification in *Tetra Laval II* that the term 'convincing evidence' merely draws 'attention to the essential function of the evidence, which is to establish convincingly the merits of an argument', this statement proves to be of limited value in identifying the applicable standard of proof under Article 101(3) TFEU.[64]

[61] Case T-86/95 *Compagnie Générale Maritime and Others v Commission*, ECLI:EU:T:2002:50, para 365.

[62] Case T-65/98 *Van den Bergh Foods v Commission*, ECLI:EU:T:2003:281, paras 136, 143.

[63] Case T-168/01 *GlaxoSmithKline Services v Commission*, ECLI:EU:T:2006:265, para 235. See also Case T-472/13 *Lundbeck v Commission*, ECLI:EU:T:2016:449, para 710.

[64] Case C-12/03 P *Commission v Tetra Laval BV (Tetra Laval II)*, ECLI:EU:C:2005:87, para 41.

Against this backdrop, the judgments handed down in *Mastercard* are of considerable interest.[65] In this case, one of the arguments that the undertakings put forward before the GCEU was that the Commission had imposed on them an excessive standard of proof, instead of the correct 'balance of probabilities' threshold that should apply in the context of Article 101(3) TFEU, and that the operation of the latter provision should be subject to the *in dubio pro reo* principle.[66] Examining these arguments, the GCEU recalled that, according to the precedent in *GlaxoSmithKline*, undertakings bear the burden of proving the benefit of Article 101(3) TFEU and must demonstrate its conditions 'by means of convincing arguments and evidence'.[67] However, the Court refrained from explicitly articulating the applicable standard of proof. Instead, it held that in the circumstances of the case, the Commission 'was properly able to conclude that [the undertakings] did not establish that the conditions for the application of Article [101(3) TFEU] were fulfilled'.[68] On this basis, it rejected the applicants' complaint.

Challenging the GCEU's judgment before the CJEU, the undertakings alleged that the GCEU committed an error of law in dismissing their claims concerning the standard of proof and the *in dubio pro reo* principle. Discussing these issues in his Opinion, AG Mengozzi proposed that the plea be rejected as inadmissible or, alternatively, as unfounded. Considering the merits of the undertakings' argument, AG Mengozzi repeated that 'it is settled case law that … the person relying on [Article 101(3) TFEU] must demonstrate, by means of convincing arguments and evidence, that the conditions for benefiting from an exemption are satisfied'.[69] Contemplating their allegation that the judgment in *GlaxoSmithKline* suggests a 'more-likely-than-not' evaluation under Article 101(3) TFEU and thus a balance of probabilities threshold, he remarked that the context of that case was substantially different, as a system of prior approvals was in force at that time and 'the analysis which the Commission was required to carry out was a prospective and forward-looking analysis of the likely advantages that the agreement notified to it would entail'.[70] Reflecting then on the operation of the *in dubio pro reo* principle, AG Mengozzi affirmed its applicability under Article 101(1) TFEU. However, he opined that this principle may not be invoked:

> [I]n an attempt to reduce the standard of proof required for the application of the exemption provided for in Article [101(3) TFEU] … It is therefore not sufficient … to adduce evidence that merely gives rise to uncertainty as to the application of Article [101(3)].[71]

[65] Case T-111/08 *MasterCard and Others v Commission (MasterCard I)* ECLI:EU:T:2012:260; and Case C-382/12 P *MasterCard and Others v Commission (MasterCard II)*, ECLI:EU:C:2014:2201.
[66] *Mastercard I* (n 65) para 195.
[67] ibid para 196.
[68] ibid para 237.
[69] *MasterCard II* (n 65), Opinion of AG Mengozzi, ECLI:EU:C:2014:42, para 141.
[70] ibid.
[71] ibid paras 146–47.

Deciding on these issues on appeal, the CJEU took the view that the complaint was essentially a repetition of the arguments put before the GCEU, seeking a re-examination of its assessment, and ultimately dismissed the plea as inadmissible.[72]

Although the CJEU declined to clarify the standard of proof that defendant undertakings must satisfy in order to discharge their legal burden under Article 101(3) TFEU, one might argue that the judgment of the GCEU in *MasterCard* points towards an evidential threshold higher than the balance of probabilities – or its equivalent level of subjective confidence. In this case, as explained in Chapter 3, the current twofold allocation of the legal onus in antitrust cases will take issue with the presumption of innocence, insofar as the latter mandates that, where the defendant is burdened with proving the elements of a defence, they must be subject to the lowest standard of proof.[73] Nevertheless, one might counter this with the idea that the perceived incompatibility of the current allocation of the burden of persuasion with the presumption of innocence could be rectified simply by reducing the undertakings' legal burden under Article 101(3) TFEU to an obligation to demonstrate the conditions of that provision to a 'balance of probabilities' standard or a similarly low degree of 'confidence'. Therefore, it is necessary to inquire whether such a threshold of evidence sufficiency is feasible in the first place, considering the Commission's obligation to establish a 'firm conviction' about the existence of an antitrust violation.

To answer this question, it is crucial to ponder on the conditions of Article 101(3) TFEU. According to Article 2 of Regulation 1/2003, undertakings seeking to benefit from that provision bear the legal burden of demonstrating all its four requirements. Therefore, it falls on them to establish not only that the conduct in question gives rise to efficiencies or other advantages, but also that it allows consumers a fair share of the resulting benefits. In the Commission's words, this condition 'implies in general that efficiencies generated by the restrictive agreement within a relevant market must be sufficient to outweigh the anti-competitive effects produced by the agreement within that same relevant market'.[74] To put it differently, the alleged efficiencies must *offset* the anti-competitive effects that have been proved by the Commission so that 'the net effect of the agreement' remains 'neutral'.[75] The specifics of this exercise remain unclear. Nevertheless, for the purposes of the argument developed here, it is important to appreciate that if the Commission has discharged its legal burden by producing evidence supporting the firm conviction that the conduct at hand restricts competition by object or by effect, then defendant undertakings entertain no real prospect of having their 'defence' upheld unless they establish an *at least equally strong* level of confidence

[72] ibid paras 215–19.

[73] See ch 3, section III.C.ii and n 94 therein.

[74] Commission Guidelines on the application of Article 81(3) of the Treaty [now Article 101(3)] [2004] OJ C101/97 (Article 101(3) TFEU Guidelines), para 43.

[75] ibid para 85.

that their conduct gives rise to objective advantages which outweigh its anti-competitive capacity or effects.

To some extent, this point was incidentally made by AG Trstenjak in her Opinion in *GlaxoSmithKline*. Pondering on what degree of probability must exist in order for an appreciable objective advantage to be found, she deliberated that 'a high degree of probability must be set here. That is because, with infringements of Article [101(1) TFEU], the existence of losses in efficiency in the form of a restriction of competition must already be postulated'.[76] Therefore, it appears that, insofar as the Commission is – rightly – subject to a threshold of persuasion which is higher than the balance of probabilities or its equivalent degree of confidence, a lower threshold of evidence sufficiency will never allow defendant undertakings successfully to invoke the 'defence' of Article 101(3) TFEU. Consequently, the undertakings' standard of proof will inevitably mirror the level of persuasion that the authority must satisfy. Since the latter is higher than a mere preponderance of the evidence or tantamount level of 'certainty', a shared allocation of the legal burden will inevitably take issue with the presumption of innocence.[77] With this in mind, it was submitted in Chapter 3 that the whole legal burden should be placed on the Commission.

B. The Standard of Proof in Merger Cases

The ambivalence over the applicable standard of proof observed in infringement proceedings has been present in merger enforcement as well. To a significant extent, the relative confusion surrounding the threshold of evidence sufficiency which governs proceedings concerning the application of the EUMR emanates from the prospective nature of merger analysis, which can make the line between substantive legal tests and the standard of proof almost indiscernible. Because merger control takes place *ex ante*, the case-by-case application of the 'significant impediment to effective competition' (SIEC) test inevitably turns into an inquiry of how likely it is that the notified transaction will give rise to restrictive effects, if allowed to proceed, in view of the available evidence.[78] As will be explained, this has created the impression that the applicable standard of proof is the balance of probabilities. The following paragraphs consider the jurisprudence of the EU Courts on the matter and contemplate whether a civil threshold of evidence sufficiency is appropriate in merger control.

[76] Joined Cases C-501/06 P, C-513/06 P, C-515/06 P and C-519/06 P *GlaxoSmithKline Services and Others v Commission and Others*, ECLI:EU:C:2009:409, Opinion of AG Trstenjak, para 193.

[77] This is especially so if one recalls that it is the Commission that weighs up the advantages and disadvantages that entail from the investigated agreement or concerted practice and that in so doing, the authority enjoys a margin of appreciation. On the contrary, defendant undertakings obviously enjoy no discretion in attempting to discharge their legal burden under art 101(3) TFEU.

[78] Bo Vesterdorf, 'Standard of Proof in Merger Cases: Reflections in the Light of the Recent Case Law of the Community Courts' (2005) 1 *European Competition Journal* 3, 19.

i. The EU Courts' Jurisprudence

Similarly to antitrust proceedings, the EU Courts have consistently underlined that merger decisions must be supported by a 'sufficiently cogent and consistent body of evidence'.[79] In the context of merger enforcement, attention was drawn for the first time to the standard of proof more than 15 years ago, when the GCEU famously annulled the Commission's decisions in *Schneider Electric*, *Airtours* and *Tetra Laval*.[80] According to the EUMR, the Commission must prohibit a concentration as incompatible with the common market if it would significantly impede effective competition and must authorise it if it would not. In this light, the GCEU stressed in *Airtours* that in the case of an alleged collective dominant position, 'the Commission is obliged to assess, using a prospective analysis of the reference market, whether the concentration which has been referred to it *leads* to a situation in which effective competition in the relevant market is significantly impeded' (emphasis added).[81] Along the same lines, the Court held in *Schneider Electric* that: 'It has not been proved to the requisite legal standard that the merger *results* in the creation of a dominant position … or, even if there should prove to be a dominant position, that it significantly *impedes* effective competition on those markets' (emphasis added).[82] Then, in *Tetra Laval I*, the GCEU took the view that the Commission must prohibit a conglomerate-type merger transaction if, in a prospective analysis of its effects, it is 'able to conclude that a dominant position would, *in all likelihood*, be created or strengthened in the relatively near future and *would lead* to effective competition on the market being significantly impeded' (emphasis added).[83] In this case, the Commission's analysis of the future dominant position must be 'particularly plausible'.[84]

The GCEU's allegedly strong language in *Tetra Laval I* caused the Commission to complain that the first instance court had unacceptably increased the standard of proof and had gone beyond its review powers.[85] Considering these allegations, AG Tizzano took the view that 'the concentration shall be prohibited when the Commission is persuaded that the notified transaction would very probably lead to the creation or strengthening of a dominant position'.[86] On appeal, however, the CJEU adopted a seemingly more relaxed test. Acknowledging the prognostic nature of merger assessment, it held that 'such an analysis makes it necessary

[79] *Impala II* (n 9) para 50; Joined Cases C-68/94 and C-30/95, *France and Société Commerciale des Potasses and de l'Azote and Entreprise Minière and Chimique v Commission (Kali & Salz)*, ECLI:EU:C:1998:148, para 228.

[80] Case T-342/99 *Airtours v Commission*, ECLI:EU:T:2002:146; Case T-310/01 *Schneider Electric v Commission*, ECLI:EU:T:2002:254; Case T-5/02 *Tetra Laval v Commission (Tetra Laval I)*, ECLI:EU:T:2002:264.

[81] *Airtours* (n 80) para 59.

[82] *Schneider Electric* (n 80) para 402. See also the wording in para 412.

[83] *Tetra Laval I* (n 80) para 153.

[84] ibid para 162.

[85] *Tetra Laval II* (n 64) para 27.

[86] ibid, Opinion of AG Tizzano, para 74.

to envisage various chains of cause and effect with a view to ascertaining which of them are the most likely'[87] and stressed that the 'evidence must support the Commission's conclusion that if such a decision were not adopted, the economic development envisaged by it would be plausible'.[88] Nevertheless, the post-*Tetra Laval II* merger jurisprudence appears to endorse a rather stricter approach. In *EDP*, for instance, the GCEU stressed that 'where, for the purposes of applying Article 2(3) of the Merger Regulation, the Commission examines a concentration, it must ascertain whether the concentration would have the direct and immediate effect of creating or strengthening a dominant position'.[89] Along similar lines, it underlined in *General Electric* that 'when the Commission relies on future conduct which it contends will be engaged in by a merged entity following a merger, it is required to establish, on the basis of convincing evidence and with a sufficient degree of probability, that the *conduct will actually occur*' (emphasis added).[90] The latter test was reiterated with identical wording in *Cisco*.[91]

This already intricate picture has been further complicated by allegations that the required degree of persuasion varies depending on whether the Commission decision authorises or prohibits the concentration, or whether it has been adopted following a Phase I or Phase II investigation. The question whether incompatibility decisions should be subject to a higher threshold of evidence sufficiency than clearance decisions arose in *Impala*. In this case, the appellants argued that merger authorisations call for a lower standard of proof compared to prohibition decisions to which a 'standard which is stricter than one based on the mere balancing of probabilities' applies, 'since a prohibition represents a serious limitation of the commercial freedom of the notifying parties and since concentrations should benefit from a presumption that they are compatible with the common market'.[92] Nevertheless, the CJEU rejected the existence of an asymmetrical standard of proof by emphasising that 'there is nothing in Article 2(2) or 2(3) of the Regulation which states that it imposes different standards of proof in relation to decisions approving a concentration, on the one hand, and decisions prohibiting a concentration, on the other' and denied the existence of a general 'presumption' of merger compatibility or incompatibility with the common market.[93]

[87] ibid para 43 (see also Case T-342/07 *Ryanair v Commission*, ECLI:EU:T:2010:280, para 27; Case T-175/12 *Deutsche Börse v Commission*, ECLI:EU:T:2015:148, para 62).

[88] ibid para 44.

[89] Case T-87/05 *EDP v Commission*, ECLI:EU:T:2005:333, para 124. See also Case T-102/96 *Gencor v Commission*, ECLI:EU:T:1999:65, paras 90–100.

[90] Case T-210/01 *General Electric v Commission*, ECLI:EU:T:2005:456, para 464. See also *Kali and Salz* (n 79) para 246 ('to assess with a sufficient degree of probability the effect which a concentration might have on competition on the relevant market, it is essential to rely on a rigorous analysis of the competitors' weight').

[91] *Cisco Systems* (n 11) para 62.

[92] *Impala II* (n 9) para 40.

[93] ibid paras 46 and 48.

Finally, in *Cisco*, the GCEU was confronted with the argument that a stricter standard of proof applies to decisions pursuant to Phase I investigations, whereby the Commission finds no serious doubts about the compatibility of the concentration with the common market than in Phase II decisions. More specifically, Cisco argued that the Commission did not enjoy any discretion when adopting a clearance decision under Article 6(1)(b) EUMR and thus that the Court 'should examine whether or not the Commission was entitled to conclude, beyond any reasonable doubt, that the concentration at issue did not give rise to competition concerns'.[94] The GCEU acknowledged that the tests in Articles 6 and 8 EUMR are different on their face: Article 6 asks for 'serious doubts' as to the compatibility of the concentration with the common market, while an Article 8 decision requires ascertaining whether the concentration 'would significantly impede effective competition' or not. However, it observed that 'the assessment criteria on which the Commission must rely when taking either an Article 6 or an Article 8 EUMR decision are the same'. Therefore, 'whether the Commission authorises … a concentration at the end of the first stage or after a second stage of examination, the standard of proof is identical'.[95]

The GCEU's ruling in *Cisco* reinforces the argument that the standard of proof governing merger analysis is uniform and does not vary depending on the progress of the proceedings.[96] By extending the scope of *Impala II* to clearance decisions pursuant to Phase I proceedings, the GCEU's approach falls in line with earlier jurisprudence on the issue. For instance, when it partially annulled the Commission's conditional authorisation of the *SEB/Moulinex* concentration in *BaByliss*, the Court noted that, given that 'an in-depth market study is not carried out in Phase I', the Commission had to demonstrate that the commitments were 'sufficient to rule out clearly any serious doubts' as to whether effective competition on the market would be significantly impeded if the transaction were to be authorised.[97] Likewise, upholding the Commission's decision to approve, subject to conditions, the *Air France/KLM* concentration a few years later in *easyJet*, the GCEU considered whether 'the Commission was entitled, without committing a manifest error of assessment, to take the view that [the proposed] commitments constituted a direct and sufficient response capable of clearly dispelling all serious doubts'.[98] Therefore, the standard of proof appears to be as high for Phase I or Phase II clearance decisions as for prohibition decisions.

[94] *Cisco Systems* (n 11) para 43.

[95] ibid para 46. Moreover, see Case T-119/02 *Royal Philips Electronics v Commission*, ECLI:EU:T:2003:101, as regards the standard of proof applicable to a referral decision. According to para 343, the Commission 'cannot decide to make such a referral, if … it is clear, on the basis of a body of precise and coherent evidence, that such a referral cannot safeguard or restore effective competition on the relevant markets'.

[96] *cf* Yves Botteman, 'Mergers, Standard of Proof and Expert Economic Evidence' (2006) 2 *Journal of Competition Law and Economics* 71, 76–77.

[97] Case T-114/02 *BaByliss v Commission*, ECLI:EU:T:2003:100, para 169.

[98] Case T-177/04 *easyJet v Commission*, ECLI:EU:T:2006:187, paras 128–29.

ii. Reflections

Considering the standard of proof for merger decisions, it is immediately apparent that a criminal threshold of evidence sufficiency is out of the question. Merger decisions do not impose financial penalties upon merging entities and the presumption of innocence does not apply to merger proceedings.[99] With this in mind, the GCEU rightly explained in *Cisco* that 'an assessment of probabilities is … involved … and not … an obligation on the Commission to show beyond any reasonable doubt that a concentration does not give rise to any competition concerns'.[100] However, the answer to the question of what degree of certainty the Commission must acquire before concluding that in the circumstances of a given case the notified concentration will or will not significantly impede effective competition if allowed to proceed has not been as clear. Based on the prognostic nature of merger analysis, the identical wording of Article 2(2) and Article 2(3) EUMR, the CJEU's proposition in *Tetra Laval II* that the Commission must base its decision on the 'most likely' competitive development and the absence of a 'presumption' of merger compatibility or incompatibility, as verified in *Impala II*, several commentators have expressed the view that merger control is subject to a balance of probabilities standard of proof.[101]

Nevertheless, the operation – and desirability, for that matter – of such an evidential threshold in merger enforcement should not be accepted at face value. First, the statement in *Tetra Laval II* that the Commission must take into account 'the most likely' development is not of much help, insofar as 'the most likely' chain of cause and effect may still be insufficiently likely for the purposes of the standard of proof.[102] Second, the language used by the EU Courts in their merger jurisprudence, as presented above, combined with the judicial prescription for the Commission to produce 'accurate, reliable, consistent and sufficient evidence',[103] appears to point towards an evidentiary threshold which is considerably higher than the balance of probabilities. A study conducted by Lyons, Menzies and Zizzo

[99] Note that in cases where the Commission has sanctioned merging entities for jumping the gun, the EU Courts' approach has been identical to that taken in antitrust proceedings (eg, Case T-332/09 *Electrabel v Commission*, ECLI:EU:T:2012:672, paras 31–32).

[100] *Cisco Systems* (n 11) para 47.

[101] Schweitzer (n 40) 141; Ó Caoimh (n 8) 281; David Bailey, 'Standard of Proof in EC Merger Proceedings: A Common Law Perspective' (2003) 40 *Common Market Law Review* 845, 887; Carles Esteva Mosso, 'Non-horizontal Mergers: A European Perspective' (2008) 31 *Fordham International Law Journal* 1442, 1447.

[102] Equally unsatisfactory is the CJEU's position that 'the evidence must support the Commission's conclusion that if such a decision were not adopted, the economic development envisaged by it would be plausible', if understood as proposing a *plausibility* standard of proof, which would be unacceptably low. This unfortunate language must be understood in the context of the CJEU's attempt to mitigate the reactions caused by the trio of Commission decision annulments and not as corresponding to the standard of proof actually applied by the Court. See Ioannis Lianos '"Judging Economists", Economic Expertise in Competition Litigation: A European View' in Ioannis Lianos and Ioannis Kokkoris (eds), *The Reform of EC Competition Law: New Challenges* (Kluwer Law International, 2010) 309.

[103] See, eg, Case T-464/04 *Independent Music Publishers and Labels Association v Commission (Impala I)*, ECLI:EU:T:2006:216, para 414.

corroborates this idea. Empirically exploring how the requirement for 'accurate, reliable, consistent and sufficient evidence' is understood in practice, the authors found that it indicates 'almost as high a standard of proof as the "beyond reasonable doubt"'.[104] Third, the civil standard of proof is driven by the principle of equality and is thus apt for proceedings where litigants are on a similar footing.[105] However, this is not the case in merger enforcement. The Commission remains an administrative authority with extensive investigative and decision-making powers in merger proceedings as well.[106] Furthermore, merger control takes place *ex ante*, before any SIEC has occurred, whereas the absence of criminal or quasi-criminal financial penalties does not eliminate the fact that the financial consequences of a merger prohibition may still be very serious for the notifying parties.[107] For these reasons, it is submitted that the civil standard of proof is neither suitable for the fairness demands of merger enforcement nor representative of the EU Courts' jurisprudence. Seeking to 'label' the applicable threshold of evidence sufficiency, the 'firm conviction' concept seems appropriate, although admittedly it has not been explicitly employed by the EU Courts in merger cases.

In any event, the operation of a high standard of proof for prohibition decisions does not imply a lower threshold for either Phase I or Phase II merger authorisations – as the EU Courts emphasised in *Impala II* and in *Cisco*. By opting for a purely symmetrical substantive legal test for assessing both the compatibility and the incompatibility of a notified concentration with the common market, the EUMR does not allow the Commission to simply clear the transaction, when the standard of proof for establishing a 'significant impediment to effective competition' has not been met. As Van Rompuy remarked, 'the Commission cannot opt for a clearance decision to be on the safe side';[108] it must be positively persuaded that the notified concentration will not pose any significant risks for competition on the market. Similarly to the imposition of a double legal burden on the authority, the operation of a uniform standard of proof across merger enforcement hints at an aversion towards both false acquittals and false convictions.[109] The endorsement of

[104] Bruce Lyons, Gordon Douglas Menzies and Daniel John Zizzo, *Professional Interpretation of the Standard of Proof: An Experimental Test on Merger Regulation* (University of East Anglia, Centre for Competition Policy, Working Paper No 2/2010) 26, available at http://competitionpolicy.ac.uk/documents/8158338/8256105/CCP+Working+Paper+10-2.pdf/40351242-7ca5-4e86-aa25-d358302f4ef1.

[105] See n 4.

[106] George Cumming, *Merger Decisions and the Rules of Procedure of the European Community Courts* (Kluwer Law International, 2011) 228–29.

[107] See ch 2, section III.B.ii.

[108] Ben Van Rompuy, 'Implications for the Standard of Proof in EC Merger Proceedings: Bertelsmann and Sony Corporation of America v. Impala (C-413/06 P) ECJ' (2008) 29 *European Competition Law Review* 608, 610. See also Pal Szilagyi, 'The ECJ Has Spoken: Where Do We Stand with the Standard of Proof in Merger Control?' (2008) 29 *European Competition Law Review* 726, 728. *cf* Kathryn Wright, 'Perfect Symmetry? *Impala v. Commission* and Standard of Proof in Mergers' (2007) 32 *European Law Review* 408, 415.

[109] See also Gisela Aigner, Oliver Budzinski and Arndt Christiansen, 'Analysis of Coordinated Effects in EU Merger Control: Where Do We Stand after Sony/BMG and Impala?' (2006) 2 *European Competition Journal* 311, 329–30.

an identical threshold of evidence sufficiency for authorisations and prohibitions alike and for both Phase I and Phase II proceedings suggests that the EU Courts attach equal importance to ensuring not only that the merging entities' right to consummate their transaction will not be unduly restricted, but also that competition will not be harmed by concentrations which were erroneously allowed to proceed.[110]

Nevertheless, it should be noted that, coupled with the symmetrical legal burden, the operation of a uniform – akin to 'firm conviction' – standard of proof in merger enforcement may place the Commission in a no-win situation. Not only is the latter faced with strict time limits and the hurdles of prognostic evaluation, but it is also expected to satisfy an elevated standard of proof and not to ever entertain doubts towards either outcome. Obviously, this is not an entirely realistic situation. For this reason, it was submitted in Chapter 3 that a finding of merger compatibility should be accepted in genuine deadlock situations.

V. The Discharge of the Standard of Proof in EU Competition Enforcement

The operation of a uniform standard of proof in EU competition enforcement by no means implies that its discharge will require the same effort in all circumstances.[111] By indicating whether the adduced information can be accepted as *proof* of a claim, the standard of proof essentially links the evidence with the substantive arguments and operates as the analytical bridge connecting the facts with the law. Accordingly, how easy or difficult it will be for the Commission – or undertakings – to satisfy it hinges on three broad parameters: first, what has to be proved; second, what evidence is available or used to this end; and, third, what facilitating mechanisms – if any – there are in place.

Indeed, not all issues are equally easy to prove. In the context of EU competition enforcement in particular, several factors may complicate or simplify the task of satisfying the standard of proof. Unsurprisingly, the nature of the conduct in question is one of them. For instance, establishing the existence of a concerted practice in parallel conduct cases will generally be more difficult than demonstrating the existence of an agreement between competitors, since the Commission will have to show that concertation constitutes 'the only plausible explanation' for

[110] Andriani Kalintiri, 'The Standard of Proof in Phase I Merger Decisions: The Lesson from the *Microsoft/Skype* Appeal' (2014) 35 *European Competition Law Review* 279.

[111] Anne-Lise Sibony, *Le Juge et le Raisonnement Economique en Droit de la Concurrence* (Librairie Générale de Droit et de Jurisprudence, 2008) 738–39 uses this expression (in French: 'effort probatoire') to argue that what matters is rather the expected intensity of the parties' effort to convince the judge rather than the debate on the appropriate standard of proof per se.

the conduct.[112] Similarly, establishing the existence of an anti-competitive vertical agreement may require a greater effort than demonstrating the existence of an anti-competitive horizontal agreement, since:

> [F]actors which … can sometimes suggest the existence of an anti-competitive agreement between competitors may prove inadequate for the purposes of establishing the existence of such an agreement in the framework of a vertical relationship between a manufacturer and a distributor, given that, in such a relationship, a certain measure of contact is lawful.[113]

Therefore, the type of conduct in question may affect how laborious the discharge of the standard of proof will be.[114]

In addition, the prospective or retrospective nature of the issue to be proved may also affect the discharge of the standard of proof. In this regard, it has been suggested that different thresholds of evidence sufficiency apply to infringement cases, where the Commission's examination focuses on past or contemporary events, compared to merger cases where competition analysis takes the form of a 'prognosis'.[115] Such differentiation, however, is inaccurate: first, the prospective or retrospective nature of the analysis is not a consideration pertinent to the *regulation* of the standard of proof, as discussed earlier; and, second, it fails to appreciate not only that certain prospective elements may be present in infringement cases, too,[116] but also that merger decision-making is grounded in the current structure of the market, the features of the existing competition and the actual commercial strength of market operators. That said, the prospective nature of the issue to be proved may indeed complicate the discharge of the standard of proof. The reason for this is that, as the CJEU explicated in *Tetra Laval II*, 'the consideration of a lengthy period of time in the future' means 'that the chains of cause and effect are dimly discernible, uncertain and difficult to establish'.[117] Therefore, 'a prospective analysis of the kind necessary in merger control must be carried out with great care' in order to ensure that it does not become 'purely speculative',[118] especially if the alleged anti-competitive effects are not certain to occur 'in a sufficiently near

[112] Joined Cases 89/85, 104/85, 114/85, 116/85, 117/85 and 125/86 to 129/85 *Ahlström Osakeyhtiö and Others v Commission (Woodpulp II)*, ECLI:EU:C:1993:120, para 71.

[113] Case C-260/09 P *Activision Blizzard Germany v Commission*, ECLI:EU:C:2011:62, paras 71–72.

[114] See also Per Hellstrom, 'A Uniform Standard of Proof in EU Competition Proceedings' in Ehlermann and Marquis (n 8) 152.

[115] Matteo Bay and Javier Ruiz Calzado, '*Tetra Laval II*: The Coming of Age of the Judicial Review of Merger Decisions' (2005) 28 *World Competition* 433, 450, who comment that: 'There is certainly a sort of paradox in requiring the Commission to be (more) convincing in proving future than past events.'

[116] See, for instance, Case C-475/99 *Ambulanz Glöckner*, ECLI:EU:C:2001:577, para 48.

[117] *Tetra Laval II* (n 64) para 44.

[118] ibid para 42: 'A prospective analysis of the kind necessary in merger control must be carried out with great care since it does not entail the examination of past events – for which often many items of evidence are available which make it possible to understand the causes – or of current events, but rather a prediction of events which are more or less likely to occur in future if a decision prohibiting the planned concentration or laying down the conditions for it is not adopted.' See also *General Electric* (n 90) para 64; and Case T-145/06 *Omya v Commission*, ECLI:EU:T:2009:27, para 33.

future'.[119] From this perspective, the more remote the contemplated effects, the more difficult it will be for the Commission to satisfy its standard of proof, since the greater the risk that such effects may ultimately not materialise.

Furthermore, the discharge of the standard of proof is informed by normality considerations. Indeed, past experience and common sense shape our perception of 'usual' and 'unusual', which may in turn influence our interpretation of the evidence and our expectations.[120] Unsurprisingly, abnormal situations will typically require a greater effort to demonstrate.[121] That said, it is interesting to note that economics may also frame our understanding of what is 'normal' and what is not.[122] For instance, cartels are generally deemed to harm competition; as such, efficiency claims will be assessed against this default premise. In this regard, economics may have a vital – even if rather indirect – contribution in the discharge of the standard of proof. Helpfully, the Commission Guidelines offer numerous examples of 'economic normality'.[123] For example, the Non-Horizontal Mergers Guidelines acknowledge that 'non-horizontal mergers are generally less likely to significantly impede effective competition than horizontal mergers'.[124] In line with this economic insight, when the Commission prohibited the *Tetra Laval/Sidel* concentration as incompatible with the common market, the GCEU emphasised that:

> Since the effects of a conglomerate-type merger are generally considered to be neutral, or even beneficial, for competition on the markets concerned, as is recognised in the present case by the economic writings cited in the analyses annexed to the parties' written pleadings, the proof of anti-competitive conglomerate effects of such a merger calls for a precise examination, supported by convincing evidence, of the circumstances which allegedly produce those effects.[125]

Therefore, the inherent 'normality' of the parties' arguments, as informed by past experience, common sense or economics, is bound to affect how easy or difficult the discharge of the standard of proof will be.

[119] *Cisco Systems* (n 11) para 121 and also para 134.

[120] Stein (n 2) 64 ff.

[121] Lord Hoffmann got this point across in a very illustrative fashion by remarking that it is less likely to see a lion in Regent's Park than to see a dog. See Laura Parret, 'Sense and Nonsense of Rules on Proof in Cartel Cases' (2008) 31 *European Competition Journal* 169, 193.

[122] The term 'economic normality' was first used by Sibony ((n 111) 746). See also Alexander Italianer, 'Quality and Quantity in Economic Assessments' (Charles River Associates Annual Conference, Brussels, 7 December 2011) 3, available at http://ec.europa.eu/competition/speeches/text/sp2011_15_en.pdf; and the interesting work of Mariateresa Maggiolino, 'Plausibility, Facts and Economics in Antitrust Law' (2014) 7 *Yearbook of Antitrust and Regulatory Studies* 107.

[123] See, eg, Guidance on the Commission's enforcement priorities in applying Article 82 of the EC Treaty to abusive exclusionary conduct by dominant undertakings [2009] OJ C45/02, paras 30, 64, 67; Commission Guidelines on the assessment of horizontal mergers under the Council Regulation on the control of concentrations between undertakings [2004] OJ C31/5, para 4.

[124] Commission Guidelines on the assessment of non-horizontal mergers under the Council Regulation on the control of concentrations between undertakings [2008] OJ C265/6, para 11.

[125] *Tetra Laval I* (n 80) para 155.

Last but not least, satisfying the applicable threshold of evidence sufficiency will generally require a greater or lesser effort depending on the complexity and novelty of the issue to be proved. Confronted, for instance, in *Impala II* with a collective dominance theory, the CJEU clarified that 'the fact that an issue of collective dominance does, or does not, arise, cannot of itself have an impact on the standard of proof which applies'; rather, 'the inherent complexity of a theory of competitive harm … is a factor which must be taken into account' when assessing the plausibility of the parties' arguments.[126] Likewise, where the authority's case is built on a novel theory of harm, meeting the required threshold of evidence sufficiency may be more challenging, as *Airtours* and *Tetra Laval* demonstrated.[127] Provided, however, that sufficient evidence is adduced, the EU Courts are not opposed to the use of alternative theories that suit the circumstances of the case. *General Electric* offers an example of this. General Electric objected, inter alia, to the Commission's definition of the market for large regional aircraft engines on the ground that its argument that engines were in indirect second-level competition on the market fell 'outside the ambit of the accepted theory of substitutability'.[128] However, scrutinising the documents on which the Commission relied, the GCEU found that its theory was supported by the evidence and upheld it.[129]

At any rate and irrespective of the specific features of the issue to be proved, the discharge of the standard of proof will be eventually contingent on the quality and quantity of the available evidence. In many respects, the process of satisfying the standard of proof resembles the process of assembling a jigsaw puzzle; unsurprisingly, the clarity of the overall picture depends on the existence of as many puzzle pieces as possible and their value. In the context of EU competition enforcement, the numerous judicial references to the characteristics that the evidence must possess leave little doubt about the significance that the EU Courts attach to its quality. In antitrust and merger cases alike, the Commission is expected to support its arguments with evidence that is 'convincing', 'consistent', 'sufficiently precise', 'cogent', 'objective', 'reliable', 'solid', 'specific', 'credible', 'contains all the information which must be taken into account' and 'is capable of substantiating the conclusions drawn from it'.[130] However, as Chapter 5 will explain, not all evidence bears the same weight. For instance, documentary evidence generally carries a stronger probative value compared to economic evidence. This does not mean that distinct standards of proof apply, as the argument sometimes goes; rather, it simply implies that in the hypothetical situation where the Commission or undertakings would wish to prove their claims solely on the basis of economic evidence, their task would become substantially more difficult.

[126] *Impala II* (n 9) para 51.

[127] See *Airtours* (n 80) para 63; and *Tetra Laval I* (n 80) paras 162, 212–14.

[128] *General Electric* (n 90) para 499. See also para 229: 'In the light of all the foregoing … the arguments based on the allegedly unorthodox nature, in terms of economic theory, of the Commission's case cannot prevail over the convincing evidence adduced by the Commission.'

[129] ibid para 503.

[130] The last two requirements are part of the marginal standard of review (*Tetra Laval II* (n 64) para 39). The symbiosis of evidence standards and standards of review is discussed in ch 7.

Finally, the discharge of the standard of proof can be eased through the use of presumptions. Technically speaking, the latter are a procedural mechanism which allows the decision-maker to accept an unknown fact as 'true' based on other facts which have been proved to the applicable threshold of evidence sufficiency. For instance, the *Anic* presumption provides that 'the undertakings participating in concerting arrangements and remaining active on the market take account of the information exchanged with their competitors when determining their conduct on that market'.[131] Another example is the *Akzo* presumption, which establishes that parent companies actually exercise decisive influence over the commercial conduct of their wholly owned subsidiaries.[132] Presumptions in EU competition enforcement are discussed in Chapter 6. However, it is already worth noting that they serve a critical mission in the process of evidence assessment, insofar as they enable the party claiming their benefit to automatically satisfy the standard of proof with regard to the presumed fact, thereby also shifting the burden of proof onto their opponent.

All in all, the discharge of the standard of proof inevitably entails some degree of construction and is not – nor can it turn into – a mechanical exercise.[133] The subject of the parties' probative efforts, the quantity and quality of the available evidence, and the operation of presumptions will determine how easy or difficult it will be for the Commission and the undertakings to meet the applicable threshold of evidence sufficiency. Against this background, how well the parties have presented their 'stories' will be critical: the more believable the story and the more sense it makes, the easier it will be to reach the conclusion that the standard of proof has been satisfied.[134]

VI. Conclusion

In brief, the standard of proof indicates how 'certain' the Commission must be before finding an infringement of Articles 101 and 102 TFEU or adopting a decision under the EUMR. In line with its function as a decision-making and risk-allocation device, the regulation of the standard of proof may not only prove determinative of the outcome of the proceedings, but may also reflect how fairness

[131] Case C-49/92 P *Commission v Anic Partecipazioni*, ECLI:EU:C:1999:356, para 121; Case C-199/92 P *Hüls v Commission*, ECLI:EU:C:1999:358, para 162.

[132] Case C-97/08 P *Akzo Nobel and Others v Commission*, ECLI:EU:C:2009:536, para 60.

[133] As evidence is evaluated by human beings, some degree of subjectivity cannot be excluded. This is what Parret ((n 121) 192–94) has called the 'X-factor'.

[134] Generally, story-telling is an inseparable part of decision-making (see Nancy Pennington and Reid Hastie, 'A Cognitive Theory of Juror Decision-Making: The Story Model' (1991–92) 13 *Cardozo Law Review* 519). It was on the basis of the Story Model that Allen suggested the reconceptualisation of the standard of proof in terms of 'relative plausibility' rather than probabilities (Ronald Allen, 'Factual Ambiguity and a Theory of Evidence' (1994) 88 *Northwestern Law Review* 604; Ronald Allen and Sarah Jehl, 'Burdens of Persuasion in Civil Cases: Algorithms v. Explanations' (2003) 4 *Michigan State Law Review* 893, 929 ff). According to this approach, the winning party should be the one with 'the more plausible story'.

and efficiency considerations are balanced in the enforcement system in question. Nevertheless, although the matter has been extensively debated, the standard of proof that governs EU competition enforcement has been rather unclear. Hence, the aim of this chapter has been to analyse how the standard of proof is, or should be, regulated in proceedings concerning the application of Articles 101 and 102 TFEU and the EUMR.

The answer to this question has been obscured by several factors. First of all, the legislative silence on the applicable threshold of evidence sufficiency in EU competition enforcement has left the matter open to interpretation, whereas the tenacious – yet vague – judicial reference to the 'requisite legal standard' to which arguments must be established has not shed much light on the issue either. Coupled with the long-lasting, albeit somewhat philosophical, dilemma over whether the standard of proof should be conceptualised in probabilistic terms or in terms of the 'inner conviction' of the judge, the absence of a clear rule has reinforced the ambivalence over its content. Last but not least, the tendency to confuse the standard of proof with the elements of the substantive legal test that the Commission must satisfy before intervening in the market is also to 'blame' for the persistent confusion over the applicable threshold of evidence sufficiency, insofar as it might create the misleading impression that varying standards of proof are in operation and it might divert the discussion about its regulation towards irrelevant thoughts.

Nevertheless, since the applicable standard of proof is an issue of law subject to full review, the EU Courts have had the opportunity to offer useful guidance on its content in both infringement and merger cases. Unsurprisingly, in proceedings concerning the application of Articles 101 and 102 TFEU, the debate over the applicable standard of proof has been dominated by arguments that the ECHR-criminal nature of antitrust fines and the presumption of innocence call for a 'beyond any reasonable doubt' threshold. However, such arguments have been dismissed by the EU Courts, which have consistently asked instead for evidence supporting the 'firm conviction' that the antitrust rules have been violated. As explained above, the latter is anything but a low threshold of evidence sufficiency. In view of the features of the EU enforcement system and EU judges' readiness to annul Commission decisions where they entertain doubts about the underlying facts, it was submitted that the 'firm conviction' concept is capable of safeguarding the effective judicial protection of the undertakings involved by being flexible enough to be stretched to an *almost* criminal standard, whilst preserving the small distance from the latter, which might be vital to the effectiveness of the regime.

In any event, the operation of an 'efficiency defence' in the context of Articles 101 and 102 TFEU begged the question of the standard of proof that defendant undertakings must satisfy in order to discharge their burden of persuasion. As explained in Chapter 3, a bifurcated allocation of the legal burden would only be compatible with the presumption of innocence if undertakings were subject to a civil standard of proof – or its equivalent level of confidence. Unfortunately, and somewhat surprisingly, the case law sheds very little light on the threshold of evidence sufficiency that undertakings must satisfy when demonstrating the existence of efficiencies or other benefits. However, as the analysis in this chapter has shown, if the Commission has discharged its burden of proof by producing evidence which supports the *firm conviction* that the agreement or concerted practice gives rise to anti-competitive effects, then defendant undertakings entertain no real prospect of having their defence upheld unless they establish an *at least equally strong* conviction that their conduct gives rise to advantages which offset these anti-competitive effects. Accordingly, the standard of proof to which defendant undertakings are subject mirrors the Commission's and is thus higher than a mere preponderance of the evidence – or the equivalent degree of conviction. On this basis, it was submitted in Chapter 3 that a bifurcated legal burden in infringement proceedings is at odds with the presumption of innocence.

Beyond antitrust proceedings, the regulation of the standard of proof has not been entirely clear in merger enforcement either. There, the absence of criminal fines and the prognostic nature of merger analysis have led some commentators to argue that merger control is subject to a mere balance of the probabilities – or a similarly low threshold of confidence. However, such a standard of proof would be problematic from a fairness point of view, insofar as it fails to account for the inequality of arms between the Commission and merging entities and the adverse consequences that a prohibition decision may have on the notifying parties' economic freedom. Furthermore, it is hardly in line with the EU Courts' jurisprudence either. Indeed, the trilogy of merger annulments in *Schneider Electric*, *Airtours*, *Tetra Laval* and subsequent case law point at a considerably higher threshold of evidence sufficiency which resembles the 'firm conviction' standard which governs antitrust cases. As *Impala* and *Cisco* have shown, the latter applies to prohibition and clearance decisions alike and to both Phase I and Phase II proceedings. However, despite its benefits, it was remarked that such a standard of proof is prone to place the Commission in a no-win situation, for which some relief could be offered by accepting a finding of merger compatibility in the case of genuine uncertainty and a decision-making deadlock.

Finally, the question of the regulation of the standard of proof should not be confused with the question of its discharge. Broadly speaking, how easy or difficult satisfying the standard of proof will be fluctuates depending on the circumstances of the case and hinges on the subject of the parties' probative efforts, the quantity or quality of the evidence and the operation of any presumptions. Accordingly, the type of conduct in question, the prospective or retrospective nature of the analysis, one's perception of normality, the complexity or novelty of the issue to be established, the amount and value of the available evidence as well as the operation of presumptions are all factors which may determine the degree of difficulty in meeting the standard of proof. Yet, this does not mean that the latter varies depending on the specific features of the case.

At any rate, the analysis of the burden of proof and the standard of proof does not answer the question as to what information can be relied upon as 'evidence' and how its probative weight is evaluated in the context of EU competition enforcement. This is the topic to which Chapter 5 will now turn.

5

Principles and Problems of Evidence Admissibility and Evaluation

I. Introduction

While the allocation of the burden of proof and the regulation of the standard of proof frame the process of evidence assessment in EU competition enforcement, the latter is heavily guided by the principles and criteria according to which evidence is admitted and weighed. Indeed, not all items of information may qualify as 'evidence' and not all evidence will bear the same probative value. With this in mind, this chapter investigates the EU Courts' jurisprudence with a view to illuminating, first, the thresholds for admitting evidence in competition proceedings and, second, the criteria for assigning probative value to admissible evidence. Accordingly, section II presents the two fundamental principles which underpin evidence admissibility and assessment in EU law in general and in EU competition enforcement in particular – namely the principle of unfettered production and the principle of unfettered evaluation of the evidence. Then, sections III and IV consider potential shortcomings in the admissibility and evaluative standards developed by the EU Courts, bearing in mind the requirements of the principle of effective judicial protection and the challenges that the use of economic evidence may entail.

II. Principles Governing Evidence Admissibility and Evaluation in EU Competition Enforcement

A. The Principle of Unfettered Production of Evidence: The *Relevance* Test

Broadly speaking, the question of admissibility indicates whether a piece of information can be relied upon as 'evidence'. Although this question is not regulated at the EU level, the GCEU confirmed in *Wabco Europe* that 'the basic principle in EU law is that evidence may be freely adduced', thereby explicitly introducing the principle of unfettered production of evidence.[1] In line with the latter, no typology of admissible and inadmissible evidence exists.[2] On the contrary, the EU Courts seem to endorse a broad understanding of the types and nature of evidence which can be included in the file, the sole criterion being the *relevance* of the piece of evidence at hand. Although the criterion of *relevance* has troubled evidence theorists because of its loose definitional scope, evidence is generally considered as 'relevant' when it can help the fact-finder decide on the contested issues, whether directly or indirectly.[3] Accordingly, both direct and circumstantial evidence are in principle admissible in competition proceedings. In the context of Article 101 TFEU in particular, the EU Courts have explained that 'the existence of an anti-competitive practice or agreement must be inferred from a number of coincidences and indicia which, taken together, may, in the absence of another plausible explanation, constitute evidence of an infringement of the competition rules'.[4] In contrast, 'evidence which has no relation to the allegations of fact and of law' is irrelevant and thus, inadmissible.[5] The rationale underpinning this approach is that investing time and resources in the assessment of information which could have no bearing on the outcome of the case would be pointless and economically inefficient.[6]

To a significant extent, the EU Courts' expansive understanding of the *relevance* criterion may be explained by the two-level structure of EU competition enforcement. Although the 'irrelevance' of the evidence is ultimately reviewed by the EU Courts, its initial appraisal is performed in the context of the administrative investigation by the Commission, which has extensive powers to decide what documents to include in the file or not.[7] However, the relevance of the evidence is

[1] Case T-380/10 *Wabco Europe and Others v Commission*, ECLI:EU:T:2013:449, para 50. See also Case C-511/06 P *Archer Daniels Midland v Commission*, ECLI:EU:C:2008:604, Opinion of AG Mengozzi, paras 112–23.

[2] Joined Cases C-310/98 and C-406/98 *Met-Trans and Sagpol*, ECLI:EU:C:2000:154, para 29 (in the context of a reference for a preliminary ruling in a case concerning the free movement of goods; confirmed in the context of competition proceedings in Case T-54/14 *Goldfish and Others v Commission*, ECLI:EU:T:2016:455, para 43).

[3] Paul Roberts and Adrian Zuckerman, *Criminal Evidence*, 2nd edn (Oxford University Press, 2010) 99.

[4] Case C-407/08 P *Knauf Gips v Commission*, ECLI:EU:C:2010:389, para 49. See also Case T-464/04 *Independent Music Publishers and Labels Association v Commission (Impala I)*, ECLI:EU:T:2006:216, para 251; Case T-336/07 *Telefónica and Telefónica de España v Commission*, ECLI:EU:T:2012:172, para 402; OECD, *Prosecuting Cartels without Direct Evidence of Agreement* (Policy Brief June 2007), available at www.oecd.org/daf/competition/prosecutionandlawenforcement/37391162.pdf.

[5] Joined Cases C-204/00 P, C-205/00 P, C-211/00 P, C-213/00 P, C-217/00 P and C-219/00 P *Aalborg Portland and Others v Commission*, ECLI:EU:C:2004:6, para 126.

[6] See, eg, Case T-13/89 *Imperial Chemical Industries v Commission*, ECLI:EU:T:1992:35, paras 289–93.

[7] Case 155/79 *AM & S v Commission*, ECLI:EU:C:1982:157, para 17, where it is confirmed that in the exercise of its investigative powers, 'it is in principle for the Commission itself, and not the undertaking concerned or any third party, whether an expert or an arbitrator, to decide whether or not a document must be produced to it'. See also Themistoklis Giannakopoulos, *Safeguarding Companies' Rights in Competition and Anti-dumping/Anti-subsidies Proceedings*, 2nd edn (Wolters Kluwer Law & Business, 2011) 95.

not to be evaluated solely by reference to its potential to support the Commission's findings. On the contrary, its usefulness for the undertakings concerned must also be taken into account. Accordingly, the EU Courts have consistently held that 'it cannot be for the Commission alone to decide which documents are of use for the defence. Where … difficult and complex economic appraisals are to be made, the Commission must give the advisers of the undertaking concerned the opportunity to examine documents which *may* be relevant so that their probative value for the defence can be assessed' (emphasis added).[8]

The use of the potential 'may' is not accidental. Indeed, an expansive interpretation of the *relevance* criterion seems to be preferred over the danger of having evidence excluded to the detriment of the parties' rights of defence – especially considering that 'such an error could not be discovered in time, before adoption of the Commission's decision'.[9] The same rationale seems to underlie the Commission's approach, which distinguishes solely between 'accessible' and 'non-accessible' evidence without regard to the *relevance* of the piece of information at hand.[10] As explicitly stated in the Commission Notice on the rules for access to the file, the parties 'will be granted access to *all* documents making up the Commission file … with the exception of internal documents, business secrets of other undertakings, or other confidential information' (emphasis added).[11] At any rate, the Commission cannot simply disregard as irrelevant pieces of information which 'appear to have some force'[12] and which were adduced by the undertakings concerned in support of their arguments. On the contrary, it must explain the reasons for not taking such evidence into account. Mere reference to the existence of the evidence in the body of the decision without proper attention to its substantive content is inadequate and may constitute a breach of the duty to state reasons.[13]

B. The Principle of Unfettered Evaluation of Evidence: The *Reliability* Test

Once a piece of information has been admitted as evidence, the ensuing question is how much probative weight it should be attributed. Broadly speaking, the probative value of an item of evidence reflects the extent to which the said evidence supports

[8] Case T-30/91 *Solvay v Commission*, ECLI:EU:T:1995:115, para 81. Note, however, Case T-240/07 *Heineken Netherland and Heineken v Commission*, ECLI:EU:T:2011:284, paras 242, 253–57 on the conditions of access to documents which are in the Commission's possession, but are not part of the investigation file.

[9] *Solvay* (n 8) para 82.

[10] Koen Lenaerts and Jan Vanhamme, 'Procedural Rights of Private Parties in the Community Administrative Process' (1997) 34 *Common Market Law Review* 531, 547.

[11] Commission Notice on the rules for access to the Commission file in cases pursuant to Articles 81 and 82 of the EC Treaty, Articles 53, 54 and 57 of the EEA Agreement and Council Regulation (EC) No 139/2004 [2005] OJ C325/07, para 10.

[12] Case C-360/92 P *Publishers' Association v Commission*, ECLI:EU:C:1995:6, para 40.

[13] ibid paras 39, 42–44.

a given proposition as opposed to another. In this sense, it ultimately indicates how much the decision-maker can rely on it to reach the conclusion that the standard of proof has been met.

In competition proceedings, the EU Courts enjoy significant discretion in assessing evidence. As AG Vesterdorf explained in his Opinion in *Rhône-Poulenc*, 'the activity of the Court of Justice and thus also that of the [GCEU] is governed by the principle of the unfettered evaluation of evidence, unconstrained by the various rules laid down in the national legal systems'.[14] Likewise, on numerous occasions, the EU Courts have declared that their assessment of the evidence is not bound by any rules. In fact, 'it is only the *reliability* of the evidence before the Court which is decisive when it comes to its evaluation'.[15] Therefore, there are no legal rules prescribing in advance how the EU Courts should evaluate the probative weight of evidence.[16] However, this does not mean that the principle of unfettered evaluation offers a free pass to judges to interpret evidence arbitrarily or in a way that compromises fundamental rights or the principle of legal certainty. On the contrary, the appraisal of the evidential weight of particular items of evidence must be based on clear, objective and transparent considerations.

Over the years, the EU Courts have identified several factors which may enhance or weaken the probative value of different types of evidence. Inevitably, however, the outcome of the evaluation is case-specific and context-specific, and one must be cautious when extrapolating guidance from past jurisprudence. The main considerations which may affect the evidential weight of different forms of relevant information, along with any shortcomings, are discussed in section IV. However, it is already worth noting that the EU Courts place special emphasis on the need to verify the probative content of *all* the evidence.[17] The significance of this is twofold. First, the reliability of a piece of evidence also depends on the extent to which the aforementioned evidence is corroborated by other items in the file. In this respect, there is an inversely proportional relationship between the

[14] Joined Cases T-1/89 to T-4/89 and T-6/89 to T-15/89 *Rhône-Poulenc v Commission*, ECLI:EU:T:1991:38, Opinion of AG Vesterdorf, at II-954.

[15] ibid II-954. Note that the *reliability* criterion is often interchanged with the requirement for *credibility* of the evidence. Although the two words are close synonyms, their meaning is not identical. Reliability refers to the trustworthiness of the evidence, while credibility is rather associated with its believability. Nonetheless, the conceptual difference lacks any practical significance; the EU Courts estimate the evidential weight of a piece of evidence by looking at both its reliability and credibility.

[16] In this sense, the principle of unfettered evaluation is grounded in the model of free proof. Models of free proof stand in contrast to systems of legal proof, where the judicial latitude in evaluating evidence is extensively curtailed by detailed legal provisions which establish hierarchical relationships among the various types of evidence and specify – almost arithmetically – the exact probative weight that must be attributed to them (Karl Kunert, 'Some Observations on the Origin and Structure of Evidence Rules under the Common Law System and the Civil Law System of Free Proof in the German Code of Criminal Procedure' (1966–67) 16 *Buffalo Law Review* 122, 144–45).

[17] Jacquelyn MacLennan, 'Evidence, Standard and Burden of Proof and the Use of Experts in Procedure before the Luxembourg Courts' in Friedl Weiss (ed), *Improving WTO Dispute Settlement Procedures: Issues and Lessons from the Practice of Other International Courts and Tribunals* (Cameron May, 2000) 269 ff.

probative value of the evidence and the need for corroboration: the less reliable the evidence, the greater the need for corroboration will be. By contrast, the better the evidence fits with other pieces of information, the greater its reliability. Second, it is now settled jurisprudence that it is not necessary for every item of evidence to satisfy the standard of proof; rather, the EU Courts have consistently adopted a holistic approach, considering instead whether 'the body of evidence relied on by [the Commission], viewed as a whole, meets that requirement'.[18]

III. Potential Shortcomings in the EU Courts' Approach to Evidence Admissibility

The combined operation of the principles of unfettered production and of unfettered evaluation has been particularly effective, in the sense that it favours the admission of as much evidence as possible and provides the EU Courts (and the Commission) with ample flexibility to assess the evidence in light of its special circumstances. Nevertheless, the judicial understanding of these principles has not always been without criticism. With this in mind, the following paragraphs consider whether the standards of evidence admissibility and evaluation, as developed by the EU Courts, may suffer from potential shortcomings.

A. Rules of Evidence *In*admissibility

The latitude afforded by the principle of unfettered production is not absolute. As AG Mengozzi eloquently observed, this principle 'cannot be construed as meaning that every item of evidence is always and, in all circumstances, usable'.[19] Indeed, evidence production is subject to a range of *in*admissibility standards which prescribe when evidence must be excluded in spite of its relevance.[20] Such standards are dispersed in the case law of the EU Courts. However, in summary, evidence may be excluded as inadmissible either on the ground that it has been unlawfully produced or that its use infringes upon the undertakings' fundamental rights, even if it has been legally obtained.[21]

[18] See, eg, *Knauf Gips* (n 4) para 47; Case T-321/05 *AstraZeneca v Commission*, ECLI:EU:T:2010:266, para 477. On this, see Fernando Castillo de la Torre and Eric Gippini Fournier, *Evidence, Proof and Judicial Review in EU Competition Law* (Edward Elgar, 2017) 78–86.

[19] *Archer Daniels Midland* (n 1) Opinion of AG Mengozzi, para 112.

[20] On the challenges of this, see Andrew Wistrich, Chris Guthrie and Jeffrey Rachlinski, 'Can Judges Ignore Inadmissible Information? The Difficulty of Deliberately Disregarding' (2005) 153 *University of Pennsylvania Law Review* 1251.

[21] For a presentation of inadmissibility standards in the context of cartel enforcement, see also Antoine Colombani, Jindrich Kloub and Ewoud Sakkers, 'Cartels' in Jonathan Faull and Ali Nikpay (eds), *The EU Law of Competition*, 3rd edn (Oxford University Press, 2014) 8.471–8.483.

Typically, evidence will not be considered if it has not been produced in accordance with the law. This may be the case in the following scenarios. First, evidence may be excluded as unlawfully produced where it was collected in the context of an unlawful investigation. Broadly speaking, investigations may be unlawful either because the rules governing their conduct have not been complied with or because the undertakings' fundamental rights have been violated. In either case, the Order of the President of the GCEU in *Hoechst* makes it clear that evidence produced in the context of illegal investigations will be excluded from judicial consideration.[22] Indeed, as was stressed more recently, 'EU law cannot … accept evidence obtained in complete disregard of the procedure laid down for gathering it and designed to protect the fundamental rights of interested persons'.[23] Second, evidence may be declared inadmissible if it has been *produced* – rather than *retrieved* – unlawfully. In EU law in general, evidence obtained illegally has been usually excluded as inadmissible,[24] although this exclusionary rule has not been always given absolute effect.[25] However, in a competition context in particular, this scenario arose only recently in *Goldfish*. There, the GCEU was asked to consider whether secret recordings of telephone conversations among cartelists, which had been collected by the Commission during a lawfully conducted inspection, should be excluded from the evidence.[26]

Addressing the matter, the Court stressed that 'evidence that the Commission has properly obtained is, in principle, admissible in an investigation into a breach of competition law'.[27] Having highlighted this, it then clarified that evidence which has been illegally produced, yet lawfully collected, will not be excluded from the file where two conditions are satisfied: 'first, the applicant was not deprived of a fair trial or of his rights of the defence and, secondly, the evidence at issue was not

[22] Case 46/87 R *Hoechst v Commission*, ECLI:EU:C:1987:167, Order of the President of the Court, para 34. See also C-94/00 *Roquette Frères*, ECLI:EU:C:2002:603, para 49. Generally, the EU Courts will not make haste to declare the Commission's investigations illegal acknowledging their importance 'as a necessary tool for the Commission in carrying out its role as guardian of the Treaty in competition matters' (Case T-66/99 *Minoan Lines v Commission*, ECLI:EU:T:2003:337, para 52). Yet, as the rulings in *Nexan France* and *Prysmian* confirm, they will closely scrutinise the lawfulness of the investigative measures (Case T-135/09 *Nexans France and Nexans v Commission*, ECLI:EU:T:2012:596, paras 39–45, 91 (confirmed on appeal in Case C-37/13 P *Nexans and Nexans France v Commission*, ECLI:EU:C:2014:2030); Case T-140/09 *Prysmian and Prysmian Cavi e Sistemi Energia v Commission*, ECLI:EU:T:2012:597, paras 34–40). See also Case 136/79 *National Panasonic v Commission*, ECLI:EU:C:1980:169, paras 26–27; Case 46/87 R *Hoechst v Commission*, ECLI:EU:C:1987:167, Order of the President of the Court, paras 26–29; Case 85/87 *Dow Benelux v Commission*, ECLI:EU:C:1989:379, para 18; Case 374/87 *Orkem v Commission*, ECLI:EU:C:1989:387, paras 13–17; Case C-36/92 P *SEP v Commission*, ECLI:EU:C:1993:928, Opinion of AG Jacobs, para 21.

[23] *Goldfish* (n 2) para 47.

[24] Joined Cases 197/80 to 200/80, 243/80, 245/80 and 247/80 *Ludwigshafener Walzmühle Erling and Others v Council and Commission*, ECLI:EU:C:1981:311, para 16; Case T-48/05 *Franchet and Byk v Commission*, ECLI:EU:T:2008:257, para 77. Also note the wording in Case C-7/95 P *Deere v Commission*, ECLI:EU:C:1998:256, para 22.

[25] Case T-192/99 *Dunnett and Others v EIB*, ECLI:EU:T:2001:72, paras 33–34; *Franchet and Byk* (n 24) paras 79–81.

[26] *Goldfish* (n 2) para 60.

[27] ibid para 59.

the only proof relied on in support of the conviction'. Applying these conditions to the facts of the case, the Court concluded that not only did the authority give all the parties the opportunity to assess the contested materials, but also that the latter did not form 'the sole basis for the Commission's belief that the applicants were guilty'.[28] The case is important because the Court held in no uncertain terms that evidence obtained illegally under the law of a Member State may be used in an EU competition investigation or in EU judicial proceedings.[29] The fact that the evidence may be inadmissible under national rules is irrelevant in the absence of a 'predominant' EU-wide 'trend' in favour of exclusion. The ruling in *Goldfish* complements and reaffirms the earlier judgment in *ADM*, where the applicant claimed that the Commission's decision should be annulled because it took into account clandestine audio and video recordings made by the FBI in the course of the latter's inquiry into the US cartel and thereby infringed its right to respect for private life.[30] While the GCEU avoided addressing the plea explicitly, it nevertheless observed that the right to respect for private life should be considered in the context of the general principle of protection against disproportionate or arbitrary intervention. With this in mind, it took into account the fact that the Commission had not relied on that evidence and that, even if the undertakings' inadmissibility claims could be upheld, 'the Commission's conclusions … would remain well-founded' in light of the other available evidence.[31]

In any event, lawfully produced evidence may still be inadmissible if its use violates the undertaking's rights of defence. For example, the right to be heard, which comprises a right to evidence disclosure, dictates that undertakings should be afforded the possibility to become fully apprised of the file and to comment on the evidence and observations proffered by the other party.[32] In this light, when the Commission admitted in *Dresdner Bank* that the applicants had not had access to the replies of the other addresses of the statement of objections on which the authority had exclusively based its finding of an infringement,[33] the GCEU excluded those documents as inadmissible. For similar reasons, the EU Courts have stressed that 'only documents cited or mentioned in the statement of objections constitute valid evidence';[34] all other evidence must be disregarded. Nevertheless, the protective scope of the rights of defence is not always clear, or absolute for that matter. For example, in infringement proceedings, the application of the right against self-incrimination has been the subject of much

[28] ibid paras 63–67.

[29] ibid para 76.

[30] Case T-224/00 *Archer Daniels Midland and Archer Daniels Midland Ingredients v Commission*, ECLI:EU:T:2003:195, para 339.

[31] ibid paras 340–42, 348.

[32] For an early statement, see Case 85/76 *Hoffmann-La Roche v Commission*, ECLI:EU:C:1979:36, para 11.

[33] Joined Cases T-44/02 OP, T-54/02 OP, T-56/02 OP, T-60/02 OP and T-61/02 OP *Dresdner Bank and Others v Commission*, ECLI:EU:T:2006:271, paras 155–60.

[34] ibid para 157. See also *Imperial Chemical Industries* (n 6) para 34; Case C-62/86 *AKZO v Commission*, ECLI:EU:C:1991:286, para 21. Note, however, Case T-50/00 *Dalmine v Commission*, ECLI:EU:T:2004:220, para 60.

contemplation.[35] Likewise, confidentiality considerations may also be factored into the outcome of the admissibility inquiry,[36] either by allowing the Commission to withdraw internal documents, business secrets of other undertakings and other confidential information, or by enabling undertakings to protect their communications with their lawyers from being used by the Commission as incriminating evidence against them.[37] Broadly speaking, however, this does not remove the evidence inadmissibility 'side-effect' that the rights of defence may have. Once a violation thereof has been established, 'contaminated' evidence will generally be excluded from consideration,[38] although this may not necessarily compromise the lawfulness of the Commission decision, unless the latter could be proved solely by reference to the inadmissible evidence.[39]

For the sake of completeness, it is worth noting that the EU Courts have also considered whether evidence obtained from another authority is admissible in EU competition proceedings. Here, one must draw a distinction between EU Member State and non-EU Member State authorities. In the former case, Regulation 1/2003 explicitly allows for exchanges of information between the Commission and the competition authorities of the Member States to be used as evidence in antitrust proceedings.[40] Furthermore, in *Dalmine* and *FSL*, the EU Courts confirmed that information produced by *other* national authorities is also admissible as evidence in the context of an EU investigation.[41] By contrast, information obtained from a non-Member State authority will be admissible only as long as undertakings have been afforded protection equivalent to that recognised under EU law.[42] Indeed, in *ADM*, the GCEU underlined that:

> [T]here is no provision that prevents the Commission from relying on a document as evidence that could be used to find that there has been a breach of Articles [101 TFEU]

[35] See generally Angus MacCulloch, 'The Privilege against Self-Incrimination in Competition Investigations: Theoretical Foundations and Practical Implications' (2006) 26 *Legal Studies* 211; Arianna Andreangeli, *EU Competition Enforcement and Human Rights* (Edward Elgar, 2008) 123 ff.

[36] See generally Luis Ortiz Blanco (ed), *EU Competition Procedure*, 3rd edn (Oxford University Press, 2013) 10.40–10.54.

[37] *AM & S* (n 7) paras 18, 20, 21, 23; Case C-550/07 P *Akzo Nobel Chemicals and Akcros Chemicals v Commission*, ECLI:EU:C:2010:512, paras 40–44.

[38] Note, however, that the EU Courts have held that voluntary responses to non-compulsory requests for information are not covered by the protective scope of the right (Case C-407/04 P *Dalmine v Commission*, ECLI:EU:C:2007:53, para 35; Case T-482/07 *Nynäs Petroleum and Nynas Petróleo v Commission*, ECLI:EU:T:2013:437, para 194); the right against *self*-incrimination may be invoked by undertakings only with respect to evidence emanating from them (Joined Cases T-25/95, T-26/95, T-30/95 to T-32/95, T-34/95 to T-39/95, T-42/95 to T-46/95, T-48/95, T-50/95 to T-65/95, T-68/95 to T-71/95, T-87/95, T-88/95, T-103/95 and T-104/95 *Cimenteries CBR and Others v Commission*, ECLI:EU:T:2000:77, paras 731–33) and that the parties' obligation 'to cooperate means that the undertaking may not evade requests for production of documents on the ground that by complying with them it would be required to give evidence against itself' (Case C-301/04 P *Commission v SGL Carbon*, ECLI:EU:C:2006:432, para 48).

[39] Case 107/82 *AEG-Telefunken v Commission*, ECLI:EU:C:1983:293, paras 24–30.

[40] See art 12.

[41] *Dalmine* (n 38) paras 62–63; Case T-655/11 *FSL and Others v Commission*, ECLI:EU:T:2015:383, paras 76–78.

[42] Case T-59/02 *Archer Daniels Midland v Commission*, ECLI:EU:T:2006:272, para 264.

> and [102 TFEU] and to set a fine, where ... the document was established in the context of a procedure which was not conducted by the Commission itself.[43]

In this case, the evidence at hand consisted of an FBI report containing a statement by a former representative of ADM made at his interview by the Grand Jury in the context of US trial proceedings. Ruling on its admissibility, the GCEU clarified that, before using evidence obtained from a third-country authority, the Commission must examine whether 'prima facie, there is serious doubt as to whether the procedural rights of the parties concerned were complied with in the procedure during which they provided such statements'. In the absence of such serious doubts, it is sufficient for the Commission to clearly indicate that it intends to rely on the evidence at hand, so as to enable undertakings to comment on its content and any irregularities or special circumstances.[44] The divergence in the approach towards evidence obtained from Member State and non-Member State authorities is unsurprising. As clarified in *Goldfish*, 'both national legal systems and EU law are deemed to incorporate the safeguards enshrined in the ECHR'.[45] However, this assumption may not be made with respect to foreign jurisdictions.

Generally, the exclusion of relevant information serves as a remedy for the unlawfulness of its production or the violation of the undertakings' fundamental rights.[46] From a CFR and ECHR perspective, the EU Courts' approach does not appear to raise any concerns. According to settled ECtHR case law, standards of evidence admissibility do not fall per se within the scope of the ECHR, being 'primarily a matter for regulation by national law'. Rather, the ECtHR's task is 'to ascertain whether the proceedings as a whole, including the way in which evidence was taken, were fair'.[47] This 'involves an examination of the "unlawfulness" in question and, where violation of another Convention right is concerned, the nature of the violation found'.[48] With respect to illegal recordings in particular, the ECtHR has not objected to their admissibility, although it noted that:

> [C]onsideration should be given as to whether [their use] deprived the applicant of a fair trial and whether the rights of defence were respected, particularly by determining whether the applicant was able to challenge the authenticity and use of that

[43] ibid para 261.
[44] ibid para 265.
[45] *Goldfish* (n 2) para 78.
[46] See Andrew Ashworth, 'Excluding Evidence as Protecting Rights' (1977) 3 *Criminal Law Review* 723; Paul Roberts, 'Excluding Evidence as Protecting Constitutional or Human Rights?' in Lucia Zedner and Julian Roberts (eds), *Principles and Values in Criminal Law and Criminal Justice: Essays in Honour of Andrew Ashworth* (Oxford University Press, 2012) 98, 171 ff.
[47] *Lucà v Italy*, ECLI:CE:ECHR:2001:0227JUD003335496, para 38.
[48] *Khan v United Kingdom*, ECLI:CE:ECHR:2000:0512JUD003539497, para 34. See also *O'Halloran and Francis v United Kingdom*, ECLI:CE:ECHR:2007:0629JUD001580902, para 53, where the ECtHR clarified that 'while the right to a fair trial under Article 6 is an unqualified right, what constitutes a fair trial cannot be the subject of a single unvarying rule but must depend on the circumstances of the particular case'.

> recording … and whether [the latter] was the only item of evidence relied on in support of the conviction.[49]

Therefore, the EU Courts' balancing approach towards evidence admissibility seems to fit well with the ECtHR's prescriptions and thus with the principle of effective judicial protection. Potential problems may arise only to the extent that the protective scope of the rights of defence is not clear-cut, as the EU Courts' understanding of the rights of defence pre-determines the outcome of the admissibility question. However, this is not a problem with the admissibility standards per se, but rather with identifying the exact protection that the CFR and the ECHR warrant in these circumstances.

B. The Right to Cross-Examine and Call Witnesses in Antitrust Cases

i. The Right to Cross-Examine and Call Witnesses before the Commission

The rights of defence do not serve only as justifications for excluding relevant evidence. At times, undertakings have also invoked their application in order to complain about the dismissal of their evidence offers. Typically, allegations to this effect are based on the right to cross-examine and call witnesses either before the Commission or the EU Courts. According to Article 6(3)(d) ECHR, everyone charged with a criminal offence has the right 'to examine or have examined witnesses against him and to obtain the attendance and examination of witnesses on his behalf under the same conditions as witnesses against him'.[50] Therefore, the question arises whether the dismissal of requests on part of defendant undertakings to cross-examine or call witnesses is incompatible with the right to a fair trial.

Generally, the right to cross-examine and call witnesses has been the subject of much controversy since the case law of the ECtHR has not been entirely clear as to its exact scope and limits.[51] Certainly, being part of the accused's minimum rights of defence, the right to confrontation – as it is also known – constitutes an essential safeguard of criminal justice. However, in the ECtHR's words:

> [T]his provision does not require the attendance and examination of every witness on the accused's behalf. Its essential aim, as is indicated by the words 'under the same conditions', is a full 'equality of arms' in the matter. With this proviso, it leaves it to

[49] *Popescu v Romania*, ECLI:CE:ECHR:2007:0426JUD007152501, para 106; *Schenk v Switzerland*, CE:ECHR:1988:0712JUD001086284, para 48.

[50] Note that the equivalent art 48(2) CFR does not list the rights of defence of the persons charged with a criminal offence, but more generally states that: 'Respect for the rights of the defence of anyone who has been charged shall be guaranteed.'

[51] See generally Stefano Maffei, *The Right to Confrontation in Europe: Absent, Anonymous and Vulnerable Witnesses* (Europa Law Publishing, 2012).

> the competent national authorities to decide upon the relevance of proposed evidence insofar as is compatible with the concept of a fair trial which dominates the whole of Article 6.[52]

Applying this rationale, the ECtHR has mitigated the absolute effect of Article 6(3)(d) by conditioning its infringement upon equality of arms considerations and the fairness of the proceedings as a whole.[53]

In EU competition enforcement, the issue arose in the wake of the broader criminalisation trend. In this context, participants in antitrust proceedings have complained about the fact that they are not afforded the possibility to directly cross-examine the authors of the statements on which the Commission relies in the course of its investigations and are only allowed subsequent access to this witness evidence as part of the file.[54] Nevertheless, the EU Courts have been unwilling to recognise a right for undertakings to cross-examine witnesses in the investigation phase. While acknowledging that the parties' rights of defence should be respected, notwithstanding the fact that the Commission cannot be classified as a 'tribunal' within the meaning of Article 6(1) ECHR,[55] the EU Courts have highlighted that what the rights of defence require is that participants in competition investigation proceedings be afforded the opportunity 'to make known their views on the truth and relevance of the facts, objections and circumstances put forward by the Commission'.[56] Since all witness statements become available to the undertakings as part of the file and can be contested on appeal,[57] the EU Courts have consistently held that the principle of respect for the rights of defence 'does not require that those undertakings be afforded, in the administrative procedure, the opportunity themselves to cross-examine the witnesses heard by the Commission'.[58] Additional considerations also seem to have influenced the judicial approach to the issue. For example, in *Coats Holding*, the GCEU took account of the general attitude and litigation choices of the applicant and remarked that although the latter had the opportunity to ask the witness questions in the investigation phase, it did not exploit it, nor did it apply to the Court for the attendance and examination of the said witness.[59] Finally, in *Aalborg Portland*, the CJEU took into account the

[52] *Engel and Others v The Netherlands*, ECLI:CE:ECHR:1976:0608JUD000510071, para 91.

[53] Pieter van Dijk et al (eds), *Theory and Practice of the European Convention on Human Rights*, 4th edn (Intersentia, 2008) 644–49.

[54] For example, in *Aalborg Portland* (n 5) para 197, Irish Cement complained that it had not been given the possibility to cross-examine the authors of two documents which the Commission produced and upon which it presumably relied in its decision.

[55] Joined Cases 100 to 103/80 *Musique Diffusion Française v Commission*, ECLI:EU:C:1983:158, para 7; Case T-439/07 *Coats Holdings v Commission*, ECLI:EU:T:2012:320, paras 171–74.

[56] *Coats Holdings* (n 55) para 174. See also Joined Cases T-122/07 to T-124/07 *Siemens Österreich and VA Tech Transmission & Distribution v Commission*, ECLI:EU:T:2011:70, paras 232–35.

[57] Case T-54/03 *Lafarge v Commission*, ECLI:EU:T:2008:255, para 149; Case T-191/06 *FMC Foret v Commission*, ECLI:EU:T:2011:277, para 139.

[58] Joined Cases C-239/11 P, C-489/11 P and C-498/11 P *Siemens v Commission*, ECLI:EU:C:2013:866, paras 318–19.

[59] *Coats Holdings* (n 55) paras 170, 176.

fact that the contested evidence 'did not constitute the *sole or decisive basis* of the findings made against Irish Cement' and that its participation in the infringement had been proved by 'other documents, which Irish Cement had the opportunity to consult and comment on'.[60]

At any rate, undertakings in competition proceedings have also relied on Article 6(3)(d) ECHR in order to establish a right to call witnesses before the Commission. For example, in *HFB and Others*, the applicants requested that the Commission examine certain employees connected with their competitors.[61] In particular, they argued that those employees could testify as to facts which would prove their innocence, and they claimed that in competition proceedings, 'the Commission is required as a matter of principle to call and hear those persons [as requested by the undertakings], even if it is unable to impose penalties in the event of non-appearance'.[62] Likewise, in *FMC Foret*, the applicant accused the Commission of not challenging the incriminating evidence provided in Solvay's statements and in the statements of an Atofina employee by calling and hearing its own employees at a cross-examination in the course of the administrative hearing.[63]

However, such pleas have been similarly ineffective. As the GCEU has explained, the Commission is required to hear a person with a sufficient interest only where the request is submitted by the person who is to provide the information – not by the undertaking in whose favour the testimony will presumably be.[64] Furthermore, although the Commission's toolbox of investigative powers includes, inter alia, the power to take statements, the authority enjoys significant latitude in the way in which it carries out the investigation.[65] Accordingly, as the EU Courts have accepted, the Commission retains a 'reasonable margin of discretion to decide how expedient it may be to hear persons whose evidence may be relevant to the investigation' and this discretion in itself does not infringe the parties' rights of defence.[66] Most importantly, however, the main reason why undertakings cannot rely on an assumed right to have witnesses called by the Commission lies in the fact that the authority itself has no power to compel persons to testify or to impose sanctions in the case of non-appearance.[67] On the contrary, both Regulation 1/2003 and the implementing Regulation 773/2004 make it absolutely clear that the consent of the testifying person is a prerequisite and that the Commission should inform

[60] *Aalborg Portland* (n 5) para 199.

[61] Case T-9/99 *HFB and Others v Commission*, ECLI:EU:T:2002:70, para 373.

[62] ibid paras 375–76.

[63] *FMC Foret* (n 57) para 129.

[64] *HFB* (n 61) para 382. See also art 13 of Commission Regulation (EC) No 773/2004 of 7 April 2004 relating to the conduct of proceedings by the Commission pursuant to Articles 81 and 82 of the EC Treaty [2004] OJ L123/19.

[65] Case T-286/09 *Intel v Commission*, ECLI:EU:T:2014:547, para 360.

[66] See *FMC Foret* (n 57) para 137; *HFB* (n 61) paras 383, 390–92.

[67] See, eg, *FMC Foret* (n 57) para 139, where it is confirmed that the Commission 'is not entitled to call witnesses to testify against the undertaking concerned without their agreement'. See also *HFB* (n 61) para 97.

the person of the voluntary nature of its testimony.[68] Consequently, pleas of a breach of the right to call witnesses before the Commission based on Article 6(3)(d) ECHR are unlikely to succeed. Again, in examining such claims, the EU Courts have paid attention to the undertakings' procedural behaviour. If the parties did not formally ask the Commission to examine the persons concerned,[69] if they did not apply for those persons to be heard as witnesses before the EU Courts[70] and if they have not indicated how 'in not hearing the persons proposed, the Commission unduly restricted the inquiry into the matter and thus limited the applicants' opportunity to provide explanations of the various aspects of the problems raised by the Commission's objections',[71] their pleas based on the right to call witnesses before the Commission have no real prospect of success.

ii. The Right to Cross-Examine and Call Witnesses before the EU Courts

A different but related argument sometimes advanced by undertakings is that they have been unlawfully denied the production of evidence before the EU Courts rather than the Commission. Indeed, Article 88(1) RPGC in force enables the parties to apply for the summoning and examination of witnesses.[72] However, such requests have been largely unsuccessful. *Dansk Rørindustri* offers a good example of this. In the appellant's view, the GCEU had infringed the then Article 68(1) RPGC and Article 6(3)(d) ECHR by dismissing its application to hear six witnesses, which would allegedly prove that the undertakings of the Group had not participated in the cartel before October 1994.[73] Responding to this plea, the CJEU recalled that in order for such a request to be granted, 'the parties have to state precisely about what facts and for what reasons the witness should be examined'.[74] However, despite the significant body of precise facts described in the application, the applicant failed to identify which precise facts would be proved by whom.[75] In addition, although the application contained references to certain persons who could allegedly witness the facts set out in those paragraphs, the names of the six persons whose testimony was requested were not mentioned there.[76] On these grounds, the CJEU was keen to dismiss the parties' complaint.

Unsurprisingly, the EU Courts' reluctance to uphold requests for the production of oral evidence has prompted the argument that it takes issue with the

[68] Regulation 1/2003, art 19(1); Regulation 773/2004, Recital (3) and art 19.

[69] Joined Cases T-109/02, T-118/02, T-122/02, T-125/02, T-126/02, T-128/02, T-129/02, T-132/02 and T-136/02 *Bolloré and Others v Commission*, ECLI:EU:T:2007:115, para 88.

[70] *FMC Foret* (n 57) para 141.

[71] *HFB* (n 61) para 383.

[72] Rules of Procedure of the General Court (RPGC) [2015] OJ L105/1.

[73] Joined Cases C-189/02P, C-202/02P, C-205/02P, C-206/02P, C-207/02P, C-208/02P and C-213/02P *Dansk Rørindustri and Others v Commission*, ECLI:EU:C:2005:408, paras 52–53.

[74] ibid para 56, quoting the text of the then art 68(1) RPGC.

[75] ibid paras 59–60.

[76] ibid paras 57–58.

undertakings' right to call witnesses based on Article 6(3)(d) ECHR. The rationale underlying such claims has been that the criminal nature of infringement proceedings places the GCEU under a *duty* to investigate the facts.[77] In *Schindler Holding*, this duty was couched in terms of an assumed 'principle of directness in the taking of evidence' that the EU Courts must comply with.[78] According to this 'principle', by not calling of their own motion all the witnesses indicated by the litigants, the EU Courts are prone to infringing the latter's rights of defence. Nevertheless, the CJEU has been unsympathetic to such claims. As reiterated in *Erste Group Bank*, it 'falls to the [GCEU] to assess the relevance of the application to the subject-matter of the dispute and the need to examine the witnesses named'.[79] Therefore, the GCEU retains significant discretion in deciding whether to grant a request for producing oral evidence or not, and this decision will predominantly depend on whether 'the evidence in the file and the explanations given during the oral procedure are insufficient to rule on the case'.[80] As the CJEU emphasised in *Dansk Rørindustri* and confirmed in *Duravit*, insofar as no absolute right to examine witnesses before a court can be derived from Article 6(3)(d) ECHR and the ECtHR's jurisprudence, the GCEU's discretion is not incompatible with the rights of defence.[81] The same point was highlighted more recently in *Telefónica*, where the Court emphasised that Article 6(3) ECHR 'does not require that every witness be called but is aimed at full equality of arms, ensuring that the procedure in issue, considered in its entirety, gave the accused an adequate and proper opportunity to challenge the suspicions concerning him'.[82]

iii. *Evaluation of the EU Courts' Approach*

The EU Courts' unwillingness to accept offers of evidence based on Article 6(3)(d) ECHR has been criticised as unsatisfactory from a due process perspective.[83] Nevertheless, any fairness concerns have been exaggerated. On a general note, the right to call and cross-examine witnesses is not unqualified. As explained previously, the ECtHR conditions its exercise upon the principle of equality of arms and the fairness of the proceedings as a whole. A similar stance has been taken by the EU Courts, which take account of all the opportunities that the undertakings had to contest the evidence against them at both the administrative and the judicial levels.[84] This flexible understanding of the protective scope of Article 6(3)(d) ECHR

[77] ibid paras 65–66.

[78] Case C-501/11 P *Schindler Holding and Others v Commission*, ECLI:EU:C:2013:522, para 40.

[79] Joined Cases C-125/07 P, C-133/07 P, C-135/07 P and C-137/07 P *Erste Group Bank and Others v Commission*, ECLI:EU:C:2009:576, para 320.

[80] *FMC Foret* (n 57) para 141.

[81] *Dansk Rørindustri* (n 73) paras 69–71; Case T-364/10 *Duravit and Others v Commission*, ECLI:EU:T:2013:477, paras 47–54.

[82] Case T-216/13 *Telefónica v Commission*, ECLI:EU:T:2016:369, para 346.

[83] Ulrich Soltesz, 'Due Process and Judicial Review: Mixed Signals from Luxembourg in Cartel Cases' (2012) 33 *European Competition Law Review* 241, 244–46.

[84] See also *Siemens* (n 58) para 325.

is rather echoed in the wording of the equivalent Article 48(2) CFR, which speaks generally of the rights of defence of any person charged.

In any event, as far as the administrative proceedings are concerned, the argument that the Commission does not have the power to force physical or legal persons to testify is compelling. Indeed, the authority cannot be accused of infringing Article 6(3)(d) ECHR by not taking action in situations not prescribed by Regulation 1/2003.[85] Therefore, if undertakings wish to claim the criminal protection afforded by Article 6(3)(d) ECHR, they should be ready to accept a corresponding broadening of the Commission's investigative powers. However, in judicial proceedings, it is important to note that things are different: unlike the Commission, which cannot examine anyone without their consent, the EU Courts have the power to summon witnesses, examine them under oath and impose sanctions in the event of non-appearance.[86] Nevertheless, from a fairness point of view, the EU Courts' refusal to grant a request for witness testimony might only be problematic if the evidence in question has been the sole or decisive basis of the Commission's decision. According to the ECtHR, in these circumstances the use of statements obtained at the pre-trial stage as evidence is not in itself inconsistent with Article 6(1) and (3)(d) ECHR and the rights of defence.[87] However, as explained in *Kostovski v The Netherlands*, 'as a rule, these rights require that an accused should be given an adequate and proper opportunity to challenge and question a witness against him, either at the time the witness was making his statement or at some later stage in the proceedings'.[88] Therefore, EU judges' reluctance to accept requests to this effect might be incompatible with the right to a fair trial – and the principle of effective judicial protection – only where the witness evidence produced in the administrative proceedings constitutes the sole or decisive basis of the Commission's decision. Indeed, imposing an unconditional obligation on the EU Courts to examine witnesses might create problems with the smooth administration of justice – as AG Léger has observed – insofar as Article 88(1) RPGC could be exploited by the parties as a procedural vehicle to delay proceedings.[89]

C. Admissibility of Economic Evidence

The principle of unfettered production of evidence implies that litigants – undertakings and the Commission alike – are not limited to particular forms of evidence when seeking to substantiate their arguments. In this context, the *relevance* criterion has worked well as the general basis of the admissibility inquiry.

[85] See *HFB* (n 61) para 392.

[86] RPGC, arts 88(1), 91, 93–95; Rules of Procedure of the Court of Justice (RPCJ) [2012] OJ L265/1, arts 64, 66–69.

[87] *Kostovski v The Netherlands*, ECLI:CE:ECHR:1989:1120JUD001145485, para 41.

[88] ibid.

[89] Case C-185/95 P *Baustahlgewebe*, ECLI:EU:C:1998:37, Opinion of AG Léger, para 121.

Nevertheless, as far as expert economic evidence is concerned, the question has been raised whether the *relevance* test is adequate or additional conditions of admissibility should be introduced.

Indeed, the use of economic evidence as a means for parties to establish their arguments has increased in recent years.[90] However, in its more complicated forms, such evidence stretches beyond judges' knowledge. Since the latter cannot be expected to know everything,[91] most legal systems provide for the possibility to engage experts with a view to assisting the fact-finder in areas calling for specialised or technical knowledge.[92] The way in which expert evidence is accommodated in different legal orders varies significantly and may range from systems of 'neutral' court-appointed experts to models of partisan experts hired by the parties. As far as the EU legal order is concerned, partisan experts are generally the rule, although their procedural status is not entirely clear.[93] Typically, parties hire their own expert and submit the latter's opinion in the form of a report or study annexed to their pleadings. Although the EU Courts may also use their case management powers to order the commissioning of an expert where they deem such a measure to be necessary, this possibility has remained largely unexploited.[94]

Broadly speaking, reliance upon expert opinion constitutes a form of what Brewer has called 'epistemic deference': the judge accepts their inferiority and turns to the epistemically 'superior' expert for assistance.[95] This form of deference certainly provides a solution to the judges' epistemic deficit. However, at the same time, it entails the risk that judges may overly rely on the expert opinion or that the expert may not be entirely bias-free.[96] In this context, admissibility rules have sometimes been used as a mechanism for 'filtering' expert testimony and regulating the epistemic gap between the expert and the judge. A good example thereof is the US practice, which has developed detailed tests for the admissibility

[90] See generally Jonathan Baker and Timothy Bresnahan, 'Economic Evidence in Antitrust: Defining Markets and Measuring Market Power' in Paolo Buccirossi (ed), *Handbook of Antitrust Economics* vol 1 (MIT Press, 2008); Jonathan Baker, 'Merger Simulation in an Administrative Context' (2011) 77 *Antitrust Law Journal* 451; Ioannis Lianos, *The Emergence of Forensic Economics in Competition Law: Foundations for a Sociological Analysis* (Centre for Law, Economics and Society, UCL, Working Paper No 5/2012), available at http://papers.ssrn.com/sol3/papers.cfm?abstract_id=2197025.

[91] Eric Barbier de la Serre and Anne-Lise Sibony, 'Expert Evidence before the EC Courts' (2008) 45 *Common Market Law Review* 941, 983.

[92] See generally Déirdre Dwyer, *The Judicial Assessment of Expert Evidence* (Cambridge University Press, 2008).

[93] Barbier de la Serre and Sibony (n 91) 965–66.

[94] Only twice have the EU Courts appointed an expert in competition proceedings: in Case 48/69 *Imperial Chemical Industries v Commission (Dyestuffs)*, ECLI:EU:C:1972:70; and in Joined Cases 89/85, 104/85, 114/85, 116/85, 117/85 and 125/86 to 129/85 *Ahlström Osakeyhtiö and Others v Commission (Woodpulp II)*, ECLI:EU:C:1993:120.

[95] Scott Brewer, 'Scientific Expert Testimony and Intellectual Due Process' (1998) 107 *Yale Law Journal* 1535, 1566 ff.

[96] Michael Mandel, 'Going for the Gold: Economists as Expert Witnesses' (1999) 13 *Journal of Economic Perspectives* 113; Richard Posner, 'The Law and Economics of the Economic Expert Witness' (1999) 13 *Journal of Economic Perspectives* 91, 93–95.

of expert testimony early on.[97] In brief, the first admissibility formula, laid out in *Frye v United States*, relied upon the general acceptance of the expert's methodology in the pertinent scientific community.[98] This standard had survived intact for half a century, when Rule 702 was introduced into the Federal Rules of Evidence, providing that:

> If scientific, technical, or other specialised knowledge will assist the trier of fact to understand the evidence or to determine a fact in issue, a witness qualified as an expert by knowledge, skill, experience, training, or education, may testify thereto in the form of an opinion or otherwise.[99]

Formulated like this and without any reference to the 'general acceptance' condition, the statutory formula gave rise to uncertainty and inconsistent interpretations, which led to the intervention of the Supreme Court in 1993. It its seminal *Daubert* ruling, the Supreme Court decided that Rule 702 has superseded the *Frye* formula, which could now serve only as an aid, and then confirmed the 'relevant and reliable' test for expert testimony.[100] More specifically, the Supreme Court held that expert testimony must satisfy the 'fit' condition, that is, it must be 'sufficiently tied to the facts of the case',[101] and underscored that its evidentiary reliability is dependent upon its scientific validity.[102]

In order to enable the judges to perform this assessment, the Supreme Court listed several pertinent factors, although it emphasised that the enumeration is by no means definitive.[103] Apart from the general acceptance criterion, other relevant considerations are whether the theories and techniques have been or can be tested; whether they have been subjected to peer review and publication; whether they have a known error rate and whether there are standards controlling their operation.[104] Applying this formula, the Supreme Court also emphasised that the focus is on the principles and methodology employed by the expert rather than on the generated conclusions.[105] In 2000, Rule 702 was amended to incorporate the *Daubert* instructions and subsequent case law,[106] and now reads that 'a witness who is qualified as an expert by knowledge, skill, experience, training, or education may testify in the form of an opinion or otherwise', provided that: (a) the expert's

[97] Andrew Gavil, 'The Challenges of Economic Proof in a Decentralized and Privatized European Competition Policy System: Lessons from the American Experience' (2008) 4 *Journal of Competition Law and Economics* 177, 186–91; Juan David Gutiérrez-Rodríguez, 'Expert Economic Testimony in Antitrust Cases: A Comparative Law and Economics Study' (2009) 14 *International Law, Revista Colombiana de Derecho Internacional* 221, 241–44.

[98] *Frye v United States*, 293 F 1013 (DC Cir 1923), 1014.

[99] Rule 702 of the Federal Rules of Evidence, prior to the 2000 amendments.

[100] *Daubert v Merrell Dow Pharmaceuticals*, 509 US 579 (1993), 588 and 589.

[101] ibid 591, quoting *United States v Downing*, 753 F 2d 1224 (CA 1985), 1242.

[102] ibid 590.

[103] ibid 593.

[104] ibid 593–94.

[105] ibid 595.

[106] Particularly *General Electric Co v Joiner*, 522 US 136 (1997); and *Kumho Tire Co v Carmichael*, 526 US 137 (1999).

scientific, technical or other specialised knowledge will help the trier of fact to understand the evidence or to determine a fact at issue; (b) the testimony is based on sufficient facts or data; (c) the testimony is the product of reliable principles and methods; and (d) the expert has reliably applied the principles and methods to the facts of the case.[107]

In stark contrast with the US emphasis on designing a workable admissibility test for expert testimony, no similar dialogue has emerged in the European scene so far. Apart from the general *relevance* test, which – as explained – is framed in very loose terms, no specific admissibility standard applies to expert economic evidence. It is submitted that this approach is correct for several reasons. First of all, account must be taken of the fact that the US and EU institutional contexts vary considerably. In the US, the introduction of a distinct admissibility filter for expert testimony was intended to ensure that so-called 'junk science' will be excluded from consideration and will not affect the jury's verdict on the facts of the case.[108] Indeed, through the admissibility enquiry, the US judges assume the role of the gatekeeper, protecting the jury from irrevocable exposure to unreliable information.[109] However, the European institutional setting is fundamentally different. No jury participates in the trial and EU judges retain full jurisdiction over both legal and factual issues. Therefore, the 'gatekeeping' rationale is absent in the EU judicial system.

Moreover, the US experience reveals the difficulties in designing an appropriate admissibility formula for expert testimony in general and economic expertise in particular. The *Frye* formula was strongly criticised for being too conservative and for preventing consideration of new and novel methodologies which had not yet gained 'general acceptance'.[110] Mindful of these criticisms, Rule 702 and the *Daubert* test were articulated in a more liberal spirit.[111] Yet, the new formula did not have the intended result.[112] In the field of competition law in particular, it was used by litigants as a vehicle for attacking economic expertise on account of one or more of the factors listed by the Supreme Court.[113] Indeed, economic expertise

[107] Rule 702 of the Federal Rules of Evidence, as amended in 2000 (further amendments in 2011 were intended to be merely stylistic and did not alter the content of the Rule).

[108] John Lopatka and William Page, 'Economic Authority and the Limits of Expertise in Antitrust Cases' (2005) 90 *Cornell Law Review* 617, 624–25, 627–28. See generally Peter Huber, *Galileo's Revenge: Junk Science in the Courtroom* (Basic Books, 1993). *cf* Gary Edmond, 'After Objectivity: Expert Evidence and Procedural Reform' (2003) 25 *Sydney Law Review* 131, 163.

[109] *cf* Brian Leiter, 'The Epistemology of Admissibility: Why Even Good Philosophy of Science Would Not Make for Good Philosophy of Evidence' [1997] *Brigham Young University Law Review* 803.

[110] Paul Giannelli, 'The Admissibility of Novel Scientific Evidence: *Frye v United States*, a Half-Century Later' (1980) 80 *Columbia Law Review* 1197; Mark McCormick, 'Scientific Evidence: Defining a New Approach to Admissibility' (1981) 67 *Iowa Law Review* 879, 905.

[111] See *Daubert* (n 100) 587 and 588.

[112] Andrew Gavil, 'After Daubert: Discerning the Increasingly Fine Line between the Admissibility and Sufficiency of Expert Testimony in Antitrust Litigation' (1997) 65 *Antitrust Law Journal* 663, 672.

[113] James Langenfeld and Christopher Alexander, '*Daubert* and Other Gatekeeping Challenges of Antitrust Experts' (2011) 25 *Antitrust* 21, 24.

proved to be particularly vulnerable, especially when adduced by plaintiffs.[114] The explanation for this largely lies in the nature of economics as part of social sciences.[115] Since the latter fall within the category of 'soft science' (as opposed to 'hard science'), testability and error rates are not always available or attainable.[116] On that account, economic expertise has often not survived the *Daubert* filter and has been excluded as inadmissible following criticisms of the employed methodology or the sufficiency of the data.[117] Indeed, *Daubert* challenges to economic expert testimony now constitute an essential part of the parties' litigation strategy in the US.[118] However, in the absence of a sufficiently apparent and acceptable test, the exclusionary effect of *Daubert* should not be taken lightly. Accordingly, the desirability of, or need for, a *Daubert*-style European test should not be taken for granted.

Additionally, in line with the principle of unfettered production of evidence and because of its contribution to achieving accuracy in fact-finding, relevant evidence should be excluded from judicial consideration only exceptionally and on the basis of clear criteria. However, the operation in the EU legal order of an admissibility formula similar to that in *Daubert* would connote an unjustifiably exclusionary attitude towards economic expert testimony. Given that economics is central in competition analysis, the practical effect of completely excluding expert economic evidence without carefully considering its probative value would be to unduly restrict the pool of evidence that parties could otherwise benefit from to substantiate their claims.[119] With this in mind, it is submitted that it is procedurally more effective and fair to handle any *Daubert*-like objections against expert testimony at the later stage of evaluating the probative weight of that evidence. In this way, the risk of erroneously and irreversibly excluding valuable evidence from judicial consideration would be avoided.

Last but not least, a further argument against the application of an admissibility formula other than the broad *relevance* inquiry is that it unnecessarily confounds the already blurred lines between the admissibility of evidence and the evaluation of its probative value. A too detailed admissibility test inevitably bleeds into the boundaries of the probative weight assessment. An admissibility test based on the

[114] ibid 21–22.

[115] See Ioannis Lianos, '"Judging Economists", Economic Expertise in Competition Litigation: A European View' in Ioannis Lianos and Ioannis Kokkoris (eds), *The Reform of EC Competition Law: New Challenges* (Kluwer Law International, 2010) 190. Note that before the ruling in *Kumho Tire*, where the Supreme Court held that 'The Daubert "gatekeeping" obligation applies not only to "scientific" testimony, but to all expert testimony', as 'Rule 702 does not distinguish between "scientific" knowledge and "technical" or "other specialized" knowledge' (at 147–49), in some cases it was contested whether economics may constitute the subject of 'expert testimony' in the meaning of this Rule.

[116] Gavil (n 112) 674.

[117] Langenfeld and Alexander (n 113) 24.

[118] Andrew Gavil, 'Daubert Comes of Age' (2000) 15 *Antitrust* 6; Christopher Hockett, Geraldine Alexis and Christina Wheeler, '*Daubert* Redux: Revisiting the Admissibility of Expert Testimony in Antitrust Cases' (2000) 15 *Antitrust* 7, 7–9.

[119] Gavil (n 112) 667.

criterion of evidence *reliability* turns this risk into reality. Moreover, in principle, expert testimony aims to compensate for judges' epistemic deficit. However, inserting a *Daubert*-style admissibility formula would have two important consequences: on the one hand, it would force judges to make a decision for which they lack the necessary knowledge because such knowledge is specialised;[120] and, on the other hand, a mistaken inadmissibility finding could not be reversed or mitigated at a later stage, but would result in the definite exclusion of the expert testimony from consideration.[121]

All in all, *Daubert* reveals a sceptical approach to expert testimony, which may be well justified by the US institutional setting and the participation of the jury in a trial. Nonetheless, the EU system is fundamentally different. In light of the difficulties in designing a generally accepted and workable admissibility formula, the absolute exclusionary effect of such a test and the possibility to better deal with the specific problems of expert testimony at the probative evaluation stage, the introduction of a *Daubert* screening in the European judicial system would have no added value; on the contrary, it would make the assessment of economic expertise unnecessarily complex.

IV. Potential Shortcomings in the EU Courts' Approach to Evidence Evaluation

The overall permissive approach of the EU Courts to evidence admissibility has shifted the focus on the subsequent step of ascertaining the probative value of the admitted evidence. According to the principle of unfettered evaluation, the sole criterion determining the probative weight of the evidence is its *reliability*. Nevertheless, this does not mean that judges are allowed to interpret evidence arbitrarily or in a way that compromises the need for a reasonable degree of predictability or fundamental rights. Over the years, the EU Courts have provided useful guidance on the factors which may affect the probative weight of different types of evidence. While no typology of evidence exists, it is helpful to identify four broad categories of relevant information that are often used in competition enforcement: documentary evidence; statements; opinion evidence; and economic evidence. The following paragraphs consider the factors which may affect their probative value and examine any potential shortcomings in the approach of the EU Courts.

[120] Roger Blair and Jill Boylston Hemdon, 'The Implications of *Daubert* for Economic Evidence in Antitrust Cases' (2000) 57 *Washington and Lee Law Review* 801, 810. *cf* Gregory Werden, 'The Admissibility of Expert Economic Testimony in Antitrust Cases' in *Issues in Competition Law and Policy* (ABA Section of Antitrust Law, 2007) 817, where he suggests that court-appointed experts or technical advisors could be employed to help judges decide what makes 'good economics' for the purposes of *Daubert* admissibility.

[121] Lianos (n 115) 284.

A. The Probative Value of Documentary Evidence

Competition cases are largely decided on the basis of documents. Documentary evidence may take various forms, ranging from meeting minutes to records of electronic or other communication among undertakings and employees to business and marketing plans, customer lists, sales data, advertising brochures, websites, press releases, industry reports and so forth. According to settled case law, 'the credibility and, therefore, the probative value of a document depends on its origin, the circumstances in which it was drawn up, the person to whom it is addressed and the soundness and reliable nature of its contents'.[122]

Helpfully, the EU Courts have elaborated on the application of these criteria in a variety of contexts.[123] First of all, it is clear that the precise source of the document – be it the undertaking under investigation, its customers or other third parties – is not decisive when determining its probative value. In *Intel*, for instance, the Court did not take issue with the fact that, in the absence of a formal exclusivity requirement, the Commission relied on the internal estimates of Dell, one of Intel's customers, as evidence of Intel's own conduct.[124] Moreover, being able to identify the author of the document might reinforce its probative value, but the fact that its identity might be unknown will not automatically deprive it of any evidential weight.[125] Likewise, the lack of a signature or date will not necessarily undermine the reliability of the document, particularly if this is normal for written evidence of that kind – for instance, notes taken in the context of an anti-competitive meeting. In *Shell*, for example, the GCEU took the view that the probative value of a note which was 'badly written, unsigned and undated' could not be diminished on that account, insofar as it was 'free of ambiguity' and bearing in mind that it was 'taken during a conversation, probably over the telephone, and the anti-competitive object of the note was a reason for its author to leave the least trace possible'.[126] Indeed, while the poor writing of a note and the fact that it is 'summary in form' or contains question marks and asterisks or 'key words' will be reasonably taken into account in determining its reliability, such considerations may not completely extinguish its evidential value.[127]

Beyond the origin of the evidence, one of the most important indicators of the reliability of a document is the time when it was produced. Unsurprisingly,

[122] *Cimenteries* (n 38) para 1053; *Rhône-Poulenc* (n 14) Opinion of AG Vesterdorf, at II-956.

[123] For a more detailed account, see Castillo de la Torre and Gippini Fournier (n 18) ch 4.

[124] *Intel* (n 65) paras 519–25. For other examples, see Joined Cases 40/73 to 48/73, 50/73, 54/73 to 56/73, 111/73, 113/73 and 114/73 *Suiker Unie and Others v Commission*, ECLI:EU:C:1975:174, para 164; Case C-413/06 P *Bertelsmann and Sony Corporation of America v Impala (Impala II)*, ECLI:EU:C:2008:392, paras 94–95; Case T-405/08 *Spar Österreichische Warenhandels v Commission*, ECLI:EU:T:2013:306, paras 149–52.

[125] Joined Cases T-305/94, T-306/94, T-307/94, T-313/94 to T-316/94, T-318/94, T-325/94, T-328/94, T-329/94 and T-335/94 *LVM v Commission*, ECLI:EU:T:1999:80, para 605; *Cimenteries* (n 38) para 901.

[126] Case T-11/89 *Shell v Commission*, ECLI:EU:T:1992:33, para 86. See also Case T-38/02 *Groupe Danone v Commission*, ECLI:EU:T:2005:367, para 288.

[127] Case T-303/02 *Westfalen Gassen Nederland v Commission*, ECLI:EU:T:2006:374, paras 105–08; *FMC Foret* (n 57) para 188; *FSL* (n 41) paras 202–03.

documents created in *tempore non suspecto* will be assigned high probative weight.[128] As pointed out by AG Vesterdorf in his Opinion in *Rhône-Poulenc*:

> [U]nder the general rules of evidence, the fact that the documents were drawn up immediately after the meetings and clearly without any thought for the fact that they might fall into the hands of third parties must be regarded as having great significance.[129]

The EU Courts have time and again endorsed the same view.[130] Generally, documents drawn up by a direct witness of the events to which they relate will be deemed more reliable than second-hand information, although the latter will still carry probative value as indirect evidence.[131] In this regard, attacks against the reliability of contemporaneous documentary evidence on the ground – for instance, that its author did not have authority to set prices,[132] was a low-level employee of the investigated undertaking[133] or did not have knowledge of the sector at hand[134] – have been insufficient to deprive it of any probative value. On the other hand, the capacity and past conduct of the author of the document may be scrutinised with a view to ascertaining its reliability.[135]

Last but not least, the EU Courts will pay great attention to the credibility and soundness of the contained account. Obviously, the greater the degree of detail in the document, the higher its reliability will be. In *Shell*, for example, a note which was badly written and lacked a signature and date was found to be reliable, among other reasons, on the ground that 'the precise, detailed nature of [the] information [it contained made] it wholly unlikely that it simply reflected market, gossip, was completely wrong or invented'.[136] That said, the credibility and accuracy of the account that a document entails may not be determined independently and in isolation from the rest of the relevant information and the features of the case; inevitably, this assessment is highly contextualised. This explains why a piece of indirect evidence may seem weak when considered alone, but when combined with others, it may help to paint a broader picture whose summative evidential force is much stronger.

B. The Probative Value of Statements

Although documentary evidence plays a crucial role in competition cases, the past few years have seen an increase in the use of statements as well. The latter are

[128] Christopher Harding and Julian Joshua, *Regulating Cartels in Europe* (Oxford University Press, 2010) ch 7.

[129] *Rhône-Poulenc* (n 14) Opinion of AG Vesterdorf, at II-956.

[130] *Coats Holdings* (n 55) para 45.

[131] *Shell* (n 126) para 86; Case T-343/06 *Shell Petroleum and Others v Commission*, ECLI:EU:T:2012:478, para 207.

[132] *FSL* (n 41) para 304.

[133] eg, *Intel* (n 65) para 1254.

[134] eg, *Cimenteries* (n 38) para 907.

[135] *FSL* (n 41) paras 205–08, 223.

[136] *Shell* (n 126) para 86.

essentially a form of witness evidence, containing *ex post* accounts of the facts produced *in tempore suspecto* – typically as a response to requests for information or in the context of interviews conducted based on Article 19 of Regulation 1/2003 or as part of a leniency application in cartel enforcement. Indeed, the launch by the Commission of its Leniency Programme with a view to luring cartelists to blow the whistle in exchange for immunity from fines or a generous penalty reduction has transformed the evidence-gathering process in cartel proceedings.[137] Nevertheless, the authority's increased reliance on statements – especially in cartel enforcement – has not been without its critics.[138] In light of the quasi-criminal nature of antitrust proceedings, the Commission has been attacked for attributing excessive probative weight to statements in breach of the principle of effective judicial protection. Against this background, the following paragraphs examine the evidential status of statements and consider whether the EU Courts' approach to their reliability falls into line with the ECHR and the CFR.

Statements may be provided either by physical persons – for example, in their capacity as lawyers, employees or former employees of the investigated undertaking – or by the company itself, usually through its legal representatives (corporate statements). As with documents, their probative value depends on their origin, the circumstances of their production and the soundness and reliability of the contained account. Indeed, according to now settled jurisprudence:

> [P]articular probative value may be attached to statements which, first, are reliable; second, are made on behalf of an undertaking; third, are made by a person under a professional obligation to act in the interests of that undertaking; fourth, go against the interests of the person making the statement; fifth, are made by a direct witness of the circumstances to which they relate; and, sixth, were provided in writing deliberately and after mature reflection.[139]

Therefore, ascertaining the probative weight of a statement requires consideration of several factors.

The source of the statement in particular as a parameter affecting its reliability has been considered in several cases. In this regard, the occasional use by the Commission of anonymous statements and its reliance on *ex post facto* evidence offered by co-accused undertakings are the two issues which have generated more controversy. Indeed, although the identity of the person who made the statement will normally be revealed to the accused undertaking, sometimes the Commission has denied disclosing the source of the evidence. In *Salzgitter Mannesmann*, for

[137] Commission Notice on Immunity from fines and reduction of fines in cartel cases [2006] OJ C298/17 (Leniency Notice), para 9(a).

[138] Julian Joshua, 'Oral Statements in EC Competition Proceedings: A Due Process Short-Cut?' (2004) 26 *Competition Law Insight* 1, 5–7; Nathalie Jalabert-Doury, 'Les Déclarations en Droit de la Concurrence: la Preuve d'Infractions Peut-Elle Se Satisfaire de "Certitudes Probables"?' (2005) 2 *Concurrences* 41, 44 ff; Jameson Dempsey, 'A Right of Confrontation for Competition Hearings before the European Commission' (2010) 75 *Brooklyn Law Review* 1489.

[139] Case T-587/08 *Fresh del Monte v Commission*, ECLI:EU:T:2013:129, para 364.

instance, the EU Courts considered the probative value of a statement made by an informant setting out the terms of a market-sharing agreement, whose identity had been kept confidential. While it was noted that the use of anonymous evidence is not excluded, the CJEU clarified that its credibility 'is necessarily reduced by the fact that the context in which it was drafted is largely unknown and because the Commission's assertions in that regard cannot be verified'.[140] Therefore, such evidence can only be used 'as one of a number of coherent indicia' corroborating other essential evidence.[141]

Unsurprisingly, undertakings have challenged the use of anonymous statements as contravening the principle of effective judicial protection and the right to a fair trial. Nevertheless, the EU Courts' approach seems well-aligned with the ECtHR's jurisprudence. As explained in *Doorson v The Netherlands*, 'even when "counterbalancing" procedures are found to compensate sufficiently the handicaps under which the defence labours, a conviction should not be based either solely or to a decisive extent on anonymous statements'.[142] Along the same lines, AG Geelhoed proposed in his Opinion in *Salzgitter Mannesmann* – and the CJEU agreed – that in order for anonymous statements to be considered, three conditions should apply: (i) the parties must be afforded the opportunity to inspect the statements and oppose them; (ii) the Commission and the GCEU must 'adopt a critical approach in assessing their probative value and look carefully into any indicia which may cast doubt on their reliability and authenticity'; and (iii) anonymous statements may not be the exclusive or predominant basis for substantiating a competition infringement.[143] Consequently, the EU Courts' approach to the probative weight of anonymous statements is sound.

Another type of statements whose use has been criticised are those made by a co-accused undertaking, typically in the context of a leniency application. Indeed, participants in cartel proceedings have repeatedly complained that statements made by leniency applicants, which are not corroborated by other evidence, should be attributed little probative value, if any. A first reason for this is their allegedly biased nature. As the applicant emphasised in *Total Raffinage Marketing*, 'such statements are by nature subjective and tend to "blame the others rather than oneself"'.[144] In addition, a second objection often raised is that, in contrast to contemporaneous documents, such statements have been produced *in tempore suspecto* by the leniency applicant's representatives with a view to mitigating its liability for the infringement found.[145] Thus, the circumstances of their production call for a lowering of their probative value. Last but not least, in *Sumitomo Metal Industries*, the applicant contested the probative value of statements produced by

[140] Case C-411/04 P *Salzgitter Mannesmann v Commission*, ECLI:EU:C:2007:54, para 46.
[141] ibid para 47.
[142] *Doorson v The Netherlands*, ECLI:CE:ECHR:1996:0326JUD002052492, para 76.
[143] Case C-411/04 P *Salzgitter Mannesmann v Commission*, ECLI:EU:C:2006:548, Opinion of AG Geelhoed, paras 62–65.
[144] Case T-566/08 *Total Raffinage Marketing v Commission*, ECLI:EU:T:2013:423, para 63.
[145] *Coats Holdings* (n 55) para 132.

the employees of the undertaking on the ground that the aforementioned employees did not have direct knowledge of the declared facts and thus that the evidential value assigned to their declarations should be diminished.[146]

Nevertheless, these arguments have proved unsuccessful. The mere fact that the information has been provided by a leniency applicant is insufficient to deprive it of any probative value.[147] Indeed, in *JFE Engineering*, the GCEU stressed that there is no prohibition in EU law preventing the use of statements originating with leniency applicants or other co-accused undertakings and further sympathised with the Commission by holding that if the use of such statements were not to be allowed, the effectiveness of the authority's ability to enforce the antitrust rules would be seriously compromised.[148] Examining specifically the argument that leniency applicants are inclined to provide distorted evidence, the EU Courts have dismissed this fear as unlikely. In *Peróxidos Orgánicos*, it was explained that an attempt to mislead the Commission runs counter the interests of the undertaking, as it 'could call into question the sincerity and the completeness of cooperation of the undertaking, and thereby jeopardise its chances of benefiting fully under the Leniency Notices'.[149] Additionally, in *Dole Food*, the GCEU highlighted that 'the existence of a personal interest in reporting the existence of a concerted practice does not necessarily mean that the person doing so is unreliable' and stressed that account must also be taken of the fact that a leniency applicant's 'admission of its participation in the cartel and the Commission's subsequent decision finding an infringement of Article [101 TFEU] exposes that undertaking to an action for damages by third parties … which may lead to serious financial consequences'.[150]

Moreover, in *Lafarge*, the GCEU held that the mere fact that the statements are prepared for the purposes of the undertaking's defence does not deprive them, as such, of the value attached to them, a position which was later confirmed in *Coats Holding*.[151] On the contrary, in *JFE Engineering*, the GCEU appreciated the fact that those statements are prepared 'deliberately and after mature reflection' and not in a rush, and the fact that the declarants can take their time to think over the content of their testimony rather significantly enhances their credibility.[152] Furthermore, as confirmed in *Bolloré*, 'statements which run counter to the interests of the declarant must in principle be regarded as particularly reliable evidence'.[153] Ruling likewise in *JFE Engineering*, the GCEU explained that where

[146] Joined Cases C-403/04 P and C-405/04 P *Sumitomo Metal Industries v Commission*, ECLI:EU:C:2007:52, para 101.

[147] *Coats Holdings* (n 55) para 45.

[148] Joined Cases T-67/00, T-68/00, T-71/00 and T-78/00 *JFE Engineering v Commission*, ECLI:EU:T:2004:221, para 192. See also Case T-59/07 *Polimeri Europa v Commission*, ECLI:EU:T:2011:361, para 52; Case T-360/09 *E.ON Ruhrgas and E.ON v Commission*, ECLI:EU:T:2012:332, para 182.

[149] Case T-120/04 *Peróxidos Orgánicos v Commission*, ECLI:EU:T:2006:350, para 70.

[150] Case T-588/08 *Dole Food and Dole Germany v Commission*, ECLI:EU:T:2013:130, paras 92–94.

[151] *Coats Holdings* (n 55) para 132; and *Lafarge* (n 57) para 379.

[152] *JFE Engineering* (n 148) para 210.

[153] *Bolloré* (n 69) para 166.

the declarant provides more information than what would be inferred from the documents available, 'that implies, a priori, in the absence of special circumstances indicating otherwise, that that person had resolved to tell the truth'.[154] Finally, as regards the lack of direct knowledge of the declarant, the EU Courts have typically dismissed such allegations on the ground that the employees make those statements as representatives of the company concerned.[155] Because of this, they are 'under a professional obligation to act in the interests of that undertaking',[156] they rely on information provided by the said company and 'in particular, by employees thereof with direct knowledge of the practices in question',[157] and they run significant legal and economic risks when making statements to the effect of admitting participation of the undertaking in an infringement, which makes it extremely unlikely that they so affirm without having inside information from employees with direct knowledge of the facts.[158]

Apart from these considerations, the reliability of statements will also be affected by the level of precision and detail they display. In *Dresdner Bank*, the GCEU held that the figures contained in the declarations of some representatives of individual banks varied widely, a fact 'which contribute[d] to their lack of precision' and eliminated the probative value of those declarations as a means for the Commission to establish its theory of the existence of a concurrence of wills on fixing a commission rate.[159] Nonetheless, as can be inferred from *FMC Foret*, minor imprecisions will most likely be tolerated where there is significant distance between the time when the events occurred and the time when the statement was made.[160]

The compatibility of the EU Courts' approach to the probative assessment of statements by co-accused undertakings or leniency applicants with the principle of effective judicial protection calls for deeper examination. As the above account illustrates, the EU Courts have consistently dismissed all concerns about the reliability of such evidence, insistently defending its probative value. However, as Joshua has pointedly observed, the judicial indicators of reliability 'seem neutral or subjective or could conceivably even be cited by ingenious defence counsel as pointing against their credibility'.[161] Indeed, most factors invoked by the EU Courts could be interpreted as reducing the probative value of corporate or leniency statements. For example, as far as leniency statements are concerned, it is doubtful whether they truly run counter to the interests of the declarant, given that such statements are made with the ulterior motive of securing full leniency

[154] *JFE Engineering* (n 148) para 212.

[155] Note ibid para 205: 'Answers given on behalf of an undertaking as such carry more weight than that of an employee of the undertaking, whatever his individual experience or opinion.'

[156] Case T-133/07 *Mitsubishi Electric v Commission*, ECLI:EU:T:2011:345, para 87.

[157] *Sumitomo Metal Industries* (n 146) para 102.

[158] ibid para 103, upholding the Opinion of AG Geelhoed at para 119.

[159] *Dresdner Bank* (n 33) para 137.

[160] *FMC Foret* (n 57) para 194.

[161] Joshua (n 138) 5.

or a generous reduction in the fine.[162] Furthermore, although the EU Courts have accepted that some caution should be exercised when evaluating the probative weight of statements made by co-accused undertakings or leniency applicants,[163] the 'caution' that the Commission and the EU Courts exercise might sometimes be minimal. As explained, the EU Courts also determine the reliability of a piece of evidence by checking whether it is corroborated by the other evidence in the file.[164] This corroboration check is critical where the accuracy of the admissions of an undertaking who is accused of having participated in an infringement is contested by several other undertakings similarly charged. In these circumstances, the GCEU stressed in *JFE Engineering* that such a statement 'cannot be regarded as constituting adequate proof of an infringement committed by the latter unless it is supported by other evidence'.[165] The need to verify the content of statements is all the more pressing considering that: (i) such statements are mostly made out of court in the course of the administrative proceedings; (ii) they are not subject to cross-examination;[166] (iii) they are not taken under oath;[167] and (iv) there are no sanctions for the provision of false or misleading information.[168]

In this light, both the Commission and the EU Courts should be truly cautious and should hesitate to assign high probative weight to such statements, or at least should demand a significantly higher degree of corroboration. Nevertheless, in *JFE Engineering*, the CJEU held that:

> [T]he degree of corroboration required in this case is lesser, in terms both of precision and of depth, in view of the reliability of Mr Verluca's statements, than would be the case if the latter were not particularly credible. Thus, it must be concluded that, if it were to be held that a body of consistent evidence was such as to corroborate the existence and certain specific aspects of the market-sharing agreement referred to by Mr Verluca … Mr Verluca's statements might be sufficient in themselves, in such a case, to constitute evidence of other aspects of the contested decision.[169]

[162] ibid 5–6.

[163] *FMC Foret* (n 57) paras 117, 119; *Dalmine* (n 34) para 88.

[164] See section II.B.

[165] *JFE Engineering* (n 148) para 219. Note that on appeal, the parties went as far as arguing that 'statements made by an undertaking accused of having participated in a cartel which are disputed by other similarly accused undertakings can be used as evidence *only if all the essential elements* of the cartel have been established on the basis of *evidence independent of those statements*' (*Sumitomo Metal Industries* (n 146) para 31 (emphasis added)).

[166] See section III.B.

[167] Note that whether statements have been made under oath is not a relevant consideration. See *FMC Foret* (n 57) paras 132–33, where the GCEU dismissed the applicant's argument that high probative value should be assigned to the statements made by its employees on the ground that they testified under oath and that the Commission should establish that the witnesses 'perjured' themselves to eliminate their evidential weight, by drawing attention to the administrative nature of the proceedings at hand.

[168] Such penalties are available only in the case of false or misleading information provided to a Commission's request for the supply of information (art 23(1)(a), (b) and (d) of Regulation 1/2003).

[169] *JFE Engineering* (n 148) para 220.

This passage therefore suggests that a statement may constitute *proof* of the infringement if it is 'particularly credible', in which case the degree of corroboration required may even amount to zero.[170] This position was echoed in *Total Raffinage Marketing*, where the GCEU reiterated that 'the degree of corroboration required may be less in view of the reliability of the statements at issue'.[171]

Considering the compatibility of the EU Courts' approach to the probative assessment of statements made by co-accused undertakings or leniency applicants with the principle of effective judicial protection and the right to a fair trial, it is submitted that the real problem is not whether such statements are particularly reliable, but whether this type of evidence can constitute the 'sole or decisive basis' of a Commission decision. In view of the ECtHR's case law on the issue, the answer should be negative. Indeed, the ECtHR held as early as in *Lucà v Italy* that:

> [W]here a deposition may serve *to a material degree* as the basis for a conviction, then, irrespective of whether it was made by a witness in the strict sense or by a co-accused, it constitutes evidence for the prosecution to which the guarantees provided by Article 6(1) and (3)(d) of the Convention apply. (Emphasis added)[172]

However, as explained earlier, essentially neither in the administrative investigation nor in the judicial proceedings may undertakings cross-examine witnesses.[173] Furthermore, the ECtHR has also drawn attention to the adverse implications of using 'evidence obtained from an accomplice by granting him immunity from prosecution' at the trial.[174] In view of this, leniency statements in particular should be assessed very strictly, since the reason why they are made by the applicant is to obtain immunity from fines or a significant penalty reduction.[175]

Against this backdrop, the approach taken in *JFE Engineering* is problematic not because the GCEU appreciated that Mr Verluca's statements were 'particularly reliable', but because it accepted that they 'might be sufficient in themselves … to constitute evidence' of the infringement.[176] The GCEU's ruling in *Del Monte* illustrates the implications of *JFE Engineering*. Despite the applicant's objection to the use of the adduced statements and the limited contemporaneous evidence, the GCEU did not take issue with the fact that the Commission relied almost

[170] Even though in that case certain documents were actually in opposition with the statements of the declarant (for example, ibid paras 220, 262–64).

[171] *Total Raffinage Marketing* (n 144) para 73.

[172] *Lucà v Italy* (n 47) para 41.

[173] See section III.B above.

[174] *X v United Kingdom*, European Commission of Human Rights' Decision of 6 October 1976 as to its admissibility.

[175] Rafael Allendesalazar, 'Evidence Gathered Through Leniency: From the Prisoner's Dilemma to a Race to the Bottom' in Claus-Dieter Ehlermann and Mel Marquis (eds), *European Competition Law Annual 2009: Evaluation of Evidence and its Judicial Review in Competition Cases* (Hart Publishing, 2010) 574. See also Ian Forrester, 'Facts are Chiels That Wanna Ding' in Barry Hawk (ed), *Fordham Competition Law Institute: International Antitrust Law and Policy* (Juris, 2011) 188–93, who worries that 'sometimes the making of a leniency request can principally be a means of harming a competitor'.

[176] See n 169.

exclusively on these statements to establish the exchange of information, on the ground that the communications between Dole and Weichert were primarily telephone conversations, of which no written record had been kept.[177] Yet, in the absence of cross-examination either at the administrative or the judicial level, it is doubtful whether the EU Courts' lenient approach to the probative treatment of statements satisfies the due process prescriptions of the ECtHR. Given that, as explained earlier, the Commission does not have the power to compel persons to testify, there seem to be only two solutions to this problem: either the EU Courts will be significantly more demanding regarding the level of corroboration required for ascertaining the probative reliability of such statements and they will refuse to uphold Commission decisions based exclusively or predominantly on statements, prompting it in this way to return to its previous document-oriented evidence practice;[178] or the GCEU itself should be willing to grant applications for examination of witnesses lodged under Article 88(1) RPGC.[179]

C. The Probative Value of Opinion Evidence

Beyond documentary evidence and statements, EU competition enforcement may also rest on opinion evidence. The latter is non-expert evidence consisting of the views of market participants – namely, competitors, suppliers, customers and consumers – and produced by means of questionnaires and surveys. Opinion evidence is different from other types of relevant information in that it allows the extraction of conclusions about the characteristics and preferences of a larger population based on the responses provided by a small sample of individuals. In this respect, questionnaires and surveys may help the authority to verify the potentially incomplete or biased data provided by the investigated undertakings and to better understand the workings of the market and the likely impact of a practice on competition. As far as the assessment of opinion evidence is concerned, the general criterion of reliability applies here as well. However, in contrast to the detailed guidance that EU judges have developed for the probative evaluation of documents and statements, the considerations underpinning the evidential weight of opinion evidence have not been articulated in a similarly explicit manner.

Although the EU Courts have relied on the results of opinion evidence as proof of an allegation on various occasions, they have only rarely elaborated on the parameters determining its probative value.[180] *Ryanair* is a notable exception.

[177] *Fresh del Monte* (n 139) paras 314, 317.

[178] Joshua (n 138) 3.

[179] Jacques Buhart and Romain Maulin, 'Proof in Cartels: State of Play and Perspectives' (2011) 4 *Concurrences* 51, 63–64.

[180] See, for instance, Case T-30/89 *Hilti v Commission*, ECLI:EU:T:1991:70, para 73; Case T-340/03 *France Télécom v Commission*, ECLI:EU:T:2007:22, paras 76, 90; Case T-151/01 *Duales System Deutschland v Commission*, ECLI:EU:T:2007:154, paras 110–59.

Among the evidence supporting the Commission's decision to prohibit the concentration between Ryanair and Aer Lingus was a passenger survey conducted by the authority at Dublin Airport by means of questionnaires.[181] One of the objections put forward by Ryanair was that the Commission assigned excessive weight to the passenger survey, which the 2007 York Aviation Report criticised as 'deficient and defective'.[182] More specifically, Ryanair attacked the design of the questionnaire as poor and as containing ambiguous and misleading questions.[183] Moreover, it claimed a number of flaws in the way in which the survey was carried out by referring to its allegedly small sample, the fact that it was not conducted on a self-completion basis, was available only in English and took place at a weekend, which seriously compromised its coverage, as business passengers normally fly on weekdays.[184] Finally, Ryanair also accused the Commission of manifest flaws in the analysis of the survey results.[185] Nevertheless, all of Ryanair's claims were dismissed by the GCEU as unfounded. Commenting on the design of the questions, the Court found that they were perfectly suitable in view of the objective of the survey, which was to ascertain whether passengers considered the two airlines as substitutes. Furthermore, the sample basis of 2,500 respondents was found to be representative, while as regards the other allegations concerning the conditions of the conduct of the survey, the Court referred to the explanations given in the Commission's decision and pointed out the strict time limits that the Commission must observe in the context of merger proceedings.[186] Last but not least, in respect of the alleged errors in the analysis of the results, the Court noted that the Commission had followed the methodology suggested by the applicant and had again reached the same main conclusions.[187]

Ryanair confirms that the general principles governing the proper design and conduct of questionnaires and surveys apply to the evaluation of the probative weight of opinion evidence in EU competition proceedings as well.[188] In this regard, the selection of population and the size of the sample, the margin of error, and the formulation of the questions and the structure of the survey may influence the reliability of such evidence.[189] The Commission learned this lesson the

[181] Miguel De la Mano, Enrico Pesaresi and Oliver Stehmann, 'Econometric and Survey Evidence in the Competitive Assessment of the Ryanair-Aer Lingus Merger' (2007) 3 *Competition Policy Newsletter* 73, 79–80.

[182] Case T-342/07 *Ryanair v Commission*, ECLI:EU:T:2010:280, para 202.

[183] ibid para 203.

[184] ibid para 204.

[185] ibid para 205.

[186] ibid paras 208–09.

[187] ibid para 210.

[188] See generally, Jon Krosnick, 'Survey Research' (1999) 50 *Annual Review of Psychology* 537.

[189] Stephen Hurley, 'The Use of Surveys in Merger and Competition Analysis' (2011) 7 *Journal of Competition Law & Economics* 45. Note also the second part of the Best Practices for the Submission of Economic Evidence and Data Collection in Cases Concerning the Application of Articles 101 and 102 TFEU and in Merger Cases (DG Competition, Staff Working Paper, 2010), which applies to survey data, although only to the extent that: (i) it is routinely collected and maintained by the parties as part of the firm's normal business operation; or (ii) it is regularly purchased from third parties

hard way in *Impala I*. One of the questions addressed to retailers as part of a questionnaire was whether record companies were aware of their competitors' public selling prices and discounts. As a result of the poor design of the question, some responses were affirmative, but did not specify of what exactly retailers were aware, namely public selling prices or discounts or both, and the Commission decided to exclude them. However, the GCEU criticised this choice and upheld the applicant's objection that positive responses should have been interpreted as covering both types.[190] By contrast, in *MasterCard*, the GCEU sided with the authority. Challenging the reliability of the merchant market survey conducted by means of requests for information, the applicants complained that merchants' answers were influenced by the fact that they knew they were being surveyed by the Commission, and that large merchants were over-represented in the sample used by the authority. Nevertheless, both claims were dismissed by the GCEU, which observed that the objectivity of merchants' answers could not be regarded as have been undermined by the fact that the Commission had disclosed its identity, and that the choice to concentrate on large merchants was justified, since these were most likely to be in a position to exert pressure on the level of the Mastercard Interchange Fee.[191]

In general, the approach of the EU Courts to the probative value of opinion evidence seems sound. As explained in *MasterCard*, in order to assess its reliability, 'regard should be had, in particular, to the circumstances in which it came into being, the person to whom it was addressed and its content'.[192] Yet, although welcome, this general statement might not fully capture the variety of factors which may affect the evidential weight of opinion evidence. In particular, the potential existence of biases of different types should be expressly acknowledged by the EU Courts. Generally, researchers have long identified various phenomena to which opinion evidence is by default susceptible – for instance, *anchoring*, that is, the tendency of respondents to adjust their answers to subsequent questions based on an initial cognitive anchor,[193] or *acquiescence response bias*, that is, 'the tendency for survey respondents to agree with statements regardless of their content'.[194] Moreover, surveys conducted in EU competition enforcement specifically might be affected by the fact that respondents might lack the necessary sophistication

(see paras 56–57). See also Kirsten Edwards, 'Estimating Diversion Ratios: Some Thoughts on Customer Survey Design' in Philip Lowe and Mel Marquis (eds), *European Competition Law Annual 2010: Merger Control in European and Global Perspective* (Hart Publishing, 2013) 36–42; Ian Thompson and James Harvey, 'When to Pop the Question(s)?: The Use of Surveys in Merger Control' (2014) 35 *European Competition Law Review* 92, 93–95. For a UK perspective, see Graeme Reynolds and Chris Walters, 'The Use of Customer Surveys for Market Definition and the Competitive Assessment of Horizontal Mergers' (2008) 4 *Journal of Competition Law & Economics* 411.

[190] *Impala I* (n 4) paras 383, 385.

[191] Case T-111/08 *MasterCard and Others v Commission*, ECLI:EU:T:2012:260, paras 155–56.

[192] ibid para 154.

[193] Hunter Gehlbach and Scott Barge, 'Anchoring and Adjusting in Questionnaire Responses' (2012) 34 *Basic and Applied Social Psychology* 417.

[194] Paul Lavrakas (ed), *Encyclopedia of Survey Research Methods* (Sage, 2008).

or specialised knowledge and may 'see' problems where none exists,[195] or by the fact that market participants' answers – especially rivals' or customers' – may be informed by their own agenda and interests.[196] Therefore, opinion evidence should not be accepted at face value. As with documents and statements, it is necessary to ensure that no undue weight is assigned to it.

D. The Probative Value of Economic Evidence

The 'more economic' approach to EU competition enforcement has been associated with an increase in the use of so-called 'economic evidence'. The precise scope of the latter is difficult to define. Indeed, economic evidence may entail a diverse array of simpler or more complex theories, models and techniques – from relatively straightforward past price correlations to intricate merger simulations.[197] This information is typically produced by economic experts commissioned by the administrative authority, the undertakings concerned or – exceptionally – by the EU Courts. Unsurprisingly, the specialised nature of economic evidence has given rise to significant challenges concerning its production, presentation and evaluation. To name but a few, whether and how generalist judges may cope with their lack of training in economics, the question how best to accommodate economic evidence institutionally and procedurally, and the role for economic experts in competition litigation are some of the themes commonly recurring in the literature.[198]

In response to these challenges, several competition authorities around the world have adopted guidelines and other soft law instruments on the submission of economic evidence.[199] Being no exception to this trend, in 2010 the Commission

[195] Nicholas Levy, 'Evidentiary Issues in EU Merger Control' in *Fordham Competition Law Institute: International Antitrust Law and Policy* (Juris, 2009) 136.

[196] See William Kolasky, 'Conglomerate Mergers and Range Effects: It's a Long Way from Chicago to Brussels' (George Mason University Symposium, Washington DC, 2001) 4–6, available at www.justice.gov/atr/public/speeches/9536.htm; Joseph Farrell, 'Listening to Interested Parties in Antitrust Investigations: Competitors, Customers, Complementors, and Relativity' (2004) 18 *Antitrust* 64, 65–67; Paul Gorecki, Cormac Keating and Brendan O'Connor, 'The Role of Economic Evidence in Merger Control in Ireland: Current and Future Practice' (2007) 3 *European Competition Journal* 345, 349 ff; Thomas Giebe and Miyu Lee, 'Competitors in Merger Control: Shall They Be Merely Heard or Also Listened to?' (2015), available at http://papers.ssrn.com/sol3/papers.cfm?abstract_id=2569832.

[197] International Competition Network, *ICN Investigative Techniques: Handbook for Merger Review* (2005), available at www.internationalcompetitionnetwork.org/uploads/library/doc322.pdf, ch 4 (as revised in 2013, available at http://internationalcompetitionnetwork.org/uploads/library/doc903.pdf).

[198] See, eg, Lisa Wood, 'Trying Antitrust Cases before Generalist Judges' (2006–07) 21 *Antitrust* 85; OECD, *Presenting Complex Economic Theories to Judges* (Competition Policy Roundtables, 2008), available at www.oecd.org/competition/abuse/41776770.pdf; Dennis Carlton, 'How Should Economic Evidence Be Presented and Evaluated?' in Ehlermann and Marquis (n 175); Michael Baye and Joshua Wright, 'Is Antitrust Too Complicated for Generalist Judges? The Impact of Economic Complexity and Judicial Training on Appeals' (2011) 54 *Journal of Law and Economics* 1.

[199] Arndt Christiansen and Christian Ewald, 'Best Practices for Expert Economic Opinions: Key Element of Forensic Economics in Competition Law' in Kai Hüschelrath and Heike Schweitzer (eds), *Public and Private Enforcement of Competition Law in Europe* (Springer, 2015) 149–57.

published its Best Practices for the submission of economic evidence and data collection in cases concerning the application of Articles 101 and 102 TFEU and in merger cases.[200] The Best Practices set minimum standards of quality with a view to excluding poor economic evidence from the outset and to improving the gathering of quantitative data. In this sense, the Best Practices constitute the equivalent of the *Daubert* test in the EU context, albeit at the administrative level. In its guidance, the Commission sketched out the key conditions that economic evidence should satisfy in order to be given weight. Among other things, it emphasised the importance of having a clear hypothesis that the submitted economic evidence aims to test, as well as the need to ensure the relevance and reliability of the data, the properness of the selected methodology, its replicability, the robustness of the analysis by checking its sensitivity, the statistical significance and practical relevance of the results, and the inherent limitations of the evidence.[201] Although the Best Practices do not have binding legal force, it is unlikely that economic evidence submitted in their defiance will be given much weight in the authority's assessment of its probative value.[202]

Turning now to the EU Courts, according to the principle of unfettered evaluation, EU judges are expected to undertake an independent assessment of the probative value of economic evidence irrespective of its source – be it the Commission or the undertakings concerned. Regrettably, however, there is relatively little guidance on the parameters which may determine the evidential weight of economic studies and reports.[203] In this regard, it is clear that economic evidence produced for the purposes of litigation will be treated with some caution, if not suspicion, at least in antitrust cases. In *Siemens*, the GCEU found that the econometric analysis produced by the applicant lacked credibility and '[could not] be regarded as a neutral and independent expert report', considering that 'it was requested and paid for by Siemens and drawn upon the basis of information provided by that company, without the accuracy or the relevance of that information being subject to any kind of independent assessment'.[204] Similarly, in *Hitachi*, the Court was not impressed with the external report submitted by the applicants, noting that it had been produced *ex post* 'for the specific needs of the parties' defence in the procedure which led to the adoption of the contested decision' and that it did 'not constitute an independent source', given that it was largely referring to statements of the addressees of the Commission's decision.[205]

Beyond the importance of the independent nature of economic evidence, further guidance on its probative assessment may be found in *Ryanair*, where

[200] Best Practices for the Submission of Economic Evidence and Data Collection in Cases Concerning the Application of Articles 101 and 102 TFEU and in Merger Cases (DG Competition, Staff Working Paper, 2010).

[201] ibid paras 16–18, 20–23, 24 ff, 32, 34–35, 37–40 (see, in particular, the first clause of para 40, which very strongly resembles the equivalent formulation of the *Daubert* test) and 41.

[202] ibid paras 23, 32.

[203] Barbier de la Serre and Sibony (n 91) 951–52.

[204] Case T-110/07 *Siemens v Commission*, ECLI:EU:T:2011:68, para 137.

[205] Case T-112/07 *Hitachi and Others v Commission*, ECLI:EU:T:2011:342, para 320.

the GCEU had the opportunity to extensively discuss the econometric evidence submitted by both the Commission and the undertaking.[206] In upholding the Commission's regression analysis, the GCEU took account of the hypothesis that this evidence aimed to test, that is, that each airline exercised a competitive impact on one another's prices, and approved the Commission's position that the fixed-effect regression technique was indeed 'the most suitable' method to evaluate whether the two airlines were in competition, as opposed to the cross-section regression technique proposed by Ryanair.[207] Moreover, the GCEU agreed that, despite the use of the fixed-effects technique, the Commission's choice of methodology satisfactorily accounted for the problem of seasonality and other exogenous shocks, and appreciated the fact that 'results would even be robust to the use of alternative methods' too.[208] In addition, the GCEU dismissed the applicant's allegation that the Commission's model was 'in contradiction with economic principles' on the ground that 'it is wrong to consider that increasing capacity leads to higher fares' and underlined the need to take account of the specific characteristics of the passenger air transport sector where 'capacity is determined before fares'.[209] Finally, the GCEU underlined the fact that the Commission had carried out 'a detailed examination of all econometric data submitted by the parties and [had] performed further tests and extensions of the baseline regressions'.[210]

The judgment in *Ryanair* is interesting. On the one hand, it certainly offers valuable glimpses into the factors which may affect the evidential weight of economic evidence. On the other hand, the Court did not perform an *independent* assessment of the probative value of economic evidence. Recalling the Commission's margin of appreciation with respect to complex economic assessments, the GCEU did not explicitly elaborate on the criteria that *it* considers appropriate for determining the technical and substantive reliability of economic evidence.[211] Rather, it confined itself to checking whether the Commission had satisfactorily addressed all the objections against its own econometric analysis, as well as against its rejection of the econometric evidence submitted by Ryanair.[212] In practice, the lack of a judicial checklist of evaluative criteria concerning economic evidence might not be as problematic following the adoption of the Commission's Best Practices, insofar as it may be conjectured that the EU Courts will endorse the criteria sensibly identified by the authority. However, what is potentially disconcerting is the

[206] For more, see de la Mano, Pesaresi and Stehmann (n 181) 73–79.

[207] *Ryanair* (n 182) para 152.

[208] ibid para 176.

[209] ibid paras 142, 174.

[210] ibid para 179. See also paras 192–194, referring to the Commission's attempt to replicate and confirm the results of the two econometric studies provided by Ryanair.

[211] Ioannis Lianos and Christos Genakos, 'Econometric Evidence in EU Competition Law: An Empirical and Theoretical Analysis' in Ioannis Lianos and Damien Geradin (eds), *Handbook on European Competition Law: Enforcement and Procedure* (Edward Elgar, 2013) 117. See also Yves Botteman, 'Mergers, Standard of Proof and Expert Economic Evidence' (2006) 2 *Journal of Competition Law and Economics* 71, 85–86.

[212] *Ryanair* (n 182) paras 146–83 and 190–95.

extension of the marginal standard of review with respect to complex economic assessments to the appraisal of the probative weight of economic evidence, as implied in *Ryanair*.

To an extent, the judicial deference to the Commission with regard to the evaluation of economic evidence could be explained by the fact that the economists preparing this evidence are often part of the authority's permanent personnel. In this sense, they contribute to the Commission's *own* expertise, which is indeed one of the main justifications for the limited judicial review of complex economic assessments.[213] Nevertheless, extending the marginal standard of review to the evaluation of the probative weight of economic evidence is inappropriate.

First of all, it should be recalled that the process of assigning weight to evidence is exclusively governed by the principle of unfettered evaluation, which requires the EU Courts to undertake an independent assessment of its reliability. In this light, it is unclear why economic evidence should be an exception to this. Although the Commission enjoys a margin of appreciation with respect to complex economic evaluations, it is settled case law that this 'does not mean that the [EU] Courts must refrain from reviewing the Commission's interpretation of information of an economic nature'; on the contrary, the EU Courts must:

> [E]stablish whether the evidence relied on is factually accurate, reliable and consistent, but also whether that evidence contains all the information which must be taken into account in order to assess a complex situation and whether it is capable of substantiating the conclusions drawn from it.[214]

Indeed, as Botteman observes, 'the Commission has a certain margin of appreciation in terms of what issues should be investigated and how; what evidence should be gathered (either qualitative or quantitative or both); and what manipulations to the economic data should be made'.[215] Nevertheless, regarding economic evidence which has been *actually* produced, there is no reason for the principle of unfettered evaluation to be qualified by the marginal standard of review.[216] Accordingly, the EU Courts should not shy away from performing their own independent appraisal of its probative value.

The argument that the EU Courts typically lack the degree of sophistication in economics that the evaluation of economic evidence assumes may not challenge this conclusion.[217] On the one hand, while experts are indeed employed in order to help judges handle their epistemic shortage, this does not inevitably imply that the EU Courts lack *any* competence to evaluate the specialised knowledge

[213] On this, see ch 7, section II.A.

[214] Case T-210/01 *General Electric v Commission*, ECLI:EU:T:2005:456, para 63.

[215] Botteman (n 211) 82.

[216] See also ch 7, section III.B.iii.

[217] This gave rise to arguments that an EU Competition Court should be established in the EU (see House of Lords, Select Committee on European Union, Fifteenth Report, *An EU Competition Court* (15th Report 2006–2007 HL Paper 75), available at www.publications.parliament.uk/pa/ld200607/ldselect/ldeucom/75/75.pdf).

presented to them.[218] On the other hand, in these circumstances, where the EU Courts are genuinely unable to ascertain the probative value of partisan expert evidence and the outcome of the case may rest on its evaluation, they can make use of the procedural possibility to commission a neutral expert – as they have already done, albeit exceptionally.[219] In this light, a deferential approach to the Commission with respect to the reliability of its economic evidence would unjustifiably entail the risk of EU judges attributing more evidential weight than is proper to the expert evidence produced by the authority.[220] However, as AG Vesterdorf noted in his Opinion in *Rhône-Poulenc*, 'the findings of economic experts cannot take the place of legal assessment and adjudication';[221] rather, the interpretation and application of the law is for the EU Courts to determine – 'and not for economic theorists'.[222] While this approach certainly applies to expert evidence produced by undertakings, similar evidence offered by the Commission should not be treated any differently. Indeed, if the concern is that partisan economic expertise may be susceptible to biases, inasmuch as it may rest on opinions and assumptions rather than 'pure' facts, economic evidence produced by the authority may well suffer from similar shortcomings compromising its reliability.

E. A de Facto 'Hierarchy' of Evidence

The principle of unfettered evaluation of the evidence signifies a system of free proof, under which relevant information is assessed independently and no formal hierarchy exists among different types of evidence. Nevertheless, not all forms of information are equally effective in practice; rather, the EU Courts' jurisprudence hints at a de facto preference for documentary evidence, followed by statements and then opinion or economic evidence.

Indeed, the relative probative 'superiority' of documents is clearly visible in the case law. Considering the evidential value of witness versus documentary evidence, the CJEU explained in *Salzgitter Mannesmann* that 'in [EU] competition law cases, oral evidence plays only a minor role, whereas written documents

[218] As Dwyer (n 92) has explained with regard to what she calls the 'limited epistemic competence' of tribunals, 'the tribunal is only required to decide whether to accept an opinion, and not to produce its own opinion', 'it is only required to assess expertise to the extent necessary to decide the case before it' and it 'must consider the expert evidence as part of the overall evidential matrix of the case' (at 108–09).

[219] See n 94.

[220] Peter Freeman, 'The Significance of Economic Evidence in Competition Cases' (IEA Beesley Lecture Series, 2009) 12, available at www.rpieurope.org/Beesley/2009/Peter%20Freeman.pdf.

[221] *Rhône-Poulenc* (n 14), Opinion of AG Vesterdorf at II-957.

[222] ibid. In addition, although no such possibility seems to exist at the moment, the cross-examination of the disagreeing experts would be equally helpful in forcing them to expose their underlying biases and assumptions, as well as the weak points of their testimony (Barbier de la Serre and Sibony (n 91) 974). See other options discussed by Lianos (n 115) 248–54; Maureen Brunt, 'Antitrust in the Courts: The Role of Economics and of Economists' in Barry Hawk (ed), *Fordham Corporate Law Institute: International Antitrust Law and Policy* (Juris, 1999) 364–66.

play a central role'.[223] Moreover, the greater weight that EU judges assign to documentary evidence and statements compared to economic evidence may be easily detected in Article 101 TFEU cases. According to the EU Courts' settled position, where the existence of concertation has been established 'unequivocally and without the need for interpretation' on the basis of documentary evidence – whether direct or circumstantial – and statements, the undertakings concerned may not simply submit 'an alternative version of the facts'.[224] Rather, economic evidence based solely on the conduct of the undertakings in the market might establish the existence of anti-competitive concertation only in the absence of *any* other plausible explanation – as already clarified in *Woodpulp*.[225] Last but not least, even in those cases where economic evidence was discussed in significant detail, its probative value was deemed to be limited. In *Ryanair*, for instance, the GCEU underscored several times that the econometric studies had played only an 'accessory role' in the Commission's analysis and that the authority itself had discounted their evidential value due to the limitations associated with their production, and had in any case sufficiently established the existence of a competitive relationship between Ryanair and Aer Lingus on the basis of other 'non-technical evidence'.[226]

That said, one might claim that the 'more economic' approach to EU competition enforcement is at odds with the de facto preference for 'traditional' forms of evidence, as opposed to 'technical evidence'. However, this argument is misplaced, insofar as it erroneously assumes that economics-grounded *legal* analysis may only be conducted on the basis of economic evidence. Indeed, the EU Courts have consistently dismissed such an idea – and rightly so. In *General Electric*, for instance, the GCEU highlighted that, while evidence of the anti-competitive effects of a merger 'may consist of economic studies establishing the likely development of the market situation and demonstrating that there is an incentive for the merged entity to behave in a particular way', 'the absence of evidence of that type is not in itself decisive' and thus the Commission's analysis was found to be 'persuasive, even in the absence of economic studies'.[227] Likewise, in *Ryanair*, the GCEU rejected the applicant's claim that 'technical' economic evidence should take priority over other types of evidence and clarified that 'it is the Commission's task to make an overall assessment of what is shown by the set of indicative factors used to evaluate the competitive situation' and that 'it is possible, in that regard, for certain items of evidence to be prioritised and other evidence to be discounted'.[228] More recently,

[223] *Salzgitter Mannesmann* (n 140) para 42. See also Case T-47/10 *Akzo Nobel and Others v Commission*, ECLI:EU:T:2015:506, para 316.

[224] *Mitsubishi Electric* (n 156) para 82.

[225] *WoodPulp II* (n 94) paras 70–71. See also *Dyestuffs* (n 94) para 66; Joined Cases 29/83 and 30/83 *CRAM v Commission*, ECLI:EU:C:1984:130, para 16; Case T-442/08 *CISAC v Commission*, ECLI:EU:T:2013:188, paras 99–104, 182.

[226] *Ryanair* (n 182) paras 156–57 and particularly para 169. See also paras 183 and 138.

[227] *General Electric* (n 214) paras 296–97, 299.

[228] *Ryanair* (n 182) paras 132, 136. See also Case T-175/12 *Deutsche Börse v Commission*, ECLI:EU:T:2015:148, paras 131–36.

in *Topps*, the GCEU explained that 'the definition of the relevant market does not require the Commission to follow a rigid hierarchy of different sources of information or types of evidence'; while the SSNIP test 'is indeed a recognised method for defining the market … it is not the only method available' to the authority, which may take into account 'other tools … such as market studies or an assessment of consumers' and other competitors' points of view'.[229]

The fact that 'traditional' evidence, such as documents and statements, appears to count more heavily in EU judges' mind than opinion and economic evidence is not inconsistent with the principle of unfettered evaluation. Rather, this de facto hierarchy may be simply explained by the somewhat bounded probative capacity of 'technical' evidence in EU competition enforcement. First of all, such evidence – especially in the form of economic reports and models – is usually employed in the context of market definition or in order to assess the effects of a practice on competition. Accordingly, in cases where a detailed definition of the market is not necessary or the existence of actual or likely restrictive effects (or lack thereof) is immaterial – for instance, cartels – it is inevitable that 'technical' evidence will be either irrelevant for the purposes of establishing the existence of an antitrust violation or of limited value. In any event, documents and statements are by default easier and more straightforward to understand than technical evidence, whose credibility depends – as explained – on the underlying data and its design, and whose findings may be susceptible to biases and interpretation. That said, the relative ease in assessing more conventional forms of evidence may not offer an excuse for unjustifiably demoting technical evidence.[230] In order for EU competition enforcement to fully benefit from opinion and economic evidence, it is important that EU judges be alert to the challenges of ascertaining its probative value and find ways to overcome them.

V. Conclusion

Since not all items of information may qualify as 'evidence' and not all evidence will bear the same probative value, the aim of this chapter has been to examine the principles and criteria which instruct the admissibility and evaluation of evidence in EU competition enforcement.

Notwithstanding the lack of systematic presentation, the investigation of the EU Courts' jurisprudence revealed the existence of a clear and balanced methodology for admitting and appraising evidence, which comprises two broad tests: the *relevance* check and the criterion of *reliability*. Combined, the principles of

[229] Case T-699/14 *Topps Europe v Commission*, ECLI:EU:T:2017:2, para 82.

[230] Note also David Gerber, 'Courts as Economic Experts in European Merger Law' in Barry Hawk (ed), *Fordham Corporate Law Institute: International Antitrust Law and Policy* (Juris, 2004) 475–94; and Barbier de la Serre and Sibony (n 91) 958–61, who have been concerned that the GCEU may assume the role of the expert itself by deciding on issues about which it lacks the necessary knowledge.

unfettered production and evaluation favour the admission of evidence, and shift the focus on the subsequent step of ascertaining its probative value. Broadly speaking, the EU Courts' approach to the admissibility and probative weight of evidence is orthodox. As regards evidence admissibility, the expansive understanding of the *relevance* threshold suits well the features of EU competition enforcement, when coupled with an appropriate set of inadmissibility rules and the absence of a special admissibility formula for economic evidence. Equally, as regards evidence assessment, understood as comprising all parameters that may increase or decrease the evidential value of an item of evidence, the *reliability* test is capable of operationalising the principle of unfettered evaluation by confining the latitude of both the Commission and the EU Courts.

Nevertheless, certain aspects of the EU Courts' approach to evidence admissibility and evaluation call for some caution. First of all, the probative treatment of statements might take issue with the principle of effective judicial protection and the right to a fair trial – especially in the context of cartel enforcement. Indeed, although the ECHR does not prescribe rules of evidence admissibility and evaluation per se, the ECtHR has stressed that evidence standards are conditioned by the overall fairness of the proceedings and are informed by the principle of equality of arms and the rights of defence. However, the high probative value that the EU Courts tend to assign to statements might be problematic from a fairness point of view in the absence of any real possibility for cross-examination, where these constitute the exclusive or predominant basis for the Commission's decision. Since the Commission lacks the power to compel a person to testify, pleas based on a breach of the undertakings' right to call and cross-examine witnesses cannot be validly raised against the authority. Yet, they might still be raised against the EU Courts, which have the power to summon witnesses, examine them under oath and impose sanctions in the event of non-appearance. Therefore, where the Commission's findings are solely or decisively supported by statements, the GCEU's unwillingness to grant applications for the examination of witnesses might be misaligned with the principle of effective judicial protection and the right to a fair trial.

Equally, some caution is also warranted with respect to the probative assessment of opinion and economic evidence. Contrary to documents and statements, for which there is abundant – and overall sound – case law explaining how their reliability is ascertained, there has been rather limited jurisprudence on the probative value of opinion and economic evidence. As a result, factors which may be critical to the credibility of such 'technical' evidence – for instance, biases – have not been fully explored yet. Since the *reliability* test is workable only when the circumstances which may inform the probative weight of the evidence are unambiguously set out, the EU Courts should be more explicit concerning the factors that may increase or decrease the evidential value of opinion and economic evidence. This is particularly important regarding the latter, given that its appraisal assumes a degree of sophistication in economics that generalist EU judges typically lack. In any event, extending the marginal standard of review with respect to complex economic assessments to the evaluation of economic evidence – as *Ryanair* suggests – is not an appropriate solution. On the contrary, it has the effect of negating the principle of unfettered evaluation by unjustifiably excluding economic evidence from its scope, whereas it entails the risk of the EU Courts improperly favouring the Commission's evidence over that produced by the undertakings.

That said, the discharge of the standard of proof depends not only on the probative value of the available evidence, but also on the existence of presumptions, insofar as the latter have the effect of enabling the party with the burden of proof to satisfy it. Accordingly, Chapter 6 will now consider the use of presumptions in EU competition enforcement.

6

Presumptions in EU Competition Enforcement

I. Introduction

The allocation of the burden of proof and the regulation of the standard of proof provide the starting point for decision-makers in their assessment of the evidence. However, the operation of these two rules is neither inflexible nor rigid; rather, it is often adjusted through the use of presumptions. Indeed, the latter are a typical component of most legal systems and EU competition enforcement is no exception. Over the years, various presumptions have come to inform the assessment of the evidence and thus the application of the competition rules. Nevertheless, despite their prevalence, there remains significant conceptual confusion about their function. With this in mind, this chapter turns its attention to the use of presumptions in EU competition enforcement. To this end, section II first offers a brief theoretical account of the concept outlining the possible rationales which may underpin their use and presenting the still inconclusive debate about their consequences for the distribution of the burden of proof. With this analysis in mind, section III distinguishes presumptions from related mechanisms, which are commonly employed in EU competition enforcement – such as proxies and premises – in an attempt to eliminate the tendency to conflate them. Section IV then examines the main presumptions developed by EU judges with a special emphasis on their foundation, their rationale and the way in which they may be rebutted – considering for the sake of completeness one non-presumption, namely the inference of concertation based on evidence of parallel behaviour. On the basis of the preceding analysis, section V reflects on the broader implications of the existing presumptions for EU competition enforcement.

II. The Concept and Significance of Presumptions

Presumptions are an all-too-familiar fixture in adjudication. Generally, to presume means 'to accept something in the absence of the further relevant information that would ordinarily be deemed necessary to establish it'.[1] Contrary to pure

[1] Nicholas Rescher, *Presumptions and the Practices of Tentative Cognition* (Cambridge University Press, 2014) 1.

assumptions, such acceptance is not without foundation; rather, presumptions are typically predicated on a preliminary issue and usually take the form of a statement that 'if A, then accept B'.

Nevertheless, the precise function of presumptions in legal proceedings has caused much debate among scholars. To a great extent, these debates stem from the tendency to confuse presumptions with other mechanisms or concepts, as well as the lack of a clear legal definition thereof. Indeed, because it lies at the heart of virtually every presumption, the bipartite configuration 'if A, then B' is often used as a compass for their detection. However, not all statements of this kind qualify as 'presumptions' in the technical meaning of the word.[2] Rather, presumptions differ from similar devices in two critical respects: first of all, they *entitle but also require* the decision-maker to draw certain procedural consequences from their operation; and, second, they are *rebuttable*, ie, they may be reversed upon the production of appropriate evidence.[3] In this light, the distinction that scholars occasionally make between 'presumptions of law' and 'presumptions of fact' is inaccurate: presumptions of fact are nothing more than factual inferences that the fact-finder is entitled – but not forced – to draw based on the evidence.[4] Equally misleading is the categorisation of presumptions into 'provisional' and 'compelling', ie, presumptions that can be reversed and those that cannot. 'Compelling presumptions' are essentially a misnomer for substantive rules of law, from which no deviation is possible: once the preliminary condition has been demonstrated to the standard of proof, the issue is settled once and for all.[5] Therefore, although a universally accepted legal definition of presumptions is still missing, one should be mindful not to confuse them with seemingly similar, but fundamentally different devices.[6]

Turning now to the rationale behind their use, presumptions may be founded upon positive or normative grounds or – usually – a combination of both.[7] From a positive perspective, common sense, past experience and ease of proof considerations offer the most compelling explanations for their use. Indeed, the well-established presumption of paternity, for instance, has a very strong positive foundation: a child born in wedlock is presumed to be the biological child

[2] This point was rather missed in the early attempts at providing a neat taxonomy of presumptions (eg, Alfred Thomson Denning, 'Presumptions and Burdens' (1945) 61 *Law Quarterly Review* 379).

[3] These two features are the defining characteristics of a presumption in the technical sense of the word.

[4] David Kaiser, 'Presumptions of Law and of Fact' (1955) 38 *Marquette Law Review* 253, 254–56; John Stumbo, 'Presumptions: A View at Chaos' (1963) 3 *Washburn Law Journal* 182, 190–94.

[5] A good example of this is the common rule that minors younger than eight years of age may not be held criminally liable. This rule is occasionally articulated in presumption-like terms ('if a minor is less than eight years old, he is presumed to be incapable of criminal liability'). In reality, however, this 'presumption' is not susceptible to rebuttal and therefore it should be more accurately classified as a provision of substantive law.

[6] Presumptions in the technical sense of the word may be either judge-made, where they have been developed by courts, or they may be established by the legislature.

[7] See Edmund Morgan, 'Presumptions' (1937) 12 *Washington Law Review and State Bar Journal* 255, 257–59; Mason Ladd, 'Presumptions in Civil Actions' (1977) *Arizona State Law Journal* 275, 279–81.

of the mother's husband because logic and experience indicate that this will be true in the overwhelming majority of cases, but also because the husband might easily provide evidence to demonstrate that the child in question is not actually fathered by him. At any rate, presumptions may be also based on normative justifications. This will be the case where their adoption is principally motivated by the need to protect a legitimate interest or promote a policy goal. The quite common presumption of death upon evidence of absence of a certain number of years is the best example of this. Indeed, the main reason behind the development of this presumption is the need to safeguard legal certainty in relation to the affairs of persons whose whereabouts have been unknown for a long time and to ensure the interests of those potentially affected by the disappearance. That said, it should be noted that most presumptions typically have both a positive and a normative basis – even if not in equal measure. The presumption of paternity, for instance, serves a policy goal as well, insofar as it is intended to secure children's rights. The presumption of death, on the other hand, is validated by the common knowledge that if a person is missing for several years without any sign of life, there is a high chance they may be dead.

Although the *need* for presumptions has been widely recognised among scholars, the *procedural consequences*, by contrast, that one must attach to their operation have caused much confusion and passionate debate. Indeed, while it is clear that presumptions instruct the decision-maker to accept an issue 'B' as true if a basic fact 'A' has been sufficiently demonstrated, the precise effect of their function on the burden and standard of proof has been less obvious. On this issue, two different theories appear to have dominated the discussion. According to the first one – principally advocated for by Thayer and Wigmore – presumptions have the effect of shifting the burden of producing evidence.[8] In practice, this means that if the party who bears the burden of persuasion with respect to issue 'B' demonstrates 'A', they are deemed to have satisfied the standard of proof in respect of 'B', unless their opponent produces evidence which calls 'A' or 'B' into question. In the latter scenario, the presumption would disappear and the party with the burden of persuasion would still have an obligation to establish 'B'. However, this approach did not find universal support. A couple of years later, a second theory – known as the 'Morgan–McCormick' theory – emerged. According to this, presumptions have the effect of shifting not only the burden of production, but also the burden of persuasion.[9] In practice, this would mean that it is no longer sufficient for the party against whom the presumption operates to produce evidence calling

[8] James Thayer, 'Presumptions and the Law of Evidence' (1889) 3 *Harvard Law Review* 141; James Thayer, *A Preliminary Treatise on Evidence at the Common Law* (Little, Brown and Co, 1898) 380–89; John Wigmore, *A Treatise on the Anglo-American System of Evidence in Trials at Common Law*, 3rd edn (Little, Brown and Co, 1940). This approach is known as the 'bubble bursting' theory.

[9] Edmund Morgan, 'Some Observations Concerning Presumptions' (1931) 44 *Harvard Law Review* 906–34; Morgan (n 7); Edmund Morgan, 'Some Further Observations on Presumptions' (1942) 16 *Southern California Law Review* 245–65.

'A' or 'B' into question; rather, it must positively disprove 'B' to make the presumption vanish. Despite the lapse of almost a century since their first assertion, both theories still hold their ground and the procedural effect of presumptions remains as contentious as ever.[10] In this light, it is hardly surprising that some authors have argued for abandoning the concept altogether.[11] Taking a definite position on this controversial issue goes beyond the scope of the present work. However, for the purposes of the subsequent analysis, one remark is necessary: where a presumption shifts the burden of persuasion, it operates akin to a defence.[12] Indeed, the only difference between persuasive presumptions and affirmative defences is that in the former case, the legal burden shifts during the trial, whereas in the latter case, it is allocated on the defendant since its beginning.

III. Distinguishing Presumptions from Similar Devices in EU Competition Enforcement

Although presumptions are thought of as a key component of EU competition enforcement, their precise operation is still poorly understood. This is hardly surprising in light of the conceptual challenges surrounding presumptions in general. Nevertheless, these difficulties have been further exacerbated in the context of competition enforcement by the tendency to conflate presumptions with similar yet distinct mechanisms – such as 'by object' legal tests and safe harbours.[13] This section will consider various devices and tools which are frequently labelled by authorities and scholars as 'presumptions' with a view to illuminating why they

[10] On the effect of presumptions, see generally Francis Bohlen, 'The Effect of Rebuttable Presumptions of Law upon the Burden of Proof' (1920) 68 *University of Pennsylvania Law Review* 307; John McBaine, 'Presumptions: Are They Evidence?' (1938) 26 *California Law Review* 519; Nigel Bridge, 'Presumptions and Burdens' (1949) 12 *Modern Law Review* 273; Charles Laughlin, 'In Support of the Thayer Theory of Presumptions' (1953) 52 *Michigan Law Review* 195; Ernest Roberts, 'An Introduction to the Study of Presumptions' (1958) 4 *Villanova Law Review* 1; Edward Cleary, 'Presuming and Pleading: An Essay on Juristic Immaturity' (1959) 12 *Stanford Law Review* 5; Richard Epstein, 'Pleadings and Presumptions' (1973) 40 *University of Chicago Law Review* 556; Charles Yablon, 'A Theory of Presumptions' (2003) 2 *Law, Probability and Risk* 227; Leonardo Raznovich, 'A Comparative Review of the Socio-legal Implications of Burden of Proof and Presumptions to Deal with Factual Uncertainty' (2008) 32 *American Journal of Trial Advocacy* 57.

[11] Ronald Allen, 'Presumptions in Civil Actions Reconsidered' (1981) 66 *Iowa Law Review* 843; Ronald Allen and Craig Callen, 'The Juridical Management of Factual Uncertainty' (2003) 7 *International Journal of Evidence and Proof* 1.

[12] David Hamer, 'Presumptions, Standards and Burdens: Managing the Cost of Error' (2014) 13 Law, Probability and Risk 221, 225–26.

[13] For a discussion of presumptions and presumption-like devices in EU competition law, see Andreas Heinemann, 'Access to Evidence and Presumptions: Communicating Vessels in Procedural Law' in Kai Hüschelrath and Heike Schweitzer (eds), *Public and Private Enforcement of Competition Law in Europe* (ZEW Economic Studies 48, 2014); David Bailey, 'Presumptions in EU Competition Law' (2010) 31 *European Competition Law Review* 362; OECD, *Safe Harbours and Legal Presumptions in Competition Law*, DAF/COMP(2017)9; Cyril Ritter, 'Presumptions in EU Competition Law' (2018) 6 *Journal of Antitrust Enforcement* 189.

do not qualify as such in the technical sense of the word, to this end drawing a distinction from related concepts – in particular *proxies* and *premises*.

A first example in this regard is the so-called 'presumption of dominance', where the undertaking enjoys a market-share of more than 50 per cent in the relevant market. Indeed, it is sometimes said that the existence of a dominant position – which is a prerequisite for the application of Article 102 TFEU – may be presumed from the existence of a market share exceeding 50 per cent. Admittedly, such claims are not groundless. In fact, they find support in *AKZO*, where the CJEU confirmed the earlier position in *Hoffmann-La Roche* that 'very large shares are in themselves, and save in exceptional circumstances, evidence of the existence of a dominant position', and clarified that 'that is the situation where there is a market share of 50%'.[14] Nevertheless, a closer look at the case law reveals that the *AKZO* statement and similar reiterations may be better understood as meaning that high market shares allow for a strong factual inference of dominance – rather than a presumption, strictly speaking.[15] On the one hand, the word 'presumption' has not been explicitly employed by the EU Courts; later judgments in particular feature the more nuanced term 'indication', which falls short of a presumption.[16] On the other hand, in all cases where the finding of dominance has been challenged – even in *AKZO* or in cases of 'super-dominance' – it is clear that the Commission and the EU Courts took additional factors into account, beyond market shares, in order to verify the existence of a dominant position.[17] Indeed, it is doubtful that merely relying on a share of over 50 per cent would enable the authority to discharge its burden of proof – and for good reason. While market shares are commonly used as a *proxy* for measuring market power in lack of a better metric, they are inevitably an imperfect indicator of an undertaking's economic strength.[18] Consequently, any inferences drawn from them must be calibrated against other parameters *before* a finding of dominance is reached.

In any event, the term 'presumption' is also frequently used in competition law in connection with 'by object' restrictions of competition or abuses of dominance. Indeed, the argument is often made that certain practices are to be prohibited by their very nature because – based on our experience – they may be 'presumed' to harm competition. However, this language is prone to obscure the operation of

[14] Case 62/86 *AKZO v Commission*, ECLI:EU:C:1991:286, para 60; Case 85/76 *Hoffman-La Roche v Commission*, ECLI:EU:C:1979:36, para 41.

[15] Jonathan Faull and Ali Nikpay (eds), *Faull and Nikpay: The EU Law of Competition*, 3rd edn (Oxford University Press, 2014) 4.160.

[16] See, eg, Case T-30/89 *Hilti v Commission*, ECLI:EU:T:1991:70, para 92; Case T-321/05 *AstraZeneca v Commission*, ECLI:EU:T:2010:266, para 243.

[17] *AKZO* (n 14) para 61; Case T-228/97 *Irish Sugar v Commission*, ECLI:EU:T:1999:246, paras 73–104; *AstraZeneca* (n 16) para 244. See also Guidance on the Commission's enforcement priorities in applying Article 82 of the EC Treaty to abusive exclusionary conduct by dominant undertakings [2009] OJ C45/02, paras 13, 15.

[18] See Louis Kaplow, 'Market Share Thresholds: On the Conflation of Empirical Assessments and Legal Policy Judgments' (2011) 7 *Journal of Competition Law & Economics* 243.

the burden of proof, whereas it has unnecessarily complicated the definition of 'by object' restrictions of competition and abuses of dominance. First of all, if the classification of a practice as a 'by object' infringement truly entailed a presumption of the *existence* of anti-competitive effects in the technical meaning of the word, it would be open to undertakings to challenge it by showing that their cartel agreement, for instance, was never implemented or that the presumed negative effects are unlikely to occur. However, the EU Courts' jurisprudence clearly illustrates that such arguments may not reverse a finding of 'by object' liability.[19] Moreover, presumptions must be compatible with the principle of effective judicial protection – as will be explained later. Considering that 'by object' liability is almost impossible to reverse, one would expect a plethora of fairness-based objections to the operation of this 'presumption'. Yet, such criticisms have never been raised by undertakings and would be rather absurd. This further indicates that, however tempting it may be, to speak of a 'presumption' in this context is inaccurate. Indeed, what is really at stake here is the proper construction of the 'by object' legal test. Inevitably, the chosen interpretation will have implications for the evidential process, insofar as the constituent elements of the legal test predetermine the negations that an undertaking may advance, but these implications are the reasonable aftermath, rather than the main focus, of the discussion.

In this regard, a better word to use is the term 'premise'. Framing the conversation about the definition of the 'by object' test around presumptions draws attention away from its main focus – that is, the appropriate scope of the substantive legal rules – and creates the impression that the matter is primarily an evidential one. By contrast, the word 'premise' describes the thinking behind not only 'by object', but also 'by effect' more accurately. A premise may be defined as an assertion or proposition which forms the basis for a decision.[20] Competition law abounds with premises. Indeed, as noted in Chapters 2 and 4, the choice between 'by object' and 'by effect' liability is heavily informed by premises about the nature of the conduct at hand. For instance, the prohibition of cartels as 'by object' restrictions of competition rests on the premise that cartels lack redeeming virtues and are thus prone to harm competition. Similarly, the 'by effect' assessment of exclusive dealing arrangements under Article 101 TFEU is also grounded in a premise, that is, that practices of this kind may have ambiguous effects on competition, which in turn implies that the optimal legal test is one providing for a case-by-case evaluation of their lawfulness.[21] While premises may be contested both by the Commission and

[19] Joined Cases C-189/02 P, C-202/02 P, C-205/02 P to C-208/02 P and C-213/02 P *Dansk Rørindustri and Others v Commission*, ECLI:EU:C:2005:408, para 145; Case C-8/08 *T-Mobile Netherlands and Others*, ECLI:EU:C:2009:343, paras 29, 31. See also the Opinion of AG Kokott at para 45. The only argument they can make is that the practice lacks the inherent capacity to harm competition (see section IV.E below).

[20] In the *Oxford Dictionaries*, the term is defined as 'an assertion or proposition which forms the basis for a work or theory' (see https://en.oxforddictionaries.com/definition/premise).

[21] Case C-234/89 *Delimitis v Henninger Brau*, ECLI:EU:C:1991:91, paras 11–13.

undertakings, they differ from presumptions in that they are not formally subject to the standard of proof and they do not automatically shift the burden of proof. Rather, they constitute part of the 'legislative facts', which guide the interpretation of the competition rules, for which exclusive authority lies with the EU Courts.[22] Accordingly, premises should not be confused with presumptions; although the two notions are conceptually related, insofar as they fall within the broader category of mental shortcuts used to facilitate legal decision-making, their function is different.

For similar reasons, the 'safe harbours' and 'bright lines' which abound in the soft law instruments published by the Commission should also be distinguished from presumptions in the technical sense of the word – although they are often classified as such. For example, the Commission Notice on the effect on trade concept establishes, on the one hand, a positive and, on the other hand, a negative 'presumption' that agreements meeting the therein specified conditions will be deemed to have or not to have an appreciable effect on trade among Member States.[23] Likewise, the Commission Guidelines on agreements of minor importance indicate that arrangements entered into between parties whose market shares do not exceed certain thresholds will be considered not to appreciably restrict competition within the meaning of Article 101(1) TFEU.[24] Similar 'safe harbours' are identified in the Commission Guidelines on horizontal cooperation agreements,[25] whereas the Guidelines on vertical restraints provide that agreements containing hardcore restrictions are 'presumed' to restrict competition in the meaning of Article 101(1) TFEU and to be unlikely to fulfil the conditions of Article 101(3) TFEU.[26] However, none of these mechanisms are presumptions in the technical meaning of the word. Apart from the fact that administrative notices and guidelines are not legally binding,[27] safe harbours and bright lines do not really shift the burden of proof, but rather articulate the premises underpinning the Commission's enforcement policy and construction of the law. In this respect, they are aimed at reinforcing the transparency of the authority's activities, and assisting businesses in self-assessing the compatibility of their conduct with the competition rules following the abolition of the compulsory notification system with the adoption of Regulation 1/2003.

[22] On this, see Kenneth Culp Davis, 'An Approach to Problems of Evidence in the Administrative Process' (1942) 55 *Harvard Law Review* 364, who observed (at 402): 'It is conventional wisdom today to observe that judges not only are charged to find what the law is, but must regularly make new law when … interpreting a statute … The very nature of the judicial process necessitates that judges be guided, as legislators are, by considerations of expediency and public policy. They must, in the nature of things, act either upon knowledge already possessed or upon assumptions, or upon investigation of the pertinent general facts, social, economic, political, or scientific.' See also ch 7, section III.B.iii.

[23] Guidelines on the effect on trade concept contained in Articles [101] and [102] of the Treaty [2004] OJ C101/81, paras 50, 53.

[24] Commission Notice on agreements of minor importance which do not appreciably restrict competition under Article 101(1) TFEU [2014] OJ C291/1, paras 8–11.

[25] Commission Guidelines on horizontal cooperation agreements [2011] OJ C11/1, paras 134, 208.

[26] Guidelines on vertical restraints [2010] OJ C130/10, para 47.

[27] However, note that they may still produce legal effects: *Dansk Rørindustri* (n 19) paras 209–11.

Last but not least, presumptions within the technical meaning of the word must be differentiated, on the one hand, from the presumptions of legality to be found in the Block Exemption Regulations and, on the other hand, from various presumption-like rules aimed at regulating the enforcement procedure so as to ensure it will not come to a standstill. Indeed, the Block Exemption Regulations provide that block categories of agreements which fulfil certain conditions are 'presumed' to satisfy the requirements of Article 101(3) TFEU and not to restrict competition within the meaning of Article 101(1) TFEU. In essence, however, such 'presumptions' are simply substantive rules of law, which rest on the *premise* that appreciable restrictive effects are unlikely to occur in the absence of market power. Strictly speaking, these presumptions are not 'rebuttable'; rather, the benefit of a block exemption may at most be withdrawn by the Commission.[28] Finally, beyond the 'presumptions' of legality established by the Block Exemption Regulations, competition enforcement features several presumption-like rules, which allow for certain procedural conclusions to be drawn, where one of the participants fails to take action or to respond with a specified period. For example, the EUMR provides that where the Commission has not adopted a decision within the specified time limits, the concentration will be 'deemed' to be compatible with the common market,[29] or that the lack of objection to a merger referral will be taken to imply consent.[30] Likewise, Regulation 773/2004 on the conduct of antitrust proceedings explains that where an undertaking misses the deadline for identifying confidential information in its submissions, the authority is entitled to assume that the documents or statements in question do not contain confidential information.[31] Although these rules are sometimes labelled as 'presumptions' because of their 'if A, then B' formulation, they do not shift the burden of proof and are merely intended to ensure the smooth running of proceedings.

IV. The Main Presumptions in EU Competition Enforcement

Bearing these clarifications in mind, this section will now identify and analyse the main presumptions – in the technical sense of the word – featuring in competition enforcement with a special emphasis on their foundation, their rationale and the way in which they may be rebutted. In this context, and for the sake of

[28] Regulation 1/2003, art 29; and Preamble, Recital 10.

[29] EUMR, art 10(6). Note also the 'presumption' that a concentration has an EU dimension, where the thresholds of art 1(2) and (3) EUMR are satisfied.

[30] ibid arts 4(4), 4(5) and 22(3).

[31] Article 16(4) of Commission Regulation 773/2004 relating to the conduct of proceedings by the European Commission pursuant to Articles [101 and 102 TFEU] [2004] OJ L123/18. Note also art 7(3), which provides that if the complainant fails to respond to the Commission's pre-rejection letter within the specified deadline, the complaint shall be deemed to have been withdrawn.

completeness, it will also consider one *non*-presumption – namely, the inference of concertation based on evidence of parallel behaviour which the EU Courts have declined to elevate into a presumption.

A. No Presumption of Concertation Based on Evidence of Parallel Behaviour

Article 101 TFEU was designed to catch not only 'agreements', but also 'concerted practices'. As the CJEU explained in *Dyestuffs*, this distinction was intended to ensure that undertakings engaging in coordination which 'knowingly substitutes practical cooperation between them for the risks of competition' will not be able to evade liability under Article 101 TFEU on the ground that their conduct falls short of an 'agreement'.[32] However, establishing the existence of a concerted practice raises significant evidential challenges for the authority, which is required to demonstrate three elements: first, some sort of direct or indirect communication among the undertakings involved, ie, concertation; second, subsequent conduct on the market; and, third, a causal connection between the established communication and the market behaviour of the undertakings concerned.[33] In this context, the question soon arose as to whether evidence of 'parallel behaviour' may be relied on to *presume* the existence of concertation. This issue was particularly salient in situations where market participants displayed the same conduct, but there was no indication of unlawful contact among them – whether direct or indirect.

Confronted with this question in *Woodpulp II*, the CJEU replied in the negative.[34] In this case, the Commission had argued that the quarterly price announcements of the operators on the pulp market were proof of an anti-competitive concertation among them. The Court, however, disagreed. Emphasising that 'parallel conduct cannot be regarded as furnishing proof of concertation unless concertation constitutes the *only* plausible explanation for such conduct' (emphasis added),[35] the Court took the view that the parallel price announcements could actually be explained by the oligopolistic nature of the market and the way in which the industry operated, and thus annulled the Commission's decision. This position was again reaffirmed in *Tournier* and *Lucazeau*, where the CJEU stressed that parallel behaviour does not give rise to a presumption of concertation if it 'can be accounted for by reasons other than the existence of concerted action'.[36]

[32] Case 48/69 *Imperial Chemical Industries v Commission* (*Dyestuffs*), ECLI:EU:C:1972:70, para 64.

[33] Case C-199/92 P *Hüls v Commission*, ECLI:EU:C:1999:358, para 161.

[34] Joined Cases C-89/85, C-104/85, C-114/85, C-116/85, C-117/85 and C-125/85 to C-129/85 *Ahlström Osakeyhtiö and Others v Commission* (*Woodpulp II*), ECLI:EU:C:1993:120; Joined Cases C-89/85, C-104/85, C-114/85, C-116/85, C-117/85 and C-125/85 to C-129/85 *Ahlström Osakeyhtiö and Others v Commission*, ECLI:EU:C:1993:120.

[35] ibid para 71.

[36] Case 395/87 *Tournier*, ECLI:EU:C:1989:319, para 24; and Joined Cases 110/88, 241/88 and 242/88 *Lucazeau and Others v SACEM and Others*, ECLI:EU:C:1989:326, paras 18–19.

In the circumstances of these cases, which concerned the compatibility with the competition rules of various collective societies' refusals to grant direct licences to users established in a different Member State, the CJEU indicated that such 'parallel conduct' might be explained away by the fact that, were they to provide direct licences, collective societies would be obliged to organise their own management and monitoring system in other countries.[37] The guidance provided by the Court in these two references for a preliminary ruling was put to the test more recently in *CISAC*.[38] In that case, the Commission found that the members of CISAC, an organisation of collecting societies managing authors' rights in their musical works, had infringed Article 101 TFEU, among others, by coordinating their behaviour in such a way that licences were confined to the domestic territory of each collecting society. However, examining the evidence, the GCEU noted that the parallel behaviour of the collecting societies could be explained by the need to ensure the effectiveness of the fight against the unauthorised use of musical works.[39] In light of the existence of an alternative plausible exegesis, their parallel conduct could not on its own support a presumption of concertation.

The judgment in *CISAC* is important because it confirms that where the Commission wishes to rely on parallel conduct alone as proof of a concerted practice,[40] the whole burden of proof remains with it. While undertakings may draw the authority's attention to specific alternative justifications for their conduct, they are neither required to do so nor obliged to produce evidence in support of their arguments. As the GCEU remarked, the authority 'cannot criticise the applicant for failing to provide further specifics regarding its other explanation'; rather, if it is not satisfied with its claims, 'it must continue the examination … or find that the concerned parties have not been capable of providing the necessary information', which did not seem to be the case in the proceedings at hand.[41] The position in *CISAC* might seem to be at odds with the EU Courts' consistent declarations that 'parallel behaviour may amount to strong evidence of a concerted practice'.[42] After all, even in the absence of a presumption, the evidence produced by the Commission may be such that it calls for a response by the undertaking concerned.[43] However, where the authority's evidence consists in parallel conduct, it seems that a counter-reply will be necessary where the parallel behaviour 'leads to conditions of competition which do not correspond to the normal conditions of competition, having regard to the nature of the products, the size and the number

[37] ibid.

[38] Case T-442/08 *CISAC v Commission*, ECLI:EU:T:2013:188.

[39] ibid paras 181–82.

[40] In *CISAC*, the authority had adduced further evidence of anti-competitive contact among the parties, but its probative value was rejected by the GCEU.

[41] *CISAC* (n 38) para 161. See also Case T-337/94 *Enso-Gutzeit v Commission*, ECLI:EU:T:1998:98, para 149.

[42] *Tournier* (n 36) para 24; *Lucazeau* (n 36) para 18.

[43] See ch 3, section III.A.ii.

of undertakings, and the volume of the said market'[44] or where 'the same operators also engage in other collusive activities at the same time'.[45]

B. The Presumptions of Participation in a Collusive Arrangement

Although the EU Courts have consistently rejected the idea of a presumption of concertation based on evidence of parallel behaviour alone, they have nevertheless eased the Commission's burden of proof by introducing another presumption, that is, that the subsequent conduct of an undertaking on the market has been informed by the content of their communications with other market participants. The origins of this presumption may be traced in the polypropylene cartel litigation. Specifically, in *Hüls* and *Commission v Anic Partecipazioni* – two judgments delivered on the same day – the CJEU held that 'subject to proof to the contrary, which it is for the economic operators concerned to adduce, there must be a presumption that the undertakings participating in concerting arrangements and remaining active on the market take account of the information exchanged with their competitors when determining their conduct on that market'.[46]

Ever since the polypropylene appeals, the presumption of a causal connection between the established concertation and the subsequent conduct of the undertakings involved has become firmly embedded in the competition jurisprudence of the EU Courts.[47] In *T-Mobile*, the CJEU clarified that the presumption may be invoked not only where the undertakings concert together on a regular basis over a long period, but even where the concerted action is the result of a single anticompetitive contact among them.[48] The wide endorsement of the *Anic* presumption is hardly surprising in view of its strong positive and normative foundation. As AG Kokott elucidated in her Opinion in *T-Mobile*, the presumed causal connection constitutes 'nothing other than a legitimate conclusion drawn on the basis of common experience'; if the existence of a concertation among two or more undertakings has been established, it is only 'natural to presume a relation of cause and effect' between the concertation and the undertakings' subsequent behaviour in the market.[49] In any event, the presumption also has a solid normative justification: it reinforces the well-established principle that 'each economic

[44] *Dyestuffs* (n 32) para 66.

[45] Case T-462/07 *Galp Energia España and Others v Commission*, ECLI:EU:T:2013:459, paras 391–92.

[46] Case C-49/92 P *Commission v Anic Partecipazioni*, ECLI:EU:C:1999:356, para 121; *Hüls* (n 33) para 162.

[47] See, eg, Case T-370/09 *GDF Suez v Commission*, ECLI:EU:T:2012:333, para 363; Case T-472/09 *SP v Commission*, ECLI:EU:T:2014:1040, para 166; Case C-286/13 P *Dole Food and Dole Fresh Fruit Europe v Commission*, ECLI:EU:C:2015:184, para 127.

[48] *T-Mobile* (n 19) para 62.

[49] ibid, Opinion of AG Kokott, para 90.

operator must determine independently the policy which he intends to adopt on the common market'.[50]

The *Anic* presumption was initially developed with a view to enabling the Commission to discharge its burden of proof with respect to concerted practices, that is, collusive arrangements falling short of an agreement. Nevertheless, it soon provided the basis for a related, yet distinct presumption, ie, that of participation in an infringement of Article 101(1) TFEU upon evidence that the undertaking has attended an anti-competitive meeting.[51] Indeed, as confirmed by the CJEU for the first time in *Aalborg Portland*, 'it is sufficient for the Commission to show that the undertaking concerned participated in meetings at which anticompetitive agreements were concluded, without manifestly opposing them, to prove to the requisite standard that the undertaking participated in a cartel'.[52] Although this presumption draws upon the *Anic* presumption, its foundations are somewhat different. From a positive perspective, the *Aalborg Portland* presumption is grounded in the idea that where an undertaking participates in an anti-competitive meeting without objecting to it, it is only reasonable that the other participants will believe that it subscribes to what was decided and that it will comply with it.[53] From a normative viewpoint, the primary aim of this presumption is to discourage passive modes of anti-competitive behaviour. As the CJEU has explained, 'a party which tacitly approves of an unlawful initiative, without publicly distancing itself from its content or reporting it to the administrative authorities, effectively encourages the continuation of the infringement and compromises its discovery'.[54]

In practice, the *Anic* presumption and the *Aalborg Portland* presumption are often invoked in conjunction. However, it should be stressed that none of these presumptions releases the Commission from its obligation to establish the anti-competitive object or effect of the communications or agreements in question. Indeed, in *Coats Holdings*, the decision of the Commission was annulled with respect to the applicant on the ground that the authority had failed to adequately demonstrate that the specific meetings in which the undertaking had participated had been of an anti-competitive nature.[55] In any event, the operation of these

[50] Joined Cases 40 to 48, 50, 54 to 56, 111, 113 and 114/73 *Suiker Unie v Commission*, ECLI:EU:C:1975:174, para 173. More recently, see Case T-180/15 *ICAP and Others v Commission*, ECLI:EU:T:2017:795, para 49. See also Ioannis Lianos and Christos Genakos, 'Econometric Evidence in EU Competition Law: An Empirical and Theoretical Analysis' in Ioannis Lianos and Damien Geradin (eds), *Handbook on European Competition Law: Enforcement and Procedure* (Edward Elgar, 2013) 92.

[51] Note that none of these presumptions releases the Commission from its obligation to demonstrate the anti-competitive nature of the communications or concluded agreements. In *Coats Holdings*, the Commission's decision was annulled with respect to the applicant on the ground that the authority had failed to establish the anti-competitive nature of the meetings in which the undertaking had participated (Case T-36/05 *Coats Holdings and Coats v Commission*, ECLI:EU:T:2007:268, paras 90–96).

[52] Joined Cases C-204/00 P, C-205/00 P, C-211/00 P, C-213/00 P, C-217/00 P and C-219/00 P *Aalborg Portland and Others v Commission*, ECLI:EU:C:2004:6, para 81.

[53] ibid para 82.

[54] ibid para 84. Note also Case C-291/98 P *Sarrió v Commission*, ECLI:EU:C:2000:265, Opinion of AG Mischo, para 45: 'it would be impossible to prevent infringements of competition law committed by cartels if it were to be accepted that an undertaking may attend such meetings with impunity'.

[55] *Coats Holdings* (n 51) paras 90–96.

presumptions was further clarified in *Eturas*, a preliminary ruling case concerning an allegedly anti-competitive concerted practice among several travel agents consisting in capping discounts for holiday packages sold via the Eturas online platform. Among other things, the CJEU was asked to provide guidance on whether the mere dispatch of an electronic message by the administrator of an online booking system informing economic operators about the forthcoming cap on discounts for products sold through the system and the subsequent implementation of a technical restriction capping such discounts were sufficient to activate the *Anic* presumption. Considering the issue, the CJEU took the view that in the absence of 'other objective and consistent indicia' that the operators were aware – or ought to have been aware – of the content of the message, the undertakings in question may not be presumed to have participated in an anti-competitive concerted practice.[56]

That said, the parallel use of the two presumptions has somewhat obscured the question how they may be rebutted. As far as the *Aalborg Portland* presumption is concerned, the EU Courts have clarified that:

> [W]here participation in [anti-competitive] meetings has been established, it is for [the] undertaking to put forward evidence to establish that its participation in those meetings was without any anticompetitive intention by demonstrating that it had indicated to its competitors that it was participating in those meetings in a spirit that was different from theirs.[57]

Indeed, according to settled jurisprudence, in order to reverse the presumption of liability based on its participation in an anti-competitive meeting, the undertaking must show that it has 'publicly distanced itself'. Nevertheless, the question remains what 'public distancing' entails. The EU Courts have stressed that the notion 'must be interpreted narrowly'.[58] In light of the case law, it seems that what is expected of an undertaking wishing to rebut the presumption of liability is either to report the infringement to the authority or – at the very least – to denounce the anti-competitive arrangement in such a way that it is clear to the other participants that it does not wish to participate in it, either at all or any longer.[59]

In this regard, what truly matters is the other participants' perception of the undertaking's intentions.[60] By contrast, arguments that the undertaking did not

[56] Case C-74/14 *Eturas and Others*, ECLI:EU:C:2016:42, paras 40–45.

[57] ibid para 81.

[58] Case T-303/02 *Westfalen Gassen Nederland*, ECLI:EU:T:2006:374, para 103.

[59] Case C-290/11 P *Comap v Commission*, ECLI:EU:C:2012:271, para 75. Note that 'public distancing' arguments are often raised by undertakings with a view to establishing that they have *ceased* their participation in the infringement – usually in an attempt to challenge the Commission's findings about the duration of their liability (see section IV.C below).

[60] Case C-634/13 P *Total Marketing Services v Commission*, ECLI:EU:C:2015:614, para 21; Case C-373/14 P *Toshiba v Commission*, ECLI:EU:C:2016:26, para 71. In light of the clandestine nature of cartels, 'the perception of the other participants must be deduced, if necessary, from the body of indicia and indirect evidence which the Commission and the Court may have' (Case T-540/08 *Esso and Others v Commission*, ECLI:EU:T:2014:630, para 46).

act on the outcome of the anti-competitive meeting, that it did not take part in all aspects of the anti-competitive scheme or that it played only a minor role are ineffective.[61] Nor will mere silent disagreement suffice to reverse the presumption of liability.[62] Internal documents stating that the undertaking wishes not to align itself with the other participants in the meeting will be insufficient.[63] Equally inadequate will be the mere fact that the representative in question left the anti-competitive meeting;[64] rather, the undertaking must 'inform the other companies represented, with sufficient clarity, that, despite appearances, it disagrees with the unlawful steps which they have taken'.[65] In *Adriatica* and *Westfalen*, for instance, the EU Courts suggested that the undertakings in question could have easily written to their competitors condemning the anti-competitive arrangements and underlining that they do not want to participate in, and be considered a party to, them.[66] In any event, irrespective of its form, the distancing must be 'firm' and 'unequivocal', and must leave the other participants in no doubt as to the undertaking's intentions.[67]

Where the presumption of liability has been triggered by the undertaking's attendance at an anti-competitive meeting, it will be extremely difficult to reverse in light of the narrow conception of the notion of 'public distancing'. By contrast, an undertaking might stand a better chance where its liability is not presumed from its participation in individual anti-competitive meetings. Indeed, in *Total Marketing*, the CJEU explained that where the infringement has taken place over several years, 'the absence of public distancing forms only one factor amongst others to take into consideration with a view to establishing whether an undertaking has actually continued to participate in an infringement or has … ceased to do so'.[68] More recently, in *Eturas*, it was reiterated that:

> [I]n a case … which does not concern an anticompetitive meeting, public distancing or reporting to the administrative authorities are not the only means of rebutting the

[61] Case T-347/94 *Mayr-Melnhof Kartongesellschaft v Commission*, ECLI:EU:T:1998:101, para 135; *Aalborg Portland* (n 52) paras 85–86; Case T-264/12 *UTi Worldwide and Others v Commission*, ECLI:EU:T:2016:112, para 126.

[62] Joined Cases T-202/98, T-204/98 and T-207/98 *Tate & Lyle and Others v Commission*, ECLI:EU:T:2001:185, paras 63–67; *Westfalen Gassen* (n 58) para 124; Case T-448/07 *YYK and Others v Commission*, ECLI:EU:T:2012:322, para 116.

[63] Case T-61/99 *Adriatica di Navigazione v Commission*, ECLI:EU:T:2003:335, para 136.

[64] Case C-510/06 P *Archer Daniels Midland v Commission*, ECLI:EU:C:2009:166, para 120.

[65] ibid para 137.

[66] ibid paras 137–38; *Westfalen Gassen* (n 58) para 103.

[67] Case T-23/99 *LR AF 1998 v Commission* ECLI:EU:T:2002:75, paras 37, 39–49, 61–62 and 150–52; Case T-360/09 *E.ON Ruhrgas and E.ON v Commission*, ECLI:EU:T:2012:332, paras 179–192. For a more detailed discussion of public distancing, see David Bailey, '"Publicly Distancing" Oneself from a Cartel' (2008) 31(2) *World Competition* 177.

[68] *Total Marketing Services* (n 60) paras 21–25. The CJEU found that the GCEU had erred in law by holding that 'public distancing constitutes the only means available to an undertaking involved in a cartel of proving that it has ceased participating in that cartel, even in the case where that company has not participated in anti-competitive meetings', but eventually concluded that this error had not invalidated the GCEU's findings.

> presumption that a company has participated in an infringement; other evidence may also be adduced with a view to rebutting that presumption.[69]

In the circumstances of the case, the CJEU suggested that the presumption of liability could be reversed upon evidence of 'a clear and express objection sent to the administrator of the Eturas system' – since each travel agent was not in a position to know who the addressees of the original message had been – or by evidence of 'a systematic application of a discount exceeding the cap in question'.[70]

C. The Presumption of Continuity

One of the greatest challenges for the Commission, when it investigates potential violations of the competition rules, is how to establish the duration of each undertaking's participation in the unlawful practice. Indeed, according to settled case law, the authority bears the burden of persuasion not only with respect to the existence of the infringement, but also its duration.[71] Identifying the starting and ending point of a violation may be difficult in the best of circumstances.[72] However, in cases concerning complex collusive arrangements involving several undertakings over longer periods of time, establishing the duration of each entity's participation in the infringement at hand becomes especially arduous.

In recognition of the existing challenges, the EU Courts have eased the authority's burden of proof in two ways. First, they have developed the doctrine of single, continuous or repeated infringement. According to this, there is one infringement – rather than several – where a series of acts forms part of an unlawful 'overall plan'.[73] The latter may be deduced:

> [F]rom the identical nature of the objectives of the practices at issue, of the goods concerned, of the undertakings which participated in the collusion, of the main rules for its implementation, of the natural persons involved on behalf of the undertakings, and lastly, of the geographical scope of those practices.[74]

Depending on how it is committed, a single infringement may be *continuous* (where it consists in continuous conduct in pursuit of a single economic aim which is intended to distort competition) or *repeated* (where the infringement was interrupted, but the undertakings concerned pursued the same objective both before

[69] *Eturas* (n 56) para 46.

[70] ibid paras 48–49.

[71] Joined Cases T-25/95, T-26/95, T-30/95 to T-32/95, T-34/95 to T-39/95, T-42/95 to T-46/95, T-48/95, T-50/95 to T-65/95, T-68/95 to T-71/95, T-87/95, T-88/95, T-103/95 and T-104/95 *Cimenteries CBR and Others v Commission*, ECLI:EU:T:2000:77, para 2802; Case T-120/04 *Peróxidos Orgánicos v Commission*, ECLI:EU:T:2006:350, paras 21 and 51.

[72] On this, see Fernando Castillo de la Torre and Eric Gippini Fournier, *Evidence, Proof and Judicial Review in EU Competition Law* (Edward Elgar, 2017) 100–16.

[73] *Aalborg Portland* (n 52) para 258; *AstraZeneca* (n 16) para 892.

[74] *ICAP* (n 50) para 221.

and after the interruption).[75] Second, the EU Courts have adopted a presumption of continuity. According to the latter, 'if there is no evidence directly establishing the duration of an infringement, the Commission should adduce at least evidence of facts sufficiently proximate in time for it to be reasonable to accept that that infringement continued uninterruptedly between two specific dates'.[76]

The doctrine of single, continuous or repeated infringement and the presumption of continuity are often engaged simultaneously, especially in cartel cases. Nevertheless, one should not lose sight of the fact that the two mechanisms are different. Despite its implications for the assessment of the evidence, the doctrine of single infringement addresses a legal question – that is, whether, as a matter of law, there are one or more infringements of the competition rules – and identifies the criteria for determining this. By contrast, the presumption of continuity is intended to assist the Commission to discharge its burden of proof with respect to the duration of the infringement and each undertaking's participation in it.[77] This presumption may be justified on both positive and normative grounds. From a positive viewpoint, experience suggests that in ongoing offences – ie, offences which are committed over longer periods of time – there is typically a link between several acts which are temporally proximate. From a normative perspective, on the other hand, the presumption of continuity aims to safeguard the effectiveness of competition enforcement by enabling the Commission to establish the duration of competition infringements in situations where there is no evidence of their existence for some periods of time. In any event, the presumption of continuity becomes activated only when the Commission establishes the existence of facts which are 'sufficiently proximate in time'. One may thus wonder what evidentiary 'gap' may prevent its operation. Unsurprisingly, the EU Courts have explained that 'the question whether or not [the period separating two manifestations of infringing conduct] is long enough to constitute an interruption of the infringement cannot be examined in the abstract';[78] rather, 'it needs to be assessed in the context of the functioning' of the infringement in question.[79] In practice, varying lengths of 'gap' have been found to preclude the Commission from relying on the presumption of continuity: seven years in *Dunlop Slazenger*;[80] 15 months in *Volkswagen*;[81]

[75] ibid paras 216–18; Case T-655/11 *FSL and Others v Commission*, ECLI:EU:T:2015:383, para 484; Joined Cases T-147/09 and T-148/09 *Trelleborg Industrie and Others v Commission*, ECLI:EU:T:2013:259, paras 85–89.

[76] Case T-43/92 *Dunlop Slazenger v Commission*, ECLI:EU:T:1994:79, para 79.

[77] Note that the existence of a single infringement and each undertaking's participation in it are two distinct issues.

[78] *ICAP* (n 50) para 220.

[79] ibid.

[80] *Dunlop* (n 76) paras 80–84. The Commission had relied on two letters prohibiting exports that Dunlop had sent in 1977 and in 1985 respectively in order to establish that the illegal conduct had continued uninterrupted in the seven-year period between them, but the GCEU dismissed this evidence as insufficient to demonstrate the existence of a continuous infringement.

[81] Case T-62/98 *Volkswagen v Commission*, ECLI:EU:T:2000:180, paras 190–92. The GCEU annulled the Commission's decision insofar as the latter found that the infringement in question, which consisted

16 months in *IMI*;[82] almost 16 months in *Quinn Barlo*;[83] more than three years in *Gosselin*;[84] two years in *Trelleborg*;[85] five months in *FSL*;[86] and seven weeks in *ICAP*.[87]

Although the assessment of sufficient temporal proximity is inevitably fact-dependent, one may extract a few guiding principles from this jurisprudence. Indeed, it is clear that the mere fact that the undertaking participated in the cartel both before and after the period concerned may be relevant, but it is not sufficient for the presumption of continuity to apply.[88] Moreover, this presumption seems less likely to be triggered where the gap considerably exceeds 'the intervals at which the undertakings … habitually manifested their respective intentions to restrict competition'.[89] In this regard, the features of the infringement and market in question may be highly pertinent. In *FSL*, for instance, the fact that 'price negotiations in the banana business occur every week' was taken into account by the GCEU when it concluded that a five-month gap prevented the Commission from presuming continuity.[90] Similarly, in *ICAP*, the fact that the LIBOR rate is set on a daily basis played a role in the GCEU's conclusion that a gap of only seven weeks did not allow the Commission to find that the infringement had continued during that period.[91] On the other hand, the fact that the content of certain contacts among the undertakings in question has not been identified may not necessarily exclude the presumption of continuity. As explained in *FMC Foret*, 'the Commission must be able to apply conclusions drawn from periods where the evidence is fairly solid to other periods where the gap between the various pieces of evidence is perhaps larger'.[92] Where there is a general pattern of anti-competitive conduct:

> [T]here will … need to be a particularly good explanation in order to convince a court of law that in a particular phase of a series of meetings things occurred which were completely different from what had transpired at earlier and subsequent meetings when those meetings were attended by the same people, took place under similar external conditions and indisputably had the same purpose.[93]

of hindering exports, had continued between October 1996 and January 1998 merely on the ground that Volkswagen had allegedly not issued a clear declaration that the unlawful measures had been cancelled after receiving the authority's statement of objections and despite the existence of evidence indicating that the violation had ceased.

[82] Case T-18/05 *IMI and Others v Commission*, ECLI:EU:T:2010:202, paras 90–96.

[83] Case T-208/06 *Quinn Barlo and Others v Commission*, ECLI:EU:T:2011:701, paras 158–65.

[84] Joined Cases T-208/08 and T-209/08 *Gosselin Group and Stichting Administratiekantoor Portielje v Commission*, ECLI:EU:T:2011:287, paras 160–68.

[85] *Trelleborg Industrie* (n 75) paras 66–67.

[86] *FSL* (n 75) paras 494–97.

[87] *ICAP* (n 50) paras 235–37.

[88] *Gosselin* (n 84) para 161.

[89] *IMI* (n 82) para 96; *Quinn Barlo* (n 83) para 165; *Gosselin* (n 84) para 166.

[90] *FSL* (n 75) para 497.

[91] *ICAP* (n 50) para 237.

[92] Case T-191/06 *FMC Foret v Commission*, ECLI:EU:T:2011:277, para 127.

[93] ibid.

Last but not least, the lack of communication for a period of time may not prevent the authority from relying on the presumption of continuity where the effects of the last-established incidence of anti-competitive behaviour extend to the weeks or months for which evidence is missing. For example, in *Villeroy & Boch and Others*, the GCEU upheld the Commission's finding of continuity of the applicant's participation in the infringement, despite the existence of a gap of about one-and-a-half years, since every meeting essentially fixed the prices by which the cartelists would abide in the following year.[94]

In any event, these broad directions are subject to an important caveat: the presumption of continuity does not relieve the Commission from the obligation positively to establish the start and the end of the undertaking's initial or resumed participation in the infringement in question.[95] In complex infringements in particular, which involve multiple products or territories, if the authority intends to hold an undertaking liable for the overall scope of the violation at hand, it must demonstrate the precise date on which the latter was – or should have been – aware of it. In *Guardian Industries*, for example, the GCEU agreed with the Commission that the applicants were responsible for the overall infringement since the first anti-competitive meeting they attended, in light of various pieces of evidence clearly showing that the cartel extended throughout the EU.[96] By contrast, in *Trafilerie* and *Fapricela*, the GCEU took the view that the applicants could not be held liable for the pan-European scope of the pre-stressing steel cartel from the beginning, since they had only taken part in meetings concerning specific countries and it was only later that they should have realised the EU-wide aspect of the anti-competitive arrangements.[97] At any rate, the Commission must specifically identify the end of the undertaking's involvement in the infringement, too. In *Solvay*, the GCEU emphasised that the authority may not 'decline to state, with supporting evidence, when the infringement ended',[98] whereas in *GDF Suez*, it underlined that the Commission may not infer the continuation of

[94] Joined Cases T-373/10, T-374/10, T-382/10 and T-402/10 *Villeroy & Boch and Others v Commission*, ECLI:EU:T:2013:455, para 272.

[95] In *Dow Chemical*, for example, the authority's finding that Dow Deutschland had taken part in a synthetic rubber cartel was partially annulled, insofar as the Commission identified 1 July 1996 as the starting date of its illegal behaviour, solely on account of the fact that on that date, an employee of another company which had participated in the cartel had been seconded to Dow. However, as the Court underlined, this fact 'does not, in itself, imply that the latter company automatically becomes a member of the cartel'. Case T-42/07 *Dow Chemical and Others v Commission*, ECLI:EU:T:2011:357, paras 88–96 and in particular para 93. See also Case T-21/09 *Dansk Rørindustri v Commission*, ECLI:EU:T:2002:74, para 62.

[96] Case T-82/08 *Guardian Industries and Guardian Europe v Commission*, ECLI:EU:T:2012:494, paras 82–91.

[97] Case T-422/10 *Trafilerie Meridionali v Commission*, ECLI:EU:T:2015:512, paras 108, 133–35, 197–98; and Case T-398/10 *Fapricela v Commission*, ECLI:EU:T:2015:498, paras 112–25.

[98] Case T-58/01 *Solvay v Commission*, ECLI:EU:T:2009:520, paras 292–304 and in particular para 302.

a violation merely from the absence of any evidence suggesting that it has been terminated.[99]

Turning now to the question of how the presumption of continuity may be reversed, undertakings may make two claims: either that the infringement in general or their participation in it in particular was interrupted; or that either was terminated at a date earlier than that identified by the Commission.[100] In practice, claims of interruption are more difficult to succeed than claims of termination. This is clearly illustrated in *Commission v Verhuizingen Coppens*, where an evidentiary gap of two years did not prevent the CJEU from upholding the Commission's finding that Coppens had continuously participated in the infringement in question for almost 11 years, in light of the lack of evidence of public distancing during the two years for which there was no evidence and of Coppens' active participation in the cartel after that period.[101] By contrast, in *Total Marketing Services*, a case concerning an alleged termination, the CJEU considered the absence of evidence of public distancing less decisive and – as noted earlier – 'only one factor amongst others to take into consideration with a view to establishing whether an undertaking has actually continued to participate in an infringement or has, on the contrary, ceased to do so'.[102] Inevitably, however, the assessment of whether the presumption of continuity should be reversed or not will be fact-specific. In *Trelleborg Industrie*, for instance, the GCEU accepted that 'the applicants' argument that they … interrupted their participation' for an intermediate period of more than two years was 'sufficiently substantiated and plausible to rebut the presumption', given the fact that during that time, 'the cartel's activity was reduced, or even non-existent, and … the lack of objective and consistent indicia that [they] intended to restart that cartel or subscribe to its objectives'.[103] Nevertheless, in general, modifications to the structure of the illegal arrangement or changes in the intensity of its operation,[104] variations in the undertakings' participation in it[105] or disagreements among the participants and tactical moves or strategies with a view to

[99] *GDF Suez* (n 47) paras 367–78. The GCEU partially annulled the authority's decision finding that a market-sharing agreement between the German and the French gas incumbents had lasted until at least 30 September 2005 in both the German and the French markets on the ground that, insofar as the burden of proof with respect to the duration of the violation rests on the Commission, the latter's argument that there was no evidence showing that the infringement in question had ended earlier on the French market could not be accepted.

[100] *Trelleborg Industrie* (n 75) para 63; Case T-423/10 *Redaelli Tecna v Commission*, ECLI:EU:T:2015:511, paras 186–88.

[101] Case C-441/11 P *Commission v Verhuizingen Coppens*, ECLI:EU:C:2012:778, para 75. For other cases involving claims of interruption, see Case T-26/06 *Trioplast Wittenheim v Commission*, ECLI:EU:T:2010:387, paras 48–49, where there was no evidence of participation in anticompetitive meetings for two years; Case T-377/06 *Comap v Commission*, ECLI:EU:T:2011:108, paras 101–03.

[102] *Total Marketing Services* (n 60) para 23.

[103] *Trelleborg Industrie* (n 75) paras 66–67.

[104] Case T-385/06 *Aalberts Industries and Others v Commission*, ECLI:EU:T:2011:114, para 105.

[105] Case T-322/01 *Roquette Frères v Commission*, ECLI:EU:T:2006:267, paras 189–202.

obtaining more concessions from the other members of the cartel[106] will not suffice to establish an interruption or termination.

D. The Presumption of Actual Exercise of Decisive Influence Over the Conduct of a Wholly Owned Subsidiary

The EU competition rules are addressed against 'undertakings'. As explained in the seminal *Höfner and Elser* case, the concept comprises 'any entity engaged in an economic activity, regardless of the legal status of that entity and the way in which it is financed'.[107] Further elaborating on this in *Hydrotherm*, the CJEU stressed that the term 'undertaking' must be understood as designating an economic – rather than a legal – unit.[108] In this regard, the existence of distinct legal entities is immaterial; what matters is – as elucidated in *Shell* – that there be a 'unitary organisation of personal, tangible and intangible elements which pursues a specific economic aim on a long-term basis and can contribute to the commission of an infringement'.[109] In the case of parent companies and subsidiaries in particular, such an economic unit will exist where 'the subsidiary does not decide independently upon its own conduct on the market, but carries out, in all material respects, the instructions given to it by the parent company'; according to settled jurisprudence, in these circumstances the anti-competitive conduct of the subsidiary may be imputed to the parent company.[110] As the CJEU confirmed in *Akzo*:

> In the specific case where a parent company has a 100% shareholding in a subsidiary which has infringed the [EU] competition rules, first, the parent company can exercise a decisive influence over the conduct of the subsidiary and, second, there is a rebuttable presumption that the parent company does in fact exercise a decisive influence over the conduct of its subsidiary.[111]

By contrast, where the parent company does not wholly own the subsidiary, it is for the Commission to demonstrate that '[decisive] influence actually was exerted … on the basis of factual evidence, including, in particular, any management power one of the undertakings may have over the other'.[112]

Relying on the *Akzo* presumption, the Commission has regularly held parent companies responsible for the anti-competitive transgressions of their wholly

[106] Case T-329/01 *Archer Daniels Midland v Commission*, ECLI:EU:T:2006:268, para 247; Case T-62/02 *Union Pigments v Commission*, ECLI:EU:T:2005:430, paras 36–42.
[107] Case C-41/90 *Höfner and Elser*, ECLI:EU:C:1991:161, para 21.
[108] Case 170/83 *Hydrotherm*, ECLI:EU:C:1984:271, para 11.
[109] Case T-11/89 *Shell v Commission*, ECLI:EU:T:1992:33, para 311.
[110] *Dyestuffs* (n 32) para 133; Case C-286/98 P *Stora Kopparbergs Bergslags v Commission*, ECLI:EU:C:2000:630, para 79.
[111] Case C-97/08 P *Akzo Nobel and Others v Commission*, ECLI:EU:C:2009:536, para 60.
[112] Case T-314/01 *Avebe v Commission*, EU:T:2006:266, para 136.

owned subsidiaries. In response, parent companies have fiercely fought back by challenging the authority's decisions before the EU Courts, usually on three grounds: first, that the rules governing parental liability are incompatible with the principle that responsibility for a competition violation is personal; second, that they pierce the corporate veil, thereby violating the principle of limited liability of company shareholders; and, third, that they contravene the principle of effective judicial protection, insofar as the presumption of decisive influence with respect to wholly owned subsidiaries is practically impossible to rebut. These concerns have been reverberated in scholarship too, with several commentators criticising the rules on parental liability in general and the *Akzo* presumption in particular.[113] However, while these two issues are certainly connected, it is crucial to appreciate that they are distinct. Indeed, the question whether the EU Courts' justification for the attribution to parent companies of liability for the anti-competitive conduct of their subsidiaries – ie, the argument that they constitute a 'single undertaking' – is sound as a matter of principle is fundamentally different from the question whether the *Akzo* presumption is appropriate for the purposes of establishing the existence of a 'single economic unit'. Regrettably, this point has been sometimes missed – as is evident in the ambiguous, yet frequent mentions of a so-called 'presumption of parental liability'.[114] The soundness of the EU Courts' justification for parental liability in EU competition law has been discussed elsewhere.[115] This section will focus only on the *Akzo* presumption.

Considering, first of all, the foundation of this presumption, it is clear that it may be justified on both positive and normative grounds. From a positive perspective, the *Akzo* presumption reflects our experience that parent companies invariably determine the way in which their wholly owned subsidiaries conduct themselves in the market due to the existence of strong links of property and control between them. From a normative perspective, on the other hand, this presumption echoes the idea that those with powers of supervision should be keeping an eye on the activities of their hierarchical subordinates to ensure

[113] See, eg, Marco Bronckers and Ann Vallery, 'No Longer Presumed Guilty? The Impact of Fundamental Rights on Certain Dogmas of EU Competition Law' (2011) 34 *World Competition* 535, 548–58; Yves Botteman, Julian Joshua and Laura Atlee, '"You Can't Beat the Percentage": The Parental Liability Presumption in EU Cartel Enforcement' [2012] *European Antitrust Review* 3; Stefan Thomas, 'Guilty of a Fault That One Has Not Committed: The Limits of the Group-Based Sanction Policy Carried out by the Commission and the European Courts in EU-Antitrust Law' (2012) 3 *Journal of European Competition Law & Practice* 11; Bettina Leupold, 'Effective Enforcement of EU Competition Law Gone Too Far? Recent Case Law on the Presumption of Parental Liability' (2013) 34 *European Competition Law Review* 570; John Temple Lang, 'How Can the Problem of the Liability of a Parent Company for Price-Fixing by a Wholly-Owned Subsidiary be Resolved?' (2014) 37 *Fordham International Law Journal* 1481, 1519–21. *cf* Lukas Solek and Stefan Wartinger, 'Parental Liability: Rebutting the Presumption of Decisive Influence' (2015) 6 *Journal of European Competition Law & Practice* 73.

[114] See, eg, the wording in Case C-521/09 P *Elf Aquitaine v Commission*, ECLI:EU:C:2011:620, para 52 and also the 'normative' justification of the presumption in para 59.

[115] Andriani Kalintiri, 'Revisiting Parental Liability in EU Competition Law' (2018) 43 *European Law Review* 145.

that their behaviour remains compliant with the law.[116] At this point, it should be noted that in the early stages of the development of the *Akzo* presumption, parent companies attempted to attack its empirical foundation by arguing that the existence of a 100 per cent shareholding may be indicative of the *ability* of the parent company to exercise decisive influence over the conduct of its subsidiary, but it is too weak to support in itself an inference that such decisive influence *actually* has been exercised.[117] However, any sympathy that the EU Courts had for this argument was rather short-lived.[118] Following *Akzo*, the typical response to similar challenges has been that a 100 per cent shareholding suffices in itself to activate the presumption that the parent company has actually shaped the conduct of its subsidiary.[119] In fact, the EU Courts have even gone two steps further: first, the parent company's stake in the subsidiary needs not be direct – indirect ownership through an intermediary company will suffice;[120] and, second, full ownership is no longer required – the presumption may be triggered even where the parent company's shareholding nears (but falls short of) 100 per cent.[121]

However, the question which has caused the greatest controversy is whether – and, if so, how – the *Akzo* presumption may be reversed. As explained already, one of the main criticisms against its operation has been that it is impossible for a parent company to show that even though it wholly owns the subsidiary, it has not actually exercised decisive influence over its conduct. This allegation is not unfounded. In practice, the *Akzo* presumption has never been successfully reversed;[122] the few instances where the Commission's decision was annulled were because the authority breached its duty to state reasons by failing to seriously examine the evidence submitted by the parent companies in question rather than because the presumption was found to have been rebutted.[123] Inevitably, the

[116] See also Case T-77/08 *Dow Chemical v Commission*, ECLI:EU:T:2012:47, para 101.

[117] *Stora Kopparbergs* (n 110) paras 22–23; *Akzo Nobel* (n 111) paras 43–47.

[118] Case C-286/98 P *Stora Kopparbergs Bergslags v Commission*, Opinion of AG Mischo, ECLI:EU:C:2000:263, para 48; Case T-325/01 *DaimlerChrysler v Commission*, ECLI:EU:T:2005:322, para 219; Joined Cases T-109/02, T-118/02, T-122/02, T-125/02, T-126/02, T-128/02, T-129/02, T-132/02 and T-136/02 *Bolloré v Commission*, ECLI:EU:T:2007:115, para 132.

[119] Since *Akzo*, the EU Courts have insisted that the reference to additional indicia in *Stora* was merely intended to identify all the elements on which the GCEU had based its reasoning (see, eg, Case T-112/05 *Akzo Nobel and Others v Commission*, ECLI:EU:T:2007:381, para 61; Joined Cases T-204/08 and T-212/08 *Team Relocations and Others v Commission*, ECLI:EU:T:2011:286, para 151).

[120] See, eg, Case C-90/09 P *General Química v Commission*, ECLI:EU:C:2011:21, paras 84–90.

[121] Case T-203/01 *Michelin v Commission*, ECLI:EU:T:2003:250, para 290; Case T-344/06 *Total v Commission*, ECLI:EU:T:2012:479, para 38; Case C-508/11 P *ENI v Commission*, ECLI:EU:C:2013:289, paras 47–49; Case C-501/11 P *Schindler Holding v Commission*, ECLI:EU:C:2013:522, para 109; Joined Cases T-389/10 and T-419/10 *SLM v Commission*, ECLI:EU:T:2015:513, para 376. Moreover, see Joined Cases T-379/10 and T-381/10 *Keramag Keramische Werke and Others v Commission*, ECLI:EU:T:2013:457, paras 313–15.

[122] In *Gosselin* (n 84) paras 51–58, the GCEU found that the presumption had been rebutted. However, the CJEU disagreed, eventually dismissing the action for annulment as unfounded: Case C-440/11 P *Commission v Stichting Administratiekantoor Portielje*, ECLI:EU:C:2013:514, paras 58–69.

[123] Case T-185/06 *L'Air liquide v Commission*, ECLI:EU:T:2011:275, paras 63–84; Case T-234/07 *Koninklijke Grolsch v Commission*, ECLI:EU:T:2011:476, paras 76–93; Case T-196/06 *Edison v Commission*, ECLI:EU:T:2011:281, paras 56–94; Case T-517/09 *Alstom v Commission*, ECLI:EU:T:2014:999, paras 97–118. See also *Elf Aquitaine* (n 114) paras 144–70.

EU Courts' repeated dismissals of the parent companies' efforts to reverse the *Akzo* presumption resulted in complaints that the latter contravenes the principle of effective judicial protection. However, EU judges have consistently defended its fairness by maintaining that even though it is difficult to rebut, the *Akzo* presumption 'remains within acceptable limits'. As explained in *Elf Aquitaine*, any evidence of the lack of actual exercise of decisive influence lies within the knowledge of parent companies and subsidiaries; accordingly, if mere unsubstantiated assertions were sufficient for its rebuttal, the presumption would be largely robbed of its usefulness.[124]

Parent companies' arguments and the EU Courts' reasoning merit deeper examination. Is the *Akzo* presumption indeed impossible to rebut and thus unfair? If not, why has no parent company succeeded in reversing it so far? To answer these questions, it is important to recall what the presumption is used for – that is, to establish the existence of a 'single economic unit' and thus an undertaking. However, the latter is independent of the question whether a connection between the unlawful outcome and the conduct of the parent company is required for liability to arise. In light of the EU Courts' insistence that competition responsibility is 'personal in nature', parent companies have – for the most part – attempted to reverse the *Akzo* presumption by arguing either that they played no role in the violation committed by their subsidiary or that they took steps to ensure that the latter would behave in compliance with Articles 101 and 102 TFEU. For instance, in *Schindler Holding*, the applicant claimed that not only did it give 'no instructions to its subsidiaries which might … have authorised or encouraged contacts contrary to Article [101 TFEU] and had no knowledge of any such contacts', but also that it had adopted a code of conduct and guidelines with the specific aim of keeping competition violations at bay.[125] Similarly, in other cases, parent companies have tried to reverse the presumption by arguing that they never operated in the sector affected by the infringement, or that their subsidiaries determined autonomously their day-to-day operations, their market acquisitions, the conclusion of contracts or their pricing policy.[126] In *Evonik Degussa*, the parent company had even explicitly instructed the sole manager of its subsidiary not to enter into agreements with competitors regarding the products in question, but its instructions had been blatantly disregarded.[127]

[124] *Elf Aquitaine* (n 114) paras 60–62; *Schindler Holding* (n 121) paras 107, 109.

[125] *Schindler Holding* (n 121) paras 85, 88.

[126] See, eg, Case T-197/06 *FMC v Commission*, ECLI:EU:T:2011:282, para 131; *ENI* (n 121) paras 64–67; *Keramag Keramische* (n 121) paras 308–322.

[127] Case C-155/14 P *Evonik Degussa v Commission*, ECLI:EU:C:2016:446, paras 15–16. In that case, the CJEU took the view that even the blatant disregard by a subsidiary of the parent company's specific instructions is insufficient to reverse the finding of a single economic unit where the subsidiary's failure to carry out those instructions 'is not the norm' (para 41). See also the Opinion of AG Mengozzi in this case: ECLI:EU:C:2015:529, paras 49–64; as well as Joined Cases C-293/13 P and C-294/13 P *Fresh Del Monte Produce v Commission*, ECLI:EU:C:2015:416, paras 96–97.

Nevertheless, all these claims have been dismissed by the EU Courts as irrelevant or insufficient. At first glance, the case law seems bizarre. However, on closer inspection, it is clear that such arguments were doomed to fail because the existence of a 'single economic unit' is not contingent on any sort of connection – whether direct or indirect – between the parent company and the violation in question. In other words, a single economic unit exists between a parent company and its wholly owned subsidiary thanks to the links of ownership and hierarchical control between them. Whether the former knew of the infringement, whether it took steps to prevent it, whether it played a more or less active role in the design of the subsidiary's commercial policy and so forth is irrelevant. What matters is whether the parent company and the subsidiary are sufficiently 'close' in financial, legal, organisational and structural terms so as to constitute a 'single economic unit'. This will almost always be the case where the parent company has a 100 per cent shareholding in the subsidiary, because of the typical 'spillover' implications this has for control. Accordingly, the *Akzo* presumption might only be reversed in exceptional circumstances. A rare example in this regard might be the case of pure financial investors: a parent company could in principle escape liability where its role was limited to providing financial assistance to the subsidiary and it lacked even the theoretical possibility of influencing in any way the latter's management.[128] Apart from this scenario, the Commission appears to have identified two further instances in which a parent company might theoretically evade liability: where it holds 100 per cent of the shares in the subsidiary only temporarily and for a short period; and where legal reasons prevent the parent company from fully exercising its control over the subsidiary.[129]

Understandably, however, these narrow circumstances will be the exception, not the norm. Therefore, contrary to the prevailing impression, the *Akzo* presumption is not fundamentally flawed. Its apparent 'irrefutability' can be largely explained, on the one hand, by the fact that parent companies and their wholly owned subsidiaries almost always constitute a 'single economic unit' and, on the other hand, by the mismatch between parent companies' perception of what they are 'blamed' for (ie, some sort of connection with the violation) and the actual rationale for the imputation of liability as developed by the EU Courts (ie, the 'single undertaking' argument). While the latter is unconvincing and problematic on several grounds, the *Akzo* presumption itself remains sound.

[128] Case C-97/08 P *Akzo Nobel and Others v Commission*, ECLI:EU:C:2009:262, Opinion of AG Kokott, fn 67; Case T-361/06 *Ballast Nedam v Commission*, ECLI:EU:T:2012:491, para 54. In practice, however, such arguments have been unsuccessful: see Case T-168/05 *Arkema v Commission*, ECLI:EU:T:2009:367, para 76; Case T-38/07 *Shell Petroleum v Commission*, ECLI:EU:T:2011:355, para 70; Case T-436/10 *Hit Groep v Commission*, ECLI:EU:T:2015:514, para 125; *ENI* (n 121) para 64. For an exception, see Case T-24/05 *Alliance One International v Commission*, ECLI:EU:T:2010:453, paras 143, 195.

[129] *Akzo Nobel* (n 128) Opinion of AG Kokott, fn 67.

E. The Presumption of Capability of Practices Which Lack Plausible Redeeming Virtues to Restrict Competition

It was explained earlier that the 'by object' classification should not be equated with a presumption of the existence of actual or likely anti-competitive effects in the market. Rather, the relevant criterion for prohibiting a practice as a 'by object' violation of the competition rules is whether it is an implausible source of efficiencies. By contrast, where the behaviour may in principle be explained on economic grounds, it may only be prohibited if it is likely to give rise to anti-competitive effects.[130] However, that said, a further qualification is necessary: once applied, the 'by object' label does activate a presumption – that is, that the practice at hand is *capable* of restricting competition or, more accurately, that it is *not incapable* of doing so. Indeed, once the Commission has established that there is a conduct which lacks a plausible procompetitive justification, it may presume that it has at the very least the capacity to restrict competition, unless the undertaking concerned produces evidence to the contrary. In other words, all the authority has to demonstrate is that the practice has been implemented; its anti-competitive potential is then presumed.

This presumption of capability may be deduced from well-established jurisprudence, although the word 'presumption' has not been explicitly employed as such by the EU Courts. In the context of Article 101 TFEU, the CJEU explained in *T-Mobile* that 'in order for a concerted practice to be regarded as having an anti-competitive object, it is sufficient that it has the potential to have a negative impact on competition'. As the Court elaborated, this means that it 'must simply be capable in an individual case, having regard to the specific legal and economic context, of resulting in the prevention, restriction or distortion of competition within the common market'.[131] The operation of such a presumption of capability is visible in the context of Article 102 TFEU as well. Indeed, the recent judgment of the CJEU in *Intel* suggests that practices which are deemed prima facie abusive are presumed to be capable of harming competition, unless the dominant undertaking challenges this conclusion 'on the basis of supporting evidence'.[132] Considering its rationale, it is clear that the presumption of capability rests on a strong positive

[130] See, eg, Case C-179/16 *F Hoffmann-La Roche and Others*, ECLI:EU:C:2018:25, para 78; Case C-67/13 P *CB v Commission*, ECLI:EU:C:2014:2204, paras 49–54. See also Luc Peeperkorn, 'Defining "By Object" Restrictions' (2015) 3 *Concurrences* 40; Pablo Ibáñez Colomo and Alfonso Lamadrid de Pablo, 'On the Notion of Restriction of Competition: What We Know and What We Don't Know We Know' in Damien Gerard, Massimo Merola and Bernd Meyring (eds), *The Notion of Restriction of Competition: Revisiting the Foundations of Antitrust Enforcement in Europe* (Bruylant, 2017); Pablo Ibáñez Colomo, 'The Future of Article 102 TFEU after *Intel*' (2018) 9 *Journal of European Competition Law & Practice* 293.

[131] *T-Mobile* (n 19) para 31.

[132] Case C-413/14 P *Intel v Commission*, ECLI:EU:C:2017:632, para 138. The CJEU held that the GCEU had committed an error of law when it refused to examine Intel's arguments that the rebates in question were not capable of restricting competition on the ground that such an analysis was not necessary.

and normative foundation. From a positive perspective, experience, common sense and economic theory tell us that conduct which lacks an economic justification has the intrinsic capacity to harm competition in the market concerned. Cartels are again a good example of this; naked price-fixing or market-sharing arrangements have an inherent anti-competitive potential, irrespective of whether they have actually given rise to – or are likely to give rise to – negative effects in the circumstances in question. From a normative viewpoint, on the other hand, the presumption of capability reinforces the idea that Articles 101 and 102 TFEU should be concerned only with conduct which may affect competition, other types of behaviour falling outside their purview.

Examining now how the presumption of capability may be reversed, the case law suggests that the undertaking in question must produce evidence showing that the practice lacks the very capacity to harm competition. To put it differently, it is necessary to demonstrate that the practice 'is not liable to impair competition'.[133] Inevitably, the question how the presumption of capability may be reversed is fact-specific and conduct-specific. Generally, a practice will not be 'liable to impair competition' in two scenarios. The first one involves situations where there is no competition – actual or potential – to restrict in the first place. This may be, for instance, the case due to the existence of national legislation eliminating any scope for competition[134] or of a de facto monopoly,[135] or due to the presence of intellectual property rights which are being lawfully exercised.[136] The second scenario involves situations where there is competition in the market, but the conduct lacks the very capacity to restrict it.

While the circumstances of the first scenario may be somewhat exceptional, challenging capability in the latter case will be genuinely more difficult. Indeed, showing incapability entails showing that there must exist no conceivable possibility for the conduct to affect competition. In this regard, the kind of the practice will play an important role. For instance, the capability of exchanges of commercially sensitive information to restrict competition will be hard to contest, considering that the harm – ie, the elimination of uncertainty in the market – becomes plausible as soon as competitors have communicated with each other. The fact that restrictive effects may not be likely to arise is insufficient for the presumption to be reversed – as *T-Mobile* and the *Bananas* cartel case clearly illustrate. Indeed, considering whether a one-off meeting where commercially sensitive information was exchanged is sufficient for a by object violation of Article 101(1) TFEU to arise, the CJEU stressed that '*the possibility could not be ruled out* that [such behaviour]

[133] Joined Cases C-403/08 and C-429/08 *Football Association Premier League and Others*, ECLI:EU:C:2011:631, para 140.

[134] *Suiker Unie* (n 50) paras 71–72; Joined Cases T-191/98 and T-212/98 to T-214/98 *Atlantic Container Line and Others v Commission*, ECLI:EU:T:2003:245, para 1130.

[135] Case T-360/09 *E.ON Ruhrgas and E.ON v Commission*, ECLI:EU:T:2012:332, paras 101–03; *GDF Suez* (n 47) paras 94–96. See also Case T-87/05 *EDP v Commission*, ECLI:EU:T:2005:333, para 117.

[136] Case T-198/98 *Micro Leader v Commission*, ECLI:EU:T:1999:341, paras 34, 56.

may, in principle, constitute a sufficient basis for the participating undertakings to concert their market conduct' (emphasis added).[137] Similarly, in the *Bananas* appeal, the EU Courts dismissed the applicants' argument that communications about price-setting factors among employees who lacked authorisation to set prices were incapable of harming competition on the ground that the information exchanges at hand '*made it possible* to reduce uncertainty for each of the participants as to the foreseeable conduct of competitors' (emphasis added).[138] For other practices, on the other hand, there might exist some greater room for manoeuvre. In relation to exclusivity rebates, for example, the CJEU acknowledged in *Intel* that the market power of the dominant undertaking, the share of the market covered by the scheme, its conditions, the duration and amount of the discounts, and the possible existence of a strategy aiming to exclude as-efficient competitors may indicate that the practice is incapable of harming competition.[139]

V. The Implications of the Presumptions Used in EU Competition Enforcement

Having examined the specifics of the main presumptions used in EU competition enforcement, it is necessary to reflect on their broader implications. In this respect, the following remarks are worth highlighting.

First of all, it is no coincidence that the most important presumptions – namely, that of a causal connection between concertation and subsequent market conduct, of participation in an anti-competitive meeting and of continuity – have been developed by the EU Courts in the context of fact-intensive proceedings, invariably involving cartels. Indeed, the main challenge of these cases lies in establishing the underlying facts; because undertakings are typically aware of the unlawfulness of their conduct, they try to minimise or destroy any evidence thereof. Since the burden of proof is borne by the Commission, its ability to enforce the antitrust rules would be seriously compromised if the authority were expected to produce evidence of every aspect and detail of the infringement. On the one hand, such evidence might not be available; on the other hand, even if it is available, its discovery may be too expensive without adding much to the overall assessment of the facts of the case. In recognition of these threats to the effectiveness and efficiency of cartel enforcement, the EU Courts progressively introduced some core presumptions with a view to easing the Commission's burden of proof. These presumptions have recalibrated the allocation of the onus of proof between the parties, shifting part of the evidentiary responsibility on undertakings. That said, it is important to note that the various presumptions are often employed cumulatively in the

[137] *T-Mobile* (n 19) para 59. See also paras 60–61.
[138] *Dole Food and Dole Fresh Fruit Europe* (n 47) paras 122, 134.
[139] *Intel* (n 132) para 139. For more, see Ibáñez Colomo (n 130) 300–03.

context of the same case – especially those involving complex infringements. For instance, the *Anic* presumption may be used in conjunction with the *Aalborg Portland* presumption and the presumption of continuity to establish an undertaking's participation in an illegal arrangement, whereas the presumption of decisive influence may be engaged in order to facilitate the imputation to parent companies of liability for the antitrust transgressions of their subsidiaries. The significance of these presumptions for the Commission may not be overstated; to a great extent, the success of cartel enforcement hinges on their operation.

Nevertheless, insofar as presumptions shift the burden of proof onto the other party, fairness issues may arise. As a matter of doctrine, the use of presumptions is not incompatible with the principle of effective judicial protection and the right to a fair trial. Drawing on the jurisprudence of the ECtHR, the EU Courts have underlined that:

> [A] presumption, even where it is difficult to rebut, remains within acceptable limits so long as it is proportionate to the legitimate aim pursued, it is possible to adduce evidence to the contrary and the rights of the defence are safeguarded.[140]

Accordingly, the fairness of the presumptions employed in EU competition enforcement seems to be contingent on the strength of their foundation, their rebuttability and on the undertakings' rights of defence being respected. As explained earlier, all the presumptions rest on solid positive and normative grounds. Their rebuttability, by contrast, calls for further examination. In principle, there is no doubt that they may be reversed; indeed, undertakings are allowed to produce evidence to that effect. However, in order to conclude on their fairness, it is necessary to consider what level of evidence is sufficient to rebut the presumption. In other words, do the presumptions developed by the EU Courts shift the burden of persuasion or do they merely shift the burden of production? In the former case, the undertakings concerned must disprove the presumed fact, whereas in the latter case, they must only bring forward evidence capable of calling it into question.[141] This discussion is not theoretical; as noted at the beginning of this chapter, presumptions which shift the burden of persuasion operate akin to defences and may thus completely change the dynamics between the parties.

Regrettably, the jurisprudence of the EU Courts is not explicit or entirely consistent on this issue. For example, the use of the phrase 'subject to proof to the contrary' in *Hüls* and *Anic*,[142] and the judicial understanding of 'public distancing'

[140] *Elf Aquitaine v Commission* (n 114) para 62, citing Case C-45/08 *Spector Photo Group v CBFA*, ECLI:EU:C:2009:806, paras 43–44; and *Janosevic v Sweden*, ECLI:CE:ECHR:2002:0723JUD003461997, para 101. See also *Salabiaku v France*, ECLI:CE:ECHR:1988:1007JUD001051983, para 28.

[141] As far as the *foundation* of the presumption is concerned, it is sufficient for undertakings to produce evidence capable of calling it into question, since the burden of proof thereof always remains with the Commission.

[142] *Anic* (n 46) para 121; *Hüls* (n 3346) para 162. See also Case C-455/11 P *Solvay v Commission*, ECLI:EU:C:2013:796, para 43.

as 'a means of excluding liability'[143] might imply that these presumptions shift the burden of persuasion. By contrast, the case law on the presumption of continuity suggests that it is at most the evidential burden which shifts on undertakings, since the duration of the conduct under examination is one of the constituent elements for establishing a violation of Articles 101 and 102 TFEU.[144] As far as the *Akzo* presumption is concerned, the emphasis placed by the EU Courts in *Elf Aquitaine* on the fact that evidence of the lack of actual exercise of decisive influence is apt to be found within the parent company's and the subsidiary's sphere of operations may connote that only the burden of production shifts. However, parent companies' and commentators' criticisms that the *Akzo* presumption is impossible to rebut reveals their perception that the latter has the effect of placing much more than merely an obligation on undertakings to produce evidence capable of calling the existence of a single economic unit into question. Last but not least, the existing jurisprudence on the presumption of capability does not allow definite conclusions on its procedural consequences. If *Intel* is any indication, it seems sufficient for undertakings to challenge the presumption 'on the basis of supporting evidence', in which case the authority is required positively to establish the capacity of the conduct to restrict competition.[145] However, Commission officials have publicly expressed a different view.[146]

Although the EU Courts have not addressed this question directly, it is submitted that in order for presumptions to be compatible with the principle of effective judicial protection, they should only impose on undertakings an obligation to adduce evidence capable of casting the issue in a different light. As noted above, a presumption 'remains within acceptable limits so long as … it is possible to adduce evidence to the contrary'. However, the possibility for undertakings to draw attention to relevant information which challenges the presumed fact does not entail the much heavier obligation which is intrinsic in the burden of persuasion. Moreover, one should not forget that most presumptions relate to the constituent elements of an antitrust offence – for instance, its duration or the entity's participation in it. Consequently, were they to shift the legal burden, the existing presumptions would contravene the principle that it is for the authority to establish the existence of an infringement, especially in cases where they are employed cumulatively. Nevertheless, the mere fact that a presumption is difficult to rebut does not mean that it operates akin to a defence or that it is unfair; it may simply convey that it has a

[143] *Westfalen Gassen* (n 58) para 103.

[144] Case T-264/12 *UTi Worldwide and Others v Commission*, ECLI:EU:T:2016:112, para 43. This explains why the burden of proof remains with the authority, even where the undertaking has argued that the limitation period has expired. See *Peróxidos Orgánicos* (n 71) para 52.

[145] *Intel* (n 132) paras 138–39.

[146] See the speech by Director-General Johannes Laitenberger, 'Accuracy and Administrability Go Hand in Hand' (CRA Conference, Brussels, 12 December 2017), available at http://ec.europa.eu/competition/speeches/text/sp2017_24_en.pdf.

strong positive basis. As explained earlier, all the presumptions developed by the EU Courts in the context of competition enforcement rest on solid positive and normative grounds. Therefore, it is unsurprising that the chances of a successful rebuttal are slim, without that impinging on their fairness.

That said, a final point is worth highlighting: presumptions as a mechanism are not a panacea. While they are hugely valuable as tools for redistributing the burden of proof and for improving the efficiency and effectiveness of the fact-finding process, they may not cure problems in the design of the law. Parental liability and exclusivity rebates exemplify this in an illustrative manner. In the case of parental liability, for instance, one might expect that abolishing the *Akzo* presumption, which has been heavily criticised as defective and unfair, would adequately address the existing concerns about the imputation to parent companies of liability for the anti-competitive behaviour of their wholly owned subsidiaries. However, such a 'solution' would be futile because the real problem lies not in the presumption – which is actually well-justified – but in the legal rule that parent companies may be held responsible for the anti-competitive acts of their subsidiaries where together they constitute a 'single undertaking'. Similarly, the existence of a rebuttable presumption that exclusivity rebates are capable of restricting competition, as per the CJEU's 'clarification' in *Intel*, may hardly compensate for the application of a legal test of prima facie illegality if the latter is not justified by the nature of the conduct at hand. The correct legal treatment of exclusivity rebates under Article 102 TFEU has been vigorously debated, with several scholars arguing that the Commission should only intervene where the practice is likely to harm competition.[147] Nevertheless, the EU Courts have consistently defended the view that exclusivity rebates offered by a dominant firm are abusive by their very nature.[148] While the 'clarification' in *Intel* is certainly welcome, insofar as it effectively obliges the authority to investigate the economic context within which the practice is implemented in greater depth, it does not (and cannot) go as far as imposing an obligation on the Commission to establish the existence of likely – rather than merely not implausible – anti-competitive effects. Consequently, the operation of a rebuttable presumption of capability in the case of exclusivity rebates may not rectify the application of an erroneous legal test, assuming that conduct of this kind should not be prohibited by its very nature.

[147] Hans Zenger, 'Loyalty Rebates and the Competitive Process' (2012) 8 *Journal of Competition Law and Economics* 717. On *Intel*, see, eg, Patrick Rey and James Venit, 'An Effects-Based Approach to Article 102: A Response to Wouter Wils' (2015) 38 *World Competition* 3; Damien Geradin, 'Loyalty Rebates after *Intel*: Time for the European Court of Justice to Overrule *Hoffman-La Roche*' (2015) 11 *Journal of Competition Law & Economics* 579; Pascale Déchamps and Gunnar Niels, 'The One Billion Euro Question for *Intel*: Moore's Law or Murphy's Law?' (2018) 9 *Journal of European Competition Law & Practice* 124. *cf* Wouter Wils, 'The Judgment of the EU General Court in *Intel* and the So-Called More Economic Approach to Abuse of Dominance' (2014) 37 *World Competition* 405.

[148] Case 85/76 *Hoffman-La Roche v Commission*, ECLI:EU:C:1979:36, para 89; *Intel* (n 132) para 137.

VI. Conclusion

Presumptions are a powerful tool in adjudication, insofar as they have the effect of redistributing the burden of proof between the parties. Nevertheless, their operation has caused much confusion. On the one hand, the lack of a clear definition has resulted in presumptions being conflated with other mechanisms, such as substantive rules and inferences. On the other hand, their procedural consequences – that is, whether they shift the burden of persuasion with respect to the presumed issue or merely the burden of production – have been long yet inconclusively debated.

In this light, the aim of this chapter has been to clarify the use of presumptions in EU competition enforcement. To this end, a crucial distinction was drawn between presumptions in the technical sense of the word – namely, inferences that the decision-maker is entitled but also required to make, and that the party against whom they operate can rebut – and related concepts, such as proxies and premises which often underpin the design, for instance, of competition legal tests and safe harbours. Focusing on the former, the following main presumptions were identified in the jurisprudence of the EU Courts: the *Anic* and *Aalborg Portland* presumptions of participation in a collusive arrangement; the *Dunlop* presumption of continuity; the *Akzo* presumption that a parent company has exercised decisive influence over the conduct of its wholly owned subsidiary; and the presumption that practices which lack plausible redeeming virtues are not incapable of restricting competition. As the analysis has demonstrated, these presumptions are well-embedded in competition enforcement and rest on solid positive and normative foundations. By contrast, the way in which they may be rebutted and their effect on the burden of proof are less clear. On this basis, it was submitted that in order for presumptions to be compatible with the principle of effective judicial protection, they should only impose on undertakings an obligation to adduce evidence capable of casting the issue in a different light. Moreover, it was stressed that presumptions are not a panacea; while they may contribute to the efficiency and effectiveness of the fact-finding process, they may not cure problems in the design of the substantive law.

In any event, the assessment of evidence in EU competition enforcement is to some extent intertwined with the control that the EU Courts exercise over the Commission's decisions. Therefore, it is necessary to consider how evidence standards and standards of judicial review operate together.

7

Evidence Standards and Standards of Judicial Review

I. Introduction

The rules on the burden and standard of proof and the principles of unfettered production and unfettered evaluation of the evidence – as fleshed out in the EU Courts' jurisprudence – compose a flexible, yet well-defined framework for assessing evidence in the context of antitrust and merger decision-making. At the same time, however, evidence standards form an intrinsic part of the judicial scrutiny to which the legality of Commission decisions may be subject. In this sense, issues of proof and issues of judicial review cannot be entirely disentangled. With this in mind, this chapter explores how standards of evidence assessment and standards of judicial review interact in EU competition enforcement. To this end, section II describes the two thresholds of control that the EU Courts traditionally apply when they scrutinise Commission decisions – namely *full* and *marginal* review – and sets out the fairness concerns against the operation of a 'manifest error of assessment' test in light of the features of the administrative model of enforcement in place. With these remarks in mind, section III then considers the interplay between evidence standards and standards of judicial review. Identifying first the evidence-related pleas that parties may submit before the EU Courts, the analysis focuses on the operation of the applicable evidence standards in the judicial scrutiny of 'complex economic appraisals' and reflects on the implications of the evidence qualification of the 'manifest error of assessment' test for marginal review.

II. Standards of Judicial Review and Fairness Concerns

A. *Full* and *Marginal* Review

The lawfulness of Commission decisions finding a violation of the antitrust rules or prohibiting or authorising a notified concentration may be scrutinised by the EU Courts in the context of an action for annulment before the GCEU or an appeal before the CJEU.[1] However, the strictness of the judicial control may vary depending on its subject matter. As explained in Chapter 2, questions of fact and issues of law are subject to comprehensive review, and the EU Courts are expected thoroughly to scrutinise Commission decisions for errors in the authority's factual findings or its interpretation of the legal rules.[2] By contrast, policy choices and complex assessments are in principle subject to marginal review.[3] The latter is thought to connote a less strict threshold of judicial scrutiny, which allows the Commission some latitude and entails checking 'whether the relevant procedural rules have been complied with, whether the statement of the reasons for the decision is adequate, whether the facts have been accurately stated and whether there has been a manifest error of appraisal or misuse of powers'.[4]

The rationales underpinning judicial deference with respect to policy choices and complex economic evaluations have been well documented in the literature.[5] As far as policy matters are concerned, the main argument for limited review derives from the allocation of competences among EU institutions. According to the Treaties, the Commission is responsible for ensuring that the competition rules are being properly enforced and for articulating competition policy. The exercise of the authority's *discretion* in this respect is manifested in multiple ways – for instance, the design of its fining strategy,[6] the setting of enforcement priorities through the handling of complaints,[7] or the choice of its preferred enforcement tool.[8] Since the Commission's power to make policy choices has constitutional foundations, a standard of review which would encroach upon its competence in the field of competition would take issue with the doctrine of powers separation, as well as the democratic principle. Accordingly, limited review in these circumstances is said to operate as a mechanism for ensuring inter-institutional balance. Each institution is confined to its allocated role; the Commission designs

[1] Article 263 TFEU; Recital 33 of Regulation 1/2003 and art 21(2) EUMR. According to art 261 TFEU, art 31 of Regulation 1/2003 and art 16 EUMR, the EU Courts have unlimited jurisdiction with regard to penalties imposed by the Commission.

[2] eg, Case C-272/09 P *KME Germany and Others v Commission*, ECLI:EU:C:2011:810, para 102; Case C-386/10 P *Chalkor v Commission*, ECLI:EU:C:2011:815, para 62.

[3] eg, Case T-201/04 *Microsoft v Commission*, ECLI:EU:T:2007:289, paras 87–88; Case T-21/05 *Chalkor v Commission*, ECLI:EU:T:2010:205, para 63.

[4] Case 42/84 *Remia v Commission*, ECLI:EU:C:1985:327, para 34; Joined Cases 142/84 and 156/84 *British American Tobacco and Reynolds Industries v Commission*, ECLI:EU:C:1987:490, para 62; Case T-271/03 *Deutsche Telekom v Commission*, ECLI:EU:T:2008:101, para 185; Case T-336/07 *Telefónica and Telefónica de España v Commission*, ECLI:EU:T:2012:172, para 69; Case T-360/09 *E.ON Ruhrgas and E.ON v Commission*, ECLI:EU:T:2012:332, para 69.

[5] For an account of the traditional reasons for judicial deference in the context of commercial regulation, see Jaime Arancibia, *Judicial Review of Commercial Regulation* (Oxford University Press, 2011) 15–32.

[6] eg, Joined Cases C-322/07 P, C-327/07 P and C-338/07 P *Papierfabrik August Koehler and Others v Commission*, ECLI:EU:C:2009:500, para 112.

[7] eg, Case T-193/02 *Piau v Commission*, ECLI:EU:T:2005:22, para 80; Case T-229/05 *AEPI v Commission*, ECLI:EU:C:2007:224, para 38.

[8] eg, DG Competition, 'To Commit or Not to Commit: Deciding between Prohibition and Commitments' (Competition Policy Brief, 2014).

and implements competition policy, whereas the EU Courts merely control its way of doing so.

Beyond policy matters, the doctrine of judicial deference also becomes engaged where the Commission's decision-making entails complex economic evaluations. In this case, the EU Courts' unwillingness to interfere with the authority's appraisals has been explained by reference to the latter's presumed superiority in terms of expertise and experience. Indeed, over the years, the Commission has improved the quality of its decision-making by introducing internal checks and balances, and has increased its capacity in economics by establishing a special department headed by the Chief Economist and run with the help of a group of highly qualified economists. Unsurprisingly, this has strengthened its ability to perform complex economic evaluations and double-check their soundness. Comparing the Commission's nature as a specialised agency with the EU judges' generalist background, it makes sense from an efficiency perspective – so the argument goes – to allow the authority a degree of leeway in its performance of complex economic evaluations. In these circumstances, its conclusions will be checked through the lens of the 'manifest error of assessment' test.[9]

B. The Fairness Concerns against Marginal Review

Nevertheless, these justifications have not prevented objections against the seemingly deferential attitude of the EU Courts towards the Commission's policy choices and complex economic assessments. Beyond its implications for the boundaries of the relationship between the two institutions, the operation of a 'manifest error of assessment' threshold of judicial control has triggered fears of an overly relaxed judicial scrutiny. The thrust of the concerns may be synopsised in the claim that the EU Courts' control over Commission decisions falls short of the prescriptions of the principle of effective judicial protection and the right to a fair trial, insofar as it fails to compensate for the 'fairness deficit' in the administrative competition proceedings.[10] The following paragraphs briefly elaborate on this claim with respect to antitrust and merger proceedings respectively.

[9] The concepts of 'discretion' and 'appreciation' are not identical: *discretion* refers to the Commission's policy choices, whereas its margin of *appreciation* pertains to complex economic evaluations. See also Case C-40/03 P *Rica Foods v Commission*, ECLI:EU:C:2005:93, Opinion of AG Léger, paras 45–49, who distinguishes between 'political' and 'technical' discretion. Note that while both policy choices and complex economic evaluations are subject to a 'manifest error of assessment' test, the criteria for identifying such an error are distinct. As AG Kokott clarified in her Opinion in *Spanish Tobacco*, the Commission's exercise of discretion is subject to the general principles of EU law and fundamental rights (Joined Cases C-628/10P and C-14/11P *Alliance One International and Others v Commission*, ECLI:EU:C:2012:11, Opinion of AG Kokott, para 48) (see, eg, Case C-441/07 P *Commission v Alrosa*, ECLI:EU:C:2010:377; Case T-133/07 *Mitsubishi Electric v Commission*, ECLI:EU:T:2011:345, para 269). By contrast, its margin of appreciation is controlled against the *Tetra Laval* formula, on which the analysis in this chapter focuses (see section III.B.i below).

[10] These concerns have led to proposals for institutional reform, including the internal separation of the Commission's investigative and decision-making powers in order to ensure its independence and

i. Fairness Concerns in Antitrust Enforcement

In the sphere of antitrust, the compatibility of the applicable standards of judicial review with Article 6(1) ECHR was questioned when the gradual imposition of ever-higher fines for violations of Articles 101 and 102 TFEU brought the fairness of the administrative model of EU competition enforcement into the spotlight.

According to the ECtHR's 'composite approach',[11] in order for administrative systems of justice to be compatible with the right to a fair trial, one of the following conditions must apply: either, at the administrative level, decisions must be made by a body that qualifies as 'an independent and impartial tribunal established by law'; or, at the judicial level, the person who has been adversely affected by a decision of the administrative authority must be afforded the possibility to appeal to a 'judicial body that has full jurisdiction and does provide the guarantees of Article 6(1)'.[12] However, as noted in Chapter 2, the Commission combines the functions of the prosecutor, the investigator and the decision-maker, and thus cannot be characterised as an 'independent and impartial tribunal established by law'.[13] Consequently, in view of the authority's current organisational structure and institutional features, the fairness of EU antitrust enforcement appears to depend on whether the EU Courts exercise 'full jurisdiction' in the meaning of the ECtHR's jurisprudence.

However, the concept of 'full jurisdiction' has proved rather enigmatic. As the ECtHR explained in *Janosevic*, this includes 'the power to quash in all respects, on questions of fact and law, the challenged decision'.[14] Yet, it is not entirely clear whether this form of judicial control can accommodate a deferential approach to policy matters or complex economic assessments.[15] The ECtHR's jurisprudence

impartiality. See, eg, Arianna Andreangeli et al, 'Enforcement by the Commission: The Decisional and Enforcement Structure in Antitrust Cases and the Commission's Fining System' in Massimo Merola and Denis Waelbroeck (eds), *Towards an Optimal Enforcement of Competition Rules in Europe: Time for a Review of Regulation 1/2003?* (Bruylant, 2010) 199–270; John Temple Lang, *Three Possibilities for Reform of the Procedure of the European Commission in Competition Cases under Regulation 1/2003* (Centre for European Policy Studies, 2011) 213 ff.

[11] *Le Compte, Van Leuven and de Meyere v Belgium*, ECLI:CE:ECHR:1981:0623JUD000687875, para 51.

[12] *Albert and Le Compte v Belgium*, ECLI:CE:ECHR:1983:0210JUD000729975, para 29.

[13] Donald Slater, Sébastien Thomas and Denis Waelbroeck, *Competition Law Proceedings before the European Commission and the Right to a Fair Trial: No Need for Reform?* (Global Competition Law Centre, College of Europe, Working Paper 04/2008) 26–29; Ian Forrester, 'Due Process in EC Competition Cases: A Distinguished Institution with Flawed Procedures' (2009) 34 *European Law Review* 817, 822–23; Nils Hauger and Christoph Palzer, 'Investigator, Prosecutor, Judge … and Now Plaintiff? The Leviathanian Role of the European Commission in the Light of Fundamental Rights' (2013) 36 *World Competition* 565.

[14] *Janosevic v Sweden*, ECLI:CE:ECHR:2002:0723JUD003461997, para 81. Note also *Compagnie des Gaz de Petrole Primagaz v France*, ECLI:CE:ECHR:2010:1221JUD002961308, paras 23–33, where the ECtHR found that judicial review which does not entail an examination of the factual issues does not comply with the requirement for 'full jurisdiction'.

[15] The ECtHR's position in *Kyprianou v Cyprus*, ECLI:CE:ECHR:2005:1215JUD007379701, has been cited as authority that a 'manifest error of assessment' test is no longer sustainable in light of the requirement for 'full jurisdiction' (eg, Donald Slater and Denis Waelbroeck, '"Marginal Review" by the

appears to suggest an affirmative answer. As acknowledged in *Bryan v United Kingdom*, 'specialised areas of law' involving 'a panoply of policy matters' call for a qualified 'approach by an appeal tribunal on questions of fact, particularly where the facts have already been established in the course of a quasi-judicial procedure governed by many of the safeguards required by Article 6, paragraph 1'.[16] In contrast, in *Tsfayo v United Kingdom*, where the dispute at hand was 'a simple question of fact', deference to the administrative body could not be justified, as the issue to be determined did not require 'a measure of professional knowledge or experience and the exercise of administrative discretion pursuant to wider policy aims', and the factual findings in this case could not 'be said to be merely incidental to the reaching of broader judgments of policy or expediency with it was for the democratically accountable authority to make'.[17] Therefore, the ECtHR's jurisprudence indicates that the concept of 'full jurisdiction' is not necessarily irreconcilable with the exercise of marginal review with respect to policy matters or complex assessments.

Against this backdrop, in *Menarini* the ECtHR scrutinised the Italian system of competition enforcement – which resembles the EU model – and found that, insofar as it provided for a full review of the facts and the law, and unlimited jurisdiction of the courts with respect to fines, it did not violate the sanctioned cartelist's right to a fair trial.[18] Yet, the ECtHR's ruling has not been sufficient to soothe concerns that the EU Courts' control fails to provide effective judicial protection to undertakings against which an infringement finding has been made and a hefty financial penalty has been imposed.[19] Although in *Schindler Holding* the EU Courts endorsed *Menarini* and explicitly declared the compatibility of their judicial review with Article 6(1) ECHR and the principle of effective

European Court of Justice in Competition Cases and its Compatibility with Fundamental Rights' in Massimo Merola and Jacques Derenne (eds), *The Role of the Court of Justice of the European Union in Competition Law Cases* (Bruylant, 2012) 288). Indeed, in its ruling, the ECtHR took the view that: 'As a court of appeal, the Supreme Court did not have full competence to deal de novo with the case, but could only review the first instance judgment for possible legal or manifest factual errors' (para 44). However, one must bear in mind not only the circumstances of the case and the 'manifest factual errors' involved (that is, the lower's court appreciation regarding the imposition of a sentence for contempt of court), but also the fact that when referred to the Grand Chamber, in delivering its judgment on 15 December 2005, the latter chose not to repeat the language of the Chamber and simply held that the Supreme Court had the power to quash the decision of the lower court, but declined to do so and thus the impartiality defect was not remedied (paras 134–35).

[16] *Bryan v United Kingdom*, ECLI:CE:ECHR:1995:1122JUD001917891, para 47; note also *Zumtobel v Austria*, ECLI:CE:ECHR:1993:0921JUD001223586, paras 31–32.

[17] *Tsfayo v United Kingdom*, ECLI:CE:ECHR:2006:1114JUD006086000, para 46.

[18] *A Menarini Diagnostics SRL v Italy*, ECLI:CE:ECHR:2011:0927JUD004350908, paras 57–67.

[19] See, eg, Lyubomir Talev, 'ECHR Implications in the EU Competition Enforcement' ('Due Process and Innovation in EU Competition Law', Centre for European Policy Studies, Brussels, 16 April 2010) 49–51; Marco Bronckers and Anne Vallery, 'Fair and Effective Competition Policy in the EU: Which Role for Authorities and Which Role for the Courts after *Menarini*?' (2012) 8 *European Competition Journal* 283, 297; Mario Siragusa, 'Annulment Proceedings in Antitrust Cases (Articles 101 and 102 TFEU) – Standard of Judicial Review over Substantive Issues' in Merola and Derenne (n 15) 135–37.

judicial protection,[20] arguments that 'full jurisdiction' is not reconcilable with any deference to the Commission have persisted. With regard to complex assessments in particular, a frequent concern has been that since such evaluations are based upon facts, a hands-off judicial scrutiny results in practice in the EU Courts declining their obligation comprehensively to review questions of fact. On this basis, it has been suggested that marginal review should be abolished as incompatible with Article 6(1) ECHR and as not reflecting the high level of scrutiny that the EU Courts exercise in reality.[21]

ii. Fairness Concerns in Merger Enforcement

Due to the criminal – or at least quasi-criminal – nature of antitrust fines, the compatibility of the administrative model of EU competition enforcement with the principle of effective judicial protection, as inspired by the right to a fair trial, has been predominantly debated by reference to antitrust proceedings. In contrast, the fairness of merger control has attracted relatively less attention – possibly because of the lack of financial sanctions and thanks to the famous trilogy of merger annulments in *Airtours*, *Schneider Electric* and *Tetra Laval*,[22] which were received by the competition community as a vivid illustration of the strict control that the EU Courts exercise over the Commission.[23]

Nevertheless, the absence of fines in decisions prohibiting a concentration does not automatically imply that judicial review in merger proceedings complies

[20] Case C-501/11 P *Schindler Holding and Others v Commission*, ECLI:EU:C:2013:522, paras 33–38. *cf* earlier Case E-15/10 *Posten Norge v ESA* [2012] EFTA Ct Rep 246, paras 84–102 and in particular paras 100–02, where, drawing on the ECtHR's jurisprudence, the EFTA Court interpreted art 6(1) ECHR as requiring that 'when imposing fines for infringement of the competition rules, ESA cannot be regarded to have any margin of discretion in the assessment of complex economic matters which goes beyond the leeway that necessarily flows from the limitations inherent in the system of legality review' and held that 'the submission that the Court may intervene only if it considers a complex economic assessment of ESA to be manifestly wrong must be rejected'.

[21] Editorial Comments, 'Towards a More Judicial Approach? EU Antitrust Fines under the Scrutiny of Fundamental Rights' (2011) 48 *Common Market Law Review* 1405, 1410–12; Wouter Wils, 'The Compatibility with Fundamental Rights of the EU Antitrust Enforcement System in Which the European Commission Acts Both as Investigator and as First-Instance Decision Maker' (2014) 37 *World Competition* 5, 16–17.

[22] Case T-342/99 *Airtours v Commission*, ECLI:EU:T:2002:146; Case T-310/01 *Schneider Electric v Commission*, ECLI:EU:T:2002:254; Case T-5/02 *Tetra Laval v Commission (Tetra Laval I)*, ECLI:EU:T:2002:264.

[23] Anthony Valcke and Francisco Todorov, 'Judicial Review of Merger Control Decisions in the European Union' (2006) 51 *Antitrust Bulletin* 339, 340; John Davies and Robert Schlossberg, '"Once More Unto the Breach, Dear Friends": Judicial Review of Antitrust Agency Merger Clearance Decisions' (2006–07) 21 *Antitrust* 17, 21; James Killick, 'Case Comment: The *GE/Honeywell* Judgment – in Reality Another Merger Defeat for the Commission' (2007) 28 European Competition Law Review 52, 60; Michael Harkera, Sebastian Peyera and Kathryn Wright, 'Judicial Scrutiny of Merger Decisions in the EU, the UK and Germany' (2011) 60 *International and Comparative Law Quarterly* 93, 117. *cf* the early approach of the EU Courts as presented by Adrian Brown, 'Judicial Review of Commission Decisions under the Merger Regulation: The First Cases' (1994) 15 *European Competition Law Review* 296, 305; Suyong Kim, Anne Vallery and Deirdre Waters, 'Judicial Review of Mergers' (2005) 10 *European Antitrust Review* 40, 42.

with the principle of effective judicial protection and the right to a fair trial. While merger control is not punitive in nature, Article 47 CFR and Article 6(1) ECHR also become engaged where 'civil rights and obligations' are involved.[24] In this regard, the problems associated with the multiple roles of the Commission are no less present in merger control than in antitrust infringement proceedings.[25] Although significant checks and balances were introduced in the last major reform of the EUMR in order to ensure due process and improve the transparency and quality of the authority's decision-making, the Commission still enjoys substantial powers – including the power to investigate a notified concentration and object to it, to gather evidence and to impose far-reaching structural and behavioural remedies on the merging undertakings.[26]

In this context, judicial review plays an important role: it serves as an essential safeguard of the fairness of merger control by ensuring that Commission decisions do not unduly encroach upon the economic freedom of undertakings. Accordingly, the question arises as to whether a marginal standard of review with respect to complex economic assessments conforms to the expectations of the principle of effective judicial protection and the right to a fair trial. This question emerges all the more forcefully because judicial deference in merger enforcement arguably emanates from the very scheme of the EUMR. Indeed, as early as in *Kali and Salz*, the CJEU clarified that:

> [T]he basic provisions of the Regulation, in particular Article 2 thereof, confer on the Commission a certain discretion, especially with respect to assessments of an economic nature. Consequently, review by the [EU] judicature of the exercise of that discretion, which is essential for defining the rules on concentrations, must take account of the discretionary margin implicit in the provisions of an economic nature which form part of the rules on concentrations.[27]

Accordingly, the existence of a margin of appreciation for the Commission seems to be an integral and indispensable feature of the merger control system.

Considered in conjunction with the Commission's double legal burden, as described in Chapter 3, it may be argued that limited review in merger enforcement is necessary to counterbalance the authority's obligation to always reach a positive finding on the compatibility or incompatibility of a concentration with the common market in accordance with the symmetrical structure of the legal test in Article 2(2) and (3) EUMR. Indeed, such an argument would find support

[24] Note that the text of art 47 CFR is not specific to criminal charges: 'Everyone whose rights and freedoms guaranteed by the law of the Union are violated has the right to an effective remedy before a tribunal in compliance with the conditions laid down in this Article.'

[25] Kyriakos Fountoukakos, 'Judicial Review and EC Merger Control: Reflections on the Effectiveness of the System with Regard to the Standard of Review and Speed' (2008) 10 *Cambridge Yearbook of European Legal Studies* 133, 136–37.

[26] See also General Electric's arguments in Case T-210/01 *General Electric v Commission*, ECLI:EU:T:2005:456, para 425.

[27] Joined Cases C-68/94 and C-30/95 *France and Société Commerciale des Potasses and de l'Azote and Entreprise Minière and Chimique v Commission (Kali and Salz)*, ECLI:EU:C:1998:148, paras 223–24.

in settled merger case law that 'the burden of proof placed on the Commission is without prejudice to its wide discretion in that sphere'.[28] However, one might protest that since merger analysis is almost entirely based on complex economic estimations about the market conditions and the prospective impact of the notified concentration on competition, marginal review essentially turns out to be the default threshold of judicial control rather than then exception. In this case, the effective judicial protection of merging entities against Commission decisions interfering with their fundamental rights might arguably be compromised.[29]

III. The Interplay between Evidence Standards and Standards of Judicial Review

Evidence assessment forms an intrinsic part of the control exercised by the EU Courts; when scrutinising the legality of a Commission decision, EU judges inevitably have regard to the relevant evidence. The question thus emerges as to how the operation of two different thresholds of judicial scrutiny – *full* and *marginal* review – may affect the assessment of the evidence and the inquiry into whether the applicable evidence standards have been complied with. The answer to this is crucial in view of the fairness concerns described above, but not obvious – particularly where 'complex economic evaluations' are involved. Does the operation of a 'manifest error of assessment' test in these circumstances signify that the Commission enjoys some degree of latitude in its interpretation of the available evidence on account of its 'experience and expertise' as a specialised agency? This section examines the interplay between evidence standards and standards of judicial review in EU competition enforcement with a view to illuminating the terms of their symbiosis.

A. Evidence-Related Pleas before the EU Courts

Broadly speaking, the burden of proof, the standard of proof and the various standards determining the admissibility and probative value of the evidence are procedural rules which the Commission must observe when assessing evidence and making decisions under Articles 101 and 102 TFEU or the EUMR. Indeed, as AG Tizzano stressed in his Opinion in *Tetra Laval II*, the EU judicature is entrusted with 'monitoring observance of the rules of law and in particular those relating to

[28] Case T-48/04 *Qualcomm v Commission*, ECLI:EU:T:2009:212, para 89; Case T-175/12 *Deutsche Börse v Commission*, ECLI:EU:T:2015:148, para 378.

[29] George Cumming, *Merger Decisions and the Rules of Procedure of the European Community Courts* (Kluwer Law International, 2011) 229–30.

procedure and the obligation to state reasons'.[30] Accordingly, whether a Commission decision has been lawfully adopted also depends on whether the applicable evidence standards have been complied with.

Evidence-related pleas before the EU Courts may take two forms: either that an issue has not been demonstrated to 'the requisite legal standard'; or that the applicable evidence standards have not been appropriately set or applied. With respect to pleas of the first type, it is settled jurisprudence that 'the General Court has exclusive jurisdiction to find and appraise the relevant facts and, in principle, to examine the evidence it accepts in support of those facts'.[31] In other words:

> Provided that the evidence has been properly obtained and the general principles of law and the rules of procedure in relation to the burden of proof and the taking of evidence have been observed, it is for the [GCEU] alone to assess the value which should be attached to the evidence produced to it.[32]

On this basis, the CJEU has frequently refused to examine pleas which it has perceived as contesting the factual assessment made by the GCEU and as calling for a re-examination of the evidence.

By contrast, pleas that the evidence rules have not been appropriately set or applied – for instance, a claim that the standard of proof was too high or that the rules on the burden of proof were disregarded – may be heard by both EU Courts. Indeed, as explained in *Timab Industries*, 'an alleged failure to have regard to the rules of evidence is a question of law which is admissible in an appeal'.[33] Accordingly, while the CJEU will not review the factual assessments made by the GCEU, it will ascertain whether the latter 'in its assessment of the facts and evidence, made an error of law by infringing general principles of law, such as the presumption of innocence and the applicable rules of evidence, such as those relating to the burden of proof'.[34] In *Commission v Keramag Keramische Werke*, for example, the CJEU set the judgment of the GCEU aside on the ground that the latter had failed to examine the probative value of certain tables, contrary to the principle of unfettered evaluation of the evidence.[35] In any event, the CJEU will also hear pleas that 'the clear sense of the evidence has been distorted' by the GCEU.[36]

[30] Case C-12/03 P *Commission v Tetra Laval (Tetra Laval II)*, ECLI:EU:C:2004:318, Opinion of AG Tizzano, para 85.

[31] Case C-89/11 P *E.ON Energie v Commission*, ECLI:EU:C:2012:738, para 64; Case C-231/14 P *InnoLux v Commission*, ECLI:EU:C:2015:451, para 59.

[32] Case C-7/95 P *Deere v Commission*, ECLI:EU:C:1998:256, para 22; Case C-185/95 P *Baustahlgewebe v Commission*, ECLI:EU:C:1998:608, paras 23–24; Joined Cases C-403/04 P and C-405/04 P *Sumitomo Metal Industries and Nippon Steel v Commission*, ECLI:EU:C:2007:52, para 38. See also Case C-644/13 P *Villeroy and Boch v Commission*, ECLI:EU:C:2017:59, para 34: 'it must be recalled that the assessment by the General Court of the evidential value of a document may not, as a rule, be subject to review by the Court of Justice in appeal proceedings'.

[33] Case C-411/15 P *Timab Industries and CFPR v Commission*, ECLI:EU:C:2017:11, para 58.

[34] ibid para 59.

[35] Case C-613/13 P *Commission v Keramag Keramische Werke and Others et Sanitec Europe*, ECLI:EU:C:2017:49, paras 64–65.

[36] Case C-373/14 P *Toshiba Corporation v Commission*, ECLI:EU:C:2016:26, para 40.

However, it is only in rare circumstances that such pleas will be upheld. Indeed, as per well-established case law, 'such a distortion must be obvious from the documents on the Court's file, without there being any need to carry out a new assessment of the facts and evidence'.[37]

That said, two clarifications are in order. First of all, the scope of judicial review is determined by the scope of the action for annulment. In other words, only those aspects of the Commission decision contested by the applicant will be reviewed by the EU Courts.[38] From an evidence perspective, EU judges will consider materials and information, insofar as they pertain to the pleadings.[39] Moreover, according to settled case law, 'review is carried out solely by reference to the elements of fact and of law existing on the date of adoption of the contested decision'.[40] A question which may arise in this regard is whether the parties may adduce new evidence relating to issues pre-dating the decision in the judicial proceedings. The case law is not entirely clear on this issue. In *GlaxoSmithKline*, the GCEU held that 'in the exercise of their rights of defence', the parties may offer evidence established after the date of adoption of Commission decision, 'but for the specific purpose of contesting or defending that decision'.[41] However, in later cases, the EU Courts seem to have taken a less restrictive view. In *Telefónica*, for instance, considering the admissibility of certain annexes, the GCEU clarified that account will be taken of:

> [A]ll the evidence adduced by the applicants, whether predating or postdating the contested decision, whether submitted in the context of the administrative procedure or for the first time in the context of the action brought before the Court, *insofar as that evidence is relevant to the review of the legality of the Commission's decision.* (Emphasis added)[42]

Arguably, this is a much lower threshold for undertakings to overcome.[43] In any event, the Commission may itself offer new information in response to the evidence produced by the applicant. Nevertheless, the authority may not alter the factual basis for its conclusions, whereas new evidence cannot make good an already inadequately reasoned decision either.[44]

[37] Case C-514/14 P *Éditions Odile Jacob v Commission*, ECLI:EU:C:2016:55, para 73.

[38] For more on this, see Fernando Castillo de la Torre and Eric Gippini Fournier, *Evidence, Proof and Judicial Review in EU Competition Law* (Edward Elgar, 2017) 228–32, 269–71.

[39] The late production of the evidence will generally result in its inadmissibility (arts 43(3), 44(1) and 46(1), 48(1) and 66(2) RPGC). See also *Baustahlgewebe* (n 32) paras 60–75.

[40] Joined Cases 15/76 and 16/76 *France v Commission*, ECLI:EU:C:1979:29, para 7; Case T-395/94 *Atlantic Container Line and Others v Commission*, ECLI:EU:T:2002:49, para 252.

[41] Case T-168/01 *GlaxoSmithKline Services v Commission*, ECLI:EU:T:2006:265, para 58. See also Case T-87/05 *EDP* v *Commission*, ECLI:EU:T:2005:333, para 158.

[42] Case T-216/13 *Telefónica v Commission*, ECLI:EU:T:2016:369, para 87, citing Case C-407/08 P *Knauf Gips v Commission*, ECLI:EU:C:2010:389, paras 87–92.

[43] Castillo de la Torre and Gippini Fournier (n 38) observe (at 274) that this jurisprudence creates an 'imbalance … in favour of the applicant'.

[44] Case 75/84 *Metro v Commission*, ECLI:EU:C:1986:399, paras 75–78; *Atlantic Container Lines* (n 40) para 254. See also Case T-464/04 *Independent Music Publishers and Labels Association v Commission (Impala I)*, ECLI:EU:T:2006:216, paras 37–40.

Second, while the Commission is the leading fact-finder in the administrative proceedings,[45] judicial proceedings are mostly adversarial, albeit with potentially extensive inquisitorial features. Indeed, it is for the parties to adduce evidence before the EU Courts, which shall then be typically disclosed to their opponent.[46] Nevertheless, EU judges may formally or informally ask questions and request the production of evidence. In particular, as per its Rules of Procedure, the GCEU may take measures of organisation and may order measures of inquiry – including, among other things, the personal appearance of the parties, requests for the production of documents and the commissioning of an expert report.[47] In this sense, and as Gippini Fournier and Castillo de la Torre have rightly observed, 'the General Court is not restricted to evidence adduced purely on the initiative of the parties'.[48] However, while EU judges *may* actively seek to clarify the facts of the case, legally they are under no obligation to do so. However broad, their inquisitorial discretion is not stretched to an active fact-finding duty. Ultimately, the legal burden remains with the parties; in the event of a fact-finding failure, EU judges may simply conclude that this has not been discharged.[49]

B. Evidence Standards, Marginal Review and Complex Economic Evaluations

i. *An Elusive Relationship*

With respect to facts, it is clear that the Commission must 'get it right'; the application of a comprehensive standard of review effectively signifies that there is only one acceptable understanding of the evidence over which EU judges have full control. By contrast, the operation of the applicable evidence standards with regard to 'complex economic evaluations' has been less obvious. As early as in *Consten and Grundig*, the CJEU explained that it 'must take account of [the] nature [of complex economic evaluations] by confining itself to an examination of the relevance of the facts and of the legal consequences which the Commission deduces therefrom'.[50]

[45] As explained in ch 2 (section III.B.i.a), the inquisitorial nature of administrative proceedings has been mitigated by the adversarial principle.

[46] In exceptional circumstances, however, the EU Courts may examine evidence without disclosing it to both parties: Castillo de la Torre and Gippini Fournier (n 38) 234–35.

[47] Rules of Procedure of the General Court [2015] OJ L105/1, ch 6.

[48] Castillo de la Torre and Gippini Fournier (n 38) 236.

[49] Joined Cases C-238/99 P, C-244/99 P, C-245/99 P, C-247/99 P, C-250/99 P to C-252/99 P and C-254/99 P *Limburgse Vinyl Maatschappij and Others v Commission*, ECLI:EU:C:2002:582, para 404; *E.ON Energie* (n 31) para 115; Case C-286/13 P *Dole Food and Dole Fresh Fruit Europe v Commission*, ECLI:EU:C:2015:184, paras 59–60. *cf* George Cumming, *Merger Decisions and the Rules of Procedure of the European Community Courts* (Kluwer Law International, 2011) 153–55, arguing in favour of an active case management duty of the EU Courts. On the fact-finding role of the EU Courts, see generally Koen Lenaerts, Ignace Maselis and Kathleen Gutman, *EU Procedural Law* (Oxford University Press, 2014) 23.57–23.72.

[50] Joined Cases 56/64 and 58/64 *Consten and Grundig v Commission*, ECLI:EU:C:1966:41, 347.

Since then, marginal review has seemingly taken a stricter form. In *Remia*, the CJEU elaborated that such review entails 'verifying whether the relevant procedural rules have been complied with, whether the statement of the reasons for the decision is adequate, whether the facts have been accurately stated and whether there has been any manifest error of appraisal or misuse of powers'.[51] Then in *Tetra Laval*, the CJEU further clarified that 'whilst … the Commission has a margin of discretion with regard to economic matters, that does not mean that the [EU] Courts must refrain from reviewing the Commission's interpretation of information of an economic nature'. On the contrary:

> [N]ot only must the [EU] Courts, inter alia, establish whether the evidence relied on is factually accurate, reliable and consistent, but also whether the evidence contains all the information which must be taken into account in order to assess a complex situation and whether it is capable of substantiating the conclusions drawn from it.[52]

Microsoft confirmed the relevance of this test – which came to be the standard formula of marginal review – not only for merger proceedings, but also for the control of Commission decisions concerning the application of Articles 101 and 102 TFEU.[53]

While these clarifications are certainly valuable, the relationship between marginal review and evidence standards remains rather elusive. First of all, the concept of 'complex economic evaluations', which arguably functions as a 'neon sign' communicating that a more relaxed scrutiny is to follow, has proved very difficult to define.[54] Over the years, the EU Courts have offered glimpses into

[51] *Remia* (n 4) para 34.

[52] Case C-12/03 P *Tetra Laval v Commission (Tetra Laval II)*, ECLI:EU:C:2005:87, para 39.

[53] *Microsoft* (n 3) paras 87-89.

[54] Several scholars have tried to delineate this concept (eg, Damien Geradin, Anne Layne-Farrar and Nicolas Petit, *EU Competition Law and Economics* (Oxford University Press, 2012) 386–87). Forwood has rightly explained that complexity 'refers more to the nature of the assessment' rather than its economic or technical aspects or its evidential implications (Nicholas Forwood, 'The Commission's "More Economic Approach" – Implications for the Role of the EU Courts, the Treatment of Economic Evidence and the Scope of Judicial Review' in Claus-Dieter Ehlermann and Mel Marquis (eds), *European Competition Law Annual 2009: The Evaluation of Evidence and its Judicial Review in Competition Cases* (Hart Publishing, 2010) 267). Bellamy has distinguished between 'facts of an economic nature' and 'facts that are entering the question of policy' (Christopher Bellamy, 'Standards of Proof in Competition Cases' in *Judicial Enforcement of Competition Law* (OECD Competition Policy Roundtable 1996) 106). Fritzsche has posited that economic evaluations are 'complex' when 'they can only be determined by interpreting multiple other simple and complex facts' and that complex economic appraisals are essentially 'factual questions as a matter of law to be answered by using scientific evidence' (Alexander Fritzsche, 'Discretion, Scope of Judicial Review and Institutional Balance in European Law' (2010) 47 *Common Market Law Review* 361, 398 and 396). Jaeger, on the other hand, has taken the view that the attribute of complexity should be accredited only to assessments involving 'elements of economic policy', which call for some degree of 'value judgement' on part of the Commission – such as the balancing of anti-competitive effects and efficiencies (Marc Jaeger, 'The Standard of Review in Competition Cases Involving Complex Economic Assessments: Towards the Marginalisation of the Marginal Review?' (2011) 2 *Journal of European Competition Law and Practice* 295, 310). For a critical discussion of the issue, see Andriani Kalintiri, 'What's in a Name? The Marginal Standard of Review of "Complex Economic Evaluations" in EU Competition Enforcement' (2016) 53 *Common Market Law Review* 1283, 1290–94).

their understanding of what a 'complex economic appraisal' is. To name but a few, the definition of the relevant market,[55] a conclusion that an undertaking holds a dominant position,[56] the weighing-up exercise under Article 101(3) TFEU[57] and ascertaining that a concentration 'would significantly impede effective competition' in the common market[58] are all examples of assessments that, according to the EU Courts, call for limited review.[59] Nevertheless, these indications are not as helpful. For one thing, given the intrinsic links of competition law with economics, one cannot easily escape the feeling that the notion of 'complex economic appraisals' is a nearly all-encompassing term. Furthermore, the case law does not reveal what affirmative features an economic assessment must have in order to be classified as 'complex'. Last but not least, the fact that complex economic evaluations, however defined, are subject to a different standard of review from issues of law and fact creates the impression that they can be meaningfully disassociated from the latter as being something entirely distinct.

At the same time, the content of the 'manifest error of assessment test' has been rather ambiguous.[60] At first glance, the qualification of 'manifestness' seems to suggest that the EU Courts will intervene only in exceptional circumstances, that is, when the Commission's conclusions are manifestly incorrect. This feeling would not be entirely unwarranted in light of the early definition of 'manifestness' provided in *RJB Mining*. Although in the context of the ECSC Treaty, the GCEU clarified that 'the term "manifest" … presupposes that the failure to observe legal provisions … appears to arise from an *obvious* error in the evaluation' (emphasis added).[61] Nevertheless, the question remains: what errors in the Commission's evaluations are 'obvious' and how can these be distinguished from other non-obvious mistakes? In this regard, the approach taken in *UFEX and Others* appears slightly more helpful. As the GCEU explained, an error of assessment is not manifest and would not suffice to warrant annulment of the contested Commission decision

[55] Case T-301/04 *Clearstream v Commission*, ECLI:EU:T:2009:317, para 47; *Microsoft* (n 3) para 482; Case T-151/05 *NVV and Others v Commission*, ECLI:EU:T:2009:144, para 53; Case T-699/14 *Topps Europe v Commission*, ECLI:EU:T:2017:2, para 80.

[56] *General Electric* (n 26) paras 60–64 and 121.

[57] *GlaxoSmithKline* (n 41) para 244.

[58] *Kali and Salz* (n 27) paras 223–24; Case T-342/07 *Ryanair v Commission*, ECLI:EU:T:2010:280, paras 29–30; Case T-119/02 *Royal Philips Electronics v Commission*, ECLI:EU:T:2003:101, para 77.

[59] See also Marco Bronckers and Anne Valery, 'Business as Usual after *Menarini*?' (2012) 3 *MLexMagazine* 44, 45.

[60] As is well known, the 'manifest error of assessment' originates from French administrative law (eg, Jean-Yves Vincent, 'L'Erreur Manifeste d'Appréciation' (1971) 142 *La Revue Administrative* 407) and has been discussed at great length in scholarship: see, eg, Bastiaan van der Esch, *Pouvoirs Discrétionnaires de l'Exécutif Européen et Control Juridictionnel* (Dalloz, 1968); Dominique Ritleng, 'Le Juge Communautaire de la Légalité et le Pouvoir Discrétionnaire des Institutions Communautaires' (1999) 9 *L'Actualité Juridique: Droit Administratif* 645; Joël Molinier, 'Le Contrôle Juridictionnel et ses Limites: À Propos du Pouvoir Discrétionnaire des Institutions Communautaires' in Joël Rideau (ed), *De la Communauté de Droit à l'Union de Droit* (LGDJ, 2000) 77–98; Aude Bouveresse, *Le Pouvoir Discrétionnaire dans l'Ordre Juridique Communautaire* (Bruylant, 2010).

[61] Case T-156/98 *RJB Mining v Commission*, ECLI:EU:T:2001:29, para 87.

'if, in the particular circumstances of the case, it could not have had a decisive effect on the outcome'.[62] This clarification is valuable, insofar as it confirms that the EU Courts are indifferent to errors which are not capable of modifying the outcome of the Commission's analysis. However, both the 'manifestness' wording and the 'obvious error' language are of limited practical value, insofar as they fail to expose *why* a given Commission appraisal may be problematic.

Last but not least, since the standards governing evidence assessment are procedural rules, one would expect that the Commission should enjoy no latitude as far as their application is concerned. Indeed, as noted earlier, marginal review entails 'verifying whether the relevant procedural rules have been complied with'. Nevertheless, what the EU Courts often utter in their judgments is that 'the Commission has not established to the requisite legal standard that … Consequently, the Commission made a manifest error of assessment in …'.[63] The emphasis placed in *Tetra Laval* on ensuring that the evidence is factually accurate, reliable and consistent, that it contains all the information which must be taken into account in order to assess a complex situation and that it is capable of substantiating the conclusions drawn from it may explain the close association of the standard of proof with marginal review. However, while there is little doubt that evidence considerations play a fundamental role in the judicial scrutiny of complex economic appraisals, the implications of the applicable evidence standards for the Commission's margin of appreciation remain rather obscure.[64]

ii. Varieties of 'Complex Economic Evaluations' and the Scope of the 'Manifest Error of Assessment' Test

The ambiguity surrounding the precise operation of evidence standards in the context of marginal review might be attributed to some extent, on the one hand, to the tendency to think of 'complex economic evaluations' as a uniform group of appraisals which are always subject to a 'manifest error of assessment' scrutiny and, on the other hand, to the assumption that marginal review is concerned with errors of a single kind and quality. However, as explained elsewhere, none of these perceptions is accurate.[65]

[62] Case T-60/05 *UFEX and Others v Commission*, ECLI:EU:T:2007:269, para 77. See also Case T-126/99 *Graphischer Maschinenbau v Commission*, ECLI:EU:T:2002:116, paras 48–49 (albeit in the context of state aid); and Joined Cases C-553/10 P and C-554/10 P *Commission and Lagardère v Éditions Odile Jacob*, ECLI:EU:C:2012:682, para 37. It is interesting to note that the EU Courts' understanding of 'manifestness' echoes settled case law, according to which violations of procedural guarantees may result in the annulment of a Commission decision only where the outcome of the administrative proceedings might have been different in the absence of the procedural defect (see Joined Cases 40–48, 50, 54–56, 111, 113 and 114/73 *Suiker Unie and Others v Commission*, ECLI:EU:C:1975:174, para 91).

[63] See, eg, *General Electric* (n 26) para 425; *Impala I* (n 44) para 449.

[64] For an excellent discussion, see Paul Craig, *EU Administrative Law*, 2nd edn (Oxford University Press, 2012) 465–73. See also Hubert Legal, 'Standards of Proof and Standards of Judicial Review in EU Competition Law' in Barry Hawk (ed), *Fordham Corporate Law Institute: International Antitrust Law and Policy* (Juris, 2006) 111–12.

[65] For a more detailed presentation of these ideas, see Kalintiri (n 54) 1295–305, 1312–15.

With respect to 'complex economic evaluations', it is crucial to appreciate that they are not performed in the abstract; rather, they form part of the intellectual process that the Commission goes through when it makes a decision on whether the conduct in question complies with the EU competition rules or not. In this context, economic appraisals may be necessary on two different levels. On the one hand, they may underpin the construction of the competition rules and the articulation of legal tests. For instance, the choice whether to prohibit exclusivity rebates by their very nature or only upon evidence of likely harm to competition may be informed by economic insights into the nature of the practice and the various ways in which it may affect competition and consumers. On the other hand, complex economic appraisals may form part of the legal qualification exercise, ie, the process of answering the question whether, in light of the available evidence, the conduct under examination fulfils the elements of the relevant legal test as identified. Indeed, this process very much resembles assembling a puzzle: the authority seeks to gather the relevant information and integrate it into a meaningful picture. However, not all puzzles are created equal. Sometimes, legally qualifying a conduct may be easy, whereas at other times it may require complex economic appraisals. The latter will most likely be the case the less accepted or more novel the economic theory on which the authority relies, the greater the number of relevant factors that it must integrate in its analysis, the more uncertain their interaction is, the more specialised the knowledge that the analysis requires and the more elaborate the argument that the authority wishes to advance.

That said, it is usually assumed that *all* complex economic evaluations are subject to marginal control. However, this is not accurate; rather, any margin of appreciation that the Commission potentially enjoys is confined to the *application* of the competition rules. By contrast, complex economic appraisals relating to their *interpretation* are treated as 'pure' questions of law and are thus subject to full review.[66] While it would not be absurd to think that the Commission is allowed some flexibility in its construction of the concepts of 'restriction of competition', 'abuse of dominance' and 'significant impediment to effective competition', given its nature as a specialised administrative agency, Article 19 TEU makes it clear that the competence to interpret EU law in an authoritative manner lies exclusively with the EU Courts. Indeed, the *meaning* and *scope* of the EU competition rules have been invariably off-limits to the Commission, regardless of whether complex economic evaluations may be involved or not.[67] On several occasions, the

[66] See also Bo Vesterdorf, 'Standard of Proof in Merger Cases: Reflections in the Light of the Recent Case Law of the Community Courts' (2005) 1 *European Competition Journal* 3, 12.

[67] Other jurisdictions have dealt with this question in a different manner. In the US, for instance, the Supreme Court has long endorsed the *Chevron* formula, which prescribes that if Congress has not directly spoken to the precise question at issue and the statute is silent or ambiguous, then 'the question for the court is whether the agency's answer is based on a permissible construction of the statute'. For a brief comparative analysis, see Paul Craig, 'Judicial Review and Questions of Law: A Comparative Perspective' in Susan Rose-Ackerman and Peter Lindseth (eds), *Comparative Administrative Law* (Edward Elgar, 2010).

EU Courts have confirmed that as a general rule, they will undertake a comprehensive review of whether or not the conditions for the application of EU competition rules are met.[68] Furthermore, they have repeatedly emphasised that in carrying out such a review, they 'cannot use the Commission's margin of discretion, by virtue of the role assigned to it in competition policy by the EU and FEU Treaties, as a basis for dispensing with the conduct of an in-depth review of the law and of the facts'.[69] Therefore, any deference to the Commission is confined to the complex economic evaluations that the authority may perform at the stage of the *application* of the competition rules, their *interpretation* being the sole prerogative of the EU Courts.

Considering now the operation of evidence standards in the judicial review of complex economic appraisals relating to the *application* of the competition rules, it is necessary to examine the scope of the 'manifest error of assessment' test. While one might be tempted to think of this test as comprising mistakes of a single quality, a closer investigation of the EU Courts' case law confirms that four different flaws have been subsumed within it and may lead to the annulment of the Commission's decision: first, a failure on part of the authority to correctly assess the material facts underpinning its analysis;[70] second, a failure to take into account key relevant factors;[71] third, taking into account an irrelevant factor which distorts the outcome of the analysis;[72] and, fourth, a failure to satisfy the standard of proof.[73] Indeed, a failure to meet the standard of proof appears to be a vice in its own right. Even where the Commission has not made erroneous factual findings and has taken into account all the pertinent factors or has not based its analysis on irrelevant parameters, its complex economic evaluations may still fail marginal review, where the authority has not produced sufficient evidence. In these circumstances, the Commission has not necessarily 'got it wrong'. However, it has not convincingly demonstrated that it has 'got it right' either.

That said, it is important to remember that judicial scrutiny is confined to a review of the *legality* of the Commission's decision. Accordingly, EU judges may

[68] eg, *Remia* (n 4) para 34; Case C-382/12 P *MasterCard and Others v Commission*, ECLI:EU:C:2014:2201, para 155.

[69] Case C-389/10 P *KME Germany and Others v Commission*, ECLI:EU:C:2011:816, para 129; Case C-386/10 P *Chalkor v Commission*, ECLI:EU:C:2011:815, para 62. See also the Opinion of AG Mengozzi in Case C-382/12 P *MasterCard*, ECLI:EU:C:2014:42, para 119, where he observed that this dictum 'has in itself the potential to neutralize de facto the very principle of the recognition of a margin of economic assessment to the Commission'.

[70] eg, Case C-62/86 *AKZO v Commission*, ECLI:EU:C:1991:286, paras 116–21, where the CJEU held that the Commission had been wrong to find that AKZO had engaged in an abusive policy of discrimination by quoting to customers of its competitor prices which were more advantageous than those it charged customers of its own, since the two categories of customers were not in fact comparable; and *Impala I* (n 44) paras 364–90, where the GCEU took issue with the Commission's finding that the market was not sufficiently transparent for collective dominance to exist.

[71] eg, Case 27/76 *United Brands v Commission*, ECLI:EU:C:1978:22, paras 252–56, where the CJEU reprimanded the Commission for not taking into account United Brand's production costs when determining whether its prices were excessive in relation to the economic value of the product.

[72] eg, *Airtours* (n 21) paras 211–15.

[73] eg, Case T-427/08 *CEAHR v Commission*, ECLI:EU:T:2010:517, paras 94–96, 119.

not annul the authority's complex economic appraisals on the ground that another possible approach to the matter was in their view 'better'. As the GCEU elaborated in *GlaxoSmithKline*, 'it is not for the Court to substitute its own economic assessment for that of the institution which adopted the decision'; it may only review its *lawfulness*.[74] This constraint is crucial for demarcating the limits of marginal review. Where complex economic assessments are involved, there may be more 'correct' ways of approaching an issue, from which the authority is in principle entitled to choose as the first instance decision-maker.[75] For example, the same concentration may give rise to both unilateral and coordinated effects. If the Commission opts to proceed on the basis of the unilateral effects theory only, the EU Courts may not find a 'manifest error of assessment' on the ground that in their view, the alternative theory was more convincing or appropriate in light of the evidence. In other words, the mere fact that the authority pursued a line of analysis that the EU Courts would not have favoured, had they been the first instance decision-maker, is insufficient to give rise to a 'manifest error of assessment'.

In any event, the Commission's margin of appreciation is not exhausted in choosing a theory of harm, but may extend to the very performance of complex economic appraisals. An illustrative example of this situation may be found in *John Deere*.[76] In this case, the Commission took issue with the information exchange system operated by UK tractor manufacturers on the ground that it increased transparency on a highly concentrated market and raised barriers to entry by enabling members to identify each competitor's sales, as well as the sales made by their dealers, where the total volume of sales for a given product and period on the territory was less than 10 units. Challenging the decision, John Deere contested the threshold of 10 units below which individualisation of information was possible as 'incomprehensible'.[77] However, none of the Courts shared its view. Taking account of the characteristics of the market, the kind of information exchanged and the fact that the disseminated information was not sufficiently aggregated, they concluded that the Commission had not committed any manifest error of

[74] *GlaxoSmithKline* (n 41) para 243. See also Joined Cases T-68, 77 and 78/89 *SIV and Others v Commission*, ECLI:EU:T:1992:38, para 160: 'It is not for the Court to carry out its own analysis of the market but that it must confine itself to verifying, as far as possible, the *correctness* of the findings in the decision which were *essential* for the assessment of the case' (emphasis added); and *General Electric* (n 26) para 312: 'It is not for the Court to substitute its own appraisal for that of the Commission, by seeking to establish what the latter would have decided if it had taken into account the deterrent effect of Article [102 TFEU].' As the CJEU indicated in Case C-67/13 P *Groupement de Cartes Bancaires v Commission*, ECLI:EU:C:2014:2204, para 46, 'the General Court must not substitute its own economic assessment for that of the Commission' because the latter 'is institutionally responsible for making those assessments'.

[75] José Carlos Laguna de Paz, 'Understanding the Limits of Judicial Review in European Competition Law' (2014) 2 *Journal of Antitrust Enforcement* 203, 217–18; Edith Loozen, 'The Requisite Legal Standard for Economic Assessments in EU Competition Cases Unravelled through the Economic Approach' (2014) 39 *European Law Review* 91, 104.

[76] Case T-35/92 *Deere v Commission*, ECLI:EU:T:1994:259.

[77] ibid para 90.

assessment in using the criterion of 10 units sold.[78] A similar conclusion may be found in the earlier judgment in *Remia*, where the CJEU considered the criteria examined by the Commission when determining the proper duration of the non-compete clause at hand and held that there was nothing to suggest that the authority had made a manifestly erroneous appraisal.[79] Therefore, one may infer that where a 'complex economic appraisal' requires setting a numerical threshold, some scope for calibration appears to be part and parcel of the Commission's margin of appreciation.[80]

iii. The Operation and Significance of Evidence Standards in Judicial Review

Against this backdrop, the following remarks are worth highlighting about the operation and significance of the applicable evidence standards in the context of the judicial review of the Commission's competition decisions.

First of all, complex economic appraisals pertaining to the *interpretation* of the substantive provisions escape the scope of the evidence rules and, in particular, of the standard of proof. Inevitably, Articles 101 and 102 TFEU, as well as the EUMR, are interpreted primarily in the context of adjudication.[81] Where the proper legal treatment of a practice is contentious, both the Commission and the undertakings concerned may be inclined to produce evidence in support of a specific construction of the law with a view to swaying judicial opinion their way. However, as explained, EU judges are typically faced with an epistemic deficit, inasmuch as they lack a specialised background in economics. As a result, they may have to rely on evidence in order to unravel the economics of a practice before deciding whether conduct of this kind should be prohibited by its very nature or only upon proof of actual or likely harm to competition following a case-by-case assessment.[82] In this respect, it would not be unreasonable to assume that the burden and standard of proof apply to the construction of the legal test, in the sense that the choice of one or the other substantive legal threshold ought to reflect a minimum degree of conviction about the underlying economics of the conduct. However, such an assumption would be mistaken in the context of EU competition enforcement. Indeed, the evidence rules apply only to so-called adjudicative facts, namely facts

[78] ibid para 92; *Deere* (n 32) paras 34–36.

[79] *Remia* (n 4) paras 25–36.

[80] See also Case T-340/03 *France Télécom v Commission*, ECLI:EU:T:2007:22, para 129: 'as the choice of method of calculation as to the rate of recovery of costs entails a complex economic assessment on the part of the Commission, the Commission must be afforded a broad discretion'.

[81] The EU competition rules are also interpreted in the context of the preliminary ruling procedure following a reference by a national court (art 267 TFEU).

[82] Admittedly, this discussion does not take place openly in EU judicial proceedings. By contrast, in the US, the economics of various practices and its implications for the design of legal tests have been explicitly considered by courts (eg, *Leegin Creative Leather Products v PSKS*, 551 US 877 (2007) on the proper legal treatment of vertical price restraints).

pertaining to the parties and practice in question. By contrast, legislative facts, ie, the underlying social and economic premises which may – more or less consciously – inform the judicial construction of the legal rules, fall outside their realm.[83] The reason for this arguably lies in Article 19 TEU, which manifests the fundamental trust of the EU institutional system in EU judges to make the 'right' choices when constructing the legal rules.[84]

Second, it is clear that any flexibility the Commission may enjoy by no means absolves the EU Courts of their obligation to *fully* review the evidence supporting its conclusions. As AG Kokott emphasised in her Opinion in *Impala II*, 'the correctness, completeness and strength of the factual material which underpins a decision must be liable to judicial review'.[85] This is critical because:

> [W]thout such a review of the factual basis for a decision it would not be possible to assess, in a meaningful way, whether the Commission had stayed within the limits of the discretion allowed to it or had committed manifest errors of assessment.[86]

This approach is consistent with the principle of unfettered evaluation of the evidence, as described in Chapter 5. As the GCEU has itself confirmed, 'it is incumbent on it … to check the nature and import of the evidence taken into consideration by the Commission'.[87] Nevertheless, the EU Courts have taken evidence review a step further: not only will they seek confirmation as to whether the evidence is factually accurate, reliable and consistent, but they will also verify whether it contains *all* the information which must be taken into account in order

[83] See Kenneth Culp Davis, 'An Approach to Problems of Evidence in the Administrative Process' (1941) 55 *Harvard Law Review* 364, 402–04 for the distinction between *legislative facts* – that is, facts that 'inform … a court's legislative judgment on questions of law and policy'– and *adjudicative facts* – that is, facts about 'what the parties did, what the circumstances were, what the background conditions were'. The reception and determination of legislative facts in judicial proceedings have given rise to difficult questions. May the court take judicial notice of legislative facts? Are legislative facts subject to the burden and standard of proof? The answer to these questions has been debated. Rule 201 of the US Federal Rules of Evidence, for instance, explicitly excludes legislative facts from judicial notice. Moreover, commentators have disagreed as to whether evidence rules should apply to legislative facts (eg, Kenneth Culp Davis, 'Facts in Lawmaking' (1980) 80 *Columbia Law Review* 931; Kenneth Karst, 'Legislative Facts in Constitutional Litigation' [1960] *Supreme Court Review* 75; Ann Woolhander, 'Rethinking the Judicial Reception of Legislative Facts' (1988) 41 *Vanderbilt Law Review* 111; Robert Keeton, 'Legislative Facts and Similar Things: Deciding Disputed Premise Facts' (1988–89) 73 *Minnesota Law Review* 1).

[84] There is nothing in the EU Courts' jurisprudence to suggest that legislative facts are subject to the applicable evidence standards – quite the opposite, given the emphasis placed on the power of EU judges to fully review questions of law (see also John Monahan and Laurens Walker, 'Social Authority: Obtaining, Evaluating and Establishing Social Science in Law' (1986) 134 *University of Pennsylvania Law Review* 477, 478, arguing that 'social science research, when used to create a legal rule, is more analogous to "law" than to "fact"'; Juliane Kokott, *The Burden of Proof in Comparative and International Human Rights Law: Civil and Common Law Approaches with Special Reference to the American and German Legal Systems* (Kluwer Law International, 1998) 36–39).

[85] Case C-413/06 P *Bertelsmann and Sony Corporation of America v Impala (Impala II)*, ECLI:EU:C:2007:790, Opinion of AG Kokott, para 179.

[86] ibid.

[87] *SIV and Others* (n 74) para 95.

to assess a complex situation and whether it is capable of substantiating the conclusions drawn from it.[88]

The potential reach of the evidence qualification of the 'manifest error of assessment' test should not be underestimated. Evidence review in the context of marginal scrutiny has armed the EU Courts with the perfect Trojan horse. On the one hand, it enables EU judges to evade potential allegations that they have unduly interfered with the Commission's margin of appreciation – after all, all they do is merely to ensure that the evidence that the authority has produced satisfies the applicable standards. At the same time, however, the *Tetra Laval* formula has the capacity to turn marginal control into a much stricter form of judicial scrutiny, which may sometimes come very close to almost entirely eliminating any 'margin of appreciation' that the Commission is said to enjoy.[89] The reason for this is twofold. First, the evidence qualification of the 'manifest error of assessment' test confirms that the Commission's *exercise*[90] of its margin of appreciation is subject to an important caveat: although the authority does possess 'a degree of latitude regarding the choice of the econometric instruments available to it and the choice of the appropriate approach to the study of any matter',[91] it is nevertheless legally required to demonstrate that its chosen approach is *justified* and thus among the 'correct' ones.[92] Second, the *Tetra Laval* formula suggests that the EU Courts remain the ultimate arbiters of the factors that *must* be taken into account in order to assess a complex situation. This is important because, as mentioned earlier,

[88] *Tetra Laval II* (n 52) para 39. See also James Venit, 'The Scope of EU Judicial Review of Commission Merger Decisions' in Philip Lowe and Mel Marquis (eds), *European Competition Law Annual 2010: Merger Control in European and Global Perspective* (Hart Publishing, 2013) 123–25. It is interesting to note that the EU Courts' understanding of marginal review in competition cases also seems to have influenced to some extent their approach in state aid and trade defence proceedings. Nevertheless, the implications of that formula in state aid judgments remain somewhat ambiguous, since the EU Courts have occasionally employed it in order to elaborate on the content of 'comprehensive review' rather than to qualify 'marginal review' (eg, Case T-565/08 *Corsica Ferries France v Commission*, ECLI:EU:T:2012:415, para 88).

[89] As remarked by Virpi Tiili and Jan Vanhamme, 'The "Power of Appraisal" (Pouvoir d'Appréciation) of the Commission of the European Communities vis-à-vis the Powers of Judicial Review of the Communities Court of Justice and Court of First Instance' (1998) 22 *Fordham International Law Journal* 885, 888, by reviewing the administrative file, the EU Courts inevitably bring themselves 'intellectually close to building their own bridge from the facts'. See, however, the concerns expressed by Hubert Legal, 'Le Contentieux Communautaire de la Concurrence Entre Contrôle Restreint et Pleine Juridiction' (2005) 2 *Concurrences* 1, 1–2.

[90] Rather than its *existence*.

[91] See eg, Case T-212/03 *MyTravel v Commission*, ECLI:EU:T:2008:315, para 83. See also Case T-699/14 *Topps Europe v Commission*, ECLI:EU:T:2017:2, paras 79–82. It is worth noting that a similar – albeit less eloquently articulated – approach has been adopted in state aid and trade defence cases too (eg, Joined Cases C-341/06 and C-342/06 P *Chronopost and La Poste v UFEX and Others*, ECLI:EU:C:2008:375, paras 149–155; Case C-290/07 P *Commission v Scott*, ECLI:EU:C:2010:480, paras 68–84; Case T-310/12 *Yuanping Changyuan Chemicals v Council*, ECLI:EU:T:2015:295, para 194).

[92] See the language used by the CJEU in Case C-510/11 P *Kone and Others v Commission*, ECLI:EU:C:2013:696, para 27; and also Paul Lasok, 'The Nature of Judicial Control' in *Celebration of 20 Years of the Court of First Instance of the European Communities* ('From 20 to 2020: Building the CFI of Tomorrow on Solid Foundations, Luxembourg 25 September 2009) 34, who observes that the Commission's latitude is confined to the outcome, rather than the process, of its decision-making.

a failure to take into consideration parameters that are not substantially relevant will *not* make for a 'manifest error of assessment'. In view of its margin of appreciation, one would expect that the Commission would have a strong say in determining what is 'relevant' and what is not. Interestingly, however, the EU Courts have employed evidence-related wording to retain this role for themselves.[93]

Obviously, whether the EU Courts actually deliver on their promise and carry out an in-depth scrutiny of the evidence is a separate issue.[94] However, this empirical question and practical difficulties do not detract from the theoretically far-reaching potential of evidence review, as the perfect 'cover' for performing a thorough inspection of the Commission's analysis without – seemingly – impinging on the authority's margin of appreciation. In this sense, evidence standards effectively serve as a mechanism for marginalising marginal review. This remark is crucial from a fairness perspective too. As explained earlier, the main criticisms against limited review stem from the assumption that the EU Courts will interfere with the Commission's complex economic appraisals only in exceptional circumstances.[95] Nevertheless, it is clear that while the Commission is arguably afforded some flexibility in its decision-making in line with the scope of judicial scrutiny as a control of the *lawfulness* of its decisions, complex economic appraisals relating to the *interpretation* of the competition rules are subject to full review as issues of law, whereas those pertaining to their *application* are subject to strict evidence requirements along the lines of the *Tetra Laval* formula. The implications of this are visible in the expansive manner in which the 'manifest error of assessment' test has been applied by the EU Courts. As noted above, a failure on the part of the authority to correctly assess the material facts underpinning its analysis, a failure to take into account key relevant factors, taking into account an irrelevant factor which distorts the outcome of the analysis, and a failure to satisfy the standard of proof may all lead to the annulment of the Commission's decision. On this basis, it is submitted that the evidence qualification of the 'manifest error

[93] In the US context, see Martin Shapiro, 'Appeal' (1979–80) 14 *Law & Society* 629, 649–50. See generally Edwin Blythe Stason, '"Substantial Evidence" in Administrative Law' (1941) 89 *University of Pennsylvania Law Review* 1026; Louis Jaffe, *Judicial Control of Administrative Action* (Little, Brown & Co, 1965).

[94] Various factors may play a role in this; eg, it is not unreasonable to think that the prospective nature of the Commission's analysis may make it more challenging for the EU Courts to identify 'manifest errors of assessment' in merger cases than in arts 101 and 102 TFEU cases, where enforcement takes place *ex post*. Several commentators have observed that the EU Courts actually exercise much stricter scrutiny over the Commission's reasoning than what one would initially expect based on the 'manifest error of assessment' formula (eg, Fernando Castillo de la Torre, 'Evidence, Proof and Judicial Review in Cartel Cases' in Ehlermann and Marquis (n 54) 390, noting that 'the "manifest" error standard in fact captures much more than decisions that are facially or self-evidently wrong'; Denis Waelbroeck, 'Le Juge Communautaire en Matière de Concentrations: "Censeur Pédagogue" ou Juge de la Légalité?' (2005) 4 *Concurrences* 2; Wouter Wils, 'The Increased Level of EU Antitrust Fines, Judicial Review, and the European Convention on Human Rights' (2010) 33 *World Competition* 5, 26–28).

[95] See, eg, Jacques Derenne, 'The Scope of Judicial Review in EU Economic Cases' in Merola and Derenne (n 15) 85: 'one can wonder why it is still acceptable and compatible with a satisfactory level of "justice" for the Court to decide that a contested act is "not manifestly incorrect"'.

of assessment' test is – at least in principle – capable of aligning the EU Courts' control over the authority's antitrust and merger decisions with the ECtHR's requirement for 'full jurisdiction'.

IV. Conclusion

Because evidence assessment is intrinsic not only to the Commission's decision-making but also to the control that the EU Courts exercise over the way in which the authority enforces the EU competition provisions, issues of proof and issues of judicial review cannot be entirely disentangled. In this context, the aim of this chapter was to investigate how standards of evidence assessment interact with standards of judicial scrutiny with a view to better understanding their operation in EU competition enforcement.

Indeed, the existence of two standards of judicial control, namely *full review* of questions of fact and law, and *marginal review* of policy choices and complex economic evaluations, has mystified to some extent the role of evidence standards in the context of the scrutiny exercised by the EU Courts. As explained above, the lawfulness of the Commission's decisions depends, among other things, on whether the rules and principles governing the evaluation of evidence have been complied with. With respect in particular to facts, there is only one 'correct' understanding of the evidence over which EU judges have full control: the Commission has either 'got it right' or 'wrong'. By contrast, the operation of the applicable evidence standards in the marginal review of so-called 'complex economic appraisals' has been less clear: on the one hand, the notion of 'complex economic appraisals' has been rather elusive, given the challenges in defining it in a positive manner; on the other hand, the reach of the 'manifest error of assessment' test – which underpins marginal review – has been somewhat ambiguous because of the vagueness of the 'manifestness' wording. At the same time, the judicial deference to the Commission with respect to policy matters and 'complex economic appraisals' has triggered criticisms that EU competition enforcement fails to comply with the principle of effective judicial protection and the right to a fair trial, insofar as the control exercised by the EU Courts allegedly falls short of the ECtHR's requirement for 'full jurisdiction'.

Nevertheless, as this chapter has explained, marginal review is far less marginal than one might assume. First of all, complex economic appraisals pertaining to the *interpretation* of the competition provisions are subject to full review as issues of law, and escape the application of the rules and principles governing evidence assessment and, in particular, of the standard of proof. Second, as far as the *application* of Articles 101 and 102 TFEU or the EUMR are concerned, the Commission does enjoy some flexibility in the sense that it is free to choose its preferred theory of harm or evidence to produce. The EU Courts are confined to a control of legality and may not annul a decision on the ground that another approach was 'better'. Accordingly, the operation of a marginal standard of review indicates that there may be more ways for the Commission to satisfy its burden and standard of proof. However, once the authority has 'exhausted' its decision-making latitude by specifying its preferred course of action, the EU Courts are fully entitled – and expected – to scrutinise whether its choices are supported by evidence which is factually accurate, reliable and consistent, which contains *all* the information that must be taken into account in order to assess a complex situation and which is capable of substantiating the conclusions drawn from it. Consequently, not only must the Commission's complex economic appraisals satisfy the applicable evidence standards, but also the authority has little say in what is relevant and what is not, since the EU Courts remain the ultimate arbiters thereof.

The far-reaching potential of the evidence qualification of marginal review is visible in the expansive manner in which the 'manifest error of assessment' test has been applied by the EU Courts. Indeed, a failure on the part of the authority to correctly assess the material facts underpinning its analysis, a failure to take into account key relevant factors, taking into account an irrelevant factor which distorts the outcome of the analysis, and a failure to satisfy the standard of proof may all lead to the annulment of the Commission's decision. With this in mind, it is submitted that the power of the *Tetra Laval* formula should not be underestimated. To the extent that it marginalises marginal review, it can effectively bring the control exercised by the EU Courts into line with the ECtHR's requirement for 'full jurisdiction', thereby eliminating the perceived 'fairness deficit' in the administrative model of enforcement.

8

Reflections

I. Introduction

The previous chapters were dedicated to understanding what rules and principles govern, or should govern, the assessment of evidence in EU competition proceedings in light of the features of EU competition enforcement. The examination of the burden and standard of proof, of the principles of unfettered production and unfettered evaluation, and of the operation of presumptions – as developed by the EU Courts and fleshed out in their jurisprudence – reveals the existence of a firmly established framework for assessing evidence which compensates for the almost complete lack of legislative guidance on these matters. At the same time, the analysis has illustrated the intricacies of defining evidence standards which are well suited to the enforcement system of which they form part.

Drawing on the discussion so far, the aim of this chapter is to offer some reflections on the broader connotations and implications of the applicable rules and principles of evidence assessment for EU competition enforcement. To this end, section II first of all ponders on the inferences one might draw for the proclivity of the regime towards risk allocation, given the function of evidence rules as decision-making devices. From a fairness perspective, then, section III contemplates the compatibility of the evidence standards in place with the principle of effective judicial protection – as inspired by the right to a fair trial – and highlights their function as a counterweight to the perceived 'fairness deficit' of the existing administrative model of enforcement. Section IV ruminates on their implications for the enforcement of Articles 101 and 102 TFEU, as well as of the EUMR, by reflecting on their operation in the context of the 'more economic' approach and by offering some remarks about their interplay with the substantive competition provisions. With these thoughts in mind, section V briefly considers how the applicable evidence standards may become translated into specific obligations for or expectations from the Commission and the EU Courts. Last but not least, section VI then turns its attention to the implications for national procedural autonomy by pointing out the existing divergence among national evidence rules and principles, and by highlighting the capacity of the evidence standards developed by EU judges to pave the way for further procedural convergence. Section VII concludes.

II. Some Connotations for the Enforcement System's Risk Proclivity

In an ideal world, the application of the competition rules would always yield correct outcomes only. However, such aspiration is unrealistic; in practice, enforcement takes place under conditions of uncertainty – whether legal or factual.[1] As such, it is inevitable that errors – either in the form of false convictions or false acquittals – will occur. Legal systems manage this risk through multiple devices – for instance, the design of substantive legal tests and the formulation of evidence rules. The systematic examination of these choices in combination might provide useful insights into a regime's proclivity towards risk. In this regard, it has been eloquently pointed out by Lao that 'ideology matters', in the sense that non-interventionist attitudes are usually accompanied not only by stricter substantive legal tests, but also by more demanding standards of proof, whereas pro-interventionist approaches favour lower substantive and evidentiary thresholds so as to facilitate governmental interference.[2] Given that evidence rules are only one of the ways in which legal regimes manage uncertainty and errors, it is not possible to draw definite conclusions about the predisposition of the EU competition enforcement system towards risk solely based on their regulation. Nevertheless, some reflections on their connotations might still be ventured.

EU antitrust enforcement has been often described as favourable to intervention – at least in its formative years. To an extent, this perception has been closely associated with different accounts about its historical and normative foundations. Ordoliberalism, for instance, and the intrinsic call for protecting a 'system of undistorted competition' has been portrayed – erroneously, for many scholars – as overly formalistic and as 'committed to a pro-regulatory stance'.[3] A similarly pro-interventionist philosophy has been attributed to the goal of market integration, insofar as the latter has been instrumental in the construction and application of the EU antitrust provisions with a view to ensuring that private actors would not be able to reinstate barriers to trade which the four freedoms aimed to abolish. Against this backdrop, the turn to a 'more economic' approach has been praised, among other things, as capable of minimising false convictions and false acquittals and of tempering the pro-interventionist attitude of early antitrust enforcement in the EU, although the extent to which this has been fully achieved remains

[1] Kenneth Heyer, 'A World of Uncertainty: Economics and the Globalisation of Antitrust' (2005) 72 *Antitrust Law Journal* 375.

[2] Marina Lao, 'Ideology Matters in the Antitrust Debate' (2014) 79 *Antitrust Law Journal* 649.

[3] Heike Schweitzer and Kiran Klaus Patel (eds), *The Historical Foundations of EU Competition Law* (Oxford University Press, 2013) 223–24. See further David Gerber, *Law and Competition in Twentieth-Century Europe: Protecting Prometheus* (Oxford University Press, 2001). *cf* Pınar Akman, 'The Role of "Freedom" in EU Competition Law' (2014) 34 *Legal Studies* 183.

under question.[4] This discussion clearly goes beyond the confines of this book. However, an interesting point to make from an evidence perspective is that in the sphere of antitrust, the applicable evidence rules overall suggest a concern with false convictions. Indeed, the legal burden of establishing an infringement rests with the Commission, whereas the 'firm conviction' standard of proof that the authority must satisfy is arguably high and evidence may be excluded from consideration where it violates undertakings' rights of defence.

At first glance, this might seem at odds with a pro-interventionist narrative, insofar as heightened evidentiary thresholds by default make intervention more difficult. Nevertheless, an enforcement system's proclivity towards risk may be more nuanced than generic labels might imply. At a primary level, the operation of high evidence standards in the EU regime appears to convey a concern with an undue interference with undertakings' economic freedom and fundamental rights. On a case-by-case basis at least, one might say that this cost seems to be prioritised over the cost of ad hoc societal harm in the event of a failure to convict because of the authority's inability to satisfy the applicable standard of proof. This interpretation makes sense if one recalls that the EU Courts developed evidence rules and principles predominantly in the context of cartel enforcement – where legal uncertainty is low and where the quasi-criminal nature of antitrust fines was first noted. Interestingly, in merger enforcement, on the other hand, the Commission's symmetrical legal burden – coupled with the operation of a fairly high threshold of evidence sufficiency – suggest a risk-neutral approach at the level of adjudication, under which false convictions and false acquittals are deemed equally serious.

In any event, caution is warranted: these limited connotations cannot be generalised into definite statements about the EU enforcement system's risk propensity or adversity. Prioritisation principles, the choice of enforcement tool and the design of substantive legal tests are, among other things, equally crucial in this evaluation. While the applicable evidence standards might refine the way in which uncertainty is managed and costs are prioritised, they may not completely override the risk choices made through other instruments.

III. The Implications for Fairness

A. The Fairness of the Applicable Evidence Standards

EU competition enforcement must respect the requirements of procedural due process. While neither the CFR nor the ECHR contains specific evidence

[4] John Fingleton and Ali Nikpay, 'Stimulating or Chilling Competition?' in Barry Hawk (ed), *Fordham Competition Law Institute: International Antitrust Law and Practice* (Juris, 2009) 388–90; Paul Lugard, 'Chilling Effects of Antitrust Law: Better Safe than Sorry?' in Barry Hawk (ed), *Fordham Competition Law Institute: International Antitrust Law and Practice* (Juris, 2009) 448.

prescriptions, evidence standards are an integral part of adjudication. Accordingly, they must be compatible with the principle of effective judicial protection, as inspired by the right to a fair trial, in both antitrust and merger proceedings.

i. *The Fairness of Evidence Standards in Antitrust Proceedings*

In the context of antitrust proceedings, the imposition of arguably high financial sanctions for violations of Articles 101 and 102 TFEU, in conjunction with the Commission's extensive investigative powers, has led to calls for the adoption of criminal procedural safeguards as necessary to compensate for the nature of antitrust fines as 'criminal charges' within the meaning of the ECHR and for the inequality of arms between the Commission and the investigated undertakings. It is thus important to consider to what extent the applicable evidence standards address these concerns and comply with the CFR – and the ECHR.

As explained in Chapter 2, the EU Courts have responded to criticisms that antitrust enforcement has acquired criminal features in two ways: on the one hand, by highlighting the application of the presumption of innocence; and, on the other hand, by stressing the need for respect of the rights of defence. Nevertheless, the analysis of the burden and standard of proof in proceedings concerning violations of the antitrust rules in Chapters 3 and 4 revealed a somewhat different picture. In principle, the presumption of innocence prevents imposing a legal burden on defendants, where its discharge entails satisfying a standard of proof higher than the balance of probabilities – or a comparable level of conviction. However, the standard of proof that undertakings must meet to prove the defence of Article 101(3) TFEU (or an equivalent Article '102(3)') mirrors the Commission's obligation to establish a 'firm conviction' about the existence of a restriction of competition by object or by effect (or of an abuse of dominance). Consequently, it is much higher than the preponderance of the evidence – or its qualitative counterpart. Insofar as they impose the legal burden of proving efficiencies on undertakings, Article 2 of Regulation 1/2003 and *Post Danmark I* are at odds with the presumption of innocence, as traditionally understood. Regarding the standard of proof, on the other hand, the EU Courts have resisted arguments that the Commission should be subject to a 'beyond any reasonable doubt' threshold of evidence sufficiency, opting instead for a 'firm conviction' standard. One might thus argue that while the EU Courts have created expectations of criminal procedural protection by insisting on the applicability of the presumption of innocence to antitrust infringement proceedings, they have stopped short of fulfilling them.

Yet, an unqualified conclusion that, as a result, the applicable evidence standards are incompatible with the principle of effective judicial protection would be rushed. While competition fines may well amount to 'criminal charges' within the meaning of the ECHR, the implications of this from a fairness standpoint must be assessed in conjunction with the administrative model of EU competition enforcement in place and the fact that the Commission lacks criminal investigative powers. Accordingly, the challenge lies in ensuring effective judicial protection for undertakings without compromising the sustainability of the enforcement system as it currently stands. Based on the analysis in Chapters 3 and 4, it is submitted that this fine balance can be achieved through a calibration of the burden of proof. As advocated in Chapter 3, Article 2 of Regulation 1/2003 and *Post Danmark I* should be 'read down' to impose only an evidential burden on undertakings, that is, an obligation to produce evidence of efficiencies in their possession. In this way, the overall responsibility for demonstrating the existence of a violation of Articles 101 and 102 TFEU will fall on the Commission, and doubts about the nature or effect of the conduct in question will act in the interests of defendant undertakings, irrespective of the level of the analysis at which they arise. Such a refined burden of persuasion would then compensate for the fact that, as expounded in Chapter 4, the 'firm conviction' threshold that the authority must satisfy in order to prove the existence of an antitrust infringement comes close to – but falls short of – the criminal standard of proof.

Beyond the shortcomings identified in the current allocation of the legal burden with respect to pro-competitive arguments and other justifications, the analysis detected only one further source of potential concern relating to the probative treatment of statements. Overall, the EU Courts' approach to the admissibility and probative value of the evidence is sound and in line with the principle of effective judicial protection. Nevertheless, given the absence of cross-examination during the administrative investigation, the reluctance of the GCEU to grant requests for the hearing and cross-examination of the author of a statement might take issue with the CFR and the ECHR, where this statement was relied upon as the sole or decisive basis for the Commission's finding of a violation of the antitrust rules. Admittedly, this scenario will be rare; typically, the authority will base its conclusions on a variety of relevant information, the statement being one of them. However, in circumstances where a statement has constituted the exclusive or predominant basis of a Commission decision finding an infringement of Articles 101 and 102 TFEU, either the EU Courts must be very demanding as to the level of corroboration required for ascertaining its probative reliability or they must be ready to allow the hearing and cross-examination of the author of the statement in the course of the judicial proceedings.

ii. Fairness of Evidence Standards in Merger Proceedings

In contrast with antitrust proceedings, whose fairness has been much debated in past years, merger enforcement has not attracted similar criticisms. The lack of financial penalties, on the one hand, and the predictive nature of merger analysis, on the other, have fortified the idea that merger proceedings are civil in nature and thus civil procedural safeguards – such as a balance of probabilities standard of proof or a similarly low level of conviction – suffice to ensure the effective judicial protection of the merging entities. However, the absence of financial sanctions in merger control should not detract attention from its regulatory nature. As explained in Chapter 2, a Commission decision declaring a concentration as incompatible with the common market interferes – whether justifiably or not – with the freedom of undertakings to engage in economic activities. Accordingly, the applicable evidence standards must be capable of safeguarding that the latter is not unduly circumscribed. This cautious approach is further compelled by the fact that merger enforcement takes place *ex ante* rather than *ex post* and that, similarly to infringement proceedings, the Commission holds multiple roles and enjoys extensive investigative powers. Therefore, while the GCEU has rightly dismissed isolated arguments that the wording of the 'serious doubts' test of Article 6(1)(b) EUMR connotes a 'beyond any reasonable doubt' standard of proof for Phase 1 merger proceedings, civil evidence standards are not acceptable either.

Commendably, the EU Courts' approach to evidence standards governing merger enforcement does not raise concerns of insufficient judicial protection for merging entities. The trilogy of merger annulments in *Schneider Electric*, *Airtours* and *Tetra Laval* set the tone early on by subjecting merger decision-making to high evidential thresholds. As explained in Chapter 3, the Commission bears the legal burden of demonstrating that a notified concentration would significantly impede effective competition on the common market if it were allowed to proceed. Furthermore, in order to discharge its burden of proof, the authority must satisfy a high standard of proof that – as the EU Courts' merger jurisprudence suggests – corresponds, or at least comes very close, to the 'firm conviction' threshold that prevails in antitrust proceedings. Last but not least, the admissibility and evaluative standards described in Chapter 5 apply to the assessment of evidence in the context of merger decision-making as well. In this regard, Fountoukakos has rightly remarked that 'apart from ensuring that procedural rules for the respect of the rights of defence are adhered to, arguably the greatest contribution of the [EU] Courts to the fairness of the Commission's administrative procedure is through the imposition of evidentiary standards'.[5]

That said, it should be noted that the evidence standards which inform merger decision-making are not entirely realistic. On the one hand, the Commission's legal burden is not exhausted to merger prohibition decisions, but extends to authorisations too. On the other hand, the standard of proof governing clearance decisions is as high as that applying to merger prohibitions, and no 'presumption' of merger compatibility or incompatibility exists. In practice, the cumulative effect of this is that the authority is not allowed to entertain any doubts whatsoever and is expected to reach a positive conclusion on the compatibility or incompatibility of the notified concentration with the common market at all times. From a fairness perspective, this approach respects the effective judicial protection of the merging entities, whereas it also has the added benefit of minimising both false acquittals and false convictions, and reinforcing public confidence in the accuracy of the Commission's decision-making. Yet, where the authority is genuinely uncertain

[5] Kyriakos Fountoukakos, 'The CFI's Contribution to a Fairer System of Merger Control' in Carl Baudenbacher et al (eds), *Liber Amicorum en l'Honneur de Bo Vesterdorf* (Bruylant, 2007) 529.

as to how to proceed with a notified transaction, it might turn merger decision-making into a vicious circle. Therefore, it was submitted that in truly deadlock situations, a finding of merger compatibility should be accepted.

B. Evidence Standards as a Remedy for the 'Fairness Deficit' of the Administrative Model of Enforcement

EU competition enforcement has been modelled upon administrative systems of justice, as explained in Chapter 2. Accordingly, the Commission acts as the 'first instance' decision-maker, whereas its decisions may be subsequently reviewed by the EU Courts. However, a recurring argument in recent years has been that this enforcement model falls short of the principle of effective judicial protection and the right to a fair trial, insofar as the authority is not an 'independently and impartial tribunal' in view of the multiple roles that it holds, nor do the EU Courts exercise 'full jurisdiction' over its decisions in view of the deference arguably shown to the agency with respect to policy matters and complex economic assessments. The criticisms against the 'fairness deficit' of the enforcement model have been more pronounced in antitrust proceedings in the wake of the 'criminalisation' trend, as marked by the gradual imposition of higher and higher fines. Nevertheless, similar concerns may also be expressed for merger enforcement – despite the lack of 'criminal' financial penalties. Not only does the Commission combine multiple roles and enjoy extensive powers in mergers proceedings as well, but also the pervasiveness of complex economic appraisals in merger decision-making arguably turns the 'manifest error of assessment' standard of review into the norm rather than the exception. Against this background, the feeling has emerged that the EU competition enforcement model suffers from a 'fairness deficit', which frustrates the effective judicial protection of undertakings finding themselves involved in antitrust and merger proceedings.

However, a closer examination into the interplay between evidence standards and standards of review reveals that this feeling may not be warranted – as explained in Chapter 7. On the one hand, not all 'complex economic appraisals' are subject to marginal control; economic evaluations pertaining to the *construction* of the competition rules – namely the choice of legal test which should govern a given practice – are treated as issues of law and are thus subject to full scrutiny, however complex they might be. On the other hand, the judicial review of complex economic assessments pertaining to the *application* of the competition rules is far less limited than one might initially believe to be the case. The explanation for this lies in the evidence qualification of the 'manifest error of assessment' test as per *Tetra Laval*. The Commission certainly enjoys a margin of appreciation with respect to its preferred course of action and may not be criticised, for instance, for relying on one theory of harm over another. However, once the authority has exercised its latitude, the EU Courts will check whether its conclusions are justified and thus 'correct' in the circumstances of the case by reviewing the probative value of the evidence supporting its findings and by verifying that it has addressed all relevant information and has satisfied the standard of proof. This finds support in the judicial application of the 'manifest error of assessment' test which seems to encompass the following types of errors: a failure on the part of the authority to correctly assess the material facts underpinning its analysis; a failure to take into account key relevant factors; taking into account an irrelevant factor which distorts the outcome of the analysis; and a failure to satisfy the standard of proof.

Accordingly, the EU Courts are not deprived of their 'power to quash in all respects, on questions of fact and law, the challenged decision'. Assuming their scrutiny conforms to their stated intention, their review of Commission antitrust and merger decisions qualifies as 'full jurisdiction' within the meaning of the ECtHR's jurisprudence. In this respect, evidence standards play a crucial role, insofar as they serve as a mechanism for marginalising marginal review and for engaging in a thorough scrutiny of the authority's findings. Consequently, they seem to provide an indirect, yet effective remedy for the 'fairness deficit' in the administrative model of enforcement.

IV. The Connotations for the Application of the Substantive Rules

A. Evidence Standards and the 'More Economic' Approach

Over the past few years, EU competition enforcement has shifted towards a so-called 'more economic' approach. While the precise meaning of this term is somewhat hazy, the gist of this transformation lies in the endorsement of mainstream economic principles to guide the design of enforcement priorities, and in the integration of economics in the interpretation and application of the competition rules. In this regard, one might wonder whether the applicable evidence standards have facilitated or potentially stalled this shift.

Based on the analysis in the previous chapters, the contribution of evidence standards seems to have been a positive one. First of all, the EU system does not subject expert evidence to special admissibility criteria – contrary to the US model, where expert testimony must satisfy the *Daubert* test for its probative value to be considered. The practical significance of this should not be underestimated. In principle, the lack of specific admissibility thresholds for expert evidence enables the Commission to rely on novel theories and economic tools, whereas it encourages the employment of complex economic evidence as a means for the parties to provide empirical support for their arguments. At the same time, the EU Courts have rightly declined to tie economics-based analysis to economic evidence. In line with the principle of unfettered production of evidence, there are no restrictions on the types of information that may be used to ascertain the nature or effects of a conduct on competition and consumers, which may further encourage the integration of economics in EU competition enforcement. That said, the EU Courts are not averse to complex economic evidence; on the contrary, EU judges have been willing to assign it some probative weight – especially where its inherent limitations have been readily acknowledged and clearly set out. Last but not least, the criticisms that a 'higher' standard of proof applies to complex theories of harm and economic evidence are unfounded. As explained in Chapter 4, the required threshold of evidential sufficiency remains the same, but the subject of proof may inevitably affect how easy or difficult its discharge will be. Therefore, the applicable rules and principles of evidence evaluation appear to have the capacity to bolster the 'more economic' approach to EU competition enforcement.

Nevertheless, while the applicable evidence standards are apt to accommodate the integration of economics in EU competition enforcement, they also serve as a quality filter by highlighting the significance of evidence-based decision-making. Indeed, the evidence qualification of the 'manifest error of assessment' test in *Tetra Laval* suggests that economics is not given a free rein in EU competition enforcement.[6] Rather, the Commission's analysis must be grounded in evidence which is factually accurate, reliable and consistent, takes all relevant considerations into account and satisfies the standard of proof, even where 'complex economic appraisals' may be involved. While the authority is entitled to choose the theory of harm that it considers to be most suitable to the circumstances of the case, 'if the evidence does not reveal that the legal tests are satisfied, [it] must accept as much, or its decision will be overturned by the Court'.[7] In this sense, the applicable evidence standards have two important implications for the 'more economic' approach to EU competition enforcement: on the one hand, coupled with the Commission's margin of appreciation, the existing rules and principles of evidence assessment allow for the extrapolation of the latest economic thinking into the discipline; however, on the other hand, the *Tetra Laval* formula sets a hard limit, insofar as it demands that the 'economics-based' application of the substantive legal tests of Articles 101 and 102 TFEU or the EUMR in any given case rest on solid ground.

B. The Symbiosis of Evidence Standards and Substantive Rules

Substantive and procedural norms are sometimes thought of as being in disconnect. This is of course sensible to the extent that they serve different functions in

[6] See also Joshua Wright, 'Abandoning Antitrust's Chicago Obsession: The Case for Evidence-Based Antitrust' (2012) 78 *Antitrust Law Journal* 241, 262–63; Simon Bishop, 'Snake-Oil with Mathematics is Still Snake-Oil: Why Recent Trends in the Application of So-Called "Sophisticated" Economics is Hindering Good Competition Policy Enforcement' (2013) 9 *European Competition Journal* 67, 71–76.

[7] Mark Clough, 'Role of Judicial Review in Merger Control' (2003–04) 24 *Northwestern Journal of International Law & Business* 729, 753.

a legal system. Broadly speaking, substantive rules create rights and obligations, and delineate the scope of permissible and impermissible behaviour. By contrast, procedural provisions dictate how substantive law may be enforced. Nevertheless, the symbiosis of substantive and procedural norms is not as airtight as one might think. At the same time, matters of substance and matters of evidence are occasionally misidentified, with undesirable consequences for their regulation and application. Drawing on the discussion so far, the following paragraphs reflect on the co-existence of evidence standards and substantive rules in EU competition enforcement, focusing on the burden of proof, the standard of proof and presumptions.

At first glance, the question 'what needs to be established' and the question 'who has to establish it' are separate; the former is a substantive issue, whereas the latter is a matter of procedure. However, as demonstrated in Chapter 3, this rigid distinction is illusive. Indeed, the current bifurcated allocation of the burden of persuasion between the Commission and undertakings goes beyond a merely evidential stipulation; rather, it may have significant implications for the ways in which Articles 101 and 102 TFEU, as well as the EUMR, are constructed and enforced. The reason for this lies in the fact that allocating the burden of persuasion with respect to pro-competitive arguments or other legitimate justifications on undertakings may create the impression either that the Commission is entitled to prohibit a conduct under Articles 101 and 102 TFEU – or a concentration under the EUMR – without any examination of its potentially beneficial aspects, or that in deciding whether a behaviour amounts to a 'restriction of competition by object or by effect', an 'abuse of dominance' or a 'significant impediment to effective competition', only certain efficiencies are relevant.

However, both options are problematic. Accepting that the Commission may discharge its burden of persuasion without considering the possibility of a legitimate explanation for the practice at hand might result in an overly expansive understanding of the prohibitive scope of the competition rules. Equally troubling is the view that in discharging its legal burden, the Commission might only take into account allocative efficiency, insofar as this approach would endorse an unjustifiably narrow conception of 'competition' in which productive and dynamic efficiencies have no role to play due to their technically being a 'defence'. Moreover, in the field of antitrust, both possible approaches sit uncomfortably with settled jurisprudence which suggests that efficiency arguments are already relevant at the 'first' level of competition analysis, the legal burden with respect to which rests on the Commission. As explained above, these complications derive from the misconception that the pro-competitive and anti-competitive aspects of a conduct can be meaningfully disassociated when assessing its impact on competition and from the failure to appreciate that efficiency considerations are built into more than one level of the analytical framework in place, although admittedly the detail in which they are examined varies depending on the stage of the analysis – moving from the implicit to the explicit and from the abstract to the concrete. To address these complications, it was submitted that the whole legal burden should remain with the Commission at all times and that undertakings should only bear an evidential burden, that is, an obligation to claim and produce evidence of any efficiencies in their knowledge.

Having said that, it is worth noting that the interplay between substantive legal tests and burdens of proof has been extensively discussed in US scholarship. As is well known, US courts have long identified two different frameworks for assessing whether a practice constitutes an unreasonable restraint of trade or monopolisation under sections 1 and 2 of the Sherman Act respectively: per se illegality and the *rule of reason* analysis. The per se test embodies a conclusive proscription of practices that have a 'pernicious effect on competition and lack … any redeeming virtue',[8] from which defendants are unable to escape by raising efficiency arguments. The rule of reason analysis, on the other hand, consists in a weighing of the anti-competitive and the pro-competitive effects of the conduct at hand with a view to determining whether it violates the antitrust rules. Nevertheless, the choice of optimal legal test has proved complicated in practice. Furthermore, while the US jurisprudence suggests that the *rule of reason* analysis may vary, taking either a 'quick look' or a 'full-blown' form, the precise scope of either approach has been rather vague.[9] Interestingly, the burden of proof has been employed in the US as a mechanism for structuring the rule of reason analysis.[10] In *Law v NCAA*, for instance, the Tenth Circuit explained that:

> [T]he plaintiff bears the initial burden of showing that an agreement had a substantially adverse effect on competition. If the plaintiff meets this burden, the burden shifts to the defendant to come forward with evidence of the procompetitive virtues of the alleged wrongful conduct. If the defendant is able to demonstrate procompetitive effects, the plaintiff then must prove that the challenged conduct is not reasonably necessary to achieve the legitimate objectives or that those objectives can be achieved in a substantially less restrictive manner. Ultimately, if these steps are met, the harms and benefits must be weighed against each other in order to judge whether the challenged behaviour is, on balance, reasonable.[11]

Nevertheless, while this framework has gained wide acceptance, it has not alleviated concerns about how to optimally formulate antitrust legal standards. In this regard, scholars have called for the adoption of 'rebuttable presumptions' of illegality or legality as a solution to the problem.[12]

[8] *White Motor Co v United States*, 372 US 253, 265 (1963).

[9] For a brief account, see 'Roundtable on Safe Harbours and Legal Presumptions in Competition Law – Note by the United States', DAF/COMP/WD(2017)85.

[10] See Andrew Gavil, 'Burden of Proof in U.S. Antitrust Law' in *Issues in Competition Law and Policy* (ABA Section of Antitrust Law, 2008).

[11] *Law v National Collegiate Athletic Association*, 5 F Supp 2d 921 (1998).

[12] Notes, 'A Suggested Role for Rebuttable Presumptions in Antitrust Restraint of Trade Litigation' [1972] *Duke Law Journal* 595; Steven Salop, 'An Enquiry Meet for the Case: Decision Theory, Presumptions and Evidentiary Burdens in Formulating Antitrust Legal Standards' (2017) Georgetown Law Faculty Publications and Other Works, available at https://scholarship.law.georgetown.edu/cgi/viewcontent.cgi?article=3025&context=facpub.

Against this backdrop, one might be tempted to draw parallels between the EU and the US approach. Nevertheless, considerable caution is warranted. For all their apparent similarities, the *by object* and *by effect* divide and the per se test and *rule of reason* analysis present conceptual and analytical differences, which have not yet been sufficiently explored.[13] A US-style 'rule of reason' assessment under Article 101(1) TFEU has been explicitly denounced in *M6 and Others*.[14] Instead, the EU Courts have developed different mechanisms for embedding pro-competitive arguments in the analysis, such as the need to consider the 'legal and economic context' of an agreement which may lead to the conclusion that it falls outside the scope of Article 101 TFEU altogether or that it is necessary to establish its effects.[15] In other words, there is more than one shade in Article 101 TFEU analysis, which arguably mitigates some of the concerns driving the calls for the introduction of 'rebuttable presumptions' in the US. In any event, one must not forget that the enforcement landscape is different too. In the EU, securing compliance with the competition rules has been a predominantly public affair so far, with administrative agencies taking the lead. By contrast, in the US, antitrust litigation is principally driven by private parties. Also, even from an institutional point of view, there exists marked divergence. In the US, the Antitrust Division of the Department of Justice follows the 'bifurcated judicial' model, whereas the Federal Trade Commission is based on the 'integrated agency' model. While the European Commission is also premised on the latter, the division of investigative and decision-making functions is much more clear-cut in its US counterpart.[16] These considerations may shape the dynamics among parties differently and thus have important implications for the allocation of the burden of proof. Accordingly, further research which goes beyond the scope of the book is required, before one might make meaningful comparisons about the interplay between substantive legal tests and burdens of proof in the EU and in the US.

Beyond the burden of proof, the discussion in the previous chapters also shed some light on the operation of presumptions and of the standard of proof in connection with substantive legal tests. As explained, economic premises about the nature of a conduct should not be conflated with presumptions in the strict, technical meaning of the word. Propositions about the impact of a practice on competition derived from economics may indeed instruct the choice of legal test in EU competition law – namely prima facie illegality versus case-by-case assessment of effects, whereas they also form part of the heuristics which may shape the

[13] For a recent effort, see Alison Jones and William Kovacic, 'Identifying Anticompetitive Agreements in the United States and the European Union: Developing a Coherent Antitrust Analytical Framework' (2017) 62 *Antitrust Bulletin* 254.

[14] Case T-112/99 *M6 and Others v Commission*, ECLI:EU:T:2001:215, paras 72–79.

[15] See also Case C-309/99 *Wouters and Others*, ECLI:EU:C:2001:390, Opinion of AG Léger, paras 102–04.

[16] Daniel Crane, *The Institutional Structure of Antitrust Enforcement* (Oxford University Press, 2011); Eleanor Fox and Michael Trebilcock (eds), *The Design of Competition Law Institutions: Global Norms, Local Choices* (Oxford University Press, 2013).

decision-maker's perception of normality and may indirectly frame the evaluation of the evidence and thus the discharge of the standard of proof. Nevertheless, procedurally speaking, they are not equivalent to presumptions – at least in the EU system, since undertakings cannot formally 'rebut' them by producing evidence to the contrary. This remark is important from the perspective of the standard of proof as well. The latter governs only adjudicative facts; by contrast, legislative facts underpinning the choice between a 'by object' or a 'by effect' legal test – economic premises included – escape its application in light of the EU Courts' exclusive competence to interpret the competition rules. Last but not least, as explained in Chapter 6, while presumptions may facilitate the fact-finding process, they are not a panacea and may not compensate for shortcomings in the design of the law.

V. The Connotations for the EU Institutions

Alongside their implications for fairness and for the application of the substantive rules, the rules and principles governing the assessment of evidence in EU competition proceedings and the evidence qualification of the 'manifest error of assessment' test may be translated into specific obligations for – or expectations from – the Commission and the EU Courts.

A. The Connotations for the Commission

Indeed, as far as the Commission is concerned, the applicable evidence standards have three important connotations: first, they call for heightened levels of administrative care in line with the right to good administration, as enshrined in Article 41 CFR; second, they set a limit to the authority's margin of appreciation; and, third, they may influence the legitimacy of its decision-making.

First of all, the evidence rules and principles that the Commission must comply with in order for its decisions to be lawful may be read to encompass specific prescriptions for the conduct of the administrative proceedings. At a minimum, the admissibility and evaluative criteria described in Chapter 5 underline the need for the authority to ensure that the collection of the evidence is not tainted by illegalities which could threaten its admissibility or diminish its probative value.[17] However, beyond this, the applicable evidence rules and principles imply that the Commission must commit to always carrying out 'a thorough and painstaking investigation', as AG Tizzano put it in his Opinion in *Tetra Laval II*.[18] While it is for

[17] See, eg, Case T-141/08 *E.ON Energie v Commission*, ECLI:EU:T:2010:516, paras 75–77.

[18] Case C-12/03 P *Commission v Tetra Laval* (*Tetra Laval II*), ECLI:EU:C:2004:318, Opinion of AG Tizzano, para 74; see also para 87.

it to decide how to run its examination,[19] the authority must search for evidence that both confirms and refutes its working hypotheses. In *Intel*, for instance, the GCEU underlined that 'it is for the Commission to conduct an investigation carefully and impartially, and it may not therefore merely gather incriminating documents and turn a blind eye to the existence of exculpatory evidence'.[20] Related to this is the authority's obligation to evaluate the available evidence objectively and spherically from the perspective of a neutral observer without any predisposition about its 'correct' interpretation.[21] People are generally 'apt to accept "confirming" evidence at face value, while subjecting "disconfirming" evidence to critical evaluation' and have the tendency to seek for information which upholds their prior beliefs and past efforts.[22] Accordingly, the Commission must be alert to biases that may prejudice its assessment of the evidence and should take appropriate steps to minimise the risk of falling prey to them.[23] Last but not least, administrative decisions finding a breach of the antitrust rules or prohibiting or authorising a notified concentration must contain a detailed analysis of the evidence so that it is clear how the standard and burden of proof have been discharged.

On a broader note, these prescriptions fall squarely in place with the right to good administration as enshrined in Article 41 CFR,[24] which encompasses,

[19] Case T-141/94 *Thyssen Stahl v Commission*, ECLI:EU:T:1999:48, para 97 (relating to proceedings pursuant to art 65 ECSC Treaty).

[20] Case T-286/09 *Intel v Commission*, ECLI:EU:T:2014:547, para 372. However, this does not mean that the Commission 'bears an obligation to obtain as many documents as possible in order to ensure that it obtain all potentially exculpatory evidence. Apart from the fact that the Commission's resources are limited, it would be impossible for the Commission to ensure that no potentially exculpatory evidence escapes its attention' (para 361). As AG Trstenjak highlighted in *GlaxoSmithKline* with respect to art 101(3) TFEU, the fact that competition proceedings are 'governed by the principle that the public authority is responsible for the procedure' does not mean that the Commission may confine itself to 'requiring from undertakings proof of the fulfilment of the requirements for the grant of the exemption but must, as a matter of good administration play its part, using the means available to it, in ascertaining the relevant facts and circumstances' (Joined Cases C-501/06 P, C-513/06 P, C-515/06 P and C-519/06 P *GlaxoSmithKline Services and Others v Commission and Others*, ECLI:EU:C:2009:409, Opinion of AG Trstenjak, para 297; see also para 301).

[21] See, eg, the bias complaints in Case T-62/98 *Volkswagen v Commission*, ECLI:EU:T:2000:180, paras 270–72; and Case T-279/02 *Degussa v Commission*, ECLI:EU:T:2006:103, paras 399–426. See also Case T-201/04 *Microsoft v Commission*, ECLI:EU:T:2007:289, para 1275.

[22] Charles Lord, Lee Ross and Mark Lepper, 'Biased Assimilation and Attitude Polarization: The Effects of Prior Theories on Subsequently Considered Evidence' (1979) 37 *Journal of Personality and Social Psychology* 2098. In the competition context, see, eg, the criticisms of Christopher Decker and George Yarrow, 'On the Discovery and Assessment of Economic Evidence in Competition Law' in *Studies in Regulation* (Regulatory Policy Institute, 2011) 40–43; and also the interesting research of Malcolm Coate and Andrew Kleit, 'Does it Matter That the Prosecutor is Also the Judge? The Administrative Complaint Process at the Federal Trade Commission' (1998) 19 *Managerial and Decision Economics* 1, 9.

[23] Wouter Wils, 'The Combination of the Investigative and Prosecutorial Function and the Adjudicative Function in EC Antitrust Enforcement: A Legal and Economic Analysis' (2004) 27 *World Competition* 201, 214–17.

[24] Although its exact protective scope is not yet fully fledged, the expectation is that the right to good administration will evolve into the equivalent of the right to a fair trial for administrative proceedings (see Case C-439/11 P *Ziegler v Commission*, ECLI:EU:C:2012:800, Opinion of AG Kokott, paras 139–51; Case T-343/06 *Shell Petroleum and Others v Commission*, ECLI:EU:T:2012:478, para 82; Case T-46/10 *Faci v Commission*, ECLI:EU:T:2014:138, paras 168–73). More generally,

inter alia, the Commission's duty to state reasons[25] and 'to examine carefully and impartially all the relevant aspects of the individual case'.[26] However, it should be clarified that although a failure to satisfy the applicable evidence standards may cost the Commission the legality of its decision, it does not automatically give rise to violations of Article 41 CFR and to non-contractual liability of the EU. *MyTravel* is a good example thereof.[27] Dismissing the applicant's argument that the Commission's failure to adduce cogent evidence in *Airtours* was a violation of its duty to state reasons, the GCEU explained that the critical issue was that 'the Airtours decision set out reasons which were adequate and which allowed the Court to review its legality, even though in terms of its substance those reasons were shown to be incorrect once that review had been carried out'.[28] Nevertheless, this does not eliminate the fact that the applicable evidence standards call for heightened levels of administrative care by the Commission.

At the same time, the existing rules and principles of evidence assessment, as developed by EU judges, have a second important implication: they effectively delimit the authority's exercise of its margin of appreciation. Being a specialised agency entrusted by the EU Treaties with securing compliance with the antitrust rules, the Commission enjoys a degree of discretion with respect to policy issues and a margin of appreciation where complex economic appraisals are involved. The way in which the authority makes use of its discretion – for instance, its choice of enforcement tool or the design of its fining policy – must comply with the principle of proportionality and fundamental rights.[29] By contrast, its exercise of its margin of appreciation is subject to the evidence qualification of the 'manifest error of assessment' test as per the *Tetra Laval* formula. In this sense, the applicable evidence standards set a hard limit to any latitude the Commission enjoys – for instance, in choosing its preferred theory of harm or econometric evidence to produce – by entailing a clear call for evidence-based administrative decision-making. Indeed, a conclusion that the competition rules are complied with or not must be grounded on evidence which is admissible and carries, on the whole, such probative weight as to satisfy the standard of proof. In this light, the applicable rules and principles of evidence assessment are embedded in the existing institutional setting as a procedural safeguard against the risk of arbitrary enforcement.

see Hanns Peter Nehl, *Principles of Administrative Procedure in EC Law* (Hart Publishing, 1999) 103 ff; Herwig Hofmann and Bucura Mihaescu, 'The Relation between the Charter's Fundamental Rights and the Unwritten General Principles of EU Law: Good Administration as the Test Case' (2013) 9 *European Constitutional Law Review* 73, 83 ff.

[25] Case C-37/13 P *Nexans and Nexans France v Commission*, ECLI:EU:C:2014:223, Opinion of AG Kokott, paras 41–42.

[26] Case T-299/08 *Elf Aquitaine v Commission*, ECLI:EU:T:2011:217, para 237; Case T-458/09 *Slovak Telekom v Commission*, ECLI:EU:T:2012:145, para 68; see also Case T-175/12 *Deutsche Börse v Commission*, ECLI:EU:T:2015:148, para 67.

[27] Case T-212/03 *MyTravel v Commission*, ECLI:EU:T:2008:315.

[28] ibid paras 72, 96.

[29] See ch 7, n 9.

Last but not least, the evidence standards in place may influence the legitimacy of the Commission's decision-making. The notion of legitimacy and its various manifestations have been the subject of vigorous debate in legal, political and psychological discourse.[30] Typically, however, the legitimacy of law enforcement is perceived in terms of outcomes (also called *output* legitimacy) and in terms of processes (known as *input* legitimacy),[31] and is often identified among the reasons why people obey the law.[32] Inevitably, the overall legitimacy of EU competition enforcement is contingent on multiple factors and is an issue which goes beyond the scope of this book.[33] Still, it is crucial to appreciate the pivotal contribution that evidence standards may make in shaping the legitimacy of antitrust and merger decision-making – both directly and indirectly. Directly, the applicable rules and principles of evidence assessment may influence input legitimacy, to the extent that they form an intrinsic component of procedural due process.[34] Indirectly, they may underpin output legitimacy by strengthening the evidence base – and thus arguably the quality – of administrative decision-making.

B. The Connotations for the EU Courts

EU judges have compensated for the almost complete lack of legislation on matters of evidence assessment by incrementally developing a comprehensive framework guiding the evaluation of evidence in EU competition proceedings. As the analysis in the previous chapters has revealed, the EU Courts have progressively formulated several rules and principles to guide the appraisal of evidence as part of antitrust and merger decision-making.

At the same time, the EU Courts have employed evidence standards as a tool for reviewing the legality of Commission decisions by conditioning the exercise of administrative latitude on heightened evidential requirements, thereby marginalising marginal review with respect to complex economic evaluations. The use of evidence standards as a Trojan horse for conducting a thorough review of the

[30] For a brief account, see Christopher Thomas, 'The Uses and Abuses of Legitimacy in International Law' (2014) 34 *Oxford Journal of Legal Studies* 729, 733–52.

[31] These terms originated in the work of Fritz Scharpf, *Governing in Europe: Effective and Democratic?* (Oxford University Press, 1999). Victor Bekkers and Arthur Edwards, 'Legitimacy and Democracy: A Conceptual Framework for Assessing Governance Practices' in Victor Bekkers et al (eds), *Governance and the Democratic Deficit: Assessing the Democratic Legitimacy of Governance Practices* (Ashgate, 2007) 35, 44–45 further developed the concept of *throughput* legitimacy, which refers specifically to the procedural dimension of input legitimacy, namely the rules and procedures by which binding decisions are made.

[32] See Tom Tyler, *Why People Obey the Law* (Princeton University Press, 2006).

[33] See generally Ingeborg Simonsson, *Legitimacy in EU Cartel Control* (Hart Publishing, 2010); Wolf Sauter, *Coherence in EU Competition Law* (Oxford University Press, 2016); Philip Lowe, Mel Marquis and Giorgio Monti (eds), *European Competition Law Annual 2013: Effective and Legitimate Enforcement of Competition Law* (Hart Publishing, 2016).

[34] See generally Tom Tyler, 'Procedural Fairness and Compliance with the Law' (1997) 133 *Swiss Journal of Economics and Statistics* 219.

authority's findings should not be underestimated. In this way, the EU Courts are, first of all, able to safeguard the effective judicial protection of the undertakings concerned by ensuring that their economic freedom is restricted only where there is strong evidence justifying administrative intervention. Second, evidence review enables the EU Courts to ensure that the Commission is held sufficiently accountable and that its decisions do not exceed the bounds of its competition competence.[35] Finally, the evidence focus of the judicial control has the capacity to increase the chances of detecting mistakes in the Commission's reasoning and can thus contribute to minimising both false convictions and false acquittals in EU competition enforcement in line with the error-correction function of judicial review.[36]

Nevertheless, the applicable evidence standards may fully realise their potential only if the EU Courts actually engage in a detailed and exhaustive examination of the evidence with a view to verifying whether the Commission's findings are supported by the available information. In this regard, consistency is crucial. Patterns of fluctuating thoroughness may reduce confidence in the ability of EU judges to scrutinise the authority's decisions, especially where complex economic appraisals are involved. Although their generalist background has been occasionally blamed for variations in the intensity of their judicial review, it is submitted that if the EU Courts have comprehensively scrutinised the Commission's conclusions in certain cases, there is no valid reason to postulate that they are unable to undertake an equally in-depth control in all cases.[37] In practice, the applicable evidence standards create an expectation from the EU Courts not to accept the authority's findings at face value, but proactively to engage with the evidence in order to verify that they are justified. In this light, the quality of judicial review hinges on the readiness of EU judges to identify and acknowledge obstacles to their ability to thoroughly scrutinise the evidence underpinning the Commission's reasoning and their willingness to engage all possible means at their disposal to overcome any difficulties. Accordingly, the judicial practice of ordering measures of inquiry must be praised.

That said, there appears to exist some room for improvement with respect to complex economic evidence at the level of the application of the competition

[35] This trend is visible in other areas of EU law as well – particularly where the fundamental rights of individuals are at risk or/and where the administrative authority's decision-making entails complex assessments, value judgements and policy choices, such as in the field of *risk regulation* (eg, Case C-269/90 *Technische Universität München v Hauptzollamt München-Mitte*, ECLI:EU:C:1991:438, paras 13–14), *state aid* (eg, Case C-525/04 P *Spain v Lenzing*, ECLI:EU:C:2007:698, paras 56–58) and *common foreign and security policy*, where restrictive measures are imposed upon individuals (eg, Joined Cases C-584/10 P, C-593/10 P and C-595/10 P *Commission and Others v Kadi*, ECLI:EU:C:2013:518, paras 119–24).

[36] Steven Shavell, 'The Appeals Process as a Means of Error Correction' (1995) 24 *Journal of Legal Studies* 379. More generally on the functions of judicial review and its importance in EU competition law, see Damien Geradin and Nicolas Petit, 'Judicial Review in European Union Competition Law: A Quantitative and Qualitative Assessment' in Massimo Merola and Jacques Derenne (eds), *The Role of the Court of Justice of the European Union in Competition Law Cases* (Bruylant, 2012) 23–44.

[37] Simon Bishop, 'Expert Economic Evidence in European Competition Law Cases' in Merola and Derenne (n 36) 303.

rules. As explained in Chapter 5, since the assessment of the evidence is solely governed by the principle of unfettered evaluation, the margin of appreciation that the Commission enjoys where complex economic appraisals are involved provides no excuse for the EU Courts to abstain from a thorough review of the supporting economic evidence. Therefore, EU judges must be prepared to make use of all available mechanisms in order to undertake an independent appraisal of the probative weight of such information.

VI. The Implications for National Procedural Autonomy

This book has focused on the standards which govern the evaluation of evidence in competition proceedings at the EU level. Nevertheless, Articles 101 and 102 TFEU may also be enforced at the national level – either by public agencies or by private parties before national courts. In fact, national competition enforcement has been on the rise in the past 15 years following two important developments: on the other hand, the adoption of Regulation 1/2003, which fully decentralised the enforcement regime;[38] and, on the other hand, the adoption of the Damages Actions Directive in 2014, which introduced minimum harmonised rules governing actions for damages suffered from an antitrust violation.[39] Against this backdrop, the question arises as to whether the evidence standards developed by the EU Courts might have any implications for national competition enforcement.

A. The Operation of Divergent Evidence Standards at the National Level

NCAs and national courts are bound by the EU Courts' jurisprudence on the interpretation of Articles 101 and 102 TFEU. By contrast, matters of procedure have been left for Member States to determine. Indeed, with some limited exceptions,[40] Regulation 1/2003 is largely silent on the procedural rules governing the enforcement of the antitrust provisions at the national level. The latitude that Member States enjoy in shaping their procedural systems as they deem appropriate derives from the well-established principle of national procedural autonomy.[41]

[38] Recitals 6–9 and arts 5 and 6 of Regulation 1/2003.

[39] Directive 2014/104/EU of the European Parliament and of the Council of 26 November 2014 on certain rules governing actions for damages under national law for infringements of the competition law provisions of the Member States and of the European Union [2014] OJ L349/1.

[40] Articles 5, 11 and 12 of Regulation 1/2003.

[41] The exact scope of the principle of national procedural autonomy has given rise to debates. See generally Constantinos Kakouris, 'Do the Member States Possess Judicial Procedural "Autonomy"?' (1997) 34 *Common Market Law Review* 1389; Walter van Gerven, 'Of Rights, Remedies and Procedures' (2000) 37 *Common Market Law Review* 501; John Delicostopoulos, 'Towards European Procedural Primacy in National Legal Systems' (2003) 9 *European Law Journal* 599.

According to the latter, unless procedural rules are provided for in primary or secondary EU law, Member States are free to adopt their own, as long as their application does not violate the principle of equivalence and does not undermine the effectiveness of EU law.[42] Briefly, the principle of equivalence requires the same remedies and procedural rules to be available to claims based on EU law as they are to analogous claims of a purely domestic nature, whereas the principle of effectiveness requires that they do not render claims based on EU law impossible or extremely difficult to enforce in practice.[43]

With the exception of the legal burden, whose allocation has been harmonised in Article 2 of Regulation 1/2003, Member States are free to apply the evidence rules of their choice. As a result, the regulation of the standard of proof, the types of admissible evidence, inadmissibility rules and the criteria for ascertaining the probative weight of the evidence may vary considerably.[44] In the UK, for instance, the applicable standard of proof that the Competition and Markets Authority (CMA) or a private claimant in the context of private litigation must satisfy is the *balance of probabilities*. Nevertheless, in proceedings against the Office of Fair Trading – the predecessor of the CMA – in *Napp*, the Competition Appeal Tribunal (CAT) stressed that in view of the quasi-criminal nature of the sanctions involved, 'strong and compelling evidence will be required before infringements of the Chapter I and Chapter II prohibitions can be found to be proved, even to the civil standard of proof'.[45] On the other hand, in civil law countries, such as Greece, France and Germany, it is the *inner conviction* of the judge which dictates whether an antitrust infringement will be deemed to have been established.

Some degree of divergence seems to exist in relation to presumptions as well. In several Member States, presumptions are recognised as a 'means of evidence', but not all of them feature presumptions specific to competition enforcement – or the same ones. For example, only some Member States – including Austria, Germany and Estonia – have statutory presumptions of dominance, which are triggered under different conditions.[46] Last but not least, national rules on the admissibility and probative value of the evidence also vary. For instance, while the protection of written communications between lawyer and client is generally recognised, its scope and the criteria for applying it may differ from Member State

[42] Case 33/76 *Rewe v Landwirtschaftskammer für das Saarland*, ECLI:EU:C:1976:188, para 5; and Case 45/76 *Comet BV v Produktschap voor Siergewassen*, ECLI:EU:C:1976:191, para 13.

[43] Case C-453/99 *Courage and Crehan*, ECLI:EU:C:2001:465, para 29; and Joined Cases C-295/04 to C-298/04 *Manfredi*, ECLI:EU:C:2006:461, para 62.

[44] Information on the rules governing actions for damages in various Member States and on the national rules for the taking of evidence is available at http://ec.europa.eu/competition/antitrust/actionsdamages/study.html and http://ec.europa.eu/competition/antitrust/actionsdamages/study.html.

[45] *Napp Pharmaceutical Holdings Limited and Subsidiaries v Director General of Fair Trading* [2002] CAT 1, para 108.

[46] Brenda Sufrin, 'The Notion of Dominance in Competition Law: An Overview of EU and National Case-Law' (2012) *e-Competitions* N° 43209.

to Member State, as the CJEU recognised in *Akzo Nobel*.[47] Inevitably, this may lead to divergent outcomes regarding the admissibility of certain items of information at the national level. As far as the probative value of the evidence is concerned, most legal systems provide for its free evaluation, although in practice there exists some variation in the assessment of the reliability of different types of evidence. For example, in *Tesco*, the CAT held that 'it would not place substantial weight upon notes of interviews where the individuals in question were not being called to give evidence before the Tribunal and whose evidence would not, therefore, be tested by cross-examination'.[48]

B. The Capacity of the EU Evidence Standards to Pave the Way for Further Procedural Convergence

The operation of divergent evidence standards at the national level is not problematic in itself. However, Member States' rules on evidence are subject to the principles of equivalence and effectiveness, as the CJEU confirmed in *Eturas*,[49] in line with earlier jurisprudence highlighting that national procedural rules must not jeopardise the effective application of Articles 101 and 102 TFEU and the scheme of Regulation 1/2003.[50] Interestingly, in its Report on the functioning of Regulation 1/2003, the Commission acknowledged that 'divergences of Member States' enforcement systems remain on important aspects' and expressed the view that this 'may merit further examination and reflection'.[51] From the perspective of private enforcement in particular, procedural variations among national legal systems become crucial, since they may drive the choice of jurisdiction in private actions. While the Damages Actions Directive injected a minimum level of harmonisation in this area, several issues – including questions of evidence assessment – remain regulated by national laws.[52] One may thus wonder whether the evidence

[47] Case C-550/07 P *Akzo Nobel Chemicals and Akcros Chemicals v Commission*, ECLI:EU:C:2010:512, paras 69–76. See also Jean-François Bellis, 'Legal Professional Privilege: An Overview of EU and National Case Law' (2011) *e-Competitions* N° 39467; Julia Holtz, 'Legal Professional Privilege in Europe: A Missed Policy Opportunity' (2013) 4 *Journal of European Competition Law & Practice* 402, 405. Note also Case T-54/14 *Goldfish and Others v Commission*, ECLI:EU:T:2016:455, paras 75–79.

[48] *Flynn Pharma Limited and Another v CMA* [2018] CAT 11, para 83, citing *Tesco v OFT* [2012] CAT 31, paras 138–39.

[49] Case C-74/14 *Eturas and Others*, ECLI:EU:C:2016:42, paras 30–32.

[50] eg, Case C-439/08 *VEBIC*, ECLI:EU:C:2010:739, para 57; Case C-360/09 *Pfleiderer*, ECLI:EU:C:2011:389, paras 23 ff; Case C-557/12 *Kone and Others*, ECLI:EU:C:2014:1317, para 33; Case C-536/11 *Donau Chemie and Others*, ECLI:EU:C:2013:366, paras 29–49.

[51] Communication from the Commission to the European Parliament and the Council, Report on the functioning of Regulation 1/2003 (COM(2009) 206 (final)) 8. See also the recommendations in Silke Brammer et al, 'Report on the Enforcement by NCAs and the ECN' in Massimo Merola and Denis Waelbroeck (eds), *Towards an Optimal Enforcement of Competition Rules in Europe: Time for a Review of Regulation 1/2003* (Bruylant, 2010).

[52] Note that the Damages Actions Directive introduced a presumption that cartel infringements cause harm (art 17(2)). Moreover, art 9 provides that final NCA decisions finding an antitrust infringement

standards developed by the EU Courts may affect the rules on evidence governing national proceedings concerning the application of Articles 101 and 102 TFEU.[53]

To begin with the burden of proof, Article 2 of Regulation 1/2003 exceptionally harmonises its application, thereby leaving no room for the principle of national procedural autonomy. According to Recital 5, its harmonisation was deemed necessary 'in order to ensure an effective enforcement of the [EU] competition rules and at the same time the respect of fundamental rights of defence'. However, the fact that Article 2 applies to EU and national proceedings alike implies that the refined approach to the allocation of the legal burden, as proposed in Chapter 3, may have an impact on the national enforcement of the EU antitrust rules too. The magnitude of this impact will depend on the premise underpinning the proposed rereading. If one accepts that a shared distribution of the burden of persuasion is prone to distort the proper construction of Articles 101 and 102 TFEU, allocating the whole legal burden on the NCA or the person alleging an antitrust violation is the inevitable solution to the problem. Admittedly, such an outcome could in principle discourage private enforcement by complicating the efforts of individuals to establish an infringement before national courts. Nevertheless, it should be noted that the bulk of competition litigation comprises standalone or follow-on actions for damages suffered as a result of the operation of a cartel. In this context, it is usually the anti-competitive effects of the cartel, issues of causation and the exact amount of the harm which are disputed, rather than the existence of efficiencies and the overall pro-competitive nature of the conduct. Therefore, one may speculate that private enforcement will not be as adversely affected by the proposed rereading of Article 2 of Regulation 1/2003. Any problems could be addressed through the introduction of appropriate presumptions which would alleviate plaintiffs' legal burden. By contrast, if one bases the suggested refinement of the current bifurcated allocation of the burden of persuasion on its incompatibility with the presumption of innocence, the impact on national competition enforcement will be less extensive. Indeed, the presumption of innocence does not apply to proceedings between private parties. Individuals requesting an injunction or bringing an action for damages for harm suffered from an antitrust violation do not dispose of investigative, decision-making and fining powers similar to those enjoyed by public agencies. Since the balance of powers between parties in private litigation is fundamentally different from that in administrative or criminal settings, the proposed rereading of Article 2 of Regulation 1/2003 would be confined to public competition enforcement only.

constitute proof thereof for the purposes of an action for damages before the courts of the Member State in question and at least prima facie evidence in all other Member States. Last but not least, according to art 17(1), Member States must ensure that neither the burden nor the standard of proof required for the quantification of harm renders the exercise of the right to damages practically impossible or excessively difficult.

[53] Since Member States have their own merger rules, the following analysis is specific to the enforcement of arts 101 and 102 TFEU.

In any event, the fact that the burden of proof is harmonised is important for a second reason. As explained in Chapter 6, the EU Courts have progressively developed various presumptions in EU competition enforcement. However, from a procedural perspective, presumptions function as a mechanism for shifting the burden of proof. With this in mind, Simonsson interestingly suggested that the presumptions established by EU judges in their competition jurisprudence could be understood as 'interpretations of the concept of "burden of proof", now regulated in Article 2'.[54] In this sense, the latter might be said to provide the gate for their transposition into national proceedings. Yet, even if this line of reasoning reads too much into Regulation 1/2003, *T-Mobile* potentially offers another route. Asked whether the referring court could apply the national rules on the burden of proof to its examination of the existence of a causal connection between concertation and subsequent market conduct, or whether it was required to apply the EU presumption according to which undertakings that remain active on the market are presumed to have taken into account the information exchanged with their competitors,[55] the CJEU held that 'the presumption of a causal connection stems from Article [101(1) TFEU], as interpreted by the Court, and it consequently forms an integral part of applicable [EU] law'.[56] Therefore, the national court was required to apply it in disregard of the national rules on the burden of proof.

T-Mobile exemplifies how blurred the line between matters of procedure and matters of substance may be. Most importantly, it lays the foundations for other presumptions similarly to disable national evidence rules on the ground that they form part of *substantive* EU competition law. Arguably, *Eturas* qualified *T-Mobile* by explaining that the reason why the *Anic* presumption is transposed into national legal systems is that it follows from the concept of a 'concerted practice' and is intrinsically linked to it.[57] By contrast, the question at hand in *Eturas* – namely whether the mere dispatch of an electronic message concerning a discount cap by the administrator of an online booking system to participating travel agents constitutes sufficient evidence to establish that its addressees were aware or ought to have been aware of its content – 'must be regarded as relating to the assessment of evidence and to the standard of proof, with the result that it is governed … by national law'.[58] Nevertheless, one might well argue that all the EU presumptions described in Chapter 6 'follow from' EU law concepts or are 'intrinsically linked' to them. For instance, the *Akzo* presumption of actual exercise of decisive influence concerns the EU notion of 'undertaking'.[59] Accordingly, they seem to have the capacity to displace national evidence rules.

[54] Ingeborg Simonsson, *Legitimacy in EU Cartel Control* (Hart Publishing, 2010) 187.
[55] Case C-8/08 *T-Mobile Netherlands*, ECLI:EU:C:2009:343, para 44.
[56] ibid para 52.
[57] *Eturas* (n 49) paras 33–34.
[58] ibid.
[59] The *Aalborg Portland* presumption concerns the issue what conduct may amount to participation in an anticompetitive agreement. The presumption of continuity is intrinsically linked to the duration of the infringement, namely one of the constituent elements of a violation. Finally, the presumption of capability follows from the 'by object' notion.

Equally interesting is the question as to whether the standard of proof as regulated at the EU level may also pave the way for further procedural convergence in national competition proceedings. The Commission Report on the functioning of Regulation 1/2003 gives this question prominence by identifying the standard of proof as one of the areas of divergence among Member States.[60] Indeed, Recital 5 expressly provides that national rules on the standard of proof are not prejudiced by Regulation 1/2003. Nevertheless, national procedural autonomy is qualified by the principle of effectiveness. The latter may confine national thresholds of evidence sufficiency in two ways. On the one hand, national standards of proof may not jeopardise the effectiveness of EU competition law.[61] In *Eturas*, the CJEU stressed that 'national rules governing the assessment of evidence and the standard of proof must not render the implementation of EU competition rules impossible or excessively difficult'.[62] Accordingly, 'the principle of effectiveness requires that an infringement of EU competition law may be proven not only by direct evidence, but also through indicia, provided that they are objective and consistent'.[63] On similar grounds, one might argue that national thresholds of evidence sufficiency which are higher than the 'firm conviction' standard endorsed by the EU Courts might not be allowed to operate in the context of national proceedings, where they would seriously undermine the ability of NCAs to enforce the antitrust rules. On the other hand, national standards of proof may not imperil the effectiveness of the CFR either.[64] In *Eturas*, for instance, the CJEU underlined that the presumption of innocence, which is now enshrined in the CFR and which 'the Member States are required to observe when they implement EU competition law', precludes a national court 'from inferring from the mere dispatch of the message at issue that the travel agencies concerned ought to have been aware of the content of that message'.[65] Similarly, national thresholds of evidence sufficiency enabling an NCA to find an infringement of Article 101 or 102 TFEU, for instance, on a balance of the probabilities may also be impermissible if they compromise the effective judicial protection of the undertakings concerned.[66]

More broadly, analogous arguments may be advanced in relation to national rules on the admissibility or probative weight of the evidence. To the extent that such rules may jeopardise the effectiveness of EU competition law or the principle

[60] Report on the functioning of Regulation 1/2003 (n 51) 8.

[61] Albeit not in the competition context; see Case 199/82 *San Giorgio*, ECLI:EU:C:1983:318, para 14. See also Takis Tridimas, *The General Principles of EU Law*, 2nd edn (Oxford University Press, 2006) 395 in relation to undertakings' rights of defence.

[62] *Eturas* (n 49) para 35.

[63] ibid para 37.

[64] According to art 51(1), the CFR is binding on Member States when they implement EU law.

[65] *Eturas* (n 49) paras 38–39. See also Case C-604/12 *N*, ECLI:EU:C:2014:302, para 41.

[66] See also Case 6/71 *Rheinmühlen Düsseldorf*, ECLI:EU:C:1971:100, para 8; Maria João Melicias, '"Did They Do it?" The Interplay between the Standard of Proof and the Presumption of Innocence in EU Cartel Investigations' (2012) 35 *World Competition* 471, 487, 507–08 on the converging potential of the presumption of innocence.

of effective judicial protection as enshrined in the CFR, they might be similarly set aside.[67] Against this backdrop, the emergence at the EU level of a comprehensive framework for evidence assessment as part of EU competition enforcement might serve in the future as a yardstick for the convergence of national evidence rules, especially where evidence matters are identified with substantive law and where the national institutional framework resembles the EU one and the fundamental rights of the undertakings involved are at risk.

VII. Conclusion

This book has sought to understand what rules and principles govern the assessment of evidence in competition enforcement at the EU level. The significance of this question derives from the fact that both the Commission – when applying the EU competition rules – and the EU Courts – when reviewing the lawfulness of the authority's decisions – rely on evidence. Drawing on the previous analysis, which was focused on identifying the foundations for a system of evidence assessment in EU competition enforcement based on the antitrust and merger jurisprudence of the EU Courts, this final chapter has offered some reflections on the connotations and implications of the applicable evidence standards for EU competition enforcement from different angles.

In this context, it was, first of all, observed that the evidence rules in place seem to indicate a preference for false convictions in antitrust enforcement and a risk-neutral approach in merger control – at least at the level of adjudication. Nevertheless, while these connotations might refine the system's overall risk proclivity or adversity, they may not override the error balancing choices made through other mechanisms – such as prioritisation principles or substantive legal tests. In any event, this chapter further highlighted the double contribution of the applicable evidence standards to the fairness of the regime: on the one hand, they are broadly speaking compatible with the principle of effective judicial protection; on the other hand, they may compensate for the 'fairness deficit' in the administrative model in place. Beyond procedural due process, their capacity to accommodate the 'more economic' approach to EU competition enforcement, whilst operating

[67] The capacity of the CFR to serve as a promising starting point for future procedural convergence has started attracting academic attention (eg, Pieter Van Cleynenbreugel, 'Judge-Made Standards of National Procedure in the Post-Lisbon Constitutional Framework' (2012) 37 *European Law Review* 90, 95–97). In the competition context in particular, strong arguments have been advanced in favour of further procedural convergence of the rights of defence available to undertakings participating in national competition proceedings (see, eg, Maciej Bernatt, 'Convergence of Procedural Standards in the European Competition Proceedings' (2012) 8 *Competition Law Review* 255; Krystyna Kowalik-Bańczyk, 'Procedural Autonomy of Member States and the EU Rights of Defence in Antitrust Proceedings' (2012) 5 *Yearbook of Antitrust and Regulatory Studies* 215; Laurence Idot, Pascal Cordonnel and Antoine Choffel, 'La Place des Droits Fondamentaux dans les Procédures de Concurrence' (Revue Concurrences, Paris, 16 January 2013)).

at the same time as a 'quality filter' calling for evidence-based decision-making, was also noted. Furthermore, although matters of substance and matters of procedure are sometimes thought of as being in disconnect, it was explained that their symbiosis is more sophisticated than one might think; the allocation of the burden of persuasion in particular may have a crucial impact on the substantive scope of the competition rules, which has been underestimated. That said, it is equally important to remember that evidence mechanisms – especially presumptions – are not a panacea and they may not eliminate problems in the articulation of the liability rules.

With these remarks in mind, some reflections were then offered on the connotations of the applicable evidence standards for the EU institutions involved in competition enforcement, namely the Commission and the EU Courts. As far as the authority is concerned, it was pointed out that the existing evidence rules and principles call for heightened levels of administrative care in line with the right to good administration, whereas they also set a limit to the Commission's margin of appreciation and may influence the legitimacy of its decision-making. For the EU Courts, on the other hand, their jurisprudence on these issues has created expectations from them of a thorough review of the evidence as part of their judicial control, which might necessitate the regular use of appropriate measures of inquiry, depending on the sufficiency and complexity of the evidence at hand. Pondering then over the implications of the EU standards for evidence assessment for national competition enforcement, the analysis highlighted their capacity to curb the autonomy of Member States in this field and to serve as a yardstick for paving the way for further procedural convergence at the national level.

All in all, this book has contributed to knowledge not only by identifying the main rules and principles governing the evaluation of evidence in competition proceedings at the EU level, but also by showing that the applicable evidence standards are not dry technicalities; rather, they are essential components of an underlying framework, which complements the substantive legal tests and may shape enforcement in its own right.

BIBLIOGRAPHY

Aigner, G, Budzinski, O and Christiansen, A, 'Analysis of Coordinated Effects in EU Merger Control: Where Do We Stand after *Sony/BMG* and *Impala*?' (2006) 2 *European Competition Journal* 311

Akman, P, 'The Role of "Freedom" in EU Competition Law' (2014) 34 *Legal Studies* 183

Albors-Llorens, A, 'The Role of Objective Justification and Effciencies in the Application of Article 82 EC' (2007) 44 *Common Market Law Review* 1727

Allen, R, 'Burdens of Proof' (2014) 13 *Law, Probability & Risk* 195

——. 'Burdens of Proof, Uncertainty and Ambiguity in Modern Legal Discourse' (1994) 17 *Harvard Journal of Law & Public Policy* 627

——. 'Factual Ambiguity and a Theory of Evidence' (1994) 88 *Northwestern Law Review* 604

——. 'The Nature of Juridical Proof' (1991) 13 *Cardozo Law Review* 373

——. 'Presumptions in Civil Actions Reconsidered' (1981) 66 *Iowa Law Review* 843

Allen, R and Callen, C, 'The Juridical Management of Factual Uncertainty' (2003) 7 *International Journal of Evidence and Proof* 1

Allen, R and Jehl, S, 'Burdens of Persuasion in Civil Cases: Algorithms v. Explanations' (2003) 4 *Michigan State Law Review* 893

Allen, R and Leiter, B, 'Naturalised Epistemology and the Law of Evidence' (2001) 87 *Virginia Law Review* 1491

Allen, R and Stein, A, 'Evidence, Probability, and the Burden of Proof' (2013) 55 *Arizona Law Review* 557

Allendesalazar, R, 'Evidence Gathered through Leniency: From the Prisoner's Dilemma to a Race to the Bottom' in CD Ehlermann and M Marquis (eds), *European Competition Law Annual 2009: Evaluation of Evidence and its Judicial Review in Competition Cases* (Hart Publishing, 2010)

Andreangeli, A, 'Between Economic Freedom and Effective Competition Enforcement: The Impact of the Antitrust Remedies Provided by the Modernisation Regulation on Investigated Parties' Freedom to Contract and to Enjoy Property' (2010) 6 *Competition Law Review* 225

——. *EU Competition Enforcement and Human Rights* (Edward Elgar, 2008)

Andreangeli, A et al, 'Enforcement by the Commission: The Decisional and Enforcement Structure in Antitrust Cases and the Commission's Fining System' in Massimo Merola and Denis Waelbroeck (eds), *Towards an Optimal Enforcement of Competition Rules in Europe: Time for a Review of Regulation 1/2003?* (Bruylant, 2010)

Andriychuk, O, *The Normative Foundations of European Competition Law* (Edward Elgar, 2017)

Arancibia, J, *Judicial Review of Commercial Regulation* (Oxford University Press, 2011)

Ashworth, A, 'Excluding Evidence as Protecting Rights' (1977) 3 *Criminal Law Review* 723

——. 'Four Threats to the Presumption of Innocence' (2006) 123 *South African Law Journal* 63

Bailey, D, '"Publicly Distancing" Oneself from a Cartel' (2008) 31(2) *World Competition* 177

——. 'Presumptions in EU Competition Law' (2010) 31 *European Competition Law Review* 362

——. 'Restrictions of Competition by Object under Article 101 TFEU' (2012) 49 *Common Market Law Review* 559

——. 'Scope of Judicial Review under Article 81 EC' (2004) 41 *Common Market Law Review* 1327

——. 'Standard of Proof in EC Merger Proceedings: A Common Law Perspective' (2003) 40 *Common Market Law Review* 845

Baker, J, 'Merger Simulation in an Administrative Context' (2011) 77 *Antitrust Law Journal* 451

——. 'Taking the Error out of the Error-Cost Analysis: What's Wrong with Antitrust's Right' (2015) 80 *Antitrust Law Journal* 1

Baker, J and Bresnahan, T, 'Economic Evidence in Antitrust: Defining Markets and Measuring Market Power' in P Buccirossi (ed), *Handbook of Antitrust Economics*, vol 1 (MIT Press, 2008)

Barbier de la Serre, E and Sibony, AL, 'Expert Evidence before the EC Courts' (2008) 45 *Common Market Law Review* 941

Bay, M and Ruiz Calzado, J, '*Tetra Laval II*: The Coming of Age of the Judicial Review of Merger Decisions' (2005) 28 *World Competition* 433

Baye, M and Wright, J, 'Is Antitrust Too Complicated for Generalist Judges? The Impact of Economic Complexity and Judicial Training on Appeals' (2011) 54 *Journal of Law and Economics* 1

Beckner, F and Salop, S, 'Decision Theory and Antitrust Rules' (1999) 67 *Antitrust Law Journal* 41

Bekkers, V and Edwards, A, 'Legitimacy and Democracy: A Conceptual Framework for Assessing Governance Practices' in V Bekkers et al (eds), *Governance and the Democratic Deficit: Assessing the Democratic Legitimacy of Governance Practices* (Ashgate, 2007)

Bellamy, C, 'Standards of Proof in Competition Cases' in *Judicial Enforcement of Competition Law* (OECD Competition Policy Roundtable, 1996)

Bellis, JF, 'Legal Professional Privilege: An Overview of EU and National Case Law' (2011) *e-Competitions* N° 39467

Bernatt, M, 'Convergence of Procedural Standards in the European Competition Proceedings' (2012) 8 *Competition Law Review* 255

Bernstein, R, *Beyond Objectivism and Relativism: Science, Hermeneutics, and Praxis* (University of Pennsylvania Press, 1983)

Bishop, S, 'Expert Economic Evidence in European Competition Law Cases' in M Merola and J Derenne (eds), *The Role of the Court of Justice of the European Union in Competition Law Cases* (Bruylant, 2012)

——. 'Snake-Oil with Mathematics is Still Snake-Iil: Why Recent Trends in the Application of So-Called "Sophisticated" Economics is Hindering Good Competition Policy Enforcement' (2013) 9 *European Competition Journal* 67

Blair, R and Boylston Hemdon, J, 'The Implications of *Daubert* for Economic Evidence in Antitrust Cases' (2000) 57 *Washington and Lee Law Review* 801

Bohlen, F, 'The Effect of Rebuttable Presumptions of Law upon the Burden of Proof' (1920) 68 *University of Pennsylvania Law Review* 307

Botteman, Y, 'Mergers, Standard of Proof and Expert Economic Evidence' (2006) 2 *Journal of Competition Law and Economics* 71

Botteman, Y, Joshua, J and Atlee, L, '"You Can't Beat the Percentage": The Parental Liability Presumption in EU Cartel Enforcement' (2012) *European Antitrust Review* 3

Bouveresse, A, *Le Pouvoir Discrétionnaire dans l'Ordre Juridique Communautaire* (Bruylant, 2010)

Brammer, S et al, 'Report on the Enforcement by NCAs and the ECN' in M Merola and D Waelbroeck (eds), *Towards an Optimal Enforcement of Competition Rules in Europe: Time for a Review of Regulation 1/2003* (Bruylant, 2010)

Brealey, M, 'The Burden of Proof before the European Court' (1985) 10 *European Law Review* 250

Brewer, S, 'Scientific Expert Testimony and Intellectual Due Process' (1998) 107 *Yale Law Journal* 1535

Bridge, N, 'Presumptions and Burdens' (1949) 12 *Modern Law Review* 273

Brodley, J, 'Proof of Efficiencies in Mergers and Joint Ventures' (1996) 64 *Antitrust Law Journal* 575

Bronckers, M and Valery, A, 'Business as Usual after *Menarini*?' (2012) 3 *MLexMagazine* 44

——. 'Fair and Effective Competition Policy in the EU: Which Role for Authorities and Which Role for the Courts after *Menarini*?' (2012) 8 *European Competition Journal* 283

——. 'No Longer Presumed Guilty? The Impact of Fundamental Rights on Certain Dogmas of EU Competition Law' (2011) 34 *World Competition* 535

Brook, J, 'Inevitable Errors: The Preponderance of the Evidence Standard in Civil Litigation' (1982) 18 *Tulsa Law Review* 79

Brown, A, 'Judicial Review of Commission Decisions under the Merger Regulation: The First Cases' (1994) 15 *European Competition Law Review* 296

Bruce, H, 'Allocating the Burden of Proof' (1997) 72 *Indiana Law Journal* 651

Brunt, M, 'Antitrust in the Courts: The Role of Economics and of Economists' in B Hawk (ed), *Fordham Corporate Law Institute: International Antitrust Law and Policy* (Juris, 1999)
Bruzzone, G and Boccaccio, M, 'Impact-Based Assessment and Use of Legal Presumptions in EC Competition Law: The Search for the Proper Mix' (2009) 32 *World Competition* 465
Buhart, J and Maulin, R, 'Proof in Cartels: State of Play and Perspectives' (2011) 4 *Concurrences* 51
Callery, C, 'Should the European Union Embrace or Exorcise Leegin's "Rule of Reason"?' (2011) 32 *European Competition Law Review* 42
Camesasca, P, 'The Explicit Efficiency Defence in Merger Control: Does it Make the Difference?' (1999) 20 *European Competition Law Review* 14
Carlton, D, 'How Should Economic Evidence Be Presented and Evaluated?' in CD Ehlermann and M Marquis (eds), *European Competition Law Annual 2009: The Evaluation of Evidence and its Judicial Review in Competition Cases* (Hart Publishing, 2010)
Carlton, D and Perloff, J, *Modern Industrial Organisation*, 4th edn (Pearson, 2015)
Castillo de la Torre, F, 'Evidence, Proof and Judicial Review in Cartel Cases' in CD Ehlermann and M Marquis (eds), *European Competition Law Annual 2009: The Evaluation of Evidence and its Judicial Review in Competition Cases* (Hart Publishing, 2010)
Castillo de la Torre, F and Gippini Fournier, E, *Evidence, Proof and Judicial Review in EU Competition Law* (Edward Elgar, 2017)
Chirita, AD, 'Procedural Rights in EU Administrative Competition Proceedings: Ex Ante – Mergers' in C Cauffman and Q Hao (eds), *Procedural Rights in Competition Law* (Springer, 2015)
Christiansen, A and Ewald, C, 'Best Practices for Expert Economic Opinions: Key Element of Forensic Economics in Competition Law' in K Hüschelrath and H Schweitzer (eds), *Public and Private Enforcement of Competition Law in Europe* (Springer, 2015)
Cleary, E, 'Presuming and Pleading: An Essay on Juristic Immaturity' (1959) 12 *Stanford Law Review* 5
Clermont, K, 'Standards of Proof Revisited' (2009) 33 *Vermont Law Review* 469
Clermont, K and Sherwin, E, 'A Comparative View of Standards of Proof' (2002) 50 *American Journal of Comparative Law* 243
Clough, M, 'Role of Judicial Review in Merger Control' (2003-2004) 24 *Northwestern Journal of International Law & Business* 729
Coate, M and Kleit, A, 'Does it Matter That the Prosecutor is Also the Judge? The Administrative Complaint Process at the Federal Trade Commission' (1998) 19 *Managerial and Decision Economics* 1
Cohen, J, *An Essay on Belief and Acceptance* (Clarendon Press, 1992)
——. *An Introduction to the Philosophy of Induction and Probability* (Clarendon Press, 1989)
——. *The Probable and the Provable* (Clarendon Press, 1977)
——. 'The Role of Evidential Weight in Criminal Proof' in Peter Tillers and Eric Green (eds), *Probability and Inference in the Law of Evidence: The Uses and Limits of Bayesianism* (Kluwer Academic Publishers, 1988)
Colley, L, 'From "Defence" to "Attack"? Quantifying Efficiency Arguments in Mergers' (2004) 25 *European Competition Law Review* 342
Collins, M, 'The Burden and Standard of Proof in Competition Litigation and Problems of Judicial Evaluation' (2004) 1 *ERA-Forum* 66
Colombani, A, Kloub, J and Sakkers, E, 'Cartels' in J Faull and A Nikpay (eds), *The EU Law of Competition*, 3rd edn (Oxford University Press, 2014)
Coombs, J and Padilla, J, 'The Use of Economic Evidence before the Courts of the European Union' in CD Ehlermann and M Marquis (eds), *European Competition Law Annual 2009: Evaluation of Evidence and its Judicial Review in Competition Cases* (Hart Publishing, 2010)
Cooper Davis, P, '"There Is a Book Out …": An Analysis of Judicial Absorption of Legislative Facts' (1987) 100 *Harvard Law Review* 1539
Craig, P, *EU Administrative Law*, 2nd edn (Oxford University Press, 2012)
——. 'Judicial Review and Questions of Law: A Comparative Perspective' in S Rose-Ackerman and P Lindseth (eds), *Comparative Administrative Law* (Edward Elgar, 2010)

Crane, D, 'Rules versus Standards in Antitrust Adjudication' (2007) 64 *Washington and Lee Law Review* 49

——. *The Institutional Structure of Antitrust Enforcement* (Oxford University Press, 2011)

Culp Davis, K, 'An Approach to Problems of Evidence in the Administrative Process' (1941) 55 *Harvard Law Review* 364

——. 'Facts in Lawmaking' (1980) 80 *Columbia Law Review* 931

Cumming, G, *Merger Decisions and the Rules of Procedure of the European Community Courts* (Kluwer Law International, 2011)

Davies, J and Schlossberg, R, '"Once More unto the Breach, Dear Friends": Judicial Review of Antitrust Agency Merger Clearance Decisions' (2006–07) 21 *Antitrust* 17

De la Mano, M, Pesaresi, E and Stehmann, O, 'Econometric and Survey Evidence in the Competitive Assessment of the Ryanair-Aer Lingus Merger' (2007) 3 *Competition Policy Newsletter* 73

De Smijter, E and Sinclair, A, 'The Enforcement System under Regulation 1/2003' in Jonathan Faull and Ali Nikpay (eds), *The EU Law of Competition*, 3rd edn (Oxford University Press, 2014)

Déchamps, P and Niels, G, 'The One Billion Euro Question for *Intel*: Moore's Law or Murphy's Law?' (2018) 9 *Journal of European Competition Law & Practice* 124

Decker, C and Yarrow, G, 'On the Discovery and Assessment of Economic Evidence in Competition Law', *Studies in Regulation* (Regulatory Policy Institute, 2011)

Decker, C, *Economics and the Enforcement of European Competition Law* (Edward Elgar, 2009)

Delicostopoulos, J, 'Towards European Procedural Primacy in National Legal Systems' (2003) 9 *European Law Journal* 599

Dempsey, J, 'A Right of Confrontation for Competition Hearings before the European Commission' (2010) 75 *Brooklyn Law Review* 1489

Denning, AT, 'Presumptions and Burdens' (1945) 61 *Law Quarterly Review* 379

Derenne, J, 'The Scope of Judicial Review in EU Economic Cases' in Merola M and Derenne, J (eds), *The Role of the Court of Justice of the European Union in Competition Law Cases* (Bruylant, 2012)

DG Competition, 'To Commit or Not to Commit: Deciding between Prohibition and Commitments' (Competition Policy Brief, 2014)

DG Economic and Financial Affairs, *The Efficiencies Defence and the European System of Merger Control* (European Economy, Reports and Studies No 5, 2001)

Dwyer, D, *The Judicial Assessment of Expert Evidence* (Cambridge University Press, 2008)

Easterbrook, F, 'Allocating Antitrust Decisionmaking Tasks' (1987–88) 76 *Georgetown Law Journal* 305

——. 'The Limits of Antitrust' (1984) 63 *Texas Law Review* 1

Editorial Comments, 'Towards a More Judicial Approach? EU Antitrust Fines under the Scrutiny of Fundamental Rights' (2011) 48 *Common Market Law Review* 1405

Edmond, G, 'After Objectivity: Expert Evidence and Procedural Reform' (2003) 25 *Sydney Law Review* 131

Edwards, K, 'Estimating Diversion Ratios: Some Thoughts on Customer Survey Design' in P Lowe and M Marquis (eds), *European Competition Law Annual 2010: Merger Control in European and Global Perspective* (Hart Publishing, 2013)

Ehlermann, CD and Marquis, M (eds), *European Competition Law Annual 2009: The Evaluation of Evidence and its Judicial Review in Competition Cases* (Hart Publishing, 2010)

Emberland, M, *The Human Rights of Companies: Exploring the Structure of ECHR Protection* (Oxford University Press, 2006)

Engel, C, 'Preponderance of Evidence versus Intime Conviction: A Behavioural Perspective on a Conflict between American and Continental European Law' (2009) 33 *Vermont Law Review* 435

Epstein, R, 'Pleadings and Presumptions' (1973) 40 *University of Chicago Law Review* 556

Esteva Mosso, C, 'Non-horizontal Mergers: A European Perspective' (2008) 31 *Fordham International Law Journal* 1442

Fackelmann, C, 'Dynamic Efficiency Considerations in EC Merger Control: An Intractable Subject or Promising Chance for Innovation' (University of Oxford, Centre for Competition Law and Policy, 2006)

Farrell, J, 'Listening to Interested Parties in Antitrust Investigations: Competitors, Customers, Complementors, and Relativity' (2004) 18 *Antitrust* 64

Faull, J and Nikpay, A (eds), *Faull and Nikpay: The EU Law of Competition*, 3rd edn (Oxford University Press, 2014)

Fingleton, J and Nikpay, A, 'Stimulating or Chilling Competition?' in B Hawk (ed), *Fordham Competition Law Institute: International Antitrust Law and Practice* (Juris, 2009)

Flemming, J, 'Burdens of Proof' (1961) 47 *Virginia Law Review* 51

Forrester, I, 'A Bush in Need of Pruning: The Luxuriant Growth of Light Judicial Review' in CD Ehlermann and M Marquis (eds), *European Competition Law Annual 2009: The Evaluation of Evidence and its Judicial Review in Competition Cases* (Hart Publishing, 2010)

——. 'Due Process in EC Competition Cases: A Distinguished Institution with Flawed Procedures' (2009) 34 *European Law Review* 81

——. 'Facts are Chiels That Wanna Ding' in B Hawk (ed), *Fordham Competition Law Institute: International Antitrust Law and Policy* (Juris, 2011)

Forwood, N, 'The Commission's "More Economic Approach": Implications for the Role of the EU Courts, the Treatment of Economic Evidence and the Scope of Judicial Review' in CD Ehlermann and M Marquis (eds), *European Competition Law Annual 2009: The Evaluation of Evidence and Its Judicial Review in Competition Cases* (Hart Publishing, 2010)

Fountoukakos, K, 'The CFI's Contribution to a Fairer System of Merger Control' in C Baudenbacher et al (eds), *Liber Amicorum en l'Honneur de Bo Vesterdorf* (Bruylant, 2007)

——. 'Judicial Review and EC Merger Control: Reflections on the Effectiveness of the System with Regard to the Standard of Review and Speed' (2008) 10 *Cambridge Yearbook of European Legal Studies* 133

Fox, E and Trebilcock, M (eds), *The Design of Competition Law Institutions: Global Norms, Local Choices* (Oxford University Press, 2013)

Friederiszick, H and Gratz, L, *Hidden Efficiencies: On the Relevance of Business Justifications in Abuse of Dominance Cases* (European School of Management and Technology Working Paper No 10/2013)

Friedman, R, 'Economic Analysis of Evidentiary Law: An Underused Tool, An Underplowed Field' (1998) 19 *Cardozo Law Review* 1531

Fritzsche, A, 'Discretion, Scope of Judicial Review and Institutional Balance in European Law' (2010) 47 *Common Market Law Review* 361

Gavil, A, 'After Daubert: Discerning the Increasingly Fine Line between the Admissibility and Sufficiency of Expert Testimony in Antitrust Litigation' (1997) 65 *Antitrust Law Journal* 663

——. 'Burden of Proof in U.S. Antitrust Law' in *Issues in Competition Law and Policy* (ABA Section of Antitrust Law, 2008)

——. 'The Challenges of Economic Proof in a Decentralized and Privatized European Competition Policy System: Lessons from the American Experience' (2008) 4 *Journal of Competition Law and Economics* 177

——. 'Daubert Comes of Age' (2000) 15 *Antitrust* 6

Gehlbach, H and Barge, S, 'Anchoring and Adjusting in Questionnaire Responses' (2012) 34 *Basic and Applied Social Psychology* 417

Geradin, D, 'Loyalty Rebates after *Intel*: Time for the European Court of Justice to Overrule *Hoffman-La Roche*' (2015) 11 *Journal of Competition Law & Economics* 579

Geradin, D and Petit, N, 'Judicial Review in European Union Competition Law: A Quantitative and Qualitative Assessment' in M Merola and J Derenne (eds), *The Role of the Court of Justice of the European Union in Competition Law Cases* (Bruylant, 2012)

Gerard, D, 'Merger Control Policy: How to Give Meaningful Consideration to Efficiency Claims?' (2003) 40 *Common Market Law Review* 1367

Gerber, D, 'Courts as Economic Experts in European Merger Law' in B Hawk (ed), *Fordham Corporate Law Institute: International Antitrust Law and Policy* (Juris, 2004)

——. *Law and Competition in Twentieth-Century Europe: Protecting Prometheus* (Oxford University Press, 2001)

Giannakopoulos, T, *Safeguarding Companies' Rights in Competition and Anti-dumping/Anti-subsidies Proceedings*, 2nd edn (Wolters Kluwer Law & Business, 2011)
Giannelli, P, 'The Admissibility of Novel Scientific Evidence: *Frye v United States*, a Half-Century Later' (1980) 80 *Columbia Law Review* 1197
Gippini Fournier, E, 'The Elusive Standard of Proof in EU Competition Cases' in CD Ehlermann and M Marquis (eds), *European Competition Law Annual 2009: The Evaluation of Evidence and its Judicial Review in Competition Cases* (Hart Publishing, 2010)
Gorecki, P, Keating, C and O'Connor, B, 'The Role of Economic Evidence in Merger Control in Ireland: Current and Future Practice' (2007) 3 *European Competition Journal* 345
Goyder, J and Albors-Llorens, A, *Goyder's EC Competition Law*, 5th edn (Oxford University Press, 2009)
Guerrin, M and Kyriazis, G, 'Cartels: Proof and Procedural Issues' in B Hawk (ed), *Fordham Corporate Law Institute: International Antitrust Law and Policy* (Juris, 1993)
Gutiérrez-Rodríguez, JD, 'Expert Economic Testimony in Antitrust Cases: A Comparative Law and Economics Study' (2009) 14 *International Law, Revista Colombiana de Derecho Internacional* 221
Hamer, D, The Civil Standard of Proof Uncertainty: Probability, Belief and Justice (1994) 16 *Sydney Law Review* 506
——. 'Presumptions, Standards and Burdens: Managing the Cost of Error' (2014) 13 *Law, Probability and Risk* 221
Harding, C and Joshua, J, *Regulating Cartels in Europe* (Oxford University Press, 2010)
Harkera, M, Peyera, S and Wright, K, 'Judicial Scrutiny of Merger Decisions in the EU, the UK and Germany' (2011) 60 *International and Comparative Law Quarterly* 93
Hauger, N and Palzer, C, 'Investigator, Prosecutor, Judge … and Now Plaintiff? The Leviathanian Role of the European Commission in the Light of Fundamental Rights' (2013) 36 *World Competition* 565
Hawk, B, 'System Failure: Vertical Restraints and EC Competition Law' (1995) 32 *Common Market Law Review* 973
Heinemann, A, 'Access to Evidence and Presumptions: Communicating Vessels in Procedural Law' in K Hüschelrath and H Schweitzer (eds), *Public and Private Enforcement of Competition Law in Europe* (ZEW Economic Studies 48, 2014)
Hellstrom, P, 'A Uniform Standard of Proof in EU Competition Proceedings' in CD Ehlermann and M Marquis (eds), *European Competition Law Annual 2009: The Evaluation of Evidence and its Judicial Review in Competition Cases* (Hart Publishing, 2010)
Heyer, K, 'A World of Uncertainty: Economics and the Globalisation of Antitrust' (2005) 72 *Antitrust Law Journal* 375
Ho, HL, 'The Presumption of Innocence as a Human Right' in P Roberts and J Hunter (eds), *Criminal Evidence and Human Rights: Reimagining Common Law Procedural Traditions* (Hart Publishing, 2012)
——. *A Philosophy of Evidence Law: Justice in the Search for Truth* (Oxford University Press, 2008)
Hockett, C, Alexis, G and Wheeler, C, '*Daubert* Redux: Revisiting the Admissibility of Expert Testimony in Antitrust Cases' (2000) 15 *Antitrust* 7
Hofmann, H and Mihaescu, B, 'The Relation between the Charter's Fundamental Rights and the Unwritten General Principles of EU Law: Good Administration as the Test Case' (2013) 9 *European Constitutional Law* Review 73
Holtz, J, 'Legal Professional Privilege in Europe: A Missed Policy Opportunity' (2013) 4 *Journal of European Competition Law & Practice* 402
Huber, P, *Galileo's Revenge: Junk Science in the Courtroom* (Basic Books, 1993)
Hurley, S, 'The Use of Surveys in Merger and Competition Analysis' (2011) 7 *Journal of Competition Law & Economics* 45
Ibáñez Colomo, P, 'The Future of Article 102 TFEU after *Intel*' (2018) 9 *Journal of European Competition Law & Practice* 293
——. 'Market Failures, Transaction Costs and Article 101(1) TFEU' (2012) 37 *European Law Review* 541

——. *The Shaping of EU Competition Law* (Cambridge University Press, 2018)
Ibáñez Colomo, P and Lamadrid de Pablo, A, 'On the Notion of Restriction of Competition: What We Know and What We Don't Know We Know' in D Gerard, M Merola and B Meyring (eds), *The Notion of Restriction of Competition: Revisiting the Foundations of Antitrust Enforcement in Europe* (Bruylant, 2017)
Idot, L, Cordonnel, P and Choffel, A, 'La Place des Droits Fondamentaux dans les Procédures de Concurrence' (Revue Concurrences, Paris, 16 January 2013)
Ilzkovitz, F and Meiklejohn, R (eds), *EC Merger Control: Do We Need an Efficiency Defence?* (Edward Elgar, 2006)
International Competition Network, *ICN Investigative Techniques: Handbook for Merger Review* (2005)
Jackson, J, 'The Effect of Human Rights on Criminal Evidentiary Processes: Towards Convergence, Divergence or Realignment?' (2005) 68 *Modern Law Review* 737
Jaeger, M, 'The Standard of Review in Competition Cases Involving Complex Economic Assessments: Towards the Marginalisation of the Marginal Review?' (2011) 2 *Journal of European Competition Law and Practice* 295
Jaffe, L, *Judicial Control of Administrative Action* (Little, Brown & Co, 1965)
Jalabert-Doury, N, 'Les Déclarations en Droit de la Concurrence: la Preuve d'Infractions Peut-Elle se Satisfaire de "Certitudes Probables"?' (2005) 2 *Concurrences* 41
Janis, M, Kay, R and Bradley, A, *European Human Rights Law*, 3rd edn (Oxford University Press, 2008)
João Melicias, M, "Did They Do It?' The Interplay between the Standard of Proof and the Presumption of Innocence in EU Cartel Investigations' (2012) 35 *World Competition* 471
Jolowicz, JA, 'Adversarial and Inquisitorial Models of Civil Procedure' (2003) 52 *International & Comparative Law Quarterly* 281
Jones, A and Kovacic, W, 'Identifying Anticompetitive Agreements in the United States and the European Union: Developing a Coherent Antitrust Analytical Framework' (2017) 62 *Antitrust Bulletin* 254
Joshua, J, 'Oral Statements in EC Competition Proceedings: A Due Process Short-Cut?' (2004) 26 *Competition Law Insight* 1
——. 'Proof in Contested EEC Competition Cases: A Comparison with the Rules of Evidence in Common Law' (1987) 12 *European Law Review* 315
Kagehiro, D and Stanton, C, 'Legal vs Quantified Definitions of Standards of Proof' (1985) 9 *Law and Human Behavior* 159
Kaiser, D, 'Presumptions of Law and of Fact' (1955) 38 *Marquette Law Review* 253
Kakouris, C, 'Do the Member States Possess Judicial Procedural "Autonomy"?' (1997) 34 *Common Market Law Review* 1389
Kalintiri, A, 'The Standard of Proof in Phase I Merger Decisions: The Lesson from the *Microsoft/Skype* Appeal' (2014) 35 *European Competition Law Review* 279
——. 'The Allocation of the Legal Burden of Proof in Article 101 TFEU Cases: A "Clear" Rule with Not-So-Clear Implications' (2015) 34 *Yearbook of European Law* 232
——. 'Revisiting Parental Liability in EU Competition Law' (2018) 43 *European Law Review* 145
——. 'What's in a Name? The Marginal Standard of Review of "Complex Economic Evaluations" in EU Competition Enforcement' (2016) 53 *Common Market Law Review* 1283
Kaplan, J, 'Decision Theory and the Fact-Finding Process' (1968) 20 *Stanford Law Review* 1065
Kaplow, L, 'Burden of Proof' (2012) 121 *Yale Law Journal* 738
——. 'Market Share Thresholds: On the Conflation of Empirical Assessments and Legal Policy Judgments' (2011) 7 *Journal of Competition Law & Economics* 243
——. 'Rules versus Standards: An Economic Analysis' (1992) 42 *Duke Law Journal* 557
——. 'The Value of Accuracy in Adjudication: An Economic Analysis' (1994) 23 *Journal of Legal Studies* 307
Karagiannis, Y, 'The Causes and Consequences of the Collegial Implementation of European Competition Law' (2013) 19 *European Law Journal* 682
Karst, K, 'Legislative Facts in Constitutional Litigation' [1960] *Supreme Court Review* 75

Karvounakis, T, 'Fair Criminal Evidence in Europe: From the European Convention on Human Rights to EU Criminal Law' (Queen Mary University of London, 2012)

Kaye, D, 'Do We Need a Calculus of Weight to Understand Proof Beyond a Reasonable Doubt?' in Peter Tillers and Eric Green (eds), *Probability and Inference in the Law of Evidence: The Uses and Limits of Bayesianism* (Kluwer Academic Publishers, 1988)

Kazazi, M, *Burden of Proof and Related Issues: A Study on Evidence before International Tribunals* (Kluwer Law International, 1995)

Keeton, R, 'Legislative Facts and Similar Things: Deciding Disputed Premise Facts' (1988–89) 73 *Minnesota Law Review* 1

Kekelekis, M, *EC Merger Control Regulation: Rights of Defence* (Kluwer Law International, 2006)

Killick, J, 'Case Comment: The *GE/Honeywell* Judgment – in Reality Another Merger Defeat for the Commission' (2007) 28 *European Competition Law Review* 52

Kim, S, Vallery, A and Waters, D, 'Judicial Review of Mergers' (2005) 10 *European Antitrust Review* 40

Kocmut, M, 'Efficiency Considerations and Merger Control: *Quo Vadis*, Commission?' (2006) 27 *European Competition Law Review* 19

Kokott, J, *The Burden of Proof in Comparative and International Human Rights Law: Civil and Common Law Approaches with Special Reference to the American and German Legal Systems* (Kluwer Law International, 1998)

Kolasky, W, 'Conglomerate Mergers and Range Effects: It's a Long Way from Chicago to Brussels' (George Mason University Symposium, Washington DC, 2001)

Korah, V, 'EEC Competition Policy – Legal Form or Economic Efficiency' (1986) 39 *Current Legal Problems* 85

Kowalik-Bańczyk, K, 'Procedural Autonomy of Member States and the EU Rights of Defence in Antitrust Proceedings' (2012) 5 *Yearbook of Antitrust and Regulatory Studies* 215

Krosnick, J, 'Survey Research' (1999) 50 *Annual Review of Psychology* 537

Kunert, K, 'Some Observations on the Origin and Structure of Evidence Rules under the Common Law System and the Civil Law System of Free Proof in the German Code of Criminal Procedure' (1966–67) 16 *Buffalo Law Review* 122

Ladd, M, 'Presumptions in Civil Actions' [1977] *Arizona State Law Journal* 275

Laguna de Paz, JC, 'Understanding the Limits of Judicial Review in European Competition Law' (2014) 2 *Journal of Antitrust Enforcement* 203

Langenfeld, J and Alexander, C, '*Daubert* and Other Gatekeeping Challenges of Antitrust Experts' (2011) 25 *Antitrust* 21

Lao, M, 'Ideology Matters in the Antitrust Debate' (2014) 79 *Antitrust Law Journal* 649

Laprévote, FC, 'Abandon All Hope, Ye Who Enter Here? Efficiencies in European Merger Control: A Few Lessons from Recent Decisional Practice' (2014) *e-Competitions* N° 65580

Lasok, P, *The European Court of Justice: Practice and Procedure*, 2nd edn (Butterworths, 1994)

——. 'The Nature of Judicial Control' in *Celebration of 20 years of the Court of First Instance of the European Communities* ('From 20 to 2020: Building the CFI of Tomorrow on Solid Foundations', Luxembourg 25 September 2009)

Laughlin, C, 'In Support of the Thayer Theory of Presumptions' (1953) 52 *Michigan Law Review* 195

Lavrakas, P (ed), *Encyclopedia of Survey Research Methods* (Sage, 2008)

Leanza, P and Pridal, O, *The Right to a Fair Trial: Article 6 of the European Convention on Human Rights* (Kluwer Law International, 2014)

Legal, H, 'Le Contentieux Communautaire de la Concurrence Entre Contrôle Restreint et Pleine Juridiction' (2005) 2 *Concurrences* 1

——. 'Standards of Proof and Standards of Judicial Review in EU Competition Law' in B Hawk (ed), *Fordham Corporate Law Institute: International Antitrust Law and Policy* (Juris, 2006)

Leiter, B, 'The Epistemology of Admissibility: Why Even Good Philosophy of Science Would Not Make for Good Philosophy of Evidence' [1997] *Brigham Young University Law Review* 803

Lempert, R, 'The Economic Analysis of Evidence Law: Common Sense on Stilts' (2001) 87 *Virginia Law Review* 1619

——. 'The New Evidence Scholarship: Analysing the Process of Proof' (1986) 66 *Boston University Law Review* 439

——. 'Modeling Relevance' (1976–77) 75 *Michigan Law Review* 1021

Lenaerts, K, 'Some Thoughts on Evidence and Procedure in European Community Competition Law' (2006) 30 *Fordham International Law Journal* 1463

Lenaerts, K, Maselis, I and Gutman, K, *EU Procedural Law* (Oxford University Press, 2014)

Lenaerts, K and Vanhamme, J, 'Procedural Rights of Private Parties in the Community Administrative Process' (1997) 34 *Common Market Law Review* 531

Leupold, B, 'Effective Enforcement of EU Competition Law Gone Too Far? Recent Case Law on the Presumption of Parental Liability' (2013) 34 *European Competition Law Review* 570

Levy, J, 'A Principled Approach to the Standard of Proof for Affirmative Defenses in Criminal Trials' (2013) 40 *American Journal of Criminal Law* 281

Levy, N, 'Evidentiary Issues in EU Merger Control' in *Fordham Competition Law Institute: International Antitrust Law and Policy* (Juris, 2009)

Lianos, I and Genakos, C, 'Econometric Evidence in EU Competition Law: An Empirical and Theoretical Analysis' in Ioannis Lianos and Damien Geradin (eds), *Handbook on European Competition Law: Enforcement and Procedure* (Edward Elgar, 2013)

Lianos, I, 'Categorical Thinking in Competition Law and the "Effects-Based" Approach in Article 82 EC' in Ezrachi A (ed), *Article 82 EC: Reflections on its Recent Evolution* (Hart Publishing, 2009)

——. *The Emergence of Forensic Economics in Competition Law: Foundations for a Sociological Analysis* (Centre for Law, Economics and Society, UCL, Working Paper No 5/2012)

——. '"Judging Economists", Economic Expertise in Competition Litigation: A European View' in I Lianos and I Kokkoris (eds), *The Reform of EC Competition Law: New Challenges* (Kluwer Law International, 2010)

Lind, A, Thibaut, J and Walker, L, 'Discovery and Presentation of Evidence in Adversary and Nonadversary Proceedings' (1972) 71 *Michigan Law Review* 1129

Loewanthal, PJ, 'The Defence of "Objective Justification" in the Application of Article 82 EC' (2005) 28 *World Competition* 455

Loozen, E, 'The Requisite Legal Standard for Economic Assessments in EU Competition Cases Unravelled through the Economic Approach' (2014) 39 *European Law Review* 91

Lopatka, J and Page, W, 'Economic Authority and the Limits of Expertise in Antitrust Cases' (2005) 90 *Cornell Law Review* 617

Lord, C, Ross, L and Lepper, M, 'Biased Assimilation and Attitude Polarization: The Effects of Prior Theories on Subsequently Considered Evidence' (1979) 37 *Journal of Personality and Social Psychology* 2098

Loucaides, L, 'Standards of Proof in Proceedings under the European Convention of Human Rights' in *Essays on the Developing Law of Human Rights* (Martinus Nijhoff Publishers, 1995)

Loucaides, L and Tulkens, F, *Judge Loukis Loucaides: An Alternative View on the Jurisprudence of the European Court of Human Rights: A Collection of Separate Opinions (1998–2007)* (Martinus Nijhoff Publishers, 2008)

Lowe, P, 'Taking Sound Decisions on the Basis of Available Evidence' in CD Ehlermann and M Marquis (eds), *European Competition Law Annual 2009: The Evaluation of Evidence and Its Judicial Review in Competition Cases* (Hart Publishing, 2010)

Lowe, P, Marquis, M and Monti, G (eds), *European Competition Law Annual 2013: Effective and Legitimate Enforcement of Competition Law* (Hart Publishing, 2016)

Luescher, C, 'Efficiency Considerations in European Merger Control: Just Another Battle Ground for the European Commission, Economists and Competition Lawyers?' (2004) 25 *European Competition Law Review* 72

Lugard, P, 'Chilling Effects of Antitrust Law: Better Safe than Sorry?' in B Hawk (ed), *Fordham Competition Law Institute: International Antitrust Law and Practice* (Juris, 2009)

Lyons, B, Menzies GD and Zizzo DJ, *Professional Interpretation of the Standard of Proof: An Experimental Test on Merger Regulation* (University of East Anglia, Centre for Competition Policy, Working Paper No 2/2010)

MacCulloch, A, 'The Privilege against Self-Incrimination in Competition Investigations: Theoretical Foundations and Practical Implications' (2006) 26 *Legal Studies* 211
MacLennan, J, 'Evidence, Standard and Burden of Proof and the Use of Experts in Procedure before the Luxembourg Courts' in Friedl Weiss (ed), *Improving WTO Dispute Settlement Procedures: Issues and Lessons from the Practice of Other International Courts and Tribunals* (Cameron May, 2000)
Maffei, S, *The Right to Confrontation in Europe: Absent, Anonymous and Vulnerable Witnesses* (Europa Law Publishing, 2012)
Maggiolino, M, 'Plausibility, Facts and Economics in Antitrust Law' (2014) 7 *Yearbook of Antitrust and Regulatory Studies* 107
Mandel, M, 'Going for the Gold: Economists as Expert Witnesses' (1999) 13 *Journal of Economic Perspectives* 113
Marenco, G, 'The Birth of Modern Competition Law in Europe' in Armin von Bogdandy, Petros Mavroidis and Yves Mény (eds), *European Integration and International Coordination: Studies in Transnational Economic Law in Honour of Claus-Dieter Ehlermann* (Kluwer Law International, 2002)
McBaine, J, 'Presumptions: Are They Evidence?' (1938) 26 *California Law Review* 519
McCormick, M, 'Scientific Evidence: Defining a New Approach to Admissibility' (1981) 67 *Iowa Law Review* 879
McNaughton, J, 'Burden of Production of Evidence: A Function of a Burden of Persuasion' (1955) 68 *Harvard Law Review* 1382
Molinier, J, "Le Contrôle Juridictionnel et ses Limites: À Propos du Pouvoir Discrétionnaire des Institutions Communautaires" in Joël Rideau (ed), *De la Communauté de Droit à l'Union de Droit* (LGDJ, 2000)
Monahan, J and Walker, L, 'Social Authority: Obtaining, Evaluating and Establishing Social Science in Law' (1986) 134 *University of Pennsylvania Law Review* 477
Monti, G, 'Article 81 EC and Public Policy' (2002) 39 *Common Market Law Review* 1057
——. *EC Competition Law* (Cambridge University Press, 2007)
Morgan, E, 'Presumptions' (1937) 12 *Washington Law Review and State Bar Journal* 255
——. 'Some Further Observations on Presumptions' (1942) 16 *Southern California Law Review* 245
——. 'Some Observations Concerning Presumptions' (1931) 44 *Harvard Law Review* 906
Motis, J, Neven, D and Seabright, P, 'Efficiencies in Merger Control' in F Ilzkovitz and R Meiklejohn (eds), *European Merger Control: Do We Need an Efficiency Defence?* (Edward Elgar, 2006)
Nazzini, R, 'Article 81 EC between Time Present and Time Past: A Normative Critique of "Restriction of Competition" in EU Law' (2006) 43 *Common Market Law Review* 497
——. *The Foundations of European Union Competition Law: The Objective and Principles of Article 102* (Oxford University Press, 2011)
——. 'The Wood Began to Move: An Essay on Consumer Welfare, Evidence and Burden of Proof in Article 82 EC Cases' (2006) 31 *European Law Review* 518
Nehl, HP, 'Article 48: Presumption of Innocence and Rights of Defence' in Steve Peers et al (eds), *The EU Charter of Fundamental Rights: A Commentary* (Hart Publishing, 2014)
——. *Principles of Administrative Procedure in EC Law* (Hart Publishing, 1999)
Neven, D, 'Competition Economics and Antitrust in Europe' (2005) 21 *Economic Policy* 741
Nicolaides, P, 'The Balancing Myth: The Economics of Article 81(1) & (3)' (2005) 32 *Legal Issues of Economic Integration* 123
Noel, PE, 'Efficiency Considerations in the Assessment of Horizontal Mergers under European and U.S. Antitrust Law' (1997) 18 *European Competition Law Review* 498
Notes, 'A Suggested Role for Rebuttable Presumptions in Antitrust Restraint of Trade Litigation' [1972] *Duke Law Journal* 595
O'Donoghue, R and Padilla, J, *The Law and Economics of Article 102 TFEU*, 2nd edn (Hart Publishing, 2013)
Odudu, O, *The Boundaries of EC Competition Law: The Scope of Article 81* (Oxford University Press, 2006)
——. 'The Wider Concerns of Competition Law' (2010) 30 *Oxford Journal of Legal Studies* 599

OECD, *Competition Policy and Efficiency Claims in Horizontal Agreements* (Competition Policy Roundtables, 1995)
——. *Presenting Complex Economic Theories to Judges* (Competition Policy Roundtables, 2008)
——. *Prosecuting Cartels without Direct Evidence of Agreement* (Policy Brief, June 2007)
——. *Safe Harbours and Legal Presumptions in Competition Law*, DAF/COMP(2017)9
Ormosi, P, 'Diminishing Incentives to Reveal Efficiency-Related Evidence: An Empirical Analysis of EC Merger Cases' (2011) 34 *World Competition* 615
Ortiz Blanco, L, 'Standards of Proof and Personal Conviction in EU Antitrust and Merger Control Procedures' in CD Ehlermann and M Marquis (eds), *European Competition Law Annual 2009: The Evaluation of Evidence and its Judicial Review in Competition Cases* (Hart Publishing, 2010)
Ortiz Blanco, L (ed), *EU Competition Procedure*, 3rd edn (Oxford University Press, 2013)
Pardo, M, 'The Nature and Purpose of Evidence Theory' (2013) 66 *Vanderbilt Law Review* 547
Parisi, F, 'Rent-Seeking through Litigation: Adversarial and Inquisitorial Systems Compared' (2002) 22 *International Review of Law and Economics* 193
Parker, J and Kobayashi, B, 'Evidence' in B Bouckaert and G de Geest (eds), *Encyclopedia of Law and Economics* (Edward Elgar, 2000)
Parr, N and Burrows, E, 'Burdens and Standards of Proof in European Community Competition Law' in *Issues in Competition Law and Policy: ABA Antitrust Section*, vol 1 (ABA Book Publishing, 2008)
Parret, L, 'Sense and Nonsense of Rules on Proof in Cartel Cases' (2008) 31 *European Competition Journal* 169
Paulis, E, 'The Burden of Proof in Article 82 Cases' in B Hawk (ed), *Fordham Competition Law Institute: International Antitrust Law and Policy* (Juris, 2007)
Peeperkorn, L, 'Defining "By Object" Restrictions' (2015) 3 *Concurrences* 40
Pennington, N and Hastie, R, 'A Cognitive Theory of Juror Decision-Making: The Story Model' (1991–92) 13 *Cardozo Law Review* 519
Posner, R, 'An Economic Approach to the Law of Evidence' (1999) 51 *Stanford Law Review* 1477
——. 'The Law and Economics of the Economic Expert Witness' (1999) 13 *Journal of Economic Perspectives* 91
Posner, R, *Economic Analysis of Law* (Aspen Publishers 2011)
Prakken, H and Sartor, G, 'Presumptions and Burdens of Proof' in Tom van Engers (ed), *Legal Knowledge and Information Systems* (JURIX, 2006)
Prete, L, 'Standard of Proof and Scope of Judicial Review in EC Merger Cases: Everything Clear after *Tetra Laval*?' (2005) 26 *European Competition Law Review* 692
Quine, WV and Ullian, JS, *The Web of Belief*, 2nd edn (McGraw-Hill Humanities/Social Sciences/Languages 1978)
Ratliff, J, 'Before the European Courts: Avoiding Double Renvoi Judicial Review in EC Competition Cases' in CD Ehlermann and M Marquis (eds), *European Competition Law Annual 2009: The Evaluation of Evidence and its Judicial Review in Competition Cases* (Hart Publishing, 2010)
Raznovich, L, 'A Comparative Review of the Socio-legal Implications of Burden of Proof and Presumptions to Deal with Factual Uncertainty' (2008) 32 *American Journal of Trial Advocacy* 57
Redmayne, M, 'Standards of Proof in Civil Litigation' (1999) 62 *Modern Law Review* 167
Reeves, T and Dodoo, N, 'Standards of Proof and Standards of Judicial Review in European Commission Merger Law' (2005) 29 *Fordham International Law Journal* 1034
Rescher, N, *Presumptions and the Practices of Tentative Cognition* (Cambridge University Press, 2014)
Rey, P and Venit, J, 'An Effects-Based Approach to Article 102: A Response to Wouter Wils' (2015) 38 *World Competition* 3
Reynolds, G and Walters, C, 'The Use of Customer Surveys for Market Definition and the Competitive Assessment of Horizontal Mergers' (2008) 4 *Journal of Competition Law & Economics* 411
Ritleng, D, 'Le Juge Communautaire de la Légalité et le Pouvoir Discrétionnaire des Institutions Communautaires' (1999) 9 *L'Actualité Juridique: Droit Administratif* 645
Ritter, C, 'Presumptions in EU Competition Law' (2018) 6 *Journal of Antitrust Enforcement* 281
Roberts, E, 'An Introduction to the Study of Presumptions' (1958) 4 *Villanova Law Review* 1

Roberts, P, 'Excluding Evidence as Protecting Constitutional or Human Rights?' in L Zedner and L Roberts (eds), *Principles and Values in Criminal Law and Criminal Justice: Essays in Honour of Andrew Ashworth* (Oxford University Press, 2012)

Roberts, P and Zuckerman, A, *Criminal Evidence* (2nd edn, Oxford University Press, 2010)

Röller, LH, 'Efficiencies in EU Merger Control: Do They Matter?' in P Lowe and M Marquis (eds), *European Competition Law Annual 2010: Merger Control in European and Global Perspective* (Hart Publishing, 2013)

Röller, LH, Stennek, J and Verboven, F, 'Efficiency Gains from Mergers' in F Ilzkovitz and R Meiklejohn (eds), *European Merger Control: Do We Need An Efficiency Defence?* (Edward Elgar, 2006)

Rousseva, E, 'Abuse of Dominant Position Defences: Objective Justification and Article 82 EC in the Era of Modernisation' in G Amato and CD Ehlermann (eds), *EC Competition Law: A Critical Assessment* (Hart Publishing, 2009)

——. 'Reflections on the Relevance and Proof of Efficiency Defences in Modern EU Antitrust Law' in J Bourgeois and D Waelbroeck (eds), *Ten Years of Effects-Based Approach in EU Competition Law: State of Play and Perspectives* (Bruylant, 2012)

Sauter, S, *Coherence in EU Competition Law* (Oxford University Press, 2016)

Scharpf, F, *Governing in Europe: Effective and Democratic?* (Oxford University Press, 1999)

Schinkel, MP, 'Forensic Economics in Competition Law Enforcement' (2008) 4 *Journal of Competition Law & Economics* 1

Schum, D, *The Evidential Foundations of Probabilistic Reasoning* (Northwestern University Press, 2001)

Schweitzer, H, 'The European Competition Law Enforcement System and the Evolution of Judicial Review' in CD Ehlermann and M Marquis (eds), *European Competition Law Annual 2009: The Evaluation of Evidence and its Judicial Review in Competition Cases* (Hart Publishing, 2010)

Schweitzer, H and Patel, KK (eds), *The Historical Foundations of EU Competition Law* (Oxford University Press, 2013)

Schweitzer, M, 'The Civil Standard of Proof: What is it, Actually?' (2016) 20 *International Journal of Evidence & Proof* 217

Scordamaglia-Tousis, A, *EU Cartel Enforcement: Reconciling Effective Public Enforcement with Fundamental Rights* (Kluwer Law International, 2013)

Shapiro, M, 'Appeal' (1979–80) 14 *Law & Society* 629

Shavell, S, 'The Appeals Process as a Means of Error Correction' (1995) 24 *Journal of Legal Studies* 379

Sibony, AL, *Le Juge et le Raisonnement Economique en Droit de la Concurrence* (Librairie Générale de Droit et de Jurisprudence, 2008)

Sibony, AL and Barbier de la Serre, E, 'Charge de La Preuve et Theorie du Controle en Droit Communautaire de la Concurrence: Pour un Changement de Perspective' (2007) 43 *Revue Trimestrielle de Droit Europeen* 205

Simonsson, I, *Legitimacy in EU Cartel Control* (Hart Publishing, 2010)

Siragusa, M, 'Annulment Proceedings in Antitrust Cases (Articles 101 and 102 TFEU): Standard of Judicial Review over Substantive Issues' in M Merola and J Derenne (eds), *The Role of the Court of Justice of the European Union in Competition Law Cases* (Bruylant, 2012)

Slater, D, Thomas, S and Waelbroeck, D, *Competition Law Proceedings before the European Commission and the Right to a Fair Trial: No Need for Reform?* (Global Competition Law Centre, College of Europe, Working Paper 04/2008)

Slater, D and Waelbroeck, D, '"Marginal Review" by the European Court of Justice in Competition Cases and its Compatibility with Fundamental Rights' in M Merola and J Derenne (eds), *The Role of the Court of Justice of the European Union in Competition Law Cases* (Bruylant, 2012)

Solek, L and Wartinger, S, 'Parental Liability: Rebutting the Presumption of Decisive Influence' (2015) 6 *Journal of European Competition Law & Practice* 73

Soltesz, U, 'Due Process and Judicial Review: Mixed Signals from Luxembourg in Cartel Cases' (2012) 33 *European Competition Law Review* 241

Stason, EB, '"Substantial Evidence" in Administrative Law' (1941) 89 *University of Pennsylvania Law Review* 1026

Stein, A, 'Criminal Defences and the Burden of Proof' (1991) 28 *Coexistence* 133
——. *Foundations of Evidence Law* (Oxford University Press, 2005)
Stumbo, J, 'Presumptions: A View at Chaos' (1963) 3 *Washburn Law Journal* 182
Stumer, A, *The Presumption of Innocence: Evidential and Human Rights Perspectives* (Hart Publishing, 2010)
Sufrin, B, 'The Notion of Dominance in Competition Law: An Overview of EU and National Case-Law' (2012) *e-Competitions* N° 43209
Svetlicinii, A, 'Assessment of Non-horizontal Mergers: Is There a Chance for the Efficiency Defence in EC Merger Control?' (2007) 28 *European Competition Law Review* 529
Szilagyi, P, 'The ECJ Has Spoken: Where Do We Stand with the Standard of Proof in Merger Control?' (2008) 29 European *Competition Law Review* 726
Talev, L, 'ECHR Implications in the EU Competition Enforcement' ('Due Process and Innovation in EU Competition Law', Centre for European Policy Studies, Brussels, 16 April 2010)
Taruffo, M, 'Rethinking the Standards of Proof' (2003) 51 *American Journal of Comparative Law* 659
Temple Lang, J, 'How Can the Problem of the Liability of a Parent Company for Price-Fixing by a Wholly-Owned Subsidiary be Resolved?' (2014) 37 *Fordham International Law Journal* 1481
——. *Three Possibilities for Reform of the Procedure of the European Commission in Competition Cases Under Regulation 1/2003* (Centre for European Policy Studies, 2011)
Thayer, J, 'The Burden of Proof' (1890) 4 *Harvard Law Review* 45
——. *A Preliminary Treatise on Evidence at the Common Law* (Little, Brown & Co, 1898)
——. 'Presumptions and the Law of Evidence' (1889) 3 *Harvard Law Review* 141
Thomas, C, 'The Uses and Abuses of Legitimacy in International Law' (2014) 34 *Oxford Journal of Legal Studies* 729
Thomas, S, 'Guilty of a Fault That One Has Not Committed: The Limits of the Group-Based Sanction Policy Carried out by the Commission and the European Courts in EU-Antitrust Law' (2012) 3 *Journal of European Competition Law & Practice* 11
Thompson, I and Harvey, J, 'When to Pop the Question(s)?: The Use of Surveys in Merger Control' (2014) 35 *European Competition Law Review* 92
Thompson, W and Schumann, E, 'Interpretation of Statistical Evidence in Criminal Trials: The Prosecutor's Fallacy and the Defence Attorney's Fallacy' (1987) 11 *Law and Human Behaviour* 167
Tiili, V and Vanhamme, J, 'The "Power of Appraisal" (Pouvoir d'Appréciation) of the Commission of the European Communities vis-à-vis the Powers of Judicial Review of the Communities Court of Justice and Court of First Instance' (1998) 22 *Fordham International Law Journal* 885
Tillers, P and Green E (eds), *Probability and Inference in the Law of Evidence* (Kluwer Academic Publishers 1988)
Townley, C, *Article 81 EC and Public Policy* (Hart Publishing, 2009)
Tribe, L, 'Trial by Mathematics: Precision and Ritual in the Legal Process' (1971) 84 *Harvard Law Review* 1329
Tridimas, T, *The General Principles of EU Law*, 2nd edn (Oxford University Press, 2006)
Twining, W, 'Evidence and Legal Theory' (1984) 47 *Modern Law Review* 261
——. *Rethinking Evidence: Exploratory Essays*, 2nd edn (Cambridge University Press, 2006)
——. *Theories of Evidence: Bentham and Wigmore* (Weidenfeld & Nicolson, 1985)
Tyler, T, 'Procedural Fairness and Compliance with the Law' (1997) 133 *Swiss Journal of Economics and Statistics* 219
——. *Why People Obey the Law* (Princeton University Press, 2006)
Underwood, B, 'The Thumb on the Scales of Justice: Burdens of Persuasion in Criminal Cases' (1977) 86 *Yale Law Journal* 1299
Valcke, A and Todorov, F, 'Judicial Review of Merger Control Decisions in the European Union' (2006) 51 *Antitrust Bulletin* 339
Van Cleynenbreugel, P, 'Judge-Made Standards of National Procedure in the Post-Lisbon Constitutional Framework' (2012) 37 *European Law Review* 90
Van der Esch, B, *Pouvoirs Discrétionnaires de l'Exécutif Européen et Control Juridictionnel* (Dalloz, 1968)

Van der Vijver, T, 'Objective Justification and Article 102 TFEU' (2012) *World Competition* 55

Van Dijk, P et al (eds), *Theory and Practice of the European Convention on Human Rights*, 4th edn (Intersentia, 2008)

Van Gerven, W, 'Of Rights, Remedies and Procedures' (2000) 37 *Common Market Law Review* 501

Van Rompuy, B, 'Implications for the Standard of Proof in EC Merger Proceedings: *Bertelsmann and Sony Corporation of America v. Impala* (C-413/06 P) ECJ' (2008) 29 *European Competition Law Review* 608

Venit, J, 'Human All Too Human: The Gathering and Assessment of Evidence and the Appropriate Standard of Proof and Judicial Review in Commission Enforcement Proceedings Applying Articles 81 and 82' in CD Ehlermann and M Marquis (eds), *European Competition Law Annual 2009: The Evaluation of Evidence and its Judicial Review in Competition Cases* (Hart Publishing, 2010)

——. 'The Scope of EU Judicial Review of Commission Merger Decisions' in L Lowe and M Marquis (eds), *European Competition Law Annual 2010: Merger Control in European and Global Perspective* (Hart Publishing, 2013)

Vesterdorf, B, 'Standard of Proof in Merger Cases: Reflections in the Light of the Recent Case Law of the Community Courts' (2005) 1 *European Competition Journal* 3

Vincent, JY, 'L'Erreur Manifeste d'Appréciation' (1971) 142 *La Revue Administrative* 407

Volpin, C, '*The Ball Is In Your Court*: Evidential Burden of Proof and the Proof-Proximity Principle in EU Competition Law' (2014) 51 *Common Market Law Review* 1159

Waelbroeck, D, 'The Assessment of Efficiencies under Article 102 TFEU and the Commission's Guidance Paper' in Federico Etro and Ioannis Kokkoris (eds), *Competition Law and the Enforcement of Article 102* (Oxford University Press, 2010)

——. 'Le Juge Communautaire en Matière de Concentrations: "Censeur Pédagogue" ou Juge de la Légalité?' (2005) 4 *Concurrences* 2

Waelbroeck, D and Bourgeois, J (eds), *Ten Years of Effects-Based Approach in EU competition Law* (Bruylant, 2012)

Waelbroeck, D and Slater, D, 'The Scope of Object vs Effect under Article 101 TFEU' in J Bourgeois and D Waelbroeck (eds), *Ten Years of Effects-Based Approach in EU Competition Law: State of Play and Perspectives* (Bruylant, 2012)

Werden, G, 'The Admissibility of Expert Economic Testimony in Antitrust Cases' in *Issues in Competition Law and Policy* (ABA Section of Antitrust Law, 2007)

Wigmore, JH, *A Treatise on the Anglo-American System of Evidence in Trials at Common Law*, 3rd edn (Little, Brown & Co, 1940)

Wils, W, 'The Combination of the Investigative and Prosecutorial Function and the Adjudicative Function in EC Antitrust Enforcement: A Legal and Economic Analysis' (2004) 27 *World Competition* 201

——. 'The Compatibility with Fundamental Rights of the EU Antitrust Enforcement System in Which the European Commission Acts Both as Investigator and as First-Instance Decision Maker' (2014) 37 *World Competition* 5

——. 'EU Antitrust Enforcement Powers and Procedural Rights and Guarantees: The Interplay between EU Law, National Law, the Charter of Fundamental Rights of the EU and the European Convention On Human Rights' (2011) 34 *World Competition* 189

——. 'The Increased Level of EU Antitrust Fines, Judicial Review, and the European Convention on Human Rights' (2010) 33 *World Competition* 5

——. 'Is Criminalization of EU Competition Law the Answer?' (2005) 28 *World Competition* 117

——. 'The Judgment of the EU General Court in *Intel* and the So-Called More Economic Approach to Abuse of Dominance' (2014) 37 *World Competition* 405

Wistrich, A, Guthrie, C and Rachlinski, J, 'Can Judges Ignore Inadmissible Information? The Difficulty of Deliberately Disregarding' (2005) 153 *University of Pennsylvania Law Review* 1251

Witt, A, 'The Enforcement of Article 101 TFEU: What Has Happened to the Effects Analysis?' (2018) 55 *Common Market Law Review* 417

——. 'From *Airtours* to *Ryanair*: Is the More Economic Approach to EU Merger Law Really about More Economics?' (2012) 49 *Common Market Law Review* 217

——. *The More Economic Approach to EU Antitrust Law* (Hart Publishing, 2016)

Wood, D, 'Proving it: The Standard and Burden of Proof in Article 82 EC Cases' (2008) 7 *Competition Law Insight* 4

Wood, L, 'Trying Antitrust Cases before Generalist Judges' (2006–07) 21 *Antitrust* 85

Woolhander, A, 'Rethinking the Judicial Reception of Legislative Facts' (1988) 41 *Vanderbilt Law Review* 111

Wright, J, 'Abandoning Antitrust's Chicago Obsession: The Case for Evidence-Based Antitrust' (2012) 78 *Antitrust Law Journal* 241

Wright, K, 'Perfect Symmetry? *Impala v. Commission* and Standard of Proof in Mergers' (2007) 32 *European Law Review* 408

Yablon, C, 'A Theory of Presumptions' (2003) 2 *Law, Probability and Risk* 227

Zander, M, 'The Criminal Standard of Proof: How Sure is Sure?' (2000) 150 *New Law Journal* 1517

Zenger, H and Walker, M, 'Theories of Harm in European Competition Law: A Progress Report' in J Bourgeois and D Waelbroeck (eds), *Ten Years of the Effects-Based Approach in EU Competition Law* (Bruylant, 2012)

Zenger, H, 'Loyalty Rebates and the Competitive Process' (2012) 8 *Journal of Competition Law and Economics* 717

Zimmer, D (ed), *The Goals of Competition Law* (Edward Elgar, 2012)

INDEX

www.ingramcontent.com/pod-product-compliance
Ingram Content Group UK Ltd.
Pitfield, Milton Keynes, MK11 3LW, UK
UKHW020249290926
15470UKWH00002B/833

9 781509 919666